The Pioneering Applications of Generative AI

Raghvendra Kumar
GIET University, India

Sandipan Sahu
Bengal Institute of Technology, India

Sudipta Bhattacharya
Bengal Institute of Technology, India

A volume in the Advances in Computational
Intelligence and Robotics (ACIR) Book Series

Published in the United States of America by
    IGI Global
    Engineering Science Reference (an imprint of IGI Global)
    701 E. Chocolate Avenue
    Hershey PA, USA 17033
    Tel: 717-533-8845
    Fax: 717-533-8661
    E-mail: cust@igi-global.com
    Web site: http://www.igi-global.com

Library of Congress Cataloging-in-Publication Data

ISBN: 979-8-3693-3278-8
EISBN: 979-8-3693-3279-5

British Cataloguing in Publication Data
A Cataloguing in Publication record for this book is available from the British Library.

The views expressed in this book are those of the authors, but not necessarily of the publisher.

For electronic access to this publication, please contact: eresources@igi-global.com.

Advances in Computational Intelligence and Robotics (ACIR) Book Series

Ivan Giannoccaro
University of Salento, Italy

ISSN:2327-0411
EISSN:2327-042X

Mission

While intelligence is traditionally a term applied to humans and human cognition, technology has progressed in such a way to allow for the development of intelligent systems able to simulate many human traits. With this new era of simulated and artificial intelligence, much research is needed in order to continue to advance the field and also to evaluate the ethical and societal concerns of the existence of artificial life and machine learning.

The **Advances in Computational Intelligence and Robotics (ACIR) Book Series** encourages scholarly discourse on all topics pertaining to evolutionary computing, artificial life, computational intelligence, machine learning, and robotics. ACIR presents the latest research being conducted on diverse topics in intelligence technologies with the goal of advancing knowledge and applications in this rapidly evolving field.

Coverage

- Heuristics
- Synthetic Emotions
- Evolutionary Computing
- Computer Vision
- Machine Learning
- Artificial Intelligence
- Algorithmic Learning
- Cyborgs
- Agent technologies
- Fuzzy Systems

IGI Global is currently accepting manuscripts for publication within this series. To submit a proposal for a volume in this series, please contact our Acquisition Editors at Acquisitions@igi-global.com or visit: http://www.igi-global.com/publish/.

Titles in this Series

For a list of additional titles in this series, please visit: www.igi-global.com/book-series

Cross-Industry AI Applications
P. Paramasivan (Dhaanish Ahmed College of Engineering, India) S. Suman Rajest (Dhaanish Ahmed College of Engineering, India) Karthikeyan Chinnusamy (Veritas, USA) R. Regin (SRM Institute of Science and Technology, India) and Ferdin Joe John Joseph (Thai-Nichi Institute of Technology, Thailand)
Engineering Science Reference • copyright 2024 • 389pp • H/C (ISBN: 9798369359518) • US $415.00 (our price)

Harnessing Artificial Emotional Intelligence for Improved Human-Computer Interactions
Nitendra Kumar (Amity Business School, Amity University, Noida, India) Surya Kant Pal (Sharda University, Greater Noida, India) Priyanka Agarwal (Amity Business School, Amity University, Noida, India) Joanna Rosak-Szyrocka (Częstochowa University of Technology, Poland) and Vishal Jain (Sharda University, Greater Noida, India)
Engineering Science Reference • copyright 2024 • 300pp • H/C (ISBN: 9798369327944) • US $335.00 (our price)

Applied AI and Humanoid Robotics for the Ultra-Smart Cyberspace
Eduard Babulak (National Science Foundation, USA)
Engineering Science Reference • copyright 2024 • 287pp • H/C (ISBN: 9798369323991) • US $305.00 (our price)

AI Algorithms and ChatGPT for Student Engagement in Online Learning
Rohit Bansal (Vaish College of Engineering, India) Aziza Chakir (Faculty of Law, Economics, and Social Sciences, Hassan II University, Casablanca, Morocco) Abdul Hafaz Ngah (Faculty of Business Economics and Social Development, Universiti Malaysia, Terengganu, Malaysia) Fazla Rabby (Stanford Institute of Management and Technology, Australia) and Ajay Jain (Shri Cloth Market Kanya Vanijya Mahavidyalaya, Indore, India)
Information Science Reference • copyright 2024 • 292pp • H/C (ISBN: 9798369342688) • US $265.00 (our price)

Applications, Challenges, and the Future of ChatGPT
Priyanka Sharma (Swami Keshvanand Institute of Technology, Management, and Gramothan, Jaipur, India) Monika Jyotiyana (Manipal University Jaipur, India) and A.V. Senthil Kumar (Hindusthan College of Arts and Sciences, India)
Engineering Science Reference • copyright 2024 • 309pp • H/C (ISBN: 9798369368244) • US $365.00 (our price)

Modeling, Simulation, and Control of AI Robotics and Autonomous Systems
Tanupriya Choudhury (Graphic Era University, India) Anitha Mary X. (Karunya Institute of Technology and Sciences, India) Subrata Chowdhury (Sreenivasa Institute of Technology and Management Studies, India) C. Karthik (Jyothi Engineering College, India) and C. Suganthi Evangeline (Sri Eshwar College of Engineering, India)

701 East Chocolate Avenue, Hershey, PA 17033, USA
Tel: 717-533-8845 x100 • Fax: 717-533-8661
E-Mail: cust@igi-global.com • www.igi-global.com

Titles in this Series

For a list of additional titles in this series, please visit: www.igi-global.com/book-series

Engineering Science Reference ● copyright 2024 ● 295pp ● H/C (ISBN: 9798369319628) ● US $300.00 (our price)

701 East Chocolate Avenue, Hershey, PA 17033, USA
Tel: 717-533-8845 x100 ● Fax: 717-533-8661
E-Mail: cust@igi-global.com ● www.igi-global.com

Table of Contents

Detailed Table of Contents

Chapter 1

Tripti Majumdar, Bengal Institute of Technology, India
Sandipan Sahu, Bengal Institute of Technology, India
Raghvendra Kumar, GIET University, India

The intersection of computer vision and natural language processing (NLP) has witnessed significant advancements in recent research, particularly in the realm of converting text into meaningful images leveraging generative AI and large language models. This review work aims to comprehensively review the progress made in text-to-image conversion. The survey covers the three primary approaches in the field, namely diffusion models (DM), GAN model approaches, and autoregressive approaches. Furthermore, the authors present a comprehensive chronology of the TIG journey, encompassing its origin and the most recent developments, providing readers with a comprehensive perspective on the field's progression. The survey focuses heavily on identifying the existing constraints of DM in picture production and offers multiple research publications and their contributions in overcoming these constraints. The survey provides useful insights into the advancements in text-to-image (TIG) generation using generative AI by focusing on key difficulties and examining how different works have addressed them.

Chapter 2

Rajneesh Ranjan, C. V. Raman Global University, India
Anjana Mishra, C. V. Raman Global University, India
Smruti Pratisruti Maharana, C. V. Raman Global University, India
Sweety Kumari, C. V. Raman Global University, India

In the past two to four years there have been significant improvements made in AI due to improvements in computing capacity, resulting in an increase in public interest and funding for research. This has led the authors to embark on a project aimed at gaining a deeper understanding of these art generator AIs using generative algorithms such as GANs and VAEs. This chapter begins by providing a brief outline of the historical context and evolution of AI in the arts, tracing its trajectory from early experiments to its current advancements in visual artistry. The subsequent sections of the chapter explore the role of generative algorithms in each artistic medium, starting with an overview of algorithmic painting, followed by an examination of algorithmic sculpture and digital art. In addition, this chapter also introduces four novel features specific to AI-Art. In this chapter, the authors have drawn upon references from various tests published by esteemed researchers and practitioners to gather the necessary insights for the investigation and deepen our understanding.

Chapter 3

Richard Shan, CTS, USA

This chapter explores the evolution and future trajectory of Python-driven generative AI, highlighting Python's role in advancing this technology. It discusses the integration of Python with emerging technologies like neuromorphic computing and reinforcement learning, focusing on their potential to revolutionize art, design, and media. Through detailed analysis of the open-source implementation of a technology platform designed, the chapter provides insights into Python's facilitation of innovative AI applications. It addresses potential challenges and ethical considerations, along with the mitigation and call to action, emphasizing the importance of responsible innovation. The narrative underscores Python's influence in making advanced AI technologies accessible and scalable, preparing readers to engage with future developments in the field of generative AI.

Chapter 4

Rabi Shankar Panda, C. V. Raman Global University, India
Anjana Mishra, C. V. Raman Global University, India
Abhishek Mohanty, C. V. Raman Global University, India

Generative artificial intelligence has enormous promise in business, marketing, finance, education, and healthcare sectors. It can have an impact on areas like consumer engagement and fraud detection. But it also poses difficult problems. Decision-making is hampered by technological barriers like data quality, explainability, and authenticity, as well as economic issues like income inequality and possible job loss. Privacy, bias, and misuse are all examples of ethical dilemmas. To address these, thorough norms that guarantee accountability, openness, and equity are needed. Meeting societal requirements and fostering collaboration requires advancing AI education and human-centric cooperation. Rules and guidelines that emphasise empathy, clarity, and ethical norms must be established to steer AI research and development toward responsible and ethical practices in order to effectively manage these obstacles.

Chapter 5

A. Firos, Rajiv Gandhi University, India
Seema Khanum, Indian Computer Emergency Response Team (ICERT), MeitY, Electronics Niketan, India

Fashion designers and brands use GANs to create new and unique patterns, styles, and textures. GANs consist of a generator and a discriminator, which work together to produce high-quality, realistic outputs. VAEs are another type of generative model that is applied to generate new fashion designs. VAEs are known for their ability to generate diverse outputs by sampling from a learned latent space. Fashion designers can use VAEs to explore different design variations and styles. StyleGAN and its successor, StyleGAN2, are advancements of GANs that specifically focus on generating high-resolution and realistic images with control over different style elements. These models have been employed in fashion to create detailed and visually appealing designs. These AI generative models have the potential to revolutionize the fashion industry by facilitating creativity and providing new avenues for artistic expression. However, it's essential to consider ethical implications, intellectual property rights, and the responsible use of AI technologies in the context of fashion design.

Chapter 6
Pooja Dehankar, Ajeenkya D.Y. Patil University, India
Susanta Das, Ajeenkya D.Y. Patil University, India

Generative AI is omnipresent in our daily lives, influencing everything from media and entertainment to personal care and healthcare. The Fourth Industrial Revolution has brought about significant developments in artificial intelligence, such as ChatGPT, which have gained prominence and changed the way data is created and produced. This chapter highlights the current use of AI in natural language processing. These models are based on machine learning. This chapter examines these models' possible benefits to the economy. The potential influence of generative AI on productivity might boost the world economy. All industry sectors will be significantly impacted by generative AI. The economy as a whole can benefit greatly from generative AI's ability to boost labor productivity. We can utilize generative AI's promise to build a more just, inclusive, and sustainable future for all people if we are aware of how it affects society. This chapter offers a comprehensive analysis of the potential exposure of generative AI, in particular to generative pre-trained transformers.

Chapter 7
Tina Babu, Alliance Univeraity, India
Rekha R. Nair, Alliance University, India
Ebin P. M., Alliance University, India

The chapter delves into the foundations of generative artificial intelligence (AI), offering an introductory overview and a nuanced understanding of its basic principles, history, and evolution. It navigates through core technologies underpinning generative AI, including neural networks, machine learning models, and key algorithms. The introduction traces generative AI's roots, unraveling its historical trajectory. It progresses to elucidate fundamental concepts, exploring neural networks' structures, functionalities, and applications. The study examines diverse machine learning models and pivotal algorithms crucial to generative AI, shedding light on their roles in generating innovative outputs. This abstract encapsulates a comprehensive journey through generative AI's core elements, serving as a foundational guide for understanding its origins, principles, and technologies.

Chapter 8
Sayak Sinha, MCKV Institute of Engineering, India
Sourajit Datta, MCKV Institute of Engineering, India
Raghvendra Kumar, GIET University, India
Sudipta Bhattacharya, Bengal Institute of Technology, India
Arijit Sarkar, MCKV Institute of Engineering, India
Kunal Das, MCKV Institute of Engineering, India

Generative AI, often known as genAI, encompasses several forms of artificial intelligence (AI) that has the ability to create unique text, images, video, or audio content. This particular iteration of artificial intelligence acquires knowledge of patterns and data arrangement from its training data, enabling it to produce novel outputs that possess similar statistical characteristics. Generative AI has a diverse range of applications, and each task requires a specialized deep-learning architecture to effectively capture the unique patterns and traits found in the training data. Generative AI models encompass various types, including generative adversarial networks (GANs), variational autoencoders (VAEs), transformers, diffusion models, normalizing flow models, and hybrid models. The configuration of a generative AI model is contingent upon the particular task and domain, encompassing elements such as the neural network's architecture, training approach, loss function, and evaluation metrics. The primary objective of generative AI is to develop autonomous systems capable of generating content that is indiscernible from information created by humans. This encompasses the production of written content, visual graphics, audio recordings, and interactive visual components. Attaining this objective would facilitate a diverse array of applications, encompassing enhanced human-computer interactions and assisting in the advancement of endeavors such as art and storytelling.

Chapter 9

Vishal Jain, Sharda University, India
Archan Mitra, Presidency University, India

This study examines the impact of Python-driven generative AI on media content creation and its ethical implications. Python's simplicity and extensive libraries have made it pivotal in AI development, enabling the generation of realistic content across various media formats. While these advancements promise significant enhancements in content creation efficiency and personalization, they also raise complex ethical issues, including concerns over authenticity, copyright infringement, and misinformation. Through surveys and case studies, this research explores the technological capabilities of generative AI, its transformative potential in the media landscape, and the ethical dilemmas it presents. The chapter advocates for a balanced approach to leveraging AI in media, emphasizing the need for frameworks that promote responsible use, ensuring innovation aligns with ethical standards and societal values.

Chapter 10

Neha Singh, Madan Mohan Malaviya University of Technology, Gorakhpur, India
Umesh Chandra Jaiswal, Madan Mohan Malaviya University of Technology, Gorakhpur, India
Ritu Singh, Madan Mohan Malaviya University of Technology, Gorakhpur, India

The growth of numerous statistical approaches used to evaluate data in educational settings has caused machine learning to recently become a novel subject of research. In this chapter, authors present a novel voting model for performance prediction that incorporates machine learning techniques and additional variables known as "student sentiment attributes." The proposed voting system was also employed to boost student test scores and improve the effectiveness of the strategies. In terms of the parameters of correlation coefficient, mean absolute error, root mean square error, time taken to build the model, relative absolute error, and root relative squared error, the supplied test set with voting method outperforms the four model evaluation methods of cross validation, use training set, supplied test set, and percentage split models. Given this, the result shows the applicability of the proposed model and computes the cost analysis of the proposed voting procedure.

The purpose of the chapter is to provide an overview of artificial intelligence (AI) to the knowledge seekers. This chapter aims to provide the historical development of AI over the years. It provides an overview of machine learning. It talks about supervised, semi-supervised, and unsupervised, reinforcement learning, and transfer learning. It delves into the generative adversarial networks (GAN). It further provides an overview of various components of neural network (NN) such as input layers, hidden layers, output layers, forward propagation, backward propagation, training, optimization, inference, fine tuning, transfer learning, etc. The chapter will leverage academic journals, conferences, and online repositories to shed light on the dynamic landscape of AI technology.

The Scikit-learn package is a popular machine-learning library in Python that provides tools for data preprocessing, feature selection, and evaluation of models. However, learning it can be hard for beginners due to its vast documentation. The goal of this chapter is to search for ways to use ChatGPT to learn the Scikit-learn package. ChatGPT's first version was used (2023). Using ChatGPT to learn Scikit-learn can help users to understand the key techniques of machine learning.

This abstract provides an overview of the fundamental concepts involved in understanding and applying machine learning models. It covers key aspects, including data preparation, training, evaluation, and deployment. The journey begins with a data preprocessing phase, emphasizing the significance of data quality, feature engineering, and addressing challenges such as missing values and outliers. Subsequently, the focus shifts to the diverse landscape of machine learning models, ranging from traditional algorithms to sophisticated architectures. The importance of selecting the most suitable model for a given task, considering factors such as interpretability, scalability, and performance, is emphasized. The process of training ML models is then elucidated, highlighting the crucial role of splitting data into training and testing sets. Essential concepts such as loss functions, optimization algorithms, and hyperparameter tuning are explored in detail. Evaluation metrics, including accuracy, precision, recall, and F1-score, are discussed to assess model performance effectively.

Preface

Generative Artificial Intelligence through Python focused on teaching readers how to implement generative AI techniques using the Python programming language. It cover topics such as generative adversarial networks (GANs), variational autoencoders (VAEs), and other methods for creating AI systems that can generate new content, such as images, text, or music.

Chapter 1 aims to comprehensively review the progress made in text-to-image conversion. Our survey coverage of the three primary approaches in the field, namely Diffusion models, GAN model approaches, and Autoregressive approaches. Furthermore, we present a comprehensive chronology of the TIG journey, encompassing its origin and the most recent developments, providing readers with a comprehensive perspective on the field's progression. Our survey focuses heavily on identifying the existing constraints of diffusion models in picture production and offers multiple research publications and their contributions in overcoming these constraints. Our survey provides useful insights into the advancements in Text-to-Image generation using Generative AI by focusing on key difficulties and examining how different works have addressed them.

Chapter 2 provides a brief outline of the historical context and evolution of AI in the arts, tracing its trajectory from early experiments to its current advancements in visual artistry. The subsequent sections of the paper explore the role of generative algorithms in each artistic medium, starting with an overview of algorithmic painting, followed by an examination of algorithmic sculpture and digital art. In addition, this paper also introduces four novel features specific to Ai-Art. In this research paper, we have drawn upon references from various tests published by esteemed researchers and practitioners to gather the necessary insights for our own investigation and deepen our understanding.

Chapter 3 addresses potential challenges and ethical considerations, along with the mitigation and call to action, emphasizing the importance of responsible innovation. The narrative underscores Python's influence in making advanced AI technologies accessible and scalable, preparing readers to engage with future developments in the field of generative AI.

Chapter 4 addresses these, thorough norms that guarantee accountability, openness, and equity are needed. Meeting societal requirements and fostering collaboration need advancing AI education and human-centric cooperation. Rules and guidelines that emphasise empathy, clarity, and ethical norms must be established to steer AI research and development toward responsible and ethical practices in order to effectively manage these obstacles.

Chapter 5 specifically focuses on generating high-resolution and realistic images with control over different style elements. These models have been employed in fashion to create detailed and visually appealing designs. These AI generative models have the potential to revolutionize the fashion industry by facilitating creativity and providing new avenues for artistic expression. However, it's essential to consider ethical implications, intellectual property rights, and the responsible use of AI technologies in the context of fashion design.

Chapter 6 examines these models' possible benefits to the economy. The potential influence of generative AI on productivity might boost the world economy. All industry sectors will be significantly impacted by generative AI. The economy as a whole can benefit greatly from generative AI's ability to boost labor productivity. We can utilize generative AI's promise to build a more just, inclusive, and sustainable future for all people if we are aware of how it affects society. This chapter offers a comprehensive analysis of the potential exposure of Generative AI, in particular to Generative Pre-Trained Transformers.

Chapter 7 encapsulates a comprehensive journey through Generative AI's core elements, serving as a foundational guide for understanding its origins, principles, and technologies.

Chapter 8 meticulously explores objective of generative AI is to develop autonomous systems capable of generating content that is indiscernible from information created by humans. This encompasses the production of written content, visual graphics, audio recordings, and interactive visual components. Attaining this objective would facilitate a diverse array of applications, encompassing enhanced human-computer interactions and assisting in the advancement of endeavors such as art and storytelling.

Chapter 9 explores the technological capabilities of generative AI, its transformative potential in the media landscape, and the ethical dilemmas it presents. The paper advocates for a balanced approach to leveraging AI in media, emphasizing the need for frameworks that promote responsible use, ensuring innovation aligns with ethical standards and societal values.

Chapter 10 proposed voting systems was also employed to boost student test scores and improve the effectiveness of the strategies. In terms of the parameters of correlation coefficient, mean absolute error, root mean square error, time taken to build the model, relative absolute error, and root relative squared error, the supplied test set with voting method outperforms the four model evaluation methods of cross validation, use training set, supplied test set, and percentage split models. Given this, the result shows the applicability of the proposed model and computes the cost analysis of the proposed voting procedure.

Chapter 11 goal is to search for ways to use ChatGPT to learn the Scikit-learn package. Methods: ChatGPT's first version was used (2023). Conclusion: Using ChatGPT to learn Scikit-learn can help users to understand the key techniques of machine learning.

Chapter 12 covers key aspects, including data preparation, training, evaluation, and deployment. The journey begins with a data preprocessing phase, emphasizing the significance of data quality, feature engineering, and addressing challenges such as missing values and outliers. Subsequently, the focus shifts to the diverse landscape of machine learning models, ranging from traditional algorithms to sophisticated architectures. The importance of selecting the most suitable model for a given task, considering factors such as interpretability, scalability, and performance, is emphasized. The process of training ML models is then elucidated, highlighting the crucial role of splitting data into training and testing sets. Essential concepts such as loss functions, optimization algorithms, and hyper parameter tuning are explored in detail. Evaluation metrics, including accuracy, precision, recall, and F1-score, are discussed to assess model performance effectively.

Chapter 13 provides an overview of the fundamental concepts involved in understanding and applying machine learning models. It covers key aspects, including data preparation, training, evaluation, and deployment. The journey begins with a data preprocessing phase, emphasizing the significance of data quality, feature engineering, and addressing challenges such as missing values and outliers. Subsequently, the focus shifts to the diverse landscape of machine learning models, ranging from traditional algorithms to sophisticated architectures. The importance of selecting the most suitable model for a given task, considering factors such as interpretability, scalability, and performance, is emphasized. The process of training ML models is then elucidated, highlighting the crucial role of splitting data into training and testing sets. Essential concepts such as loss functions, optimization algorithms, and hyperparameter tuning are explored in detail. Evaluation metrics, including accuracy, precision, recall, and F1-score, are discussed to assess model performance effectively.

Raghvendra Kumar

GIET University, India

Sandipan Sahu

Bengal Institute of Technology, India

Sudipta Bhattacharya

Bengal Institute of Technology, India

Acknowledgment

Raghvendra Kumar dedicates this book to his sons, Prakhar Pandey & Pranay Pandey, and his wife, Priyanka Pandey.

Sandipan Sahu dedicates this book to his father, Kalipada Sahu, Mother, Sefali Sahu and brother, Late Dibyendu Sahu.

Sudipta Bhattacharya dedicates this book to his parents and family.

Chapter 1
A Comprehensive Survey of Hypermedia System for Text– to–Image Conversion Using Generative AI

Tripti Majumdar
Bengal Institute of Technology, India

Sandipan Sahu
Bengal Institute of Technology, India

Raghvendra Kumar
GIET University, India

ABSTRACT

The intersection of computer vision and natural language processing (NLP) has witnessed significant advancements in recent research, particularly in the realm of converting text into meaningful images leveraging generative AI and large language models. This review work aims to comprehensively review the progress made in text-to-image conversion. The survey covers the three primary approaches in the field, namely diffusion models (DM), GAN model approaches, and autoregressive approaches. Furthermore, the authors present a comprehensive chronology of the TIG journey, encompassing its origin and the most recent developments, providing readers with a comprehensive perspective on the field's progression. The survey focuses heavily on identifying the existing constraints of DM in picture production and offers multiple research publications and their contributions in overcoming these constraints. The survey provides useful insights into the advancements in text-to-image (TIG) generation using generative AI by focusing on key difficulties and examining how different works have addressed them.

DOI: 10.4018/979-8-3693-3278-8.ch001

INTRODUCTION

In the ever-expanding realm of artificial intelligence, the fusion of NLP and computer vision has led to remarkable advancements, particularly in the domain of TIG. This fusion not only bridges the gap between linguistic and visual understanding but also opens doors to novel applications ranging from content creation to assistive technologies. Over the past few decades, researchers have embarked on a fascinating journey, striving to enhance the capability of machines to understand, interpret, and generate visual content from textual descriptions.

The aim of this paper is to provide a thorough exploration of the development of TIG techniques from their nascent stages to the state-of-the-art models of today. By delving into the historical developments, breakthrough methodologies, and current trends, we endeavour to shed light on the progression of this interdisciplinary field. From early attempts utilizing simplistic rules and heuristics to the recent emergence of deep learning architectures, the landscape of TIG has witnessed a profound transformation, propelled by advancements in both computational power and algorithmic sophistication.

Our review will navigate through significant milestones, encompassing the inception of Generative Adversarial Network (GAN) s and their subsequent adaptations designed for generating images from text. We will explore pivotal research papers, seminal contributions, and benchmark datasets that have shaped the trajectory of this field. Furthermore, we will analyse the challenges encountered, such as fidelity, diversity, and semantic coherence, and discuss the innovative approaches devised to address these hurdles.

As we embark on this journey through the annals of TIG, it becomes evident that the quest for imbuing machines with the capacity to translate textual descriptions into visually compelling representations is far from over. With the burgeoning interest from academia and industry alike, fueled by the promise of applications in art, design, e-commerce, and beyond, the field stands poised at the brink of unprecedented possibilities.

Through this paper, we invite readers to join us in unraveling the multifaceted evolution of TIG, as we navigate through the historical landmarks and contemporary paradigms that have sculpted this captivating domain.

Brief Discussion on Text-to-Image Generation

In this paper, we illustrate upon the intricacies and advancements within the realm of TIG, with a particular focus on the utilization of diverse GAN models and DM. This investigation builds upon a foundation of prior research, aiming to delve deeper into the fusion of textual input and visual output through the lens of sophisticated computational techniques.

Drawing upon a diverse array of scholarly sources, empirical studies, and technical documents, we aim to offer a nuanced understanding of the mechanisms underlying text-to-image synthesis.

By elucidating the work of various GAN models and the diffusion model, we seek to underscore the diversity of approaches and the spectrum of possibilities inherent in TIG. Through a detailed examination of these models, we aim to highlight their respective strengths, limitations, and comparative efficacy in generating visually compelling images from textual inputs.

In summary, this paper represents a comprehensive endeavour to expound upon the work of TIG using various GAN models and the diffusion model. By meticulously synthesizing existing literature and empirical evidence, our goal is to enhance the collective understanding of this dynamic field, thereby laying the groundwork for future advancements and innovations in text-to-image synthesis.

Some Recent Application and Its Advancement

Recent advancements in TIG have spurred a plethora of innovative applications across diverse domains, revolutionizing fields such as multimedia content creation, e-commerce, virtual reality, and more. Below, I'll outline some notable applications and advancements, supported by relevant citations.

The advent of GANs has marked a pivotal moment in the trajectory of TIG, ushering in a new era characterized by the ability to train neural networks to maketrue images from textual descriptions. This transformative capability finds its roots in seminal research, epitomized by the ground breaking work (Reed et al., 2016), whose Generative Adversarial Text-to-Image Synthesis (GATIS) model stands as a cornerstone in the application of GANs to this domain. This landmark contribution has set the stage for subsequent advancements, propelling the field forward with innovations that push the boundaries of fidelity and diversity in generated imagery.

The evolutionary journey of TIG has been marked by a rich tapestry of models and methodologies, each contributing uniquely to the ongoing narrative of progress. Early milestones such as StackGAN (Zhang et al., 2017) and AttnGAN (Xu et al., 2018) further underscore the transformative potential of attention mechanisms and multi-stage conditioning in enhancing the quality and richness of generated images. These innovations not only showcase the power of GANs but also illustrate the iterative refinement and expansion of techniques aimed at bridging the semantic gap between text and image modalities.

The evolutionary trajectory of TIG witnessed further diversification with the introduction of variational autoencoders (VAEs) and their integration with GANs, leading to the emergence of hybrid architectures like VQ-VAE-2 (Razavi et al, 2019) and DALL-E (Brock et al., 2018). These hybrid models represent a synthesis of disparate techniques, leveraging the strong point of both GANs and VAEs to achieve unprecedented levels of fidelity, resolution, and semantic control in generated imagery. The advent of such hybrid architectures not only expands the scope of TIG but also opens up new avenues for creative exploration and manipulation of visual content.

As we traverse the annals of TIG, from its nascent beginnings to the frontiers of contemporary research, it becomes increasingly apparent that each model and methodology contributes a distinct chapter to the unfolding narrative of innovation. From the foundational principles of GANs to the intricate fusion of attention mechanisms and variational inference, the evolution of TIG serves as a testament to the collective ingenuity, perseverance, and collaborative spirit of the research community. In this ever-evolving landscape, the quest for generating realistic and semantically meaningful images from textual prompts continues to inspire and drive forward the boundaries of artificial intelligence and computational creativity.

Synthetic image generation holds several advantages, particularly in addressing the prevalent challenge of scarce or unavailable image data in various business contexts as well as medical fields also. By employing sophisticated algorithms and techniques, synthetic image generation can effectively overcome the limitations posed by data scarcity. This approach involves creating synthetic image data that closely mimics real-world images, thus mitigating the impact of insufficient data availability.

In the realm of thermal imaging, particularly valuable for nocturnal threat detection such as suspects, dogs, or other hazards to first responders, its applications extend to locating lost children, fugitives, and animals in dense foliage or darkness. In a recent study (Pavez et al., 2023), authors introduce an advanced system employing deep learning techniques to create high-fidelity artificialupdraft face images. Their methodologyassimilates a thermally fine-tuned Stable Diffusion Model with a Vision Transformer (ViT) classifier, complemented by a Prompt Designer and Prompt Database, enabling exact control over image generation. Extensive testing across various scenarios demonstrates the system's ability to produce accurate and high-quality thermal images. A noteworthy contribution of this research is the creation of aartificial thermal face image database, beneficial for training thermal detection models. Evaluation using a facial detection model confirms the effectiveness of their synthetic images, producing results akin to authentic thermal face images, a detector adjusted with genuine thermal images attains a 97% accuracy rate when evaluated with synthetic images. Conversely, a detector exclusively trained on synthetic data achieves a 98% accuracy rate.

One significant application of synthetic image generation is in the realm of conversational chatbots. These chatbots, powered by artificial intelligence (AI), rely on TIG techniques to dynamically produce contextual images in response to user input. By integrating synthetic images seamlessly into conversational interfaces, chatbots can enhance user engagement and provide more enriching experiences.

Uniqueness of Our Work

Our survey effort makes a distinct and valuable contribution to the current body of knowledge on TIG in multiple ways. 1. Covering all approaches: Our survey differs from earlier ones by providing a full coverage of the three primary approaches in the field, namely DM (Cao, 2024; Croitoru, 2023; Yang, 2023; Zhang, 2023; Zhang, 2023), GAN model approaches (Ullah, 2022; Frolov, 2021; Zhou, 2021), and Autoregressive approaches (Regis, 2022; Chen, 2021). 2. Complete time journey: Furthermore, we present a comprehensive chronology of the TIG journey, encompassing its origin and the most recent developments, providing readers with a comprehensive perspective on the field's progression. 3. Emphasis on Limitations and Solutions: Our survey focuses heavily on identifying the existing constraints of DM in picture production and offers multiple research publications and their contributions in overcoming these constraints. Our survey provides useful insights into the advancements in TIG using Generative AI by focusing on key difficulties and examining how different works have addressed them.

The remainder of this paper is structured as follows- Section 2 discuss different GAN models for TIG and also briefly introduce the architecture of basic GAN model, we have discussed pioneering works of GAN model for TIG. Section 3 introduce Diffusion model, Discuss background and basic working functionalities of diffusion model. We have discussed all the significant DM used in TIG. Section 4 further discusses Autoregressive models for TIG and also briefly introduce the architecture of basic Autoregressive model. We have discussed ground-breaking works of Autoregressive model for TIG. In Section 5, we re-examine diverse applications beyond TIG, and in Section 6, we explore the challenges alongside future opportunities. Finally, we conclude in section 7.

TEXT-TO-IMAGE GENERATION USING GAN

The structure of TIG epitomize a ground-breaking merger of NLP and computer vision, orchestrating the conversion of textual explanations into visually captivating images. This interdisciplinary domain has seen notablegrowth driven by the continuous evolution of deep learning methodologies and generative modelling techniques. At the heart of TIG models lies the intricate orchestration of sophisticated neural networks, often leveraging architectures such as GANs and Autoregressive Transformers.

Currently, multiple projects are in progress to create a new and innovative deep architecture and GAN (Reed et al. 2016) formulation that will successfully connect the progress made in text and picture modelling. The goal is to convert visual ideas from letters into pixels.

These architectures empower the models with the cognitive prowess to comprehend and decipher textual input, subsequently engendering images that faithfully encapsulate the semantic essence conveyed within the provided descriptions.

The domain of text-to-image synthesis has experiencedanextraordinary evolution, galvanized by the advent of GAN technology. It was in the year 2014 when Ian Goodfellow, alongside his esteemed collaborators, introduced the revolutionary concept of GANs (Goodfellow et al., 2014). This paradigm-shifting model swiftly garnered attention as a seminal advancement in the domain of unsupervised machine learning, promising unparalleled capabilities in generating synthetic data distributions.

In the broader landscape of machine learning, the predominant objective often revolves around the generation of accurate predictions. This iterative process entails the ingestion of data into the model, facilitating the generation of output. Subsequently, the predicted outcomes are juxtaposed against the desired outputs gleaned from the provided training dataset. This perpetual cycle of comparison and refinement embodies a continuous process of optimization, wherein the model dynamically adjusts its parameters to achieve optimal predictive performance. Such a methodology epitomizes the essence of supervised learning, wherein the model's learning process is guided by the labeled data inputs.

In stark contrast, GANs represent a paradigmatic departure from conventional supervised learning frameworks, epitomizing an instance of unsupervised learning. Unlike their supervised counterparts, GANs operate autonomously, devoid of external labels to guide the learning process. Instead, GANs harness their intrinsic adversarial mechanism to self-supervise and iteratively refine their performance.

The original formulation of the GAN framework planned by Ian Good fellow and his colleagues in 2014 is referred to as a Vanilla GAN. In a Vanilla GAN (Goodfellow, 2016, pp. 47-80), two neural networks are employed: the generator and the discriminator as described in Figure 1. Arbitrary noise serves as contribution for the generator, which then generates fake data samples, such as images, based on this noise.

The Generator endeavours to synthesize truthful data samples that closely mirror the authentic data distribution observed in the training dataset. Concurrently, the Discriminator meticulously scrutinizes these generated samples, discerning between genuine data and synthetic counterparts. Through this adversarial interplay, the Generator continually refines its output to deceive the Discriminator, while the Discriminator evolves to enhance its discernment capabilities. This perpetual dance between the Generator and the Discriminator underpins the learning dynamics within the GAN framework, culminating in the creation of high-fidelity synthetic data distributions that closely approximate real-world phenomena.

Figure 1. GAN ARCHITECTURE

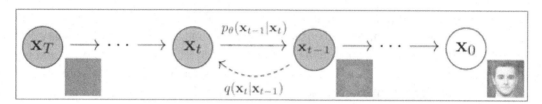

Newly, there has been notable interest in generative models, particularly focused on GANs. Significant advancements have been made in both theoretical understanding and practical applications, leading to the introduction of numerous GAN variants.

The generated samples are evaluated by the discriminator, which distinguishes between real and fake data. Throughoutpreparation, the generator aims to produce samples that are indistinguishable from real data, while the discriminator aims to correctly classify real and synthetic samples. The training process of a Vanilla GAN entails a competitive interaction between the generator and the discriminator, with both networks being trained simultaneously. This adversarial approach fosters the improvement of the generator's capability to produce lifelike samples over time, while at the same time enhancing the discriminator's skill in discerning among genuine and artificial samples.

Benefits of GAN Models

Unsupervised Learning: GANs provide a robust framework for unsupervised learning, eliminating the need for labelled data(Goodfellow et al., 2014).

Data Generation: GANs possess the ability to produce artificial data that closely resembles authentic data, rendering them extremely valuable for tasks such as generating images, synthesizing text into images, and augmenting data.

Enhanced Creativity: GANs foster creativity by enabling the creation of novel and diverse content. They explore the latent space of data distributions to produce unique outputs.

Data Augmentation: GANs are used for data augmentation, which enhances the robustness and generalization of machine learning models by generating extra training samples.

Privacy Preservation: GANs can generate synthetic data for privacy-preserving purposes, enabling research and analysis in fields where data privacy is crucial, such as healthcare and finance.

While GANs have garnered acclaim for their capacity to generate high-fidelity data, it's imperative to acknowledge certain drawbacks (Borji, 2019, pp. 41-65) associated with this technology.

Firstly, GANs pose significant challenges in terms of training complexity. The inherent adversarial nature of GANs, wherein the generator and discriminator networks continually compete against each other, often leads to instability and sluggish training progress.

Moreover, the effectiveness of GANs hinges on the availability of substantial training data. Generating satisfactory results with GANs typically necessitates access to extensive datasets. This requirement can pose a hindrance when adequate data is either not readily accessible or the dataset size is insufficient.

Moreover, GANs are prone to a phenomenon called manner collapse, wherein the generator network generates a partial range of outputs, failing to capture the intended diversity in generated samples.

In essence, while GANs offer unparalleled capabilities in generating realistic data, addressing challenges such as training complexity, data requirements, and mode collapse remains crucial for maximizing their potential in various applications.

The distinct benefit of GANs lies in their skill to construct a generator directly from real data, bypassing the necessity for a predetermined mathematical model. Nonetheless, this approach is not without its challenges, largely stemming from the inherent unpredictability of the data. In traditional GANs, the resultant output is solely contingent upon the random vector input, lacking any inherent mechanism for precise control over the generated content. Consequently, GAN networks often struggle to produce satisfactory images, particularly when tasked with generating high-resolution visuals or intricate objects.

Pioneering Text-to-Image Generation GAN Model

TIG Generation (Ramzan et al., 2022), facilitated by GAN (Goodfellow et al., 2016) models, is a significant breakthrough in artificial intelligence. It allows for the transformation of written descriptions into highly realistic visuals. GANs, firstlyprojected by Ian Goodfellow and his colleagues in 2014, have subsequently emerged as a fundamental component in the domain of generative modeling. This revolutionary technology has been applied in various fields, such as generating high-quality photographs, fostering artistic expression, and aiding in design endeavors.

Deep Convolutional GAN (DC-GAN)

DCGAN is a type of GAN that employs deep convolutional neural networks (CNNs) for both the generator and discriminator networks. DCGANs were introduced by Radford et al. in 2015 (Radford et al., 2015), aiming to progress the stability and standard of generated images compared to traditional GAN architectures.

DCGAN presents numerous advantages over traditional GAN architectures in the work of TIG. Firstly, DCGANs produce superior image quality (Reed et al., 2016), thanks to their utilization of deep convolutional networks.In fashion design and virtual try-on systems, DCGANs have been employed to generate clothing items based on textual descriptions. By providing descriptions of clothing attributes such as color, style, and texture, DCGANs can generate corresponding images, facilitating virtual try-on experiences for users.

These networks excel at capturing spatial dependencies, resulting in more realistic and detailed images. Moreover, DCGANs address common training challenges such as mode collapse and vanishing gradients, thereby ensuring more stable training processes.

Furthermore, DCGANs learn hierarchical image representations, enabling them to capture both low-level and high-level features. This capability enhances the meaningfulness of the generated images by incorporating intricate details and overall context. Additionally, DCGANs simplify architecture design by relying on convolutional layers, eliminating the necessity for manually crafted feature extractors. This simplification streamlines the implementation process and reduces the complexity of model development.

Advantage of DCGANs is their scalability and adaptability to various image generation tasks. They can accommodate different resolutions without imposing significant increases in computational complexity, making them versatile tools for a wide range of applications in TIG. Another notable advantage of DCGAN is Fashion Design and Virtual Try-On-That is in fashion design and virtual try-on systems, DCGANs have been employed to generate clothing items based on textual descriptions. By providing descriptions of clothing attributes such as color, style, and texture, DCGANs can generate corresponding images, facilitating virtual try-on experiences for users.

Conditional Generative Adversarial Networks (CGANs)

Recognizing the limitations of traditional GANs and DCGAN, efforts have been made to refine the generation process. One notable advancement in this regard is the introduction of CGANs by (Mirza et al., 2014). This ground breaking extension augments GANs with a conditional framework, affording greater control over the generation process (Zhou et al., 2021). By incorporating additional information, such as class labels or context, CGANs enable more precise and targeted generation, addressing the shortcomings observed in traditional GAN architectures. The configuration of CGAN is illustrated in Figure 2.

Figure 2. Architecture of CGAN

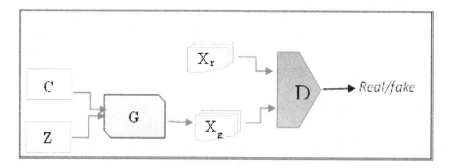

The architecture of CGANs bears resemblance to that of traditional GANs, albeit with a crucial distinction: both the generator (G) and the discriminator (D) in CGAN are trained on supplementary information denoted as C. This additional information, which could encompass various forms of supplementary data like class labels or response from different modalities, serves to guide the generation process towards more targeted outcomes. By incorporating both the latent input vector Z and the conditioning information C, CGANs offer enhanced control over the generated outputs.

In practical terms, this means that CGANs have the ability to harness both the inherent randomness of the latent space (Z) and the structured information provided by the conditioning data (C) to produce more tailored and contextually relevant outputs. Despite this augmentation, the fundamental loss function of CGAN remains akin to that of traditional GANs, ensuring continuity in the adversarial training framework.

CGANs provide controlled generating abilities by conditioning the generator on supplementary proof, namely class labels or attributes, enabling the synthesis of data customized to specific situations. This conditioning improves stability during training, resulting in quicker convergence and enhanced overall performance in comparison to conventional GANs. Furthermore, CGANs have the ability to generate multiple modes or variations for each given condition, thus addressing the problem of mode collapse that is commonly observed in conventional GANs. Furthermore, CGANs have the capability to facilitate semi-supervised learning tasks. This means that the discriminator may accurately categorize real samples into several classes and utilize both labeled and unlabeled data to improve performance. This is especially beneficial in situations where there is a scarcity of labeled data. CGANs are particularly effective in performing cross-domain translation responsibilities, such as converting images from one style to another, adding color to black and white images, and carrying out other transformations across different domains. In a wide range of applications the mentioned model can be used by adjusting the generator and discriminator to different types of information, such as class labels, text descriptions, or other modalities. This makes them suitable for various domains, including image generation and NLP.

CGANs are naturally more intricate than regular GANs because of the supplementary conditioning mechanism, which augments computational demands for training and inference, as well as the intricacy of the model architecture. Although CGANs have enhanced stability in comparison to conventional GANs, they are nevertheless susceptible to training instability, such as mode collapse or oscillations. Furthermore, CGANs necessitate labeled data for conditioning, which may not always be accessible or practical to acquire, unlike classic GANs that do not have this prerequisite. While conditioning on extra information can partially alleviate mode collapse, it does not completely eradicate this problem. CGANs have several shortcomings in comparison to standard GANs, specifically in terms of complexity, conditioning requirements, and training instability. The selection between CGANs and regular GANs is contingent upon the particular demands and limitations of the generating task being undertaken.

Structural Generative Adversarial Networks (SGANs)

SGANs is a specialized category of GANs designed for TIG, aiming to produce outputs with specific structural properties. Unlike traditional GANs that focus on generating realistic images, SGANs are tailored to adhere to predefined structural constraints such as object shapes, spatial arrangements, or semantic consistency.

SGAN utilizes an unsupervised segmentation module to extract structural information, enabling discriminators to evaluate images based on their structure. This compels the generators to produce images with coherent structural content, enhancing genuineness. The multistage framework allows SGAN to generate images with increasing resolution. Experimental results demonstrate that SGAN outperforms baseline methods, producing high-resolution, realistic, and structurally coherent remote sensing images consistent with given text descriptions.

SGANs introduce additional constraints or guidance to the GAN framework to ensure that generated outputs possess desired structural properties. These properties can vary depending on the application domain. For instance, in image generation tasks, structural constraints might include object shapes, spatial arrangements, or semantic consistency.

The structural coherence of ground objects in remote sensing images is crucial for authenticity; for example, real bridges are typically straight. To address this challenge, Author of the paper (Zhao & Shi, 2021) propose a multistage SGAN as described in Figure 3that synthesizes isolated sensing images in aorganisedway guided by text descriptions.

In this scholarly discourse (Deng et al., 2017), the author initiates an exploration into the novel realm of SGANs within the context of semi-supervised conditional generative modelling. SGANs emerge as a ground-breaking framework poised to revolutionize the landscape of generative modelling by harnessing the power of two independent latent variables: y and z.

Central to the SGAN paradigm is the assumption that the observed data x is intricately linked to these latent variables, each imbued with distinct functionalities. While y serves as a conduit for encoding the designated semantics, acting as a beacon of meaning within the data, z assumes the role of a repository housing the manifold other factors of variation, thereby enriching the tapestry of generated samples with diversity and nuance.

Figure 3. Outline of the planned SGAN for text-to-remote-sensing-image generation

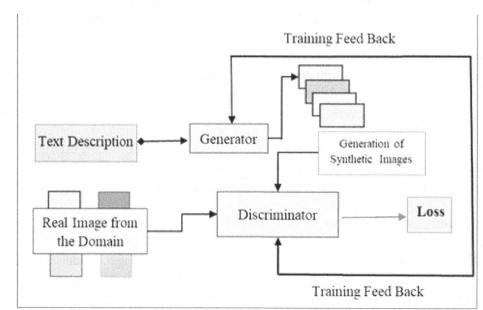

(Zhao, & Shi, 2021)

To navigate the intricate terrain of disentangled semantics embodied by y and z, SGAN orchestrates a symphony of collaboration within the hidden space. Here, two collaborative games are meticulously crafted, each tailored to minimize the reconstruction error associated with either y or z. Through this intricate dance, SGAN endeavors to distill the essence of semantics while preserving the nuanced variations inherent within the data, thus fostering a deeper understanding of its underlying structure.

The journey of SGAN transcends the boundaries of mere reconstruction, delving into the realm of adversarial games in pursuit of equilibrium. These adversarial games, comprising a crucial aspect of SGAN's training regime, are instrumental in guiding the model towards convergence at the elusive stage of true joint data distributions: $p(x, z)$ and $p(x, y)$. In doing so, SGAN deftly navigates the treacherous terrain of probability distribution, steering clear of the diffuse dispersion that plagues traditional maximum likelihood estimation (MLE)-based methodologies.

The efficacy of SGAN is not merely conjecture but substantiated through rigorous evaluation encompassing the scrutiny of trained networks and their performance in downstream tasks. Through meticulous analysis, SGAN emerges as a paradigm of excellence, boasting a highly controllable generator and disentahjg ngled representations. Moreover, SGAN distinguishes itself by achieving state-of-the-art results across multiple datasets, particularly in the domain of semi-supervised image classification. (Deng et al., 2017) Notable achievements include unprecedented error rates of 1.27%, 5.73%, and 17.26% on the MNIST, SVHN, and CIFAR-10 datasets respectively, under varying label constraints.

The true brilliance of SGAN lies not only in its performance metrics but also in its inherent versatility. By virtue of its adeptness in separately modeling y and z, SGAN emerges as a virtuoso capable of crafting images imbued with high visual fidelity while adhering steadfastly to designated semantics. Beyond the realm of image generation, SGAN's potential extends to a myriad of applications, encompassing realms such as style transfer and beyond, thus heralding a new era of innovation and possibility.

Attention Generative Adversarial Network (AttnGAN)

Another variation of the traditional GAN architecture is AttnGANthat incorporates attention mechanisms to enhance the generation process. While there isn't a single canonical paper or reference specifically dedicated to Attention GAN, several papers and works have explored the integration of attention mechanisms within GANs for several tasks, such as image generation, image-to-image translation, and text-to-image synthesis.

The paper (Zhang et al., 2019) authors introduces the Self-Attention GAN (SAGAN) as a technique for attention-driven, long-range dependency modelling in image generation tasks. Previous convolutional GANs create high-resolution facts by relying exclusively on spatially local points within lower-resolution feature maps. Nevertheless, SAGAN facilitates the production of specific information by taking into account cues from every feature location. Furthermore, the authors emphasize that the discriminator can validate the steadiness of detailed features across distant parts of the image. Recent research findings indicating the influence of generator conditioning on GAN performance are also discussed. In response to this insight, spectral normalization is applied to the GAN generator, resulting in observed enhancements in training dynamics. The authors state that the proposed SAGAN outperforms previous methods, specifically achieving a higher Inception score of 52.52 compared to the previous best score of 36.8. Additionally, it reduces the Frechetstart distance from 27.62 to 18.65 on the challenging ImageNet dataset. Picturing of the attention layers illustrates that the generator utilizes neighbourhoods corresponding to object forms rather than local regions with fixed shapes.

The authors of this paper (Xu et al., 2018) introduce the AttnGAN, a method that enables the generation of good quality images from text by incorporating attention-based, multi-stage refinement techniques. AttnGAN utilizes an innovative attentional generative network to generate detailed information in different parts of the image. It achieves this by prioritizing related words in the natural language description. In addition, they suggest utilizing a comprehensive attentional multimodal parallel model to compute a precise image-text matching loss for the purpose of training the generator. The authors of AttnGAN illustrate that it achieves notable advancements compared to the previous cutting-edge models. It enhances the highest reported commencement score by 14.14% on the CUB dataset and by 170.25% on the more demanding COCO dataset. Additionally, they conduct a comprehensive analysis by visualizing the attention layers of AttnGAN, revealing its capability to automatically select conditions at the word level for generating different parts of the image, which is confirmed for the first time.

Controllable Text-to-Image Generative Adversarial Network (ControlGAN)

ControlGAN is a specific variant of GANs designed for TIG tasks. It intentions to improve the control and variety of created images based on textual descriptions. It addresses the limitations of traditional GANs in makingvaried and controllable images from textual elaborations. ControlGAN incorporates a control mechanism that enables users to manipulate specific attributes of the generated images through textual inputs.

This control mechanism allows users to specify desired attributes such as object color, shape, size, position, or other visual properties in the textual descriptions. ControlGAN typically containsa generator and a discriminator network, similar to other GAN architectures.

In the paper (Lee, & Seok, 2019)authors describe how ControlGAN addresses limitations in TIG by enhancing the guidance provided to the generator. It introduces a novel architecture that separates the feature classifier from the discriminator and employs data augmentation techniques to improve classifier performance. Evaluated on the CIFAR-10 dataset, ControlGAN outperforms existing models, generating diverse samples with superior quality. Additionally, it demonstrates the ability to generate intermediate and reverse features for both interpolated and extrapolated input labels, enhancing the variety of generated images.

The generator receipts as input both a disorganised noise vector sampled from a predefined distribution and the textual description containing control signals. The generator learns to produce images that match both the provided textual description and the desired control signals.

ControlGAN undergoes adversarial training, wherein the generator endeavors to generate images that are blurry from real ones based on textual descriptions and control signals. The discriminator provides feedback to the generator by distinguishing between genuine and synthesized images. As the generator fine-tunes its parameters to minimize the discriminator's ability to discern real from generated images, the discriminator, conversely, strives to enhance its discriminative capability.

ControlGAN has various applications in TIG tasks, such as generating images based on specific user preferences or semantic descriptions. It can be used in e-commerce platforms for generating product images based on textual descriptions, in virtual fashion try-on applications, or in creative design tools for generating visual content based on user input.

In the paper (Lyu et al., 2019), The authors introduces a novel ControlGAN capable of synthesizing high-quality images while allowing users to manipulate object attributes independently of other content generation. ControlGAN comprises three key components. Firstly, it incorporates a word-level spatial and channel-wise attention-driven generator, leveraging an attention mechanism to synthesize image subregions corresponding to the most relevant words. The generator follows a multi-stage architecture, progressively refining image quality from coarse to fine. Secondly, ControlGAN incorporates a word-level discriminator that examines the relationship between words and image sub regions to separate various visual attributes. This enables the generator to receive detailed training signals regarding visual characteristics. Additionally, ControlGAN utilizes perceptual loss in TIG todecreasearbitrariness in the creation process as well as encourage the generator to uphold visual consistency with the original text.

Mirror Generative Adversarial Network (MirrorGAN)

For text-to-image synthesis introduces a pioneering two-stage training approach aimed at enhancing the quality and diversity of generated images. This innovative method addresses some of the key challenges in text-to-image creation, like generating images with diverse styles and attributes that faithfully represent the textual input.

In the first phase of MirrorGAN's(Reed et al., 2016) training, a generator network is trained using an adversarial loss function to generate initial images from textual descriptions. These initial images may lack diversity and fine-grained details due to the limited training data available initially. However, they serve as a starting point for the subsequent refinement stage.

In the second stage, MirrorGAN introduces a mirror discriminator, which evaluates both real images from the dataset and the generated images from the generator. Additionally, the mirror discriminator is tasked with distinguishing among different styles within the generated images. This response loop encourages the generator to explore various modes of the data distribution and produce images with diverse styles and attributes.

One of the notable benefits of MirrorGAN is its capability to make images that capture the rich semantic information present in the textual descriptions. By leveraging the mirror discriminator's feedback, the generator can refine its output to better match the desired attributes specified in the text.

MirrorGAN has establishedstrikingoutcomes in various text-to-image synthesis tasks, comprising generating images from detailed textual descriptions and conditional image generation. It has been uncovered to produce good-quality images with diverse styles and attributes, outperforming previous approaches in terms of both visual feature and diversity.

In modern times, creating an image based on a provided text description involves accomplishing two main target: pictorial authenticity and semantic coherence. Although considerable development has been achieved in generating good and graphically authentic images through GAN, maintaining semantic coherence between the text description and visual representation remains a substantial challenge.

The authors of the paper (Qiao et al., 2019) address this challenge by introducing a novel framework named MirrorGAN, designed to achieve global-local attention and semantic preservation in text-to-image synthesis. MirrorGAN adopts the concept of learning TIG through redescription and consists of three primary modules: a Semantic Text Embedding Module (STEM), a Global-Local Collaborative Attentive Module for Cascaded Image Generation (GLAM), and a Semantic Text Regeneration and Alignment Module (STREAM). STEM is responsible for creating word- and sentence-level embeddings. GLAM employs a cascaded architecture to generate target images from coarse to fine scales, utilizing both local word attention and global sentence attention to progressively enhance the diversity and semantic coherence of the produced images. STREAM focuses on regenerating the text description from the created image, ensuring semantic alignment with the provided text description.

Extensive tests conducted on two public benchmark datasets underscore the superiority of MirrorGAN over other state-of-the-art approaches, demonstrating its efficacy in achieving both visual realism and semantic consistency in text-to-image synthesis.

Dynamic Memory-GAN (DM-GAN)

DC-GAN which stands for Diverse Image Generation via Dynamic Memory-based GANs, is an innovative approach to text-to-image synthesis. It introduces a dynamic memory mechanism to generate diverse and good-quality images from textual explanations. The method addresses the challenge of producing varied images that accurately represent the semantics of the input text.

The key idea behind DM-GAN is the incorporation of a dynamic memory module within the generator network. This memory module stores and updates information about the generated images and their corresponding textual descriptions during training. By dynamically updating the memory based on the feedback from the discriminator, DM-GAN encourages the generator to produce diverse images while maintaining consistency with the input text.

DM-GAN's dynamic memory mechanism allows the generator to adaptively adjust its generation process based on the evolving content stored in the memory. This allows the production of images with diverse styles, poses, and attributes, resulting in a more comprehensive coverage of the image space.

Moreover, DM-GAN leverages a conditional Wasserstein GAN framework, which conditions the generator on the input text to ensure that the generated images are semantically consistent with the textual descriptions. By combining dynamic memory with conditional GANs, DM-GAN achieves state-of-the-art performance in terms of both qualityof imageand diversity in text-to-image synthesis tasks.

In this study, our focus lies on the generation of realistic images from textual descriptions. Current methodologies typically commence by generating an initial image with rudimentary shape and color, followed by refining this initial image to achieve higher resolution. However, prevalent text-to-image synthesis techniques encounter two primary challenges. Firstly, these processes are acutely reliant on the quality of the initial images. Suboptimal initialization often leads to subsequent processes struggling to improve the image to anappropriate level of excellence. Secondly, each word within a text description holds varying degrees of importance in depicting different aspects of an image, yet existing approaches employ unchanged text representations throughout the image refinement process.

To address these issues, authors of the paper (Zhu et al., 2019) propose DM-GAN for generating superior images. Our novel way incorporates a dynamic memory module, which facilitates the refinement of indistinct image content, particularly when the initial images are inadequately generated. A memory writing gate is devised to selectively capture crucial text information based on the content of the preliminary image, enabling our approach to precisely translate text descriptions into images. Furthermore, we employ a response gate to dynamically fuse information retrieved from the memories with image features.

Authors also conduct extensive evaluations of the DM-GAN model using the Caltech-UCSD Birds 200 dataset and the Microsoft Common Objects in Context dataset. The investigational results exhibit that our proposed DM-GAN model outperforms state-of-the-art approaches in terms of image quality and fidelity.

DIFFUSION MODEL IMAGE GENERATION

DM are a category of generative models employed in the fields of machine learning and statistics to represent the progression of data across time. DM aim to replicate the gradual dissemination or dispersion of information or uncertainty throughout the data space. DM are utilized in the field of text-to-image creation to produce lifelike visuals based on textual descriptions. The approach entails iteratively enhancing an initial noise vector to produce progressively lifelike visuals that correspond to the provided text description. During each iteration, the noise vector is dispersed or expanded to capture the semantic meaning of the text. This process produces high-quality images that accurately depict the textual input. DM commonly utilize probabilistic frameworks to represent the diffusion process, enabling the production of varied and lifelike samples. In addition, they can utilize sophisticated methods like attention processes and dynamic memory mechanisms to improve the quality and coherence of the created visuals.

DM have been investigated in the field of deep learning as a viable alternative to other generative frameworks such as GANs or VAEs. DM do not provide an outcome all at once; instead, they incrementally develop their outputs across numerous steps, progressively improving them.

Fundamental of Diffusion Model

The origin of the DDPM (Ho et al., 2020) may be primarily attributed to two key efforts: the investigation of score-based generative models (SGM)(Song, & Ermon, 2019)and the introduction of diffusion probabilistic models (DPM) (Sohl-Dickstein et al., 2015) as early as 2015. Therefore, it is essential to review the operational concepts of DPM (Sohl-Dickstein et al., 2015) and SDE (Song, & Ermon, 2019) before discussing the introduction of DDPM.

DPM is an innovative method that integrates adaptability and accountability in generative modeling, taking inspiration from non-equilibrium statistical physics. The fundamental concept entails deliberately deteriorating the arrangement within a data distribution by means of a progressive diffusion process, then subsequently acquiring knowledge of a reverse diffusion process to reinstate the original arrangement. This method allows for the quick acquisition, selection, and assessment of probability in deep generative models with intricate structures.

The objective is to create a progressive spreading mechanism that simplifies intricate data distributions into a manageable format, and then acquire a reversible mechanism that functions as the distribution model for generating data. The method explores both the advancing (inference) diffusion process and the reverse (generative) diffusion process, emphasizing their training and application in probability assessment. Furthermore, it discusses the establishment of limits for the amount of disorder in the reverse process and the possible use of the acquired distributions in calculating probabilities that come after, such as filling in missing parts or reducing noise in images.

Score-based generative models (SGM) present a novel technique for generative modeling known as score-based generative modeling. This method entails approximating the gradients of the data distribution by score matching and producing samples by employing Langevin dynamics. The authors tackle the difficulties of score-based generative modeling by introducing varying levels of Gaussian noise to the data and training a single conditional score network to predict scores across all noise levels. They also suggest a sampling technique using annealed Langevin dynamics. The essay explores toy experiments, the production of images using diverse datasets, image inpainting by annealed Langevin dynamics, and includes several illustrations illustrating samples and outcomes.

Denoising Diffusion Probabilistic Model (DDPM)

DDPM (Ho et al., 2020) is a ground-breaking advancement in the development of diffusion probabilistic models (Sohl-Dickstein et al., 2015). The work conducted by DDPM focuses on the application of diffusion probabilistic prototypes for the purpose of generating high-quality images. This paper presents a new relationship between DM and denoising score matching using Langevin dynamics. It suggests a parameterization that enhances the quality of samples and explores the gradual lossy compression abilities of DM. Experimental results exhibit exceptional performance on diverse datasets. The paper additionally presents comprehensive information regarding the model's design, training procedure, and selection of hyperparameters.

DDPMs employ dual Markov chains to model both the forward and reverse processes (Ho, 2020; Sohl-Dickstein, 2015). Data diffusion with preset noise, such as Gaussian noise, happens in the forward phase. In the opposite process, deep neural networks(DNN) are used to systematically remove noise and restore the original data.

Forward Pass

Figure 4. By applying the Markov assumption, the joint distribution of the latent variables can be obtained by multiplying the Gaussian conditional chain transitions

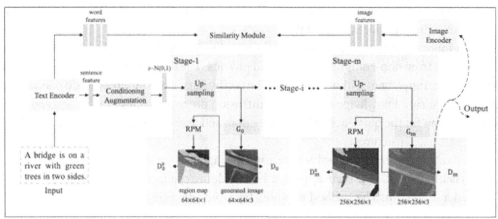

(Ho et al., 2020)

Assume the existence of a pristine data point, denoted as x_0, which is randomly selected from a data distribution known as $q(x_o)$. Subsequently, the onward diffusion process gradually disrupts the initial clean data distribution by introducing Gaussian noise, finally reaching the conventional Gaussian distribution z_T. During the diffusion step T, the latent variables $x_1, x_2, x_3, \ldots x_T$ are generated using noise. Put simply, it produces x_T by utilizing a sequential transition kernel $q(x_t | x_{t-1})$, which can be expressed as follows:

$$q(x_t | x_{t-1}) := \mathrm{N}\left(x_t; \sqrt{1 - \beta_t} x_{t-1}, \beta_t \mathrm{I}\right), \forall t \in \{1, \ldots, T\} \quad 1$$

Thus, the forward process is characterized by the utilization of a sequence of transition kernels:

$$q(x_{1:T} | x_0) := \prod_{t=1}^{T} q(x_t | x_{t-1}) \quad 2$$

The variance schedule $\beta_t \in (0,1)$ governs step sizes, and I represent the identity matrix with dimensions equivalent to the input data x_t. Additionally, N(x, ; μ, σ) denotes the Gaussian distribution of x with mean μ and covariance σ. Assume $\alpha_t := 1 - \beta_t$ and $\overline{\alpha}_t := \prod_{s=1}^{t} \alpha_s$ and α_s and ϵ as a Gaussian noise, It becomes possible to obtain a noisy sample from any step of the distribution, given the original input x_0 (Vignac et al., 2022), in the following manner:

$$q(x_t|x_0) := N\left(x_t; \sqrt{\overline{\alpha}_t}\, x_0, \sqrt{1 - \overline{\alpha}_t}\, \mathbf{I}\right) \quad 3$$

$$whwre\; x_t = \sqrt{\overline{\alpha}_t}\, x_0 + \sqrt{1 - \overline{\alpha}_t}\, \epsilon \quad 4$$

Reverse Process

In the reverse process, noise is eliminated at each step in the reverse time direction until the initially degraded data is restored. We commence with $p_\theta(x_T)$ to produce $p_\theta(x_0)$, adhering to the true data distribution $q(x_0)$. Once more, $x_T \sim N(O, I)$. A sequence of reverse Gaussian transition kernels p_θ, where θ Denotes the parameters that can be acquired through learning, is expressed in the structure of a DNN as follows:

$$p_\theta(x_{0:T}) := p(x_T) \prod_{t=1}^{T} p_\theta(x_{t-1}|x_t) \quad 5$$

$$p_\theta(x_{t-1}|x_t) := N\left(x_{t-1}; \mu_\theta(x_t, t), \sigma_\theta(x_t, t)\mathbf{I}\right) \quad 6$$

Furthermore, the model parameters include both the mean $\mu_\theta(x_t, t)$ and the variance $\sigma_\theta(x_t, t)$. The model aims to approximate the true data distribution throughout the reverse process by optimizing the variational upper bound on negative log-likelihood (NLL).

$$\mathbb{E}\left[-log\, p_\theta(x_0)\right] \le \mathbb{E}_q\left[-log\frac{p_\theta(x_{0:T})}{q(x_{1:T}|x_0)}\right] = \mathbb{E}_q\left[-log\, p(x_T) - \sum_{t \ge 1} log\frac{p_\theta(x_{t-1}|x_t)}{q(x_t|x_{t-1})}\right] \quad 7$$

It can be reformulated using the Kullback–Leibler divergence (KL divergence) as follows.

$$\mathbb{E}_q\left[\underbrace{D_{KL}(q(x_T|x_0)p(x_T))}_{L_T} + \sum_{t>1} \underbrace{D_{KL}(q(x_{t-1}|x_t, x_0))\big\| p_\theta(x_{t-1}|x_t)}_{L_{t-1}} - \underbrace{log\, p_\theta(x_0|x_1)}_{L_0}\right]$$

8

The equation mentioned above is divided into three components. Initially, L_T minimizes the KL divergence between $q(x_T|x_0)$ and a standard Gaussian distribution $p(x_T)$. Subsequently, in L_{t-1}, $p_\theta(x_{t-1}|x_t)$ can be computed against the posteriors from the forward process. Finally, the last term L_0 represents a negative log-likelihood. Particularly, L_{t-1} on x_0 which make it manipulable:

$$q(x_{t-1} | x_t, x_0) = N\left(x_{t-1}; \overline{\mu}_t(x_t, x_0), \overline{\beta}_t \mathbf{I}\right) \quad 9$$

$$where \, \overline{\mu}_t(x_t, x_0) := \frac{\sqrt{\overline{\alpha}_{t-1}} \beta_t}{1 - \overline{\alpha}_t} x_0 + \frac{\sqrt{\overline{\alpha}_t}(1 - \overline{\alpha}_{t-1})}{1 - \overline{\alpha}_t} x_t \, and \, \overline{\beta}_t = \frac{1 - \overline{\alpha}_{t-1}}{1 - \overline{\alpha}_t} \beta_t \quad 10$$

Taking into account equations 6, 9, and 10, the term Lt−1 in equation 8 can be restated as:

$$L_{t-1} = \mathbb{E}_q\left[\frac{1}{2\sigma_t^2}\left\{\overline{\mu}_t(x_t, x_0) - \mu_\theta(x_t, t)\right\}^2\right] + C \quad 11$$

Where C is independent of θ and so considered a constant. (Ho et al., 2020) emphasize that instead of parameterizing the average $\mu_\theta(x_t, t)$, it is more effective to enhance training efficiency and improve sample quality by anticipating the noise vector ϵ at each time step t throughout the forward process, parameterizing it as $\mu_\theta(x_t, t)$. The equation 11 is reformulated in the following manner:

$$\mathbb{E}_{t \sim u(1,T), x_0 \sim q(x_0), \epsilon \sim N(0,I)} \lambda(t) \left\{\epsilon - \epsilon_\theta(x_t, t)\right\}^2 \quad 12$$

In this expression, $u(1, T)$ represents a constant distribution, $\lambda(t)$ serves as a weighting function for uniformly adjusting the scales of noise, and ϵ_θ is a deep parameterized model predicting Gaussian noise $\epsilon \sim N(\mathbf{O}, \mathbf{I})$. Once trained, it generates samples of x_0 resembling the original data.

Although DDPM is initially designed for continuous data like images and audio, its applicability can extend beyond these domains.

Groundbreaking Text-to-Image Diffusion Modelling

This section delves into innovative text-to-image frameworks that utilize DM. The frameworks are classified into two main categories based on the location where the diffusion prior is applied: the pixel space or the latent space. The initial group of techniques directly produces pictures from the high-dimensional pixel level, as demonstrated by GLIDE (Nichol et al., 2021)and Imagen (Saharia et al., 2022). On the other hand, another method includes first reducing the picture to a space with less dimensions before training the diffusion model. Some notable approaches that fall under the area of latent space include Stable Diffusion (Rombach et al., 2022), VQ-diffusion (Gu et al., 2022), and DALL-E 2 (Ramesh et al., 2022).

Pixel Space Diffusion Models

GLIDE: is an innovative project that explores the field of Text-to-Image -T2I synthesis using DM(Nichol et al., 2021).GLIDE was proposed by Nichol et ail. (Nichol et al., 2021) In 2021 and represents a significant progress in the field of T2I generation. T2I is based on the concept of using text descriptions to influence the formation of images. This involves substituting class labels with textual prompts in conditional deep learning models, which allows for more directed and controlled sampling throughout the image synthesis process. GLIDE demonstrates improved photorealism and caption similarity in its produced samples by utilizing classifier-free guiding instead of CLIP(Radford et al., 2021) guidance. The process entails the training of a diffusion model with a massive parameter count of 3.5 billion. This model is enhanced by incorporating a text encoder that utilizes a transformer (Vaswani et al., 2017) architecture. GLIDE surpasses current models such as DALL-E (Ramesh et al., 2021) in both human and automatic assessments, notably in terms of Frechet Inception Distance (FID) and the quality of images as evaluated by humans. Furthermore, GLIDE's functionality goes beyond simple picture creation, since it also includes activities such as image inpainting and fine-tuning for text-driven image modification. The comparison with other models highlights the effectiveness of GLIDE in many situations, which strengthens its status as an innovative effort in the field of T2I synthesis utilizing DM. Figure 6 displays example pictures created using GLIDE. Figure 6 displays example pictures created using GLIDE. Figure 7demonstrates the practical ability of GLIDE to alter pre-existing pictures by including text prompts, introducing new elements such as objects, shadows, and reflections as needed.

Imagen: Imitating GLIDE (Nichol et al., 2021), Imagen (Saharia et al., 2022) employs a classifier-free approach to guide picture production. Imagen was introduced by (Saharia et al., 2022) and represents a state-of-the-art approach in the discipline of text-to-image synthesis. The analysis of Imagen and GLIDE provides insight into the progress and improvements made in the field of T2I production through the utilization of DMs with classifier-free guiding. Imagen demonstrates exceptional effectiveness in producing photorealistic pictures by utilizing advanced techniques such as massive transformer language models and high-fidelity DM. It efficiently uses pretrained language models such as BERT (Devlin et al., 2018), T5 (Raffel et al., 2017), and CLIP (Radford et al., 2021) as text encoders, utilizing their weights without modification to save computing resources. This enables the process of embedding text without requiring an internet connection, which in turn reduces the amount of computer resources needed while training the text-to-image diffusion prior in real-time.

GLIDE and Imagen differ significantly in their approaches to text encoding. GLIDE simultaneously instruct the text encoder and the diffusion prior using paired image-text data. In contrast, Imagen utilizes a pre-trained and fixed big language model, simplifying the training procedure and maximizing processing resources. Furthermore, Imagen's decision to utilize exclusively text-based collections of data for training the language model brings about a wide-ranging and varied distribution of textual information. This, in turn, enhances the accuracy and congruity between images and their corresponding text descriptions.

Imagens's performance on the COCO (Lin et al., 2014) dataset is superior than other contemporary approaches in terms of sample quality as well as image-text alignment, as demonstrated by the comparison study. Furthermore, the implementation of DrawBench, ainclusive benchmark for text-to-image models, highlights Imagen's supremacy by demonstrating its strength and effectiveness across many assessment parameters.

Both Imagen and GLIDE are notable breakthroughs in T2I synthesis employing DMs. Imagen, in particular, demonstrates improved efficiency and performance by utilizing pretrained language models and dynamic thresholding strategies. These findings highlight the changing nature of T2I synthesis and lay the groundwork for future study and advancements in this field. Figure 8 shows the Imagen model diagram. Imagen employs a large frozen T5-XXL encoder to convert the input text into embeddings. A conditional diffusion model transforms the text embedding into a 64×64 picture. Imagen employs text-conditional super-resolution DM to increase the resolution of the picture from 64×64 to 256×256 and from 256×256 to 1024×1024. Figure 9 shows 1024 × 1024 image examples for different text inputs.

Figure 8. Visualization of Imagen model diagram

(Saharia et al., 2022)

Figure 9. Choose 1024 × 1024 image examples for different text inputs

(Saharia et al., 2022)

latent Space Diffusion Model

Stable Diffusion: Stable diffusion (SD) is a significant achievement in the field of latent space. SD is a representational framework which trains DM on latent space. It is an enlarged version of the Latent Diffusion Model (LDM) Proposed by(Rombach et al., 2022). SD is a model that converts text into pictures. It has been trained using 512x512 images from a specific portion of the LAION-400M dataset, as described in reference (Schuhmann et al., 2021). This approach improves the efficiency of training and sampling in DM, guaranteeing that picture synthesis retains a high degree of visual accuracy. The architecture of Latent LDMs consists of a two-stage process: first, a diffusion model is trained to remove noise from the input picture, and then a generative model is conditioned on the output of the diffusion model to generate the final image. Conditioning may be utilized in many ways, using cross-attention processes to guarantee effective conditioning.

LDMs employ a dual-stage methodology. During the initial phase, an autoencoder is utilized to train a perceptual compression model (Zhang et al., 2018). Figure 10 presents the model overview where, the model acquires knowledge of a lower-dimensional latent space that is perceptually indistinguishable from the picture space. The compression model employs a blend of a perceptual loss and a patch-based adversarial objective to guarantee authentic reconstructions. The latent space derived from this compression model is more suited for likelihood-based generative models. During the second stage, DM are trained using the compressed latent space.DM are stochastic models that estimate a data distribution by removing noise from a variable that follows a normal distribution. The DMs' ability to generate is strengthened by the inductive biases derived from their UNet design (Dhariwal et al., 2021; Ronneberger et al., 2015). LDMs employ a modified version of the variational lower bound to train the DM. By doing this, the models may focus on the crucial semantic elements of the data and train in a space that has fewer dimensions and is computationally efficient. LDMs can also be conditioned on other inputs such as textual data or semantic maps. This is accomplished by enhancing the UNet backbone of the DM with a cross-attention mechanism. The cross-attention mechanism, as described in reference (Vaswani et al., 2017), enables models to learn attention-based models for different input modalities, hence enhancing the capability of generating images conditionally with more flexibility.

Figure 10. Stable diffusion model overview

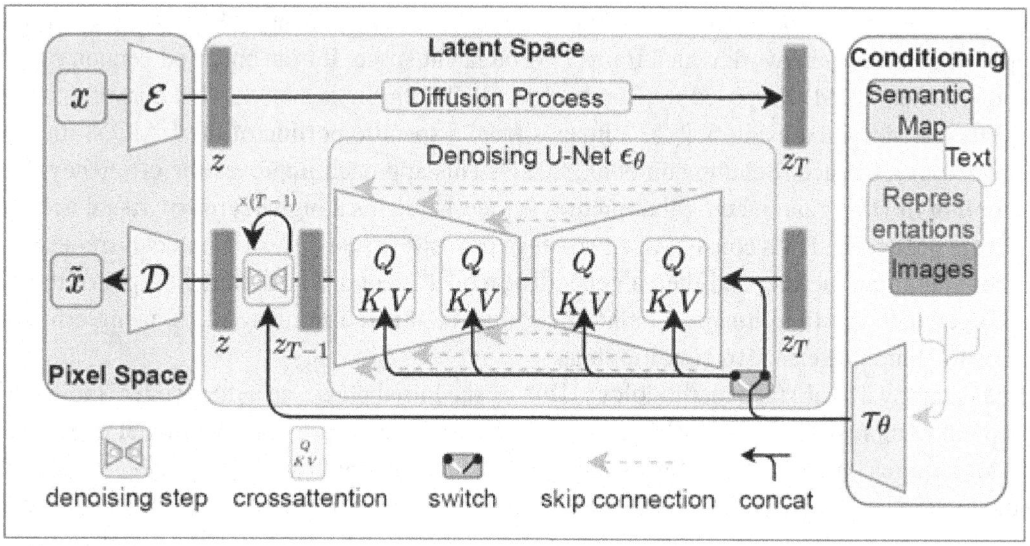

Vector Quantized Diffusion Model (VQ-Diffusion): Another crucial pioneering model in latent space for TIG is the VQ-Diffusion model, was introduced by (gu et al., 2022). This model leverages a vector quantized variational autoencoder (VQ-VAE)(Van et al., 2017), wherein its latent space is organized by a conditional variant of the recently introduced DDPM(Ho et al., 2020).The model integrates the VQ-VAE model with the diffusion model, overcoming limitations of existing methods by mitigating unidirectional bias and preventing accumulated prediction errors. Figure 11 shows the overall framework of the VQ-Diffusion model. The overall structure begins with the VQVAE. The VQ-Diffusion model represents the discrete latent space by applying a reverse diffusion process that gradually corrupts the input using a predetermined Markov chain. It demonstrates notably superior performance compared to traditional autoregressive models and previous GAN-based text-to-image approaches. The model architecture comprises a text encoder, a diffusion image decoder, and a VQ-VAE(Van et al., 2017) model. The VQ-Diffusion model primarily addresses the issue of unidirectional bias and cumulative prediction mistakes that are frequently observed in current text-to-image generating techniques DALL-E (Ramesh et al., 2021), CogView(Ding et al., 2021 and M6 (Lin et al., 2021). The model does this by employing a vector quantized variational autoencoder (VQ-VAE) and a conditional version of the DDPM(Ho et al., 2020) to represent the hidden space. The VQ-Diffusion model utilizes a mask-and-replace diffusion method to prevent the buildup of errors and enhance convergence. The strategy presented in this study overcomes the constraints of current approaches and offers a superior and more efficient way for producing good-quality photographs based on textual explanations. The model exhibits superior picture quality and adeptly manages complexity, all while outperforming conventional autoregressive approaches in terms of speed. Although VQ-Diffusion model does not have explicit limitations, still potential drawbacks may include dependence on pre-trained models, the necessity for extensive datasets for training, and the trade-off between inference speed and output quality.

DALLE-2: Another category of text-to-image DM, such as DALLE-2(Ramesh et al., 2022), includes the integration of multimodal latent spaces using multimodal contrastive models (Radford, 2021; Jia, 2021; Yuan, 2021). DALLE-2, introduced by Ramesh et al. from OpenAI (Ramesh et al., 2022) in 2022, emerged around the same period as the aforementioned models -Diffusion and VQ-DM. These approaches synchronize picture embeddings and text encodings in a shared representation space. The CLIP framework, which is a cutting-edge method for learning multimodal representations, has been widely used in many models that convert text into images. DALLE-2, also known as unCLIP(Ramesh et al., 2022), is an example of such an application. It utilizes the CLIP text encoder and replaces the CLIP picture encoder with a diffusion model to generate images from the CLIP latent space. The proposed model, unCLIP, consists of two main components: Prior model and a decoder model, Figure 12. Prior Model: The prior model generates CLIP image embeddings conditioned on text captions. The previous model may take the form of either an autoregressive (AR) model or a diffusion model. In the AR approach, the model transforms the CLIP image embedding into a sequence of discrete codes and predicts them sequentially based on the caption. Conversely, the diffusion model directly represents the continuous vector form of the CLIP image embedding using a Gaussian diffusion model conditioned on the caption. The prior model can also be conditioned on the CLIP text embedding in addition to the caption. The AR prior is trained using Principal Component Analysis (PCA) (Pearson, 1901, pp. 559-572) to reduce the dimensionality of the CLIP image embeddings, while the diffusion prior is trained using a decoder-only Transformer model. Decoder Model: The decoder model generates images conditioned on CLIP image embeddings and optionally text captions. DM(Ho, 2020; Song, 2020) are used in the decoder to produce images conditioned on the CLIP image embeddings. The architecture of the decoder is modified from the original GLIDE model by adding CLIP embeddings to the prevailing timestep embedding and projecting them into extra tokens of context. The decoder model also includes diffusion upsampler models (Nichol, 2021; Saharia, 2022) to generate high-resolution images. During training, classifier-free guidance (Ho, &Salimans, 2022) is enabled by randomly setting CLIP embeddings to zero and randomly dropping the text caption. The combination of the prior model and the decoder model allows for text-conditional image generation. The prior model generates CLIP image embeddings from captions, and the decoder model uses these embeddings to generate images. The joint training of these two components enables the generation of diverse images while preserving the semantics and style of the input captions, Figure 13. Overall, explicitly generating image representations improves image diversity by leveraging the rich latent space of CLIP embeddings and allowing for variations in non-essential details while preserving the semantics and style of the images. The unCLIP paradigm, as currently presented, has many shortcomings. These limitations encompass restricted control over created pictures, absence of clear semantic comprehension, reliance on CLIP's performance, computational intricacy, and inadequate explanation of the generated images. The model has challenges in associating qualities with objects, maintaining coherence in text creation, and accurately representing intricate features in intricate scenarios. Furthermore, there are potential hazards linked to the production of misleading or detrimental material. Future research should focus on addressing these constraints in order to improve the capabilities and reduce the dangers associated with the unCLIP model.

Figure 11. Overall framework of VQ-diffusion model

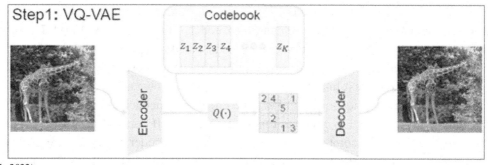

(Gu et al., 2022)

Figure 12. An overview of the unCLIP model architecture at a high level

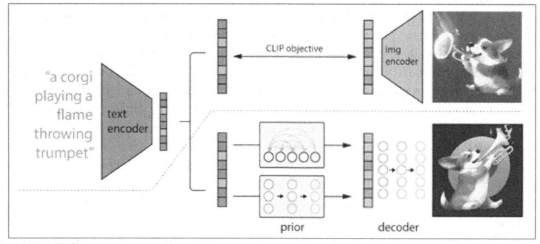

(Ramesh et al., 2022)

Figure 13. Different renditions of an input image are generated by encoding it with CLIP and subsequently decoding it using a DM—These variations maintain semantic features such as the existence of a clock in the image and the overlapping strokes in the logo, along with stylistic elements like the surrealism in the painting and the color gradients in the logo, while altering non-essential details

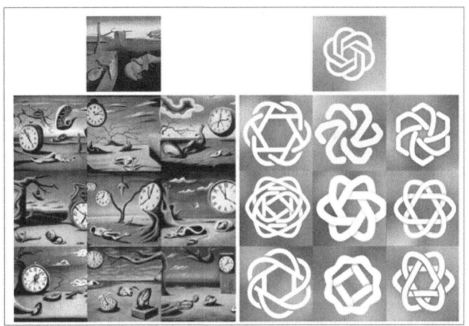

(Ramesh et al., 2022)

TIG USING AUTOREGRESSIVE (VAR) MODEL

One way to address the challenge of generating truthful images from textual descriptions is by using autoregressive models. These models have been shown to be real at capturing the intricate relationships between different types of data. Autoregressive models are a type of statistical models that utilize the sequential pattern of data to produce outputs one by one. Each output is dependent on the preceding ones. Autoregressive models provide a potential framework for generating images from textual descriptions in the domain of text-to-image creation. These replicas are able to successfully capture the complex connections between words and visual elements.

Fundamental of Autoregressive Model

An autoregressive (AR) model is a statistical model that uses past values of a time series to predict upcoming values. The underlying principle of this approach is that the existing value of the time series is affected by its previous data, and this relationship is determined by a set of coefficients. The AR model was first coined by (Van. Et al., 2016) of google deepMind. The authors introduced Pixel Recurrent

Neural Networks, a type of DNN capable of representing the probability distribution of natural images. The objective was to calculate a probability distribution for natural images that can be easily utilized to determine the likelihood of images and to create new ones.

Autoregressive models employ linear regression by using lagged variables of its output obtained from earlier time steps. Autoregressive models differ from typical linear regression in that they solely depend on previously predicted outcomes and do not take into account additional independent variables. This technique is expressed by the subsequent formula.

$$p(x) = \prod_{i=1}^{n} p\left(x_i \middle| x_1, x_2, \ldots x_{i-1}\right) = \prod_{i=1}^{n} p(x_i | x_{<i})$$

Where $x_{<i} = [x_1, x_2, \ldots x_{i-1}]$ represent the vector of random variables with an index smaller than i.

When formulated probabilistically, an autoregressive model assigns probabilities to independent variables across n possible steps, operating under the assumption that preceding variables conditionally impact the outcome of the subsequent ones. The equation below can also be used to represent autoregressive modelling.

$$y_t = c + \varnothing_1 y_{t-1} + \varnothing_2 y_{t-2} + \ldots + \varnothing_p y_{t-p} + \epsilon_t$$

In this context, y represents the predicted outcome which is calculated by multiplying several orders of prior results by their corresponding coefficients, ϕ. The coefficient denotes the weights or characteristics that influence the significance of the predictor in determining the new outcome. The method also accounts for stochastic noise that may impact the forecast, suggesting that the model is not perfect and can be further enhanced.

Pathways Autoregressive Text-to-Image Model (Parti)

In 2022, Yu et al. (Yu et al., 2022) introduced Parti at Google, offering a unique text-to-image methodology distinct from existing approaches like Google's Imagen (Saharia et al., 2022) and DALLE-2 (Ramesh et al., 2022). Unlike these methods, Parti diverges from DM, opting instead for an autoregressive architecture in its text-to-image synthesis process. Autoregressive models for TIG continue to be attractive due to the considerable previous research on scaling big language models (Pont-Tuset, 2020; Brown, 2020; Thoppilan, 2022; Du, 2022; Chowdhery, 2023) and the progress made in discretizing other modalities, such as images and audio, allowing them to be considered as language-like tokens. Parti utilizes a sequence-to-sequence modelling technique, similar to machine translation. In this paradigm, the system utilizes contextual cues to accurately generate subsequent words or image tokens by predicting them based on prior ones. Parti approaches TIG as a sequence-to-sequence modelling challenge, akin to machine translation. This strategic alignment enables it to leverage advancements in large language models, particularly those enabled by scaling both data and model sizes. Here, the target outputs represent sequences of image tokens, rather than text tokens in a foreign language. Leveraging the robust image tokenizer ViT-VQGAN (Yo et al., 2021), Parti encodes images into sequences of discrete tokens. It harnesses the tokenizer's capability to reconstruct such sequences into high-quality, visually diverse images.

The PARTI model for TIG achieves significant improvements in quality by increasing the size of Parti's encoder-decoder architecture to support up to 20 billion parameters. Additionally, it achieves state-of-the-art zero-shot FID (Heusel et al., 2017)scores, with an impressive score of 7.23, and additional improves to a finetuned FID score of 3.22 on the MS-COCO (Lin et al., 2014) dataset. Furthermore, the model exhibits exceptional efficacy across various categories and levels of difficulty, as demonstrated by its performance in studies conducted on Localized Narratives and PartiPrompts. These analyses were part of a complete benchmark that included over 1600 English prompts introduced in this study.

Parti operates as a two-stage model, consisting of an image tokenizer and an autoregressive model, as illustrated in Figure 14. In the initial stage, a tokenizer is trained to convert images into sequences of discrete visual tokens during training, which are later used to reconstruct images during inference. Subsequently, the second stage involves training an autoregressive sequence-to-sequence model, which generates image tokens based on input text tokens.

Figure 14. Overview of Parti autoregressive model

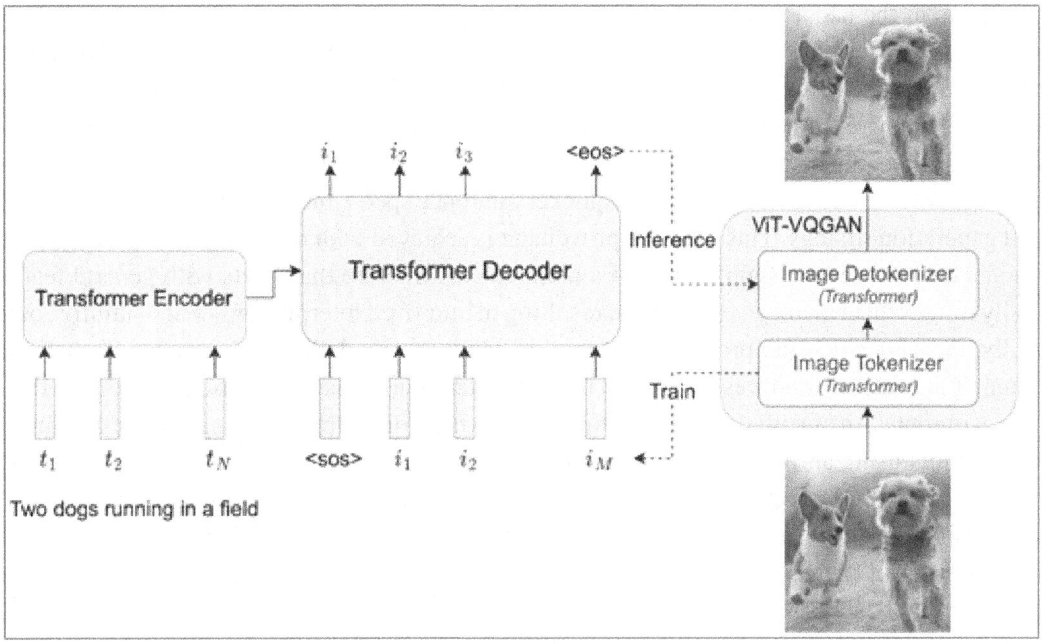

(Ramesh et al., 2022)

Although Parti has showcased various capabilities, it is important to take into account its limits. Firstly, despite its novel architecture, Parti utilizes autoregressive modelling, which can provide scalability difficulties. Autoregressive models sometimes necessitate sequential generation, which can result in slower inference times, particularly when dealing with extensive datasets or intricate picture synthesis tasks. Furthermore, while Parti has demonstrated favourable outcomes in terms of image quality and accuracy, its performance may differ depending on the type of textual inputs. Further investigation is required to explore the model's capacity to precisely convert a wide range of textual descriptions into top-notch visuals, especially in niche or specialized fields. Furthermore, Parti's dependence on an autoregressive technique may restrict its ability to adequately capture global contextual information. Autoregressive models typically prioritize analysing the immediate relationships within a sequence, which may result in disregarding the wider semantic contexts that exist in the textual descriptions. Moreover, similar to several deep learning models, Parti's performance is greatly influenced by the caliber and variety of the training data. The presence of biases or limits in the training dataset can result in the propagation of these issues to the generated images, hence impacting the model's ability to generalize and maintain resilience. Although Parti has demonstrated encouraging outcomes on benchmark datasets like MS-COCO, its practicality in real-world situations and many applications has yet to be thoroughly investigated. To improve Parti's effectiveness and expand its usefulness in text-to-image generating tasks, it is important to address these limitations.

Vector Quantized Autoregressive (VQ-AR)

In the current scenarios, Vector Quantized AutoRegressive (VQ-AR) (Fei et al., 2022) models have demonstrated impressive performance in generating images from text by accurately predicting discrete image tokens in the latent space, following a left-to-right, top-to-bottom order. Despite its simplicity, the generative process has remarkable effectiveness.The VQ-AR presents an innovative approach to generating high-quality images from text, with the goal of enhancing current methods such as VQ-AR models. This iterative framework produces novel image elements in a step-by-step fashion, utilizing the current environment in a simultaneous manner, hence improving the process of image generation. The suggested method produces a significantly quicker inference speed, more than 13 times faster, by using a parallel generation strategy. This speed improvement is achieved with minimal sacrifice in performance. The model emphasizes the significance of a hierarchical structure that starts with general features and gradually refines them in image production, resulting in improved interpretability and intuitive outcomes. Typically, they approach the problem as a type of language modelling and employ Transformer-like (Vaswani et al., 2017) structures to acquire the understanding of the connection between verbal inputs and visual outputs. An essential element of these methods involves transforming each image into a series of distinct units using an image tokenizer based on VQ-VAE (Va &Vinyals, 2017), such as VQ-GAN (Yu, 2021; Esser, 2021), RQ-VAE (Lee et al., 2022), and ViT VQGAN (Yu et al., 2021).

One limitation of the proposed progressive model for TIG lies in its reliance on the predefined generation order of image tokens. While the top-down hierarchy offers interpretability and computational efficiency benefits, it may not always capture the complex interdependencies between different image features effectively. Additionally, the variant scoring strategies used to determine the generation order might not always generalize well across diverse datasets or text prompts, potentially leading to suboptimal results in certain scenarios. Furthermore, the incorporation of image token revision into the progressive framework, although improving model performance, may introduce additional complexity and computational overhead, especially when dealing with large-scale datasets or real-time applications. Therefore, while the proposed progressive model shows promising results in terms of perceptual quality and inference speed, further research is needed to address its limitations and ensure its applicability across a wide range of TIG tasks and settings.

EXPLORING TEXT-TO-IMAGE GENERATION AND ITS APPLICATIONS

The progress in Text-to-Image Generation (TIG) models has sparked interest in a range of captivating uses beyond generating images from text. These activities encompass artistic painting, video production, and picture alteration that are guided by textual input.

Text-Driven Artistic Creation

Generative models have made great progress in the field of artistic painting, specifically in overcoming the issues encountered by GAN-based painting methods, such as training instability and model collapse (Jabbar et al., 2021). Current endeavors have focused on DM, which have produced remarkable outcomes in generating a wide range of digital artworks. Multimodal guided artwork diffusion (MGAD) (Huang et al., 2022) improves the generating process by integrating textual and visual inputs, leading to the creation of digital artworks that are both high-quality and diverse. DiffStyler(Huang et al., 2024) presents an alternative method that utilizes a configurable dual diffusion model with learnable noise to maintain the overall content of input images. This approach achieves outstanding outcomes in terms of both quantitative measurements and manual assessment. In order to improve the originality of the Stable Diffusion model (We, 2022, pp. 59-80), techniques have been suggested to extend the textual conditions and retrain the model using the Wikiart dataset. This allows users to generate new images from renowned painters. In addition, there have been attempts to customize the production of text-to-image by personalizing aesthetic styles (Gallego, 2022, pp. 59-80) and expanding the range of created pictures to include Scalable Vector Graphics (SVGs) for digital applications (Jain et al., 2023). Computation efficiency is improved by using retrieval-augmented DM, which recover neighbors from specialized datasets to have precise control over image style (Rombach et al., 2022). Additional improvements, such as the implementation of supervised style advice and self-style guidance techniques, allow for the definition of more detailed style characteristics (Pan et al., 2023), leading to the creation of images with a wide range of visual styles.

Text-to-video generation is the process of producing videos using text inputs. It serves as a connection between text-to-image and video generation models. Two prominent methodologies in this field are Make-A-Video (Singer et al., 2022) and Video Imagen. Make-A-Video utilizes pretrained text-to-image models to produce superior films by integrating temporal data and developing spatial super-resolution and frame interpolation models. By utilizing unsupervised learning techniques on video data, Make-A-Video enhances the speed of training without the need for coupled text-video data. However, Video Imagen (Ho et al., 2022a) employs cascaded video DM(Ho et al., 2022b) to synthesize videos from text. The statement implies that the latest discoveries in text-to-image models, such as utilizing frozen encoder text conditioning, can be utilized for generating videos. Moreover, the utilization of video DM, such as the v-prediction parameterization, enhances the advancement of overall DM.

The production of three-dimensional things has distinct difficulties in comparison to the fabrication of two-dimensional images. DeepFusion(Poole et al., 2022) was the first to use DM for synthesizing 3D objects, taking inspiration from previous research such as Dream Fields (Jain et al., 2022). The NeRF(Mildenhall et al., 2021) model was developed via distillation using a pretrained 2D diffusion model called Imagen. Nevertheless, Magic3D (Lin et al., 2023) pointed up concerns regarding DeepFusion(Poole et al., 2022), specifically mentioning subpar outcomes and inefficient optimization caused by the use of low-resolution picture guidance and the sluggish processing of NeRF. Magic3D suggested an optimization technique that starts with rough representations and gradually improves mesh representations using high-resolution diffusion priors. In addition, Magic3D implemented a sparse 3D hash grid structure to accelerate the generating process. A 3DDesigner (Li et al., 2022) who prioritizes consistency in creating 3D objects, with a particular focus on ensuring that they correlate accurately when viewed from different angles. By using low-resolution NeRF-based findings as priors, this method deployed a two-stream asynchronous diffusion module to improve consistency and provide consistent outcomes in a 360-degree setting.

Text-Driven Image Editing

DiffusionCLIP(Kim et al., 2021) was the first to include DMinto picture manipulation tasks. The system employs a pre-trained deep learning model to convert images into a latent space. This latent space is then refined in reverse using a loss function that combines local directional CLIP (Gal et al., 2022) loss and identity loss. This process guides image alteration while ensuring that important characteristics are preserved. LDEdit(Gallego, 2022, pp. 59-80) streamlines this procedure by integrating deterministic forward diffusion with latent space manipulation based on target text, demonstrating strong performance in a range of editing tasks. Prompt-to-Prompt (Hertz et al., 2022) tackles the problem of text prompt sensitivity by utilizing cross-attention maps during diffusion to capture the relationships between pixels and words. Studies on image-to-image (Tumanyan et al., 2023) translation have investigated semantic characteristics in the diffusion latent space, showcasing the ability to manipulate spatial features and self-attention to exert control over the translation process. DiffusionIT(Kwon et al., 2022) utilizes style-content disentanglement to accomplish unsupervised image translation. CycleDiffusion(Wu & De, 2022) integrates many generative models by redefining the latent space of DM, allowing for GAN-like guiding. Direct Inversion (Elarabawy et al., 2022) is a method that converts images into noise vectors and then reconstructs modified images. EDICT (Wallace et al., 2023) is a technique that enhances the quality of reconstruction by keeping the noise vectors linked together during the diffusion process. Null-text Inversion (Mokady et al., 2023) improves picture editing by utilizing diffusion pivotal inversion and null-text optimization (Song et al., 2020), thereby reducing mistake propagation problems in DDIM-based editing.

The 3DDesigner (Lin et al., 2022)is at the forefront of developing a technique that allows for 360-degree manipulation using single-view editing. This involves creating text embeddings from a combination of blended noises and then mapping them to a space that is not dependent on the specific perspective. DATID-3D (Kim, & Chun, 2023)tackles the difficulties associated with adapting 3D objects to a certain domain using text guidance. These obstacles include the loss of diversity, establishing connection between language and images, and maintaining high picture quality. The proposed method utilizes DM to generate a wide range of target images that are aware of different poses. It improves the quality of the images by enhancing the CLIP and filtering processes. The results obtained from this method surpass those achieved by state-of-the-art generators such as EG3D(Chan et al., 2022), producing high-resolution images that are consistent across several views.

CHALLENGES AND RESEARCH DIRECTION

Although there have been significant breakthroughs in generative DM for organised data, still some issues are noticed that need to be addressed. This calls for further research in this subject.

Customized Designs for Structured Data: Generative DM are highly dependent on parameters such as architectural design, training technique, and noise scheduling. However, the majority of methods for handling structured data simply incorporate or make minor adjustments to existing techniques from other modalities. Modifying these features has the potential to greatly improve the ability to create models and solve the problem of generative modelling, which involves ensuring high-quality, diverse, and fast sampling(Xiao et al., 2021).

Contributory learning and counterfactual reasoning: approaches into DM, their performance can be improved(Moraffah et al., 2021). Causal learning is a process that helps to identify the cause-and-effect links between variables. It is particularly useful in tasks such as financial forecasting or modelling the evolution of diseases. Counterfactual reasoning is a method that allows us to forecast outcomes by considering alternate conditions. It provides valuable insights into potential scenarios. Utilizing cause-and-effect linkages or counterfactual estimation can enhance the effectiveness and resilience of DM.

Dataset Bias: The presence of inherent bias in publicly accessible datasets, namely in demographic characteristics and bioelectrical signals, has a negative effect on the ability of models to generalize and be applicable(Liu, 2024; Duan, 2023; Meng, 2022). To address these problems, it is essential to have datasets that are varied and well-balanced, or to develop new methodologies that can eliminate biases.

Expanding Multi-modality Learning: Incorporating structured data with other modalities improves model performance and allows for new tasks to be accomplished. Future research could prioritize the development of approaches that effectively integrate numerous data modalities and investigate unexplored topics(Muthukumar, 2021; Liu, 2018).

Miscellaneous Challenges: It is crucial to develop advanced methodologies for modelling both continuous and categorical data types in tabular data modelling. An all-encompassing framework that includes generation, imputation, and forecasting for modelling tabular and time-series data can be advantageous. Integrating medical oncology and unpredictable(Niu et al., 2022) visit intervals can enhance performance in medical applications. Furthermore, it is essential to tackle the issue of extended inference durations in relation to GAN-based techniques, since this is vital for the real-time or on-chip implementation of medical devices. Consequently, enhancements are required to ensure practical applicability.

CONCLUSION

To summarize, TIG models have exhibited impressive performance and adaptability in a wide range of applications, highlighting their extraordinary potential. Nevertheless, the field of generative models designed specifically for structured data has not been thoroughly investigated in comparison to other types of data. In order to fill this void and promote advancement in this field, we have undertaken an extensive assessment on TIG employing generative models such as GANs, Diffusion, and autoregressive models. Our survey gives a concise examination of the fundamental principles behind these generative models and provides a brief overview of the current body of research in each area. Furthermore, we have delineated the existing obstacles and put-up prospective avenues for research in the future, with the goal of encouraging additional investigation and progress in the subject. This survey is expected to be a great resource for researchers and amateurs interested in TIG. It will encourage further innovation and progress in this interesting field.

REFERENCES

Borji, A. (2019). Pros and cons of gan evaluation measures. *Computer Vision and Image Understanding*, 179, 41–65. 10.1016/j.cviu.2018.10.009

Brock, A., Donahue, J., & Simonyan, K. (2018). Large scale GAN training for high fidelity natural image synthesis. arXiv preprint arXiv:1809.11096.

Brown, T., Mann, B., Ryder, N., Subbiah, M., Kaplan, J. D., Dhariwal, P., & Amodei, D. (2020). Language models are few-shot learners. *Advances in Neural Information Processing Systems*, 33, 1877–1901.

Cao, H., Tan, C., Gao, Z., Xu, Y., Chen, G., Heng, P. A., & Li, S. Z. (2024). A survey on generative diffusion models. *IEEE Transactions on Knowledge and Data Engineering*, 1–20. 10.1109/TKDE.2024.3361474

Chan, E. R., Lin, C. Z., Chan, M. A., Nagano, K., Pan, B., De Mello, S., & Wetzstein, G. (2022). Efficient geometry-aware 3d generative adversarial networks. In *Proceedings of the IEEE/CVF conference on computer vision and pattern recognition* (pp. 16123-16133). IEEE.

Chen, Y., Koch, T., Lim, K. G., Xu, X., & Zakiyeva, N. (2021). A review study of functional autoregressive models with application to energy forecasting. *Wiley Interdisciplinary Reviews: Computational Statistics*, 13(3), e1525. 10.1002/wics.1525

Chowdhery, A., Narang, S., Devlin, J., Bosma, M., Mishra, G., Roberts, A., & Fiedel, N. (2023). Palm: Scaling language modeling with pathways. *Journal of Machine Learning Research*, 24(240), 1–113.

Croitoru, F. A., Hondru, V., Ionescu, R. T., & Shah, M. (2023). Diffusion models in vision: A survey. *IEEE Transactions on Pattern Analysis and Machine Intelligence*, 45(9), 10850–10869. 10.1109/TPAMI.2023.326198837030794

Deng, Z., Zhang, H., Liang, X., Yang, L., Xu, S., Zhu, J., & Xing, E. P. (2017). Structured generative adversarial networks. *Advances in Neural Information Processing Systems*, 30.

Devlin, J., Chang, M. W., Lee, K., & Toutanova, K. (2018). Bert: Pre-training of deep bidirectional transformers for language understanding. arXiv preprint arXiv:1810.04805.

Dhariwal, P., & Nichol, A. (2021). Diffusion models beat gans on image synthesis. *Advances in Neural Information Processing Systems*, 34, 8780–8794.

Ding, M., Yang, Z., Hong, W., Zheng, W., Zhou, C., Yin, D., & Tang, J. (2021). Cogview: Mastering text-to-image generation via transformers. *Advances in Neural Information Processing Systems*, 34, 19822–19835.

Du, N., Huang, Y., Dai, A. M., Tong, S., Lepikhin, D., Xu, Y., & Cui, C. (2022, June). Glam: Efficient scaling of language models with mixture-of-experts. In *International Conference on Machine Learning* (pp. 5547-5569). PMLR.

Duan, Y., Zhou, J., Wang, Z., Chang, Y. C., Wang, Y. K., & Lin, C. T. (2023). *Domain-specific denoising diffusion probabilistic models for brain dynamics*. arXiv preprint arXiv:2305.04200.

Elarabawy, A., Kamath, H., & Denton, S. (2022). *Direct inversion: Optimization-free text-driven real image editing with diffusion models*. arXiv preprint arXiv:2211.07825.

Esser, P., Rombach, R., & Ommer, B. (2021). Taming transformers for high-resolution image synthesis. In *Proceedings of the IEEE/CVF conference on computer vision and pattern recognition* (pp. 12873-12883). IEEE.

Fei, Z., Fan, M., Zhu, L., & Huang, J. (2022). *Progressive Text-to-Image Generation.* arXiv preprint arXiv:2210.02291.

Frolov, S., Hinz, T., Raue, F., Hees, J., & Dengel, A. (2021). Adversarial text-to-image synthesis: A review. *Neural Networks*, 144, 187–209. 10.1016/j.neunet.2021.07.01934500257

Gal, R., Patashnik, O., Maron, H., Bermano, A. H., Chechik, G., & Cohen-Or, D. (2022). Stylegan-nada: Clip-guided domain adaptation of image generators. *ACM Transactions on Graphics*, 41(4), 1–13. 10.1145/3528223.3530164

Gallego, V. (2022). *Personalizing text-to-image generation via aesthetic gradients.* arXiv preprint arXiv:2209.12330.

Goodfellow, I. (2016). *Nips 2016 tutorial: Generative adversarial networks.* arXiv preprint arXiv:1701.00160.

Goodfellow, I., Pouget-Abadie, J., Mirza, M., Xu, B., Warde-Farley, D., Ozair, S., & Bengio, Y. (2014). Generative adversarial nets. *Advances in Neural Information Processing Systems*, 27.

Gu, S., Chen, D., Bao, J., Wen, F., Zhang, B., Chen, D., & Guo, B. (2022). Vector quantized diffusion model for text-to-image synthesis. In *Proceedings of the IEEE/CVF Conference on Computer Vision and Pattern Recognition* (pp. 10696-10706). IEEE. 10.1109/CVPR52688.2022.01043

Hertz, A., Mokady, R., Tenenbaum, J., Aberman, K., Pritch, Y., & Cohen-Or, D. (2022). *Prompt-to-prompt image editing with cross attention control.* arXiv preprint arXiv:2208.01626.

Heusel, M., Ramsauer, H., Unterthiner, T., Nessler, B., & Hochreiter, S. (2017). Gans trained by a two time-scale update rule converge to a local nash equilibrium. *Advances in Neural Information Processing Systems*, 30.

Ho, J., Chan, W., Saharia, C., Whang, J., Gao, R., Gritsenko, A., & Salimans, T. (2022). Imagen video: High definition video generation with diffusion models. arXiv preprint arXiv:2210.02303.

Ho, J., Jain, A., & Abbeel, P. (2020). Denoising diffusion probabilistic models. *Advances in Neural Information Processing Systems*, 33, 6840–6851.

Ho, J., & Salimans, T. (2022). Classifier-free diffusion guidance. arXiv preprint arXiv:2207.12598.

Ho, J., Salimans, T., Gritsenko, A., Chan, W., Norouzi, M., & Fleet, D. J. (2022). Video diffusion models. *Advances in Neural Information Processing Systems*, 35, 8633–8646.

Huang, N., Tang, F., Dong, W., & Xu, C. (2022, October). Draw your art dream: Diverse digital art synthesis with multimodal guided diffusion. In *Proceedings of the 30th ACM International Conference on Multimedia* (pp. 1085-1094). ACM. 10.1145/3503161.3548282

Huang, N., Zhang, Y., Tang, F., Ma, C., Huang, H., Dong, W., & Xu, C. (2024). Diffstyler: Controllable dual diffusion for text-driven image stylization. *IEEE Transactions on Neural Networks and Learning Systems*, 1–14. 10.1109/TNNLS.2023.334264538198263

Jabbar, A., Li, X., & Omar, B. (2021). A survey on generative adversarial networks: Variants, applications, and training. *ACM Computing Surveys*, 54(8), 1–49. 10.1145/3463475

Jain, A., Mildenhall, B., Barron, J. T., Abbeel, P., & Poole, B. (2022). Zero-shot text-guided object generation with dream fields. In *Proceedings of the IEEE/CVF conference on computer vision and pattern recognition* (pp. 867-876). IEEE. 10.1109/CVPR52688.2022.00094

Jain, A., Xie, A., & Abbeel, P. (2023). Vectorfusion: Text-to-svg by abstracting pixel-based diffusion models. In *Proceedings of the IEEE/CVF Conference on Computer Vision and Pattern Recognition* (pp. 1911-1920). IEEE. 10.1109/CVPR52729.2023.00190

Jia, C., Yang, Y., Xia, Y., Chen, Y. T., Parekh, Z., Pham, H., & Duerig, T. (2021, July). Scaling up visual and vision-language representation learning with noisy text supervision. In *International conference on machine learning* (pp. 4904-4916). PMLR.

Kim, G., & Chun, S. Y. (2023). Datid-3d: Diversity-preserved domain adaptation using text-to-image diffusion for 3d generative model. In *Proceedings of the IEEE/CVF Conference on Computer Vision and Pattern Recognition* (pp. 14203-14213). IEEE. 10.1109/CVPR52729.2023.01365

Kim, G., & Ye, J. C. (2021). *Diffusionclip: Text-guided image manipulation using diffusion models.* Academic Press.

Kwon, M., Jeong, J., & Uh, Y. (2022). *Diffusion models already have a semantic latent space.* arXiv preprint arXiv:2210.10960.

Lee, D., Kim, C., Kim, S., Cho, M., & Han, W. S. (2022). Autoregressive image generation using residual quantization. In *Proceedings of the IEEE/CVF Conference on Computer Vision and Pattern Recognition* (pp. 11523-11532). IEEE.

Lee, M., & Seok, J. (2019). Controllable generative adversarial network. *IEEE Access : Practical Innovations, Open Solutions*, 7, 28158–28169. 10.1109/ACCESS.2019.2899108

Li, G., Zheng, H., Wang, C., Li, C., Zheng, C., & Tao, D. (2022). 3ddesigner: Towards photorealistic 3d object generation and editing with text-guided diffusion models. arXiv preprint arXiv:2211.14108.

Lin, C. H., Gao, J., Tang, L., Takikawa, T., Zeng, X., Huang, X., & Lin, T. Y. (2023). Magic3d: High-resolution text-to-3d content creation. In *Proceedings of the IEEE/CVF Conference on Computer Vision and Pattern Recognition* (pp. 300-309). IEEE.

Lin, J., Men, R., Yang, A., Zhou, C., Ding, M., Zhang, Y., & Yang, H. (2021). *M6: A chinese multimodal pretrainer.* arXiv preprint arXiv:2103.00823.

Lin, T. Y., Maire, M., Belongie, S., Hays, J., Perona, P., Ramanan, D., & Zitnick, C. L. (2014). Microsoft coco: Common objects in context. *Computer Vision–ECCV 2014: 13th European Conference, Zurich, Switzerland, September 6-12, 2014Proceedings*, 13(Part V), 740–755.

Liu, L., Wang, Y., & Xu, Y. (2024). A practical guide to counterfactual estimators for causal inference with time-series cross-sectional data. *American Journal of Political Science*, 68(1), 160–176. 10.1111/ajps.12723

Liu, T., Wang, K., Sha, L., Chang, B., & Sui, Z. (2018, April). Table-to-text generation by structure-aware seq2seq learning. *Proceedings of the AAAI Conference on Artificial Intelligence*, 32(1). 10.1609/aaai.v32i1.11925

Lyu, H., Sha, N., Qin, S., Yan, M., Xie, Y., & Wang, R. (2019). Advances in neural information processing systems. *Advances in Neural Information Processing Systems*, 32.

Meng, C., Trinh, L., Xu, N., Enouen, J., & Liu, Y. (2022). Interpretability and fairness evaluation of deep learning models on MIMIC-IV dataset. *Scientific Reports*, 12(1), 7166. 10.1038/s41598-022-11012-235504931

Mildenhall, B., Srinivasan, P. P., Tancik, M., Barron, J. T., Ramamoorthi, R., & Ng, R. (2021). Nerf: Representing scenes as neural radiance fields for view synthesis. *Communications of the ACM*, 65(1), 99–106. 10.1145/3503250

Mirza, M., & Osindero, S. (2014). Conditional generative adversarial nets. arXiv preprint arXiv:1411.1784.

Mokady, R., Hertz, A., Aberman, K., Pritch, Y., & Cohen-Or, D. (2023). Null-text inversion for editing real images using guided diffusion models. In *Proceedings of the IEEE/CVF Conference on Computer Vision and Pattern Recognition* (pp. 6038-6047). IEEE. 10.1109/CVPR52729.2023.00585

Moraffah, R., Sheth, P., Karami, M., Bhattacharya, A., Wang, Q., Tahir, A., Raglin, A., & Liu, H. (2021). Causal inference for time series analysis: Problems, methods and evaluation. *Knowledge and Information Systems*, 63(12), 3041–3085. 10.1007/s10115-021-01621-0

Muthukumar, P., & Zhong, J. (2021). *A stochastic time series model for predicting financial trends using nlp*. arXiv preprint arXiv:2102.01290.

Nichol, A., Dhariwal, P., Ramesh, A., Shyam, P., Mishkin, P., McGrew, B., & Chen, M. (2021). *Glide: Towards photorealistic image generation and editing with text-guided diffusion models*. arXiv preprint arXiv:2112.10741.

Nichol, A. Q., & Dhariwal, P. (2021, July). Improved denoising diffusion probabilistic models. In *International conference on machine learning* (pp. 8162-8171). PMLR.

Niu, K., Lu, Y., Peng, X., & Zeng, J. (2022). Fusion of sequential visits and medical ontology for mortality prediction. *Journal of Biomedical Informatics*, 127, 104012. 10.1016/j.jbi.2022.10401235144001

Pan, Z., Zhou, X., & Tian, H. (2023). Arbitrary style guidance for enhanced diffusion-based text-to-image generation. In *Proceedings of the IEEE/CVF Winter Conference on Applications of Computer Vision* (pp. 4461-4471). IEEE. 10.1109/WACV56688.2023.00444

Pavez, V., Hermosilla, G., Silva, M., & Farias, G. (2023). Advanced Deep Learning Techniques for High-Quality Synthetic Thermal Image Generation. *Mathematics*, 11(21), 4446. 10.3390/math11214446

Pearson, K. (1901). LIII. On lines and planes of closest fit to systems of points in space. *The London, Edinburgh and Dublin Philosophical Magazine and Journal of Science*, 2(11), 559–572. 10.1080/14786440109462720

Pont-Tuset, J., Uijlings, J., Changpinyo, S., Soricut, R., & Ferrari, V. (2020). Connecting vision and language with localized narratives. *Computer Vision–ECCV 2020: 16th European Conference, Glasgow, UK, August 23–28, 2020Proceedings*, 16(Part V), 647–664.

Poole, B., Jain, A., Barron, J. T., & Mildenhall, B. (2022). Dreamfusion: Text-to-3d using 2d diffusion. arXiv preprint arXiv:2209.14988.

Qiao, T., Zhang, J., Xu, D., & Tao, D. (2019). Mirrorgan: Learning text-to-image generation by redescription. In *Proceedings of the IEEE/CVF conference on computer vision and pattern recognition* (pp. 1505-1514). IEEE.

Radford, A., Kim, J. W., Hallacy, C., Ramesh, A., Goh, G., Agarwal, S., & Sutskever, I. (2021, July). Learning transferable visual models from natural language supervision. In *International conference on machine learning* (pp. 8748-8763). PMLR.

Radford, A., Metz, L., & Chintala, S. (2015). *Unsupervised representation learning with deep convolutional generative adversarial networks.* arXiv preprint arXiv:1511.06434.

Raffel, C., Luong, M. T., Liu, P. J., Weiss, R. J., & Eck, D. (2017, July). Online and linear-time attention by enforcing monotonic alignments. In *International conference on machine learning* (pp. 2837-2846). PMLR.

Ramesh, A., Dhariwal, P., Nichol, A., Chu, C., & Chen, M. (2022). Hierarchical text-conditional image generation with clip latents. arXiv preprint arXiv:2204.06125.

Ramesh, A., Pavlov, M., Goh, G., Gray, S., Voss, C., Radford, A., & Sutskever, I. (2021, July). Zero-shot text-to-image generation. In *International conference on machine learning* (pp. 8821-8831). PMLR.

Ramzan, S., Iqbal, M. M., & Kalsum, T. (2022). Text-to-Image Generation Using Deep Learning. *Engineering Proceedings*, 20(1), 16.

Razavi, A., Van den Oord, A., & Vinyals, O. (2019). Generating diverse high-fidelity images with vq-vae-2. *Advances in Neural Information Processing Systems*, 32.

Reed, S., Akata, Z., Lee, H., & Schiele, B. (2016). Learning deep representations of fine-grained visual descriptions. In *Proceedings of the IEEE conference on computer vision and pattern recognition* (pp. 49-58). IEEE. 10.1109/CVPR.2016.13

Reed, S., Akata, Z., Yan, X., Logeswaran, L., Schiele, B., & Lee, H. (2016, June). Generative adversarial text to image synthesis. In *International conference on machine learning* (pp. 1060-1069). PMLR.

Regis, M., Serra, P., & van den Heuvel, E. R. (2022). Random autoregressive models: A structured overview. *Econometric Reviews*, 41(2), 207–230. 10.1080/07474938.2021.1899504

Rombach, R., Blattmann, A., Lorenz, D., Esser, P., & Ommer, B. (2022). High-resolution image synthesis with latent diffusion models. In *Proceedings of the IEEE/CVF conference on computer vision and pattern recognition* (pp. 10684-10695). IEEE. 10.1109/CVPR52688.2022.01042

Rombach, R., Blattmann, A., & Ommer, B. (2022). *Text-guided synthesis of artistic images with retrieval-augmented diffusion models.* arXiv preprint arXiv:2207.13038.

Ronneberger, O., Fischer, P., & Brox, T. (2015). U-net: Convolutional networks for biomedical image segmentation. In *Medical image computing and computer-assisted intervention–MICCAI 2015: 18th international conference, Munich, Germany, October 5-9, 2015, proceedings, part III 18* (pp. 234-241). Springer International Publishing.

Saharia, C., Chan, W., Saxena, S., Li, L., Whang, J., Denton, E. L., & Norouzi, M. (2022). Photorealistic text-to-image diffusion models with deep language understanding. *Advances in Neural Information Processing Systems*, 35, 36479–36494.

Saharia, C., Ho, J., Chan, W., Salimans, T., Fleet, D. J., & Norouzi, M. (2022). Image super-resolution via iterative refinement. *IEEE Transactions on Pattern Analysis and Machine Intelligence*, 45(4), 4713–4726.36094974

Schuhmann, C., Vencu, R., Beaumont, R., Kaczmarczyk, R., Mullis, C., Katta, A., & Komatsuzaki, A. (2021). Laion-400m: Open dataset of clip-filtered 400 million image-text pairs. arXiv preprint arXiv:2111.02114.

Singer, U., Polyak, A., Hayes, T., Yin, X., An, J., Zhang, S., & Taigman, Y. (2022). Make-a-video: Text-to-video generation without text-video data. arXiv preprint arXiv:2209.14792.

Sohl-Dickstein, J., Weiss, E., Maheswaranathan, N., & Ganguli, S. (2015, June). Deep unsupervised learning using nonequilibrium thermodynamics. In *International conference on machine learning* (pp. 2256-2265). PMLR.

Song, J., Meng, C., & Ermon, S. (2020). *Denoising diffusion implicit models*. arXiv preprint arXiv:2010.02502.

Song, Y., & Ermon, S. (2019). Generative modeling by estimating gradients of the data distribution. *Advances in Neural Information Processing Systems*, 32.

Song, Y., & Ermon, S. (2020). Improved techniques for training score-based generative models. *Advances in Neural Information Processing Systems*, 33, 12438–12448.

Thoppilan, R., De Freitas, D., Hall, J., Shazeer, N., Kulshreshtha, A., Cheng, H. T., & Le, Q. (2022). *Lamda: Language models for dialog applications*. arXiv preprint arXiv:2201.08239.

Tumanyan, N., Geyer, M., Bagon, S., & Dekel, T. (2023). Plug-and-play diffusion features for text-driven image-to-image translation. In *Proceedings of the IEEE/CVF Conference on Computer Vision and Pattern Recognition* (pp. 1921-1930). IEEE. 10.1109/CVPR52729.2023.00191

Ullah, U., Lee, J. S., An, C. H., Lee, H., Park, S. Y., Baek, R. H., & Choi, H. C. (2022). A review of multi-modal learning from the text-guided visual processing viewpoint. *Sensors (Basel)*, 22(18), 6816. 10.3390/s2218681636146161

Van Den Oord, A., Kalchbrenner, N., & Kavukcuoglu, K. (2016, June). Pixel recurrent neural networks. In *International conference on machine learning* (pp. 1747-1756). PMLR.

Van Den Oord, A., & Vinyals, O. (2017). Neural discrete representation learning. *Advances in Neural Information Processing Systems*, 30.

Vaswani, A., Shazeer, N., Parmar, N., Uszkoreit, J., Jones, L., Gomez, A. N., & Polosukhin, I. (2017). Attention is all you need. *Advances in Neural Information Processing Systems*, 30.

Vignac, C., Krawczuk, I., Siraudin, A., Wang, B., Cevher, V., & Frossard, P. (2022). *Digress: Discrete denoising diffusion for graph generation.* arXiv preprint arXiv:2209.14734.

Wallace, B., Gokul, A., & Naik, N. (2023). Edict: Exact diffusion inversion via coupled transformations. In *Proceedings of the IEEE/CVF Conference on Computer Vision and Pattern Recognition* (pp. 22532-22541). IEEE. 10.1109/CVPR52729.2023.02158

Wu, C. H., & De la Torre, F. (2022). *Unifying Diffusion Models' Latent Space, with Applications to CycleDiffusion and Guidance.* arXiv preprint arXiv:2210.05559.

Wu, X. (2022, October). Creative painting with latent diffusion models. In *Proceedings of the Second Workshop on When Creative AI Meets Conversational AI* (pp. 59-80). Academic Press.

Xiao, Z., Kreis, K., & Vahdat, A. (2021). Tackling the generative learning trilemma with denoising diffusion gans. arXiv preprint arXiv:2112.07804.

Xu, T., Zhang, P., Huang, Q., Zhang, H., Gan, Z., Huang, X., & He, X. (2018). Attngan: Fine-grained text to image generation with attentional generative adversarial networks. In *Proceedings of the IEEE conference on computer vision and pattern recognition* (pp. 1316-1324). IEEE. 10.1109/CVPR.2018.00143

Yang, L., Zhang, Z., Song, Y., Hong, S., Xu, R., Zhao, Y., Zhang, W., Cui, B., & Yang, M. H. (2023). Diffusion models: A comprehensive survey of methods and applications. *ACM Computing Surveys*, 56(4), 1–39. 10.1145/3626235

Yu, J., Li, X., Koh, J. Y., Zhang, H., Pang, R., Qin, J., & Wu, Y. (2021). Vector-quantized image modeling with improved vqgan. arXiv preprint arXiv:2110.04627.

Yu, J., Xu, Y., Koh, J. Y., Luong, T., Baid, G., Wang, Z., & Wu, Y. (2022). Scaling autoregressive models for content-rich text-to-image generation. arXiv preprint arXiv:2206.10789, 2(3), 5.

Yuan, L., Chen, D., Chen, Y. L., Codella, N., Dai, X., Gao, J., & Zhang, P. (2021). Florence: A new foundation model for computer vision. arXiv preprint arXiv:2111.11432.

Zhang, C., Zhang, C., Zhang, M., & Kweon, I. S. (2023). Text-to-image Diffusion Models in Generative AI: A Survey. arXiv 2023. arXiv preprint arXiv:2303.07909.

Zhang, H., Goodfellow, I., Metaxas, D., & Odena, A. (2019, May). Self-attention generative adversarial networks. In *International conference on machine learning* (pp. 7354-7363). PMLR.

Zhang, H., Xu, T., Li, H., Zhang, S., Wang, X., Huang, X., & Metaxas, D. N. (2017). Stackgan: Text to photo-realistic image synthesis with stacked generative adversarial networks. In *Proceedings of the IEEE international conference on computer vision* (pp. 5907-5915). IEEE. 10.1109/ICCV.2017.629

Zhang, R., Isola, P., Efros, A. A., Shechtman, E., & Wang, O. (2018). The unreasonable effectiveness of deep features as a perceptual metric. In *Proceedings of the IEEE conference on computer vision and pattern recognition* (pp. 586-595). IEEE. 10.1109/CVPR.2018.00068

Zhang, T., Wang, Z., Huang, J., Tasnim, M. M., & Shi, W. (2023). *A Survey of Diffusion Based Image Generation Models: Issues and Their Solutions.* arXiv preprint arXiv:2308.13142.

Zhao, R., & Shi, Z. (2021). Text-to-remote-sensing-image generation with structured generative adversarial networks. *IEEE Geoscience and Remote Sensing Letters*, 19, 1–5.

Zhou, R., Jiang, C., & Xu, Q. (2021). A survey on generative adversarial network-based text-to-image synthesis. *Neurocomputing*, 451, 316–336. 10.1016/j.neucom.2021.04.069

Zhu, M., Pan, P., Chen, W., & Yang, Y. (2019). Dm-gan: Dynamic memory generative adversarial networks for text-to-image synthesis. In *Proceedings of the IEEE/CVF conference on computer vision and pattern recognition* (pp. 5802-5810). IEEE.

Chapter 2
AI in Visual Arts:
Exploring Generative Algorithm

Rajneesh Ranjan
C. V. Raman Global University, India

Anjana Mishra
C. V. Raman Global University, India

Smruti Pratisruti Maharana
C. V. Raman Global University, India

Sweety Kumari
C. V. Raman Global University, India

ABSTRACT

In the past two to four years there have been significant improvements made in AI due to improvements in computing capacity, resulting in an increase in public interest and funding for research. This has led the authors to embark on a project aimed at gaining a deeper understanding of these art generator AIs using generative algorithms such as GANs and VAEs. This chapter begins by providing a brief outline of the historical context and evolution of AI in the arts, tracing its trajectory from early experiments to its current advancements in visual artistry. The subsequent sections of the chapter explore the role of generative algorithms in each artistic medium, starting with an overview of algorithmic painting, followed by an examination of algorithmic sculpture and digital art. In addition, this chapter also introduces four novel features specific to AI-Art. In this chapter, the authors have drawn upon references from various tests published by esteemed researchers and practitioners to gather the necessary insights for the investigation and deepen our understanding.

INTRODUCTION

It's a well known Fact that Art has constantly evolving along with the evolution of Science and Technology. Throughout the history, art has maintained a continual evolution and embraced new technological innovations, artists have gradually given up on using their old methods and tools they used to create artworks from and avert to the newest innovations and tools as a substitute medium to create artworks.

DOI: 10.4018/979-8-3693-3278-8.ch002

This interaction has significantly influenced how viewers interpret and engage with art, impacting their approach based on their unique understanding and perspective towards the art. Similar to the inventions and findings of printing press, computers, photography, film rolls, AI is seen as a new technological revolution that will revolutionized the way how people create artwork and enhance our potential and imagination capabilities.

The first look at AI tools may make one think that they mechanize the artistic process completely, reiterating the same concerns about new technologies that were previously experienced. But some historical examples indicate a more complicated situation. Earlier instances of technological disruption did not mean the end of art; they provoked massive changes in creators' responsibilities and practices, thereby reshaping modern media aesthetics.

To illustrate this point, when photography was invented in the 19th century it initially seemed to be a menace towards traditional painting. Nevertheless, instead of replacing paintings altogether, photography fostered an era of artistic freedom which gave birth to movements like Impressionism and Modern Art. On the other hand, portrait photography did take over portraiture to some degree, leading to an interim decline in employment for classical portrait painters and artists. However, these similarities within history point out a common dynamic: new tools confront established creative canons and labor market structures thereby creating opportunities for the emergence of other forms of art or variants in which artists can operate.

Unlike past disruptions, however, generative algorithms operate by analyzing existing artistic media and extracting statistical patterns to generate new art. However, this process also raises concerns about the human-made data on which it is based, its impact on the resulting outputs and its significance with respect to authorship. Generative algorithms challenge conventional thinking about authorship, ownership as well as creative inspiration by automating certain aspects of the creative process. In doing so, they blur the boundaries between originality and derivation that define media production. Considering how generative algorithms affect aesthetics, culture and legal frameworks becomes imperative. These questions demand careful thought given their implications for ownership, credit and future of creative work. To comprehend the changing map of artistic creation through which generative algorithms operate, it is crucial to have these talks, which are outlined in this white paper.

A BRIEF REVIEW ON AI IN VISUAL ARTS

"Creativity takes courage"

- Henri Matisse

Visual Arts

Visual art is a multidimensional field that captures the spirit of human expression via diverse means such as painting, sculpture and digital arts. At its centre, visual arts is a potent medium of communication that goes beyond cultural and language confines by touching the hearts and minds of audiences. Symbolizing our natural ability to see and understand things in life, the human eye represents the visible element of this discipline. Visual arts being a looking glass that reflects on various hues of human experiences, faith systems and dreams which are complex just like life.

Correspondingly, art has been with us since time immemorial where ancient civilizations used primitive techniques for decorating cave walls and sacred objects. Thus, the early artwork was not only visually appealing but also carried information about their way of life prior to death and religion they held. Since prehistoric cave drawings up until classical period sculptures, art has always changed over time while preserving its basic function as a man's means of expression in all ages as referred in Figure 1.

It is the visual arts that play a key role in shaping our perception, challenging social norms and fostering cultural exchange by using different techniques, styles and materials. Visual art has the ability to provoke thought, emotion and change; it can be seen through the evocative strokes of brushes, tactile forms of sculptures or even immersive digital landscapes of virtual realities. In today's world, visual artists are still stretching their boundaries towards creativity while incorporating technology advancements and adopting new trends in their artistic works.

Ai In Visual Arts

Artificial intelligence, AI is transforming the visual arts to open a new era of creativity and innovation that pushes the borders of artistic expression to heights never reached before. By fusing deep neural networks, machine learning algorithms and AI technologies, artists venture into uncharted territories and as such are discovering new dimensions for art and creating new forms of art Throughout the History as Shown in Table 1.

Table 1. Impact of AI on visual arts and art accessibility over time (1800s–2020s)

Time Period	AI Influence on Visual Arts	Increase in People Affected by Art	Increase in Art Accessibility
1800s	None	Limited	Limited (Physical Galleries, Private Collections)
Early 1900s (Pre-WWII)	None	Limited	Limited (Galleries, Salons)
Mid-1900s (Post-WWII)	None	Growth (Rise of Middle Class, Public Art)	Increase (Museums expand, Art in Public Spaces)
1960s-1980s	Early seeds of AI art concepts	Growth	Increase (Expansion of art markets and globalization)
1990s-2000s	Development of AI art algorithms	Growth	Significant Increase (Internet access to art)
2010s-2020s	Explosion of AI art tools and applications	Substantial Growth (Generative algorithms like GANs and VAEs)	Dramatic Increase (Social Media, Online Galleries)

One prominent reflection of how AI affects the visual arts is seen in a technique called neural style transfer. This innovative method allows artists to incorporate one image with the styles of other images resulting in visually engaging compositions that transcend traditional art boundaries. Thus for example in google's 'DeepDream' project where surreal and dream like images are created through using neural networks which enhance or modify existing images thereby blurring the line between human imagination and computational creativity. An amalgamation between technology and art brings out fresh ways through which art has been expressed capturing audiences by their mesmerizing nature(DeepDream - a code example for visualizing Neural Networks, 2015).

The use of AI in the visual art has led to the creation of hyper-realistic digital paintings. This is done by artists such as Robbie Barrat who use machine learning algorithms to come up with highly detailed works that are no different from those done by traditional means. With large sets of data, made up of paintings, photographs as well as other visual media, these artists can produce realistic landscapes and portraits that were unimaginable before now. Consequently, digital artistry has become better than ever and it challenges the traditional concepts behind making an artwork.

In addition, AI has given rise to interactive and immersive art experiences. Examples include The Next Rembrandt by Microsoft in collaboration with ING bank where machine learning technology was used to study famous artists' work and then generate new pieces based on their styles. Such artworks have been created through a process that requires human artists' input but which relies heavily on artificial intelligence (AI) systems; thereby, enabling viewers to experience them physically or digitally. It also redefines artistic collaborations in this electronic age because one cannot tell whether it is real or not (Liam, 2020).

What's more, AI allows artists to venture into novel media and methods that were previously closed to them. "GANPaint Studio," developed by MIT scientists, is a tool for fine arts that allows artists to work on styles, colors and textures in real time using generative adversarial networks (GANs). This ground-breaking tool opens up new opportunities for infinite creativity by enabling the artist to break out of traditional forms and go wild with boundless ideas typical of AI in Visual Arts (CSI framework, 2019).

AI has also totally transformed art curation and exhibition as one of its new roles. Such platforms as Artrendex use machine learning algorithms to analyze art trends, forecast market demand and enable informed decisions for collectors & galleries. By delivering AI-driven insights, these platforms allow stakeholders to influence the direction of the art world, promote greater inclusivity and pluralism in global culture through democratizing the digital age access of fine arts (Artrendex, 2021).

EXPLORING GENERATIVE ALGORITHMS

Exploring Generative Algorithms delves into a fascinating realm of artificial creativity that mirrors human ingenuity in generating diverse content autonomously. This emerging field covers many algorithms and methods used to create different types of contents such as pictures, songs, texts and videos. The basis of Generative Algorithms is the comprehension of basic structures like Generative Adversarial Networks (GANs), Variational Autoencoders (VAEs) among other genius models.

GANs was introduced in 2014 by Ian Goodfellow and colleagues as an innovative concept in generative AI. GANs comprise a generator and discriminator network interacting in an adversarial game with the objective of producing synthetic data which cannot be distinguished from real samples. On one hand, the generator uses random noise to create realistic outputs while on the other hand, the discriminator learns how to differentiate between real and fake data thus making the generator continuously improve its output quality.

In addition to GANs, VAEs add a probabilistic structure to generative modeling. In that direction, VAEs achieve input data encoding into a latent space thereby enabling sampling as well as reconstruction which in turn generates various outputs. When the variational lower bound on the data likelihood is optimized, VAEs capture important characteristics of the input distribution hence promoting smooth and continuous generation.

Apart from GANs and VAEs, there exist other generative approaches such as autoregressive models, flow-based models, and attention-based models that have unique strengths and capabilities. For example, autoregressive models generate data one at a time in sequence while flow based models learn reversible mappings between data space and latent space. For instance, attention-based models exploit their ability to focus on relevant parts of an input during generation; this makes them scalable or parallelizable among other qualities.

Generative Adversarial Networks (GANs) and Variational Auto-Encoders (VAEs)

A neural network program called Deep Dream, which was initially created by Google, was trained in 2016 by importing thousands of images for image classification and generating artistic images. The goal of the Generative Adversarial Networks (GAN) program is to teach computers to recognize and replicate historical masterpieces. Scientists developed the Creative Adversarial Networks (CAN) program in 2017, which is built on the original GAN and allows computers to produce art on their own rather than just mimicking human behavior.

The generative algorithms such as Generative Adversarial Networks (GAN's) and Variational Auto-encoders (VAE's), both of which provide different ways to create and change images. The GANs were described as working by connecting two neural networks—the generator and the discriminator—who tirelessly try to outdo each other. Through adversarial training like this, GANs can produce even more lifelike pictures since the generator is continuously being adjusted in accordance with feedback from discriminator. GANs have played a significant role in generating photo-realistic images, thus becoming a buzzword in AI-generated art.

On the other hand, Diederik Kingma and Max Welling introduced Variational Auto-encoders (VAEs), in 2014 that offer a different approach towards generative modeling.

From the previous paragraph, we know that encoder network and decoder network constitute VAEs to learn a low-dimensional latent space representation of input data. The encoders try to create an efficient data representation while decoders seek to build the original data from this learned latent space. Unlike GANs which are aimed at generating realistic images, VAEs are designed mainly for image denoising, data compression and anomaly detection because they prioritize on these latter two objectives.

GANs and VAEs, though both being powerful generative modeling tools, perform best in different areas and contexts. For instance, GANs are commonly used on image-oriented or visual datasets as they aim at achieving naturalistic pictures or modifying the ones already existing. Conversely, VAEs make for excellent applications of signal processing tasks which encompass anomaly detection and predictive maintenance among others that necessitates acquiring an efficient knowledge about data. Moreover, today's genitive AI has seen the development of a wide range of techniques including diffusion models, transformers e.g., OpenAI's ChatGPT as well as neural radiance fields (NeRFs) that have stretched beyond traditional GANs and VAEs thereby expanding the scope of generative modeling. These avenues create new methods for constructing and optimizing images, text, 3D media thereby furthering the boundaries of generative algorithms.

In 3D object generation context GANs have helped to identify strong computer vision and graphics techniques. As an illustration through GAN networks such studies can find out 3D objects like Yu et al.'s network which processes unlabelled unclear data. In addition, there has been development of GAN-based architectures for better quality and sharper images as well as for 2D to 3D conversion. These inventions demonstrate that GANs are so versatile across the fields from computer vision to medical imaging.

Again, GANs have made a contribution in the field of image processing such as ultrasound image resolution enhancement and lesion class generation from small sample sizes. By using deep convolutional GANs, researchers provided a faster analysis of medical images and bettered match between low-resolution and high-resolution image volumes. In holography, GANs create unique holographic images via digital holography microscopy.

Nonetheless, these models have challenges like mode collapse or training instability outlined in the preceding paragraph. The future directions of research aim at solving these problems and making GAN models more powerful. To overcome the problem of training stability and quality output by GAN-produced outputs, it is suggested that techniques like weight pruning, Nash Equilibrium as well as new loss functions be used. Other possibilities include incorporating attention mechanisms and reinforcement learning strategies to expand the reach of GANs and circumvent the limitations arising from their discrete nature.

To summarize, generative algorithms is an emerging field that utilizes VAEs and GANs as its cutting-edge technologies for image production, signal processing and manipulation. In the meantime, further developments in generative algorithms such as advancements in GANs and VAEs or other novel techniques provide a great opportunity for ground-breaking innovations across various fields including fine arts, design, health care among others. For any society to benefit from generative algorithms it therefore requires responsible use of GAN/VAEs by researchers who ought to follow all ethical considerations thereof in order discover new potentialities that underlie this concept.

Generative Algorithms in Painting

"Generative art is the ceding of control by the artist to an autonomous system" -Cecilia Di Chio

The use of generative algorithms has grown dramatically in painting, giving artists new ways of improving their creative prowess. The arrival of these generative algorithms like the Generative Adversarial Networks (GANs) and Variational Autoencoders (VAEs) changed how we understand visual arts. These algorithms enable artists to produce new works, try out various styles and challenge conventional norms in art.

Michael Hansmeyer's thoughts on Generative algorithms highlights a paradigm shift in creativity where there is more emphasis on processes rather than final products. This approach creates an atmosphere of artificial serendipity with unexpected results and fresh ideas that occur spontaneously as shown in Figure 3. In this regard, Hansmeyer's design of a grotto set for Mozart's opera foregrounds these principles indicating how computational tools can facilitate quicker exploration, optimization and experimentation with creative thoughts hence maximizing opportunities for innovative practices.

According to the cognitive scientist Margaret Boden, 95% of professional artists and scientists are doing experimental work, a fact that indicates the potential benefits of generative systems. These systems provide a good foundation for quick investigations and as well as rapid testing thus allowing people who practice art or science to explore larger creative spaces at magnitudes that have never been imagined before.

This artistic revolution is being spearheaded by generative artists like Anders Hoff and Mark J. Stock who each take different approaches in relation to how nature, computation and art can be merged together. While Hoff breaks perfect structures apart slowly because he is interested in patterns, Stock's "Sprawl" compares natural growth patterns with artificial ones; this therefore reflects on the conflict between human-made environment and living beings' evolution.

The democratization of generative art through tools such as R package GenerativeArt empowers masses of people to generate numerous diverse images based upon random parameters resulting in a culture of experimentation and creativity. Other pioneers such as Draves (2013) bring about massive change using generative algorithms by leveraging collective intelligence capable of generating infinite abstract animations.

Generative Algorithms in Sculpture

Generative algorithms have found compelling applications in sculpture, offering artists unprecedented opportunities to explore new forms, shapes, and textures. By leveraging the principles of generative design, sculptors can push the boundaries of traditional sculptural techniques, creating dynamic and innovative artworks that challenge conventional notions of form and materiality. Painting, visual arts and some other domains were significantly altered by generative algorithms like GANs and VAEs. In sculpture, they make it possible for artists to come up with intricate designs which are very complicated in nature, hence creating room for experimentation.

A major advantage of using generative algorithms in sculpture is that they allow designers to automate the process of creation while still providing space for their artistic input. The possibilities presented by algorithmic design are limitless; this enables artists to generate diverse forms of sculptures each with its own aesthetic values and spatial arrangements. This method allows sculptors to rapidly explore many options, thereby facilitating rapid prototyping and experimentation.

Additionally, generative algorithms provide a medium for sculptors to create statues which go beyond the realms of normal geometric shapes and forms. With GANs, artists can come up with organic and biomimetic sculptures that imitate natural forms and textures thereby blurring the line between art and nature. Through this merger of computational design principles with organic structures, new possibilities are created which enable artists to explore growth, development as well as metamorphosis in their sculptures.

Generative algorithms also allow the exploration of parametric design techniques applied in sculpture. On top making a decision about imaging software to work on, the artist also defines some critical parameters needed by the program like its resolution, field size or bit depth among others. The presented paper evaluates these types of art applications focusing on their differences following varying conceptual needs based on various theories pertaining to sculptural representation through time.

In addition, the incorporation of generative algorithms and digital fabrication processes has changed the way sculptures are made. Conjoining algorithmic design with advanced manufacturing methods like 3D printing and robotic fabrication allows artists to convert complex models into real works with precision and speed. This continuous flow from digital to physical world removes barriers for sculptors in terms of form making or materiality as well as virtual/tangible divide in sculpture forms.

Michael Hansmeyer's ground-breaking work in generative art and architecture (Figure 4) also demonstrates the possibilities of algorithms in sculptural creation. Through application of complicated computational algorithms, he creates three-dimensional shapes that are intricate and visually arresting, which challenge conventional modes of production. The iconic designs such as The White Tower and Zauberflöte by Hansmeyer show how art can be integrated with technology and architecture to create new directions for sculpture. Besides, 3D printing combined with algorithmic design exposes the architectural complexity involved in precision construction, minimizing the boundary between digital and material worlds. By this inventive method, Hansmeyer helps us discern how generative algorithms can contribute towards a transformation in sculptural practice hence creating room for novel ideas in the realm of artistic expression and making.

Generative Algorithms in Digital Art

Generative Algorithms have revolutionized the field of digital art and design by enabling artists and designers to explore new creative frontiers. Generative models have opened up intriguing new possibilities for producing stunning and distinctive digital artwork by utilizing the power of artificial intelligence and machine learning. This is where we will look into the world of generative Algorithms in digital art, exploring its promise, obstacles and future trends. To this end, generative algorithms have greatly reshaped various artistic domains like painting, sculpture and visual arts as explained in the previous paragraph. These algorithms enable artists creating immersive experiences in digital art that blend virtual with physical realms.

One of the prominent applications of generative Algorithms in digital art is the use of GAN's. GAN's which consist of two neural networks: a generator network that creates new content, and a discriminator network that tries to distinguish between real and generated content. The counterbalanced relationship urges the generator towards more realistic, quality outputs that surpass those of previous generations. Generative AI technology has been variously used in the field of digital art and design. Artists have made use of generative models for image synthesis and style transfer, enabling them to come up with visually appealing artworks with rare designs. Nonetheless, other areas have investigated text-to-image generation as generative models change textual descriptions into corresponding visual representations. Other than this, drawings can be converted into actual images or 3D models and animations generated using generative AI techniques thus broadening the horizons of digital art production.

Numerous artists and designers have turned to generative Algorithms during their creative process which has resulted in some remarkable artworks. The boundary between human creativity and machine intelligence was blurred by the art produced as a result of collaborations between artists and AI systems. In addition, several tools and platforms have come up for facilitating creation of generative AI based digital arts enabling artists with accessible and powerful tools for experimenting for an expression.

There are several advantages that Generative Algorithms brings into the world of digital art. It provides artists with new sources of inspiration, generates vast numbers of diverse ideas, and makes it possible to explore unknown territories. Furthermore, if used well, generative algorthms can help automate certain aspects of the creative process working as a collaborator rather than a substitute. Nonetheless, responsible and inclusive creative practices need to address ethical concerns; training data could be biased thus leading to non-inclusive practices while generative models have limitations that must be overcome.

The future of arts and design is about to experience many changes in terms of generative algorithms. Changes in the fields of design, art, and entertainment are bringing about new courses for development and creativity through which it will be possible to co-create and interact across disciplines. Continued research, ethics, and responsible practices will make generative Algorithms more useful in increasing human artistic potentials. Generative Algorithms embraced for exploration and collaboration between artists opens up new horizons and helps to set new exciting frontiers for art from a global perspective.

MODERNIZATION OF APPROACHING ART

"A picture is worth a thousand words"

-Henrik Ibsen

In the past, traditional artworks are usually stored indoors, and the artist's thoughts and emotions are always hidden in the works which are kept away from the common audience, which make the meaning expression passive and indirect. In addition to this, the audience must always keep a certain distance from the art piece to watch and experience it. The meaning expression of AI in Visual Arts, nevertheless, has special advantages. Through the use of network and remote communication technologies, creators can communicate with the audience beyond physical and temporal boundaries, while also directly expressing their thoughts and emotions through computer vision, speech recognition, and sensing technologies. These technologies also have aesthetic and practical value, as they can satisfy people's actual needs while incorporating the concepts of beauty and artistic style into products. Thus, AI in the visual arts, with its many purposes such as finding the truth, illuminating thought, and identifying objective laws, can not only amuse people, but also foster sentiment, control emotions, and maintain hormonal balance. In addition, it may be used to cure mental illnesses and diseases in the future.

THE ATTRIBUTES OF ARTIFICIAL INTELLIGENCE IN VISUAL ARTS

The emerging features of AI in Visual Arts primarily encompass four dimensions: SYNESTHETIC EXPERIENCE, FLUIDITY AND ADAPTABILITY, INTERACTION AND ENGAGEMENT, and PERMEATION AND ASSIMILATION. A graphical representation of these AI in Visual Arts traits is depicted in Figure 5. (AiArt: Towards Artificial Intelligence Art, 2020)

AI in Visual Arts is a form of art, and therefore it bears the same features of traditional art like creativity, historicity and aesthetics. However, a new route for AI in the visual arts will be interactivity, which is the result of combining cutting-edge technology with creativity in artistic advancements. It differs from earlier art genres with its novel features. The new features of AI in Visual Arts mainly comprise of four key aspects:

Synesthesia-Experience, Flowability and Changeability, Communication and Interaction, and Penetration and Integration.

Synesthetic Experience

The traditional art provides for the experiential meeting, usually limited to personal sensations like those of sight or sound which are often shallow, incomplete and passive. The conventional art doesn't enable viewers to fully understand the artist's message or emotions of the artwork that it presents.

On the other hand, AI in Visual Arts gives a whole multisensory experience including visual, auditory as well as cognitive psychology element.

In digital painting, Magenta's "Sketch-RNN" thingy shows how AI can make drawings from words. It learnt from many human drawings so it can know what you mean when you write stuff. You know? When you say "tree" it takes that into account and comes up with different types of trees drawn in different colors and textures. It's like turned words into pictures, mingling how we look at things with how we read them (Magenta, 2018).

Also, Magenta's "NSynth" project goes into making new sounds using AI. By remixing some sounds in interesting ways, new audio fragments are created through this system. This means musicians and artists have access to new soundscapes they've never experienced before; kind of like seeing sounds in colors or feeling them like textures is an apt analogy.It is a situation where an artist's palette has been expanded by adding more colors for music makers in terms of sound though instead of paint (NSynth: Neural audio synthesis, 2017).

In sculpture, Google's "DeepDream" stuff provides a different form of mixing the senses. Originally it was designed to assist computers see better but now it makes fantastic pictures from nothing by finding patterns within images. Artist can use this for producing strange statues that look like fantasy worlds or abstract art. With DeepDream, AI defies the rules we have come to know concerning how we see things, thereby allowing people to delve into crazy and wild ideas (Inceptionism: Going deeper into neural networks, 2015).

This total immersion enables one feel more about the intentions of the creator, by vividly showing their thoughts and feelings and will through direct and effective means of artistic expression. These efforts also, push the boundaries of artistic research beyond what has been known before and redefines human-machine relations.

Fluidity and Adaptability

AI's fluidity and adaptability, however, have profoundly transformed the creative landscape, offering artists with never-before-seen tools and techniques to explore their imaginations. This fusion of technology and art has resulted into remarkable innovations that blur these demarcation points between human and machine creativity.

One such example is AI in Visual Arts in digital art where artificial intelligence algorithms generate original artworks. It simply talks about how things are changing. According to Roy Ascot the British artist, art is not focused on appearance but immanence because it is an active process that shifts from the outermost visible form through to the innermost form. AI in Visual Arts is a kind of art that changes infinitely: moving art.

In the field of digital painting, AI-powered tools such as DeepDream have revolutionized artistic workflows. DeepDream was developed by Google for interpreting and modifying images using neural networks, resulting in dream-like compositions with intricate details. Beeple among others uses DeepDream to create surreal digital paintings that venture into offbeat styles and expand digital art's possibilities (Creativity with AI, 2015).

Additionally, the AI has made tremendous progress in sculpture using methods like 3D printing. Through the application of AI algorithms artists can create intricate 3D models that are built up by layers on top of layers using 3D printers. Ioan Florea, an artist, employs the use of artificial intelligence algorithms with 3D printing equipment to produce sculptures that captivate audiences and defy conventional distinctions between physical and digital realms while showing how art blends into technology (Ai Weiwei: Circle of Animals, 2016).

Interaction and Engagement

In Visual Arts, audiences do not talk or touch the artworks only. They can also connect with the artists spiritually and even contribute to the reassembly of pieces. This interaction may be audible or taciturn as well as direct or indirect and cover a range of distances made possible by AI technology that makes viewers become participants in what they are seeing. Thus, this change release an artist from being bound by creativity as it helps to understand interactive art more inclusively and diversely. Artificial Intelligence in Visual Arts blurs borders between art and life; act of creation and act of viewing exemplify "Social Sculpture" advocated by Joseph Beuys, where everyone is an artist.

For instance, envision an AI in Visual Arts painting whereby viewers could interact with digital canvas through voice prompts resulting into altering colors, shapes and forms thus co-creating the artwork with AI system. This collaboration subverts traditional conceptions of authorship inviting viewers to enter into a dynamic conversation with the work itself.

In the same way as, in the realm of AI in Visual Arts sculpture, it is also possible for individuals to interact with sculptures having sensors and AI algorithms implanted in them, which enable them to manipulate their form and movement through movements or presence to act as co-creators. Such an interactive experience has no line between real physical world and the digital one thus encouraging people to explore fresh ways of creating art and being a part of art.

Permeation and Assimilation

The world of digital art has been penetrated and absorbed by artificial intelligence software that changes the way artists create, engage with and perceive art. A case in point is AI in Visual Arts, where algorithms of artificial intelligence are used to create works of art thus merging the difference between human creative ability and machine intelligence.

For AI in Visual Arts, an example would be: using AI algorithms to analyze enormous data sets of images and other forms of art that already exist out there, learn the artistic styles and techniques involved within them by which they create their own original works without any human intervention. This process not only demonstrates the potentiality of AI in generating visually appealing art pieces but also challenges established forms of authorship as well as creativity.

Among the examples that show us how AI in Visual Arts can be done in real life by the Google Magenta project. The intersection between AI and creative thinking is what informs the development of programs that generate music, visual art and other types of creative output like those produced by Magenta. Using machine learning methods, Magenta makes visually attractive works that are conceptually compelling thus showing that AI can function as a tool for creativity (Magenta, 2024).

AI has influenced the traditional approaches to painting and spread across them. The Portrait of Edmond de Belamy (Figure 2), which was done by Obvious, an art collective using a machine learning system Generative Adversarial Networks (GANs) is a case in point. It attracted great attention when Christie's auctioned this AI-created artwork in 2018, which raised questions on whether AI has any place in art or if humanity is losing value as computer age advances (Art's next Medium, 2020).

Similarly, when it comes to sculpture, AI has integrated itself into the creation process thus enabling artists to explore new directions in form and expression. One such example is an interactive sculpture created by artist Daniel Rozin. Sensors and AI algorithms help Rozin create sculptures that respond to viewer movements thereby turning static objects into dynamic, participatory artworks. In his work

"Mirror No.10", he uses a grid of rotating tiles that reflects the viewer's image resulting into blurred distinctions between real and virtual worlds (Smithsonian Magazine, 2024).

The work of artist Ai Weiwei is another example, who uses digital fabrication techniques and AI algorithms in his sculptures that are both intricate and thought-provoking. His sculpture Circle of Animals / Zodiac Heads based on the Chinese zodiac signs made from today's materials with modern technologies addressing the place where tradition meets innovation in contemporary art (ZODIAC: A Graphic Memoir, 2024). These examples illustrate where AI has pervaded and assimilated within digital art, painting, and sculpture, transforming artistic practices and widening frontiers for creative practice.

ART KNOWS NO BOUNDS: DEFYING GRAVITY AND SPACE

Art, in its many forms, can break free from the rules of gravity and space. imagine paintings seem to float in mid-air or sculptures that break through the barriers of physics. It is AI that creates room for artists to explore unconventional ideas and challenge the limits.

An illustrative instance of this is in using AI in digital art installations. Artists can use algorithms to create stunning visual effects that seem to warp space and twist reality. These usually incorporate elements such as light, sound or movement that take the viewers into an otherworldly experience. An example is the "Infinity Room" by Yayoi Kusama where mirrors and lights produce an illusion of infinite space thus creating a blurred line between reality and fiction as shown below in (Figure 6).

Another example is seen in how VR experiences are created with AI tools. An artist can build complete worlds outside our physical realm hence allowing people access incredible environments together with impossible things. For instance, there exists a virtual reality experience called Tilt Brush where painting happens in three dimensions which results into works of art that appear to defy the laws of physics.

Moreover, AI can be used to generate art that challenges our perceptions of space and gravity. For example, generative adversarial networks (GANs) can produce surreal images that play with perspective and scale, creating scenes that feel simultaneously familiar and otherworldly.

Examples of Art Knows No Bounds

"THE IMPOSSIBLE STATUE"

The Impossible Statue became a reality thanks to innovative AI modeling and state of the art manufacturing techniques. Constructed from stainless steel, its intricate precision challenged Sandvik's advanced digital manufacturing solutions and cutting tools.

According to Peter Skogh, "Impossible statue is a perfect example of what modern technology combined with human genius can achieve", Director at Tekniska museet. "We want to create more awareness on what technology can do and encourage young people to pursue careers in STEM fields. And this project meets all these criteria" (Creating the impossible statue, 2023).

The statue involved training of multiple artificial intelligence models using the works from five of the greatest and most famous sculptors, blending together some of their most famous characteristics:

Michelangelo's dynamic off-balance poses (Italy, 1475-1564)

Rodin's musculature and reflectiveness (France, 1840-1917)

Käthe Kollwitz' expressionist feeling (Germany, 1867-1945)

Takamura Kotaro's focus on momentum and mass (Japan, 1883-1956)

Augusta Savage's defiance in her figures (USA, 1892-1962).

Sandvik utilized advanced techniques, including depth estimators, human pose estimators, videogame algorithms, and specialized AI, to transform a 2D design that consolidated the styles of five artists to a detailed three-dimensional mode. The complex design was managed with the assistance of Mastercam software renowned for its computer aided manufacturing abilities into an actual statue consisting over nine million polygons and intricate details.

The manufacturing process of the statue demonstrated Sandvik's end-to-end digital capabilities as Vericut software was used to simulate safe, reliable and efficient tooling and machining by Sandvik Coromant. Digital perfection before machining eliminated need for scrapping and remaking any parts. A digital simulation decreased trial and verification time six-fold compared to conventional manual processes leading to reduction in the use of stainless steel by twice the amount. Just three simulations were necessary for the final piece while 100 were needed for the first one. Machining with Sandvik Coromant tools made it possible to make 17 different parts that had a superior surface quality with almost invisible seam borders. The steel consumption of the statue was reduced due to sectioning, which resulted in all removed material being recycled back into the supply chain through Alleima, Sandvik's material supplier.iuy

To create this statue, we employed professionals who are knowledgeable in CAD modeling, CAM programming, and machining. CNC machines were directed during production using a daunting 40 million lines G- code generated. Metrology software from Metrologic Group under Sandvik ensured that every minor detail of the statue was maintained. As a result, this final statue weighs around 500 kg and measures at 150 cm high in terms of precision is concerned; there is an ideal variation from its digital design within less than 30 microns (0.03 mm), comparable with such minuteness found in Swiss watchmaking contexts. This precision was achieved through virtual simulations, utilizing digital twin technology and optimizing tool paths.

"DIO"

- Artist: Ben Snell

AI art is currently in the spotlight, with record-breaking auctions, artistic controversies, and discussions about creativity. However, a unique development has emerged: an AI-generated sculpture crafted from the ground-up remains of the computer that conceived it.

It's the work of New York artist Ben Snell. Dio was designed by AI trained on hundreds of classical sculptures.

Snell's piece, named Dio, just like Snell's earlier works, follows the same methodology. Thus in this case the machine learning algorithms have been programmed to scan through a historical artwork database and produce similar outputs as what they have previously observed which is guided by the artist.

For instance, training data for Dio consisted of over a thousand classical sculptures (including such canonical works as Discobolus and Michelangelo's David), though Snell neglects to mention his participation in shaping the algorithmic predictions. "I would rather not go into any more details about technique and implementation, because I see them as alienating," Snell said to The Verge via email. "I don't want to render the behavior of Dio in human terms; rather, I want it to appear just like ours ". My goal is not to make Dio more human; instead, I aim at understanding ourselves as computational beings.

Snell believes he's the artist, not the computer. Yet, he's excited about how his algorithms work. He says the computer tries to remember sculptures it's seen before and imagines new ones when he asks it to. He uses figurative language to help people understand these digital processes better. But whatever the relation between Snell and his machine learning systems, he says Dio will be the "first and last" output from his algorithms (Vincent, 2019).

Snell, after he had finished creating the 3D model, took apart the computer he worked with and crushed it into pieces in a vacuous box. Among other things that were part of the computer are its casing, hard drive, RAM and graphics processing unit. He also made a mold of Dio using 3D printing technology and then using resin plus ground remains of the computer he casted the sculpture into this mold alone.

Snell wanted to reduce his influence over the algorithms. By destroying the data and training model used to make Dio, he ensured the sculpture became a one-of-a-kind piece that can't be replicated."And voila!" says Snell. "Dio emerges with a newfound physical agency."

CONCLUSION

AI & Art can dominate and influence audience everywhere. In conclusion, the relationship between art and technology has long been intertwined, evolving alongside the advancements in science and technology. Over the years, artists have embraced new technological innovations, gradually shifting from traditional methods to utilizing the latest tools as alternative mediums for creative expression. This interaction has not only influenced the creation of artworks but has also transformed how viewers interpret and engage with art, shaping their understanding based on their unique perspectives.

Just as the invention of the printing press, computer and photography changed art forever, artificial intelligence (AI) is claimed to be a forthcoming technical revolution anticipated to change how artwork is made and increase our capacity for imagination. The introduction of generative algorithms has brought about huge improvements in AI fostered by increased computing power, application of big data and creation of new models.

Nowadays, AI has gained a new meaning in visual arts thanks to developments in deep learning and big data. This fusion between art and AI has resulted into a rising trend characterized by many exhibitions exploring the crossovers between these two disciplines. However, even though AI practices have been applied in visual art circles, academicians have not paid much attention to these issues resulting in some gaps thus necessitating further investigation on the relationship between artificial intelligence and art.

In this paper, we have explored various aspects of AI in visual arts, ranging from the introduction of generative algorithms like GANs and VAEs to their implementation in painting, sculpture, and digital art. We have also delved into the modern approach towards art, emphasizing the limitless possibilities of artistry in defying gravity and space, exemplified by real-life implementations such as the "Infinity Room", "THE IMPOSSIBLE STATUE" and "DIO".

Looking ahead, we envision continued progress through experimentation and refinement of theories, models, and tools in AI in visual arts development. By further exploring the potential for creativity and innovation in this emerging field, we aim to unlock new dimensions of artistic expression and redefine the boundaries of art in the digital age.

FUTURE SCOPE FOR IMPROVEMENT

Enhancing the training and stability of GANs is one key area for improvement. Nevertheless, while GANs have been able to generate realistic images impressively; these models usually suffer from issues like mode collapse and instability in training. In future, researchers should focus on developing new approaches for training, regularization and architecture design that prevent these problems by making GAN models stronger and robust.

Similarly, there's much room for enhancing how expressive and flexible VAEs are. Although VAEs provide a theoretically sound framework for learning latent representations of data, they may not be effective in capturing complex high-dimensional distributions. Prospective developments may include tuning loss functions, exploring alternative priors and incorporating additional constraints which will lead to better diversity/ quality in generated samples.

Furthermore, deep learning architectures; computation resources; optimization algorithms can also drive progress in both GANs and VAEs. As the hardware becomes more advanced while computational techniques become more complicated day by day, it is possible for researchers to exploit this progress to develop superior and faster generative models.

In addition to technical advancements, there is a growing need for interdisciplinary cooperation and application focused research in the area of generative algorithms. Researchers can develop better and more effective generative systems, if they cooperate with other professionals such as artists, designers and entertainers to get precise specifications and challenges required in real life situations.

Figure 3.

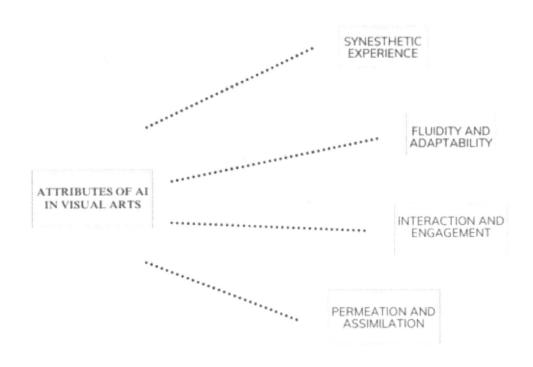

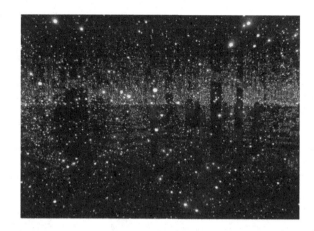

Figure 7.

REFERENCES

Ai, W. (2016, July 26). *Circle of animals / zodiac heads*. Carnegie Museum of Art. https://carnegieart .org/exhibition/ai-weiwei-circle-of-animals-zodiac/

AiArt. (2020). *Towards artificial intelligence art*. Research Gate. https://www.researchgate.net/publication/ 342642793_AiArt_Towards_Artificial_Intelligence_Art

Art's next medium. (2020). Christie's. https://www.christies.com/en/stories/a-collaboration-between-two -artists-one-human-one-a-machine-0cd01f4e232f4279a525a446d60d4cd1

Artrendex. (2021). Artrendex. https://www.artrendex.com/

Brings together new 2024 papers. (2020). Ebin.Pub. http://ebin.pub

Chen, W. (2020). *AiArt: Towards artificial intelligence art*. Research Gate. https://www.researchgate .net/publication/342642793_AiArt_Towards_Artificial_Intelligence_Art

Creating the impossible statue. (2023, April). Sandvik. https://www.home.sandvik/en/stories/articles/ 2023/04/creating-the-impossible-statue/

Deepart Io. (n.d.). (2023). *Creativity with AI*. https://creativitywith.ai/deepartio/

DeepDream. (2015, July). *A code example for visualizing neural networks*. Google AI Blog. https://ai .googleblog.com/2015/07/deepdream-code-example-for-visualizing.html

Di Chio, C. (Ed.). (2011). *Generative art is the ceding of control by the artist to an autonomous system*.

DigitalCommons@UNO. (2021). *The institutional repository of the University of Nebraska Omaha*. Unomaha.edu. http://digitalcommons.unomaha.edu

DIO - Artist. Ben Snell. (2018). This AI-generated sculpture is made from the shredded remains of the computer that designed it. The Verge. https://www.theverge.com/tldr/2019/4/12/18306090/ai-generated -sculpture-shredded-remains-ben-snell-dio

Fox, A. (2020, May 5). Bronze Age chieftain's remains found beneath U.K. skate park. *Smithsonian Magazine*. https://www.smithsonianmag.com/arts-culture/daniel-rozin-interactive-art-180974810/

Framework, C. S. I. (2019). Ganpaint.Io. https://ganpaint.io/

IBSE. (2019). Iitm.Ac.In. http://ibse.iitm.ac.in

Inceptionism: Going deeper into neural networks. (2015, June). Google AI Blog. https://ai.googleblog .com/2015/06/inceptionism-going-deeper-into-neural.html

Is artificial intelligence set to become art's next medium? (n.d.). (2023). Christie's. https://www.christies .com/features/A-collaboration-between-two-artists-one-human-one-a-machine-9332-1.aspx

Liam, M. O. (2020, October 6). *The next Rembrandt developed by AI*. Liam M OBrien. https://www .liammobrien.com/rembranbt-ai/

Long, X. (2023). *Common features of Henri Matisse's painting concept and ancient Chinese pictorial thought.* Человек и Культура.

Magazine, S. (2023). Arts & culture. *Smithsonian Magazine.* https://www.smithsonianmag.com/category/arts-culture/

Matisse, H. (2023, November 15). Creativity takes courage. *The Socratic Method.* https://www.socratic-method.com/quote-meanings-french/henri-matisse-creativity-takes-courage

NSynth. (2017, April 6). *Neural audio synthesis.* Magenta. https://magenta.tensorflow.org/nsynth

StatusNeo. (2022, September 18). *Accelerated time to value.* StatusNeo - Cloud Native Technology Services & Consulting. http://statusneo.com

Vincent, J. (2019, April 12). This AI-generated sculpture is made from the shredded remains of the computer that designed it. *The Verge.* https://www.theverge.com/tldr/2019/4/12/18306090/ai-generated-sculpture-shredded-remains-ben-snell-dio

We like to build AI things. (2024, February 24). Growthsetting. http://growthsetting.com

Wikipedia contributors. (2024, February 4). *A picture is worth a thousand words.* Wikipedia, The Free Encyclopedia. https://en.wikipedia.org/w/index.php?title=A_picture_is_worth_a_thousand_words&oldid=1203266294

Your all-in-one collaborative workspace. (2024). Coda. http://coda.io

Zodiac: A graphic memoir. (2023). Ai Weiwei Films. https://www.aiweiwei.com/zodiac

Chapter 3
Navigating Uncharted Waters:
Emerging Technologies and Future Challenges in Generative AI With Python

Richard Shan
CTS, USA

ABSTRACT

This chapter explores the evolution and future trajectory of Python-driven generative AI, highlighting Python's role in advancing this technology. It discusses the integration of Python with emerging technologies like neuromorphic computing and reinforcement learning, focusing on their potential to revolutionize art, design, and media. Through detailed analysis of the open-source implementation of a technology platform designed, the chapter provides insights into Python's facilitation of innovative AI applications. It addresses potential challenges and ethical considerations, along with the mitigation and call to action, emphasizing the importance of responsible innovation. The narrative underscores Python's influence in making advanced AI technologies accessible and scalable, preparing readers to engage with future developments in the field of generative AI.

INTRODUCTION

In an era defined by rapid technological acceleration, the domain of generative artificial intelligence (GenAI) emerges as a frontier rich with transformative potential. Amidst a myriad of programming languages and tools, Python distinguishes itself as not just a facilitator but as a pivotal force in the advancement of generative AI. This chapter endeavors to explore the profound impact Python has had on this dynamic field, particularly focusing on how it continues to shape and catalyze technological breakthroughs that are set to redefine industries across art, design, and media.

The narrative of Python in AI is one of empowerment and accessibility. Renowned for its simplicity and readability, Python has democratized the field of AI, enabling a broad spectrum of users—from academic researchers to industry practitioners—to implement complex algorithms effectively. The language's extensive library ecosystem, including TensorFlow, PyTorch, and Keras, provides a versatile foundation for building sophisticated generative models. These models, ranging from Generative Adversarial Networks (GANs) to transformer-based architectures, have been instrumental in pushing the boundaries of what machines can create and imagine.

DOI: 10.4018/979-8-3693-3278-8.ch003

As we stand on the brink of what many consider to be a new era in technological evolution, it is imperative to chart the course of generative AI facilitated by Python. This involves not only a retrospective look at the milestones achieved but also a forward-looking perspective into the potential challenges and opportunities that lie ahead. This chapter will delve into the transformative impacts these technologies are poised to have on art, design, and media, assessing the broader societal implications while navigating through the complexities of ethical, technical, and regulatory landscapes.

Python's journey in the realm of generative AI is marked by significant milestones that reflect its evolving capability and the expanding ambitions of the developers who wield it. From the early days of simple algorithmic procedures to today's advanced neural network architectures, Python has been a constant companion to innovation. The development of generative models like GANs, Variational Autoencoders (VAEs), and more recently, large-scale foundation models such as GPT, DALL-E, Claude, and others, highlight a trajectory of rapid advancement and increasing complexity. These models, powered by Python's accessible frameworks, have not only enhanced the feasibility of complex AI tasks but have also made such technologies accessible to a wider audience, thus fostering a culture of innovation.

In this chapter, we aim to synthesize insights from leading technologists, futurists, and practitioners to forecast the trajectory of Python-driven generative AI. We will explore cutting-edge developments and speculate on their future implications, particularly in how they might revolutionize the creative industries. The discussion will extend beyond mere technological advancements, delving into the ethical dimensions and societal impacts of these emergent technologies. By addressing both the potential and the pitfalls of Python in generative AI, this chapter seeks to equip readers with a comprehensive understanding of this dynamic field, encouraging responsible innovation and foresight in navigating the uncharted waters of tomorrow's technological landscapes.

Thus, as we delve deeper into the specifics of Python's role in advancing generative AI, we not only acknowledge its current state but also prepare to embrace the challenges and opportunities that lie ahead. This introductory exploration sets the stage for a detailed discussion on emerging technologies, potential future scenarios enabled by Python, and the strategic navigation required to harness these advancements responsibly. As we transition into a deeper analysis in the following sections, we remain focused on Python's integral role in shaping the future of generative AI, ensuring that the journey through this evolving landscape is as informed as it is innovative.

PYTHON'S EVOLUTION IN GENERATIVE AI

The evolution of Python within the realm of generative AI is a narrative of groundbreaking advancements and pivotal shifts in computational approaches. This journey from rudimentary script-based solutions to the sophisticated ecosystems of today has solidified Python's position as a cornerstone in AI development. This section provides a comprehensive overview of the milestones in Python's integration with generative AI technologies, elucidating how its frameworks and libraries have played a crucial role in shaping the capabilities of generative models.

Early Beginnings: Python's Entry Into AI

The initial foray of Python into AI was marked by its simplicity and ease of use, traits that made it an appealing choice for academic settings and early-stage developers. Python's syntax and dynamic nature allowed for quick iteration and prototyping—a crucial advantage in the nascent stages of AI research. Simple algorithmic procedures (Hou et al., 2023) in Python paved the way for more complex endeavors, setting a foundational stage upon which the future of generative AI would be built.

The Rise of Libraries and Frameworks

As the AI field burgeoned, so did Python's toolkit. The development and widespread adoption of libraries such as NumPy and SciPy provided the mathematical backbone needed for advanced computations. However, the real transformation came with the advent of TensorFlow, PyTorch, and Keras. These frameworks offered not just robust tools for building and training neural networks but also a modular approach that significantly lowered the barrier to entry for creating sophisticated AI models.

TensorFlow, developed by Google, became synonymous with deep learning due to its flexible, yet powerful, graph-computation model. PyTorch, with its dynamic computation graphs, offered a more intuitive and interactive approach, which was particularly suited for academia and research. Keras, on the other hand, functioned as a high-level API that enabled fast and easy prototyping of deep learning applications. Together, these tools propelled Python to the forefront of AI research and application, enabling the creation of more complex generative models.

Pioneering Generative Models

The true testament to Python's role in generative AI came with the development of Generative Adversarial Networks (GANs) and Variational Autoencoders (VAEs). These models, which allowed machines to generate new data instances that mimic real data, opened up new possibilities in art, design, and other creative sectors (What's the next word in large language models?, 2023). Python's frameworks made these models accessible and modifiable, allowing a wide range of applications (Ferrara, 2023) from automated content creation to complex data augmentation tasks.

The progression didn't stop there. The introduction of transformer-based models like OpenAI's GPT series redefined what generative AI could achieve. These models, which were primarily developed using Python, showcased an ability to handle diverse data types beyond images—extending generative capabilities to text, code, and even mixed-media formats. The scalability and versatility of Python played a critical role in enabling these models to learn from vast datasets, thus improving their generative capabilities.

Foundation Models and Beyond

More recently, the focus has shifted towards foundation models such as BERT, DALL-E, Stable Diffusion, and various successors. The Stanford Institute for Human-Centered Artificial Intelligence's (HAI) Center for Research on Foundation Models (CRFM) coined the term "foundation model" in August 2021 to mean "any model that is trained on broad data (generally using self-supervision at scale) that can be adapted (e.g., fine-tuned) to a wide range of downstream tasks" (Bommasani, 2021). Python's role in these developments has been twofold: firstly, as the primary language for building and training these models, and secondly, as a tool for the broader community to engage with and extend these technologies.

These foundation models have further solidified Python's position at the cutting edge of AI. They have not only enhanced the generative capabilities of AI systems but have also democratized access to these technologies, enabling a broader range of creators to experiment with AI-driven art and design.

As we anticipate further advancements, Python's continuous evolution alongside AI is evident in the emerging trends such as neuromorphic computing and quantum machine learning. Python's adaptability and the robust ecosystem of libraries are likely to remain central as these technologies develop.

In short, Python's journey through the milestones of generative AI underscores its vital role in this field. From facilitating early experiments to enabling complex, large-scale generative models, Python has proven indispensable. The historical context provided in this section sets the stage for understanding how Python will continue to drive the frontiers of generative AI, impacting various industries and reshaping creative practices worldwide. As we move forward, the narrative of Python and AI will undoubtedly evolve, promising new possibilities and challenges alike.

IMAGINING FUTURE SCENARIOS

The potential transformations that Python-driven generative AI can bring to various industries are vast and varied. This section employs a creative and speculative lens to paint scenarios that might unfold due to advancements in Python-driven generative AI, particularly in how these technologies could reshape the creative industries such as graphic design, film, and education.

Transforming Graphic Design

Imagine a world where graphic designers collaborate with AI to instantly generate and iterate on visual concepts. Python-driven AI tools can analyze current design trends and user feedback in real-time, enabling designers to create visuals that are not only aesthetically pleasing but also highly personalized and context-aware. For example, a campaign for an eco-friendly product can be visually aligned with consumer values and preferences, dynamically adapting its design elements to resonate more effectively with different demographics.

Revolutionizing the Film Industry

In the film industry, Python-driven generative AI could play a pivotal role in both pre-production and post-production phases. Scriptwriting AI could analyze vast amounts of film scripts to suggest plot twists and character developments that are unique yet contextually appropriate, potentially speeding up the scriptwriting process. During post-production, AI could generate realistic digital actors and environments, reducing the need for costly sets and on-location shoots. This could democratize film production, allowing smaller studios to create visually stunning films with significantly lower budgets.

Personalized Learning Environments

The education sector stands to benefit immensely from advancements in generative AI. Python could facilitate the development of personalized learning environments where educational content is tailored to the learning pace and style of each student. AI-driven tutors could provide real-time feedback and support, adapting educational materials to address students' specific weaknesses and strengths. For instance, a student struggling with mathematical concepts could be taught through customized problems that gradually increase in complexity, all generated and moderated by AI to perfectly match the student's evolving competence.

AI in Performing Arts

Beyond traditional media, Python-driven AI could transform performing arts by enabling real-time generative performances where music, dance, and visual art are created and altered dynamically in response to audience reactions. This could lead to entirely new forms of interactive performances, where the boundary between the performer and the audience blurs, creating a collaborative, immersive artistic experience.

The Role of Low-Code and No-Code Platforms

Python's flexibility and robustness might be further amplified through the increased use of low-code and no-code platforms that make AI tools accessible to non-programmers, like Joget DX. These platforms could empower artists, designers, educators, and filmmakers to implement complex AI functionalities through simple graphical user interfaces. This would not only democratize access to advanced technologies but also spur innovation across sectors by allowing more people to experiment with and benefit from AI capabilities.

While these scenarios illustrate the potential of Python-driven AI, they also raise significant ethical and societal questions. Issues such as the authenticity of AI-generated art, the displacement of jobs, and the implications of AI in shaping cultural norms must be carefully considered. It will be crucial to develop guidelines and frameworks to ensure that these technologies are used responsibly and that their benefits are distributed equitably across society.

The possibilities envisioned in this section represent just a fraction of what might be achieved with Python-driven generative AI. As we continue to explore and develop these technologies, their potential to reshape industries and redefine creative expression remains both an exciting prospect and a profound responsibility. The scenarios imagined here provide a glimpse into a future where Python not only enhances human creativity but also collaborates in the creation of new forms of art and interaction, highlighting the need for thoughtful integration of technology into the fabric of human activity.

EXPLORING PYTHON-DRIVEN GENAI ADVANCEMENTS

Emerging technologies within the domain of Python-driven generative AI present a horizon brimming with potential. This section explores the cutting-edge research, emerging trends, and innovations that Python is poised to facilitate, especially in the fields of art, design, and media, as illustrated in Figure

1. It also examines how these technological advancements might impact these fields, bringing about a transformative shift in creativity and production processes.

Enhanced Computational Models: Neuromorphic Computing and AI

One of the most significant advancements on the horizon is the integration of neuromorphic computing with generative AI. Neuromorphic computing, which mimics the neural structure of the human brain, offers unprecedented computational power and efficiency, such as Intel's Hala Point. Python's role in this integration is crucial as it provides the necessary tools and libraries for simulation and experimentation. This can lead to the development of AI models that not only process information faster but also with greater energy efficiency, enabling more sustainable AI operations.

Autonomy in Creative Processes: Reinforcement Learning and Generative Design

Python is also at the forefront of employing reinforcement learning (RL) algorithms in creative problem-solving. RL algorithms, which learn optimal actions through trial and error, are being used to develop autonomous agents capable of creating complex and nuanced designs. For instance, in the realm of architectural design, these agents can generate multiple design alternatives based on specific criteria, significantly speeding up the creative process while adhering to aesthetic and functional requirements, such as DvArch.

Figure 1. Progression of Python-based generative AI

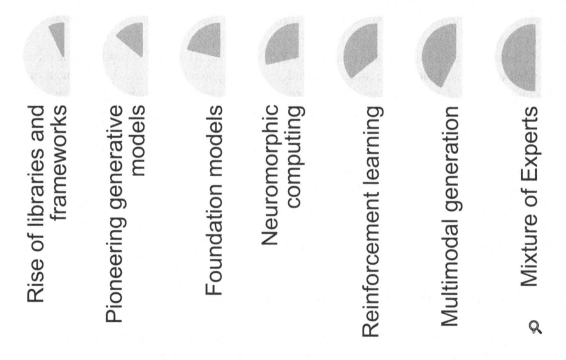

Advancements in Multimodal Generation

The potential of Python in advancing AI-generated art and media is particularly exciting. With the increasing sophistication of generative models like GANs and transformer-based architectures, artists and designers are equipped with tools that can generate highly detailed and contextually relevant artworks. Python's libraries such as TensorFlow and PyTorch offer the scalability necessary to handle intricate computations and vast datasets, enabling the creation of artworks that are not only unique but also resonate with a broad audience.

Moreover, the development of multimodal AI models (Bewersdorff et al., 2024) — capable of understanding and integrating multiple forms of data (text, image, sound) — is transforming content creation. These models, facilitated by Python's versatile ecosystem, allow for a more nuanced integration of different media types, leading to richer, more immersive creations. For instance, an AI can generate a soundtrack based on the mood of a visual piece, or vice versa, creating a cohesive artistic experience that is dynamically generated in real-time, like what is in Adobe Project Music GenAI Control.

Mixture of Experts (MoE) and Contextual AI Content

Looking further, the Mixture of Experts (MoE) models represent another frontier for Python-driven AI. These models, which employ a dynamic routing of tasks to specialized experts within a larger network, can handle tasks requiring a mixture of different skills and knowledge areas via agents (Yang & Liu, 2024). This is particularly pertinent in the context of generative AI, where the demand for highly contextual and personalized content is rising. Python's ability to integrate with MoE frameworks allows for the creation of content that is not only diverse but also tailored to specific user preferences and contexts, such as what was built in the architecture of Gemini and Grok-1.

While the advancements are promising, they also introduce new challenges. The increasing complexity of AI models necessitates more robust computational resources (Li et al., 2022) and more sophisticated development tools. Python's ecosystem will need to evolve to support these demands, ensuring that it remains an effective tool for innovation in generative AI.

In essence, the advancements in Python-driven AI are setting the stage for a future where creative processes are more autonomous, nuanced, and intertwined with technological innovation. As these technologies continue to evolve, they will undoubtedly redefine the landscape of art, design, and media, creating new opportunities for creativity and expression. This exploration not only highlights the potential of these advancements but also underscores the need for continuous development and adaptation of Python tools and libraries to meet the emerging demands of generative AI.

NAVIGATING OPEN-SOURCE SOLUTIONS FOR GENERATIVE AI

In the realm of generative artificial intelligence (AI), Python stands out not only for its simplicity and readability but also for the richness of its open-source ecosystem. This ecosystem, powered by a community-driven approach to innovation, has given rise to numerous frameworks, libraries, and packages specifically tailored for generative AI. In this section, we delve into some of these open-source resources, such as Streamlit, Chainlit, LangChain, LlamaIndex, ACME, JAX, Diffusers, SingleStore

Notebook, and Haystack, examining their features, uses, and how they contribute to advancing the capabilities of generative AI.

Technology Platform

The GenAI technology platform is designed as a comprehensive ecosystem to facilitate the development, deployment, and operation of generative AI applications. This system is structured in a layered architecture with two supporting pillars that provide a robust foundation for both development and operational processes, as displayed in Figure 2.

Figure 2. Technology platform of Python-based generative AI

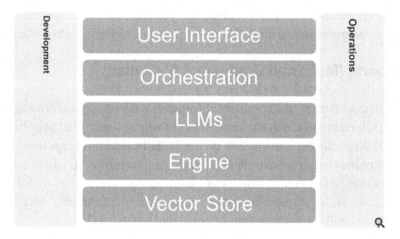

Middle Stack: Core Layers of the Platform

User Interface Layer: At the top of the stack, the User Interface layer is where users interact with the system. This layer is designed to be intuitive and accessible, providing tools and features that allow users to seamlessly create, modify, and interact with AI-generated content. Open-source frameworks like Streamlit can be integrated here to enable rapid prototyping and deployment of user-friendly interfaces.

Orchestration Layer: Below the User Interface, the Orchestration layer manages the flow of data and operations across the platform. It coordinates the interactions between the user interface, underlying AI models, and the data repository, ensuring efficient processing and execution of tasks. Tools like Apache Airflow or Kubernetes can be utilized in this layer to manage complex workflows and maintain high availability.

LLMs (Large Language Models) Layer: Central to the platform, this layer hosts the large language models that drive the generative capabilities of the platform. Open-source models such as GPT or BERT can be deployed here, providing powerful natural language processing capabilities that can be tailored to specific tasks or industries.

Engine Layer: The Engine layer is the computational backbone of the platform, responsible for executing AI models and handling the heavy lifting of data processing. This layer often employs machine learning frameworks like TensorFlow or PyTorch, which are well-suited for building and running sophisticated AI models.

Vector Store Layer: At the base of the stack, the Vector Store layer manages the storage and retrieval of vector data used and generated by AI models. This layer is crucial for the performance of search and retrieval operations within the platform, utilizing systems like Faiss or Annoy for efficient similarity search in high-dimensional spaces.

Supporting Pillars: Development and Operations

Development Pillar: This pillar focuses on the tools and processes that support the development of AI applications. It includes version control systems like Git, integrated development environments (IDEs) such as VS Code, and continuous integration/continuous deployment (CI/CD) tools like Jenkins or GitLab. The Development pillar ensures that AI models and applications are developed in a structured and efficient manner, promoting code reuse, maintainability, and collaboration among developers.

Operations Pillar: The Operations pillar encompasses the tools and practices required to maintain and scale AI applications. This includes monitoring tools like Prometheus or Grafana to track system performance and operational metrics, as well as deployment tools such as Docker or Ansible for automating the deployment and scaling of AI applications. The focus here is on ensuring reliability, performance, and security of the platform in a production environment.

Together, these layers and pillars form a cohesive platform that supports the entire lifecycle of generative AI applications, from development through deployment to ongoing operation. By leveraging open-source components across the stack, the platform not only fosters innovation and flexibility but also ensures that it remains cost-effective and adaptable to changing technologies and business needs, as highlighted in Figure 3.

Figure 3. Open-source components for tech platform

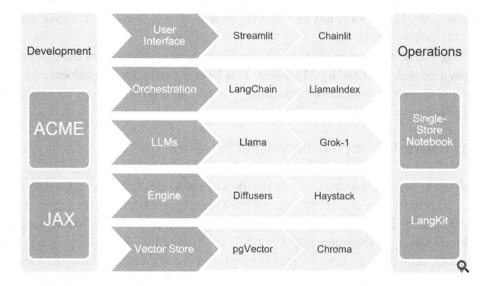

Next we will dive deep to selected component in the technology platform.

Streamlit: Simplifying Data Science and Machine Learning Applications

Streamlit is an open-source app framework specifically designed for machine learning and data science teams. It allows data scientists and developers to create beautiful, interactive web applications quickly and with minimal coding. One of the key features of Streamlit is its ability to turn scripts into shareable web apps with simple Python APIs. This feature is incredibly useful for generative AI projects, where visualizing data and model outputs can be as crucial as the analysis itself.

Key Features and Applications:

- Rapid Prototyping: Streamlit's design philosophy centers around speed and simplicity. Developers can go from data scripts to app deployment in a matter of hours, significantly accelerating the iterative processes typical of generative AI projects.
- Interactivity: Without the need for callbacks, Streamlit apps update automatically as users interact with them. This is particularly advantageous for generative AI applications, where user inputs can dynamically influence model outcomes.
- Component Ecosystem: Streamlit supports custom components built with React, allowing developers to extend their applications' capabilities and integrate other data visualization libraries like Plotly or Bokeh.

Streamlit's ease of use and flexibility make it an excellent choice for showcasing generative AI models, facilitating stakeholder interaction with AI functionalities, and gathering feedback on AI-generated outputs in real time.

Chainlit: Enhancing GenAI Interactions

While not as widely recognized as Streamlit, Chainlit is an emerging framework that aims to integrate blockchain technology with artificial intelligence. Chainlit is an innovative, open-source asynchronous Python framework designed specifically for developing scalable conversational AI and agentic applications, which provides developers with the tools needed to build sophisticated AI-driven interfaces, such as ChatGPT-like applications, embedded chatbots, software copilots, and customized frontends for unique agentic experiences. Chainlit also includes robust API support, allowing for seamless integration into existing systems or the creation of new projects from the ground up.

Key Features and Applications:

- Rapid Development and Integration: Chainlit is engineered to facilitate quick development, enabling seamless integration with an existing codebase or the ability to start a project from scratch within minutes. This feature is crucial for businesses looking to rapidly deploy conversational AI capabilities without extensive downtime or integration challenges.
- Embedded AI Copilots: With Chainlit, developers can embed AI-powered software copilots into applications. These copilots can assist with a range of tasks, from code completion and debugging to sophisticated decision support, making them invaluable across various sectors including software development, customer support, and data analysis.
- Customizable Frontends: Chainlit supports the development of custom frontends, allowing creators to tailor their conversational AI applications to deliver unique user experiences. This flexibility is key for brands or services requiring a specific user interaction model that aligns with their operational needs and aesthetic values.
- Data Persistence: Chainlit includes functionality to collect, monitor, and analyze data interactions between users and the AI. This ability to track and store user interactions is vital for refining AI responses, understanding user behavior, and enhancing overall engagement strategies (Bandi et al., 2023).
- Visualization of Multi-Step Reasoning: One of the standout features of Chainlit is its capability to visualize the reasoning process behind AI-generated responses. This visualization helps developers and end-users alike to understand the intermediate steps that lead to a particular output, enhancing transparency and trust in AI decisions.
- Iterative Prompt Engineering: Chainlit's Prompt Playground feature allows developers to experiment with and refine prompts used in conversational AI applications. This tool is particularly useful for diagnosing and correcting errors in AI responses, thereby improving the accuracy and relevance of conversational outputs over time.

Chainlit is not just a tool for building AI applications; it is a comprehensive platform that empowers developers to create intelligent, responsive, and adaptable AI systems that can truly transform user interactions and operational efficiencies. As AI continues to evolve, Chainlit's role in fostering accessible, powerful, and trustworthy AI solutions is likely to grow, making it a cornerstone of innovative AI development in the Python community.

LangChain: Bridging Language Models and Application Development

LangChain is a library designed to facilitate the development of applications that leverage LLMs. It abstracts much of the complexity involved in integrating these models into various applications, making it easier for developers to focus on the higher-level logic of their projects.

Key Features and Applications:

- Modular Components: LangChain offers modular components for common operations needed when working with language models, such as chaining multiple models together or integrating external knowledge sources.
- Ease of Integration: The library provides tools for connecting language models with APIs, databases, and other external systems, which is particularly useful in creating sophisticated generative AI applications that require a combination of text generation and real-world data interaction.

LangChain is especially relevant in today's AI landscape where language models like GPT-4 are being used to generate human-like text. It supports the rapid development of applications ranging from automated content creation to AI-powered conversational agents.

LlamaIndex: Facilitating Efficient Search and Retrieval in Large Models

LlamaIndex is another innovative tool in the generative AI space, designed to improve the efficiency of information retrieval from large language models. By optimizing how data is indexed and retrieved, LlamaIndex enhances the performance of AI applications that need to process and generate responses from large datasets.

Key Features and Applications:

- Performance Optimization: LlamaIndex improves the speed and accuracy of search operations within large datasets, a critical factor in applications such as interactive AI-driven tutorials or customer service bots.
- Scalability: It is built to scale with the growing size of language models and datasets, ensuring that the retrieval processes do not become bottlenecks as the amount of data increases.

LlamaIndex exemplifies the kind of tool that becomes increasingly necessary as businesses and researchers work with ever-larger models and more complex data structures in their generative AI applications.

Diffusers: Streamlining the Use of Diffusion Models

Diffusers, by Hugging Face, is a library designed to simplify the use and deployment of diffusion models in generative AI. Diffusion models are a class of generative models that have shown great promise in generating high-quality images, audio, and other forms of media.

Key Features and Applications:

- Pre-trained Models: Diffusers provide access to a range of pre-trained models, making it easier for developers to implement state-of-the-art diffusion models without extensive computational resources.
- Pipeline Integration: It offers easy integration with existing AI pipelines, enhancing the capacity to produce AI-generated media with minimal setup.

Diffusers is particularly popular among developers looking to create advanced generative artworks or media content that requires high fidelity and nuanced detail.

Haystack: Building Powerful Search Engines for AI Applications

Haystack is an open-source framework designed to enable scalable and flexible search engines over large text documents. It is built to assist developers in creating powerful search applications that can leverage the latest language models for deep understanding and rich information retrieval.

Key Features and Applications:

- Deep Learning Integration: Haystack facilitates the integration of state-of-the-art language models, enhancing search capabilities with deep semantic understanding.
- Modular Setup: It allows for a highly customizable setup, letting developers choose and configure different components such as document stores, retrieval techniques, and reader models according to their specific needs.

Haystack is particularly effective in generative AI applications where complex information retrieval is necessary, such as in legal document analysis or automated research systems.

These libraries and tools collectively enhance the Python ecosystem, providing developers with powerful options for building and deploying generative AI models. Each brings distinct advantages, whether in improving computational efficiency, simplifying model deployment, or enhancing data interaction capabilities. As the field of generative AI continues to evolve, the role of these open-source resources will undoubtedly expand, offering more refined and specialized functionalities tailored to the burgeoning needs of AI practitioners.

The Python ecosystem is a rich landscape of frameworks, libraries, and packages that are continually evolving to meet the demands of generative AI. Various tools not only facilitate the development of AI applications but also push the boundaries of what these applications can achieve. Whether it's enhancing interactivity, ensuring security, simplifying the integration of complex models, or optimizing performance, these open-source resources are vital to the progression of generative AI. As we look to the future, the role of these tools will undoubtedly expand, further cementing Python's place at the heart of innovation in generative AI.

ACME: A Library for Reinforcement Learning

ACME is a library designed for building scalable and efficient reinforcement learning (RL) (Liu, Han, Ma et al, 2023) agents, developed by DeepMind. It focuses on providing a clean and simple API for RL that supports both research prototypes and production-ready systems. ACME is particularly useful in generative AI for creating models that can learn complex behaviors from their environment, thereby enhancing their ability to generate creative and contextually appropriate outputs.

Key Features and Applications:

- Modular Design: ACME's modular design allows for flexibility in experimenting with different components of an RL system, such as various algorithms and network architectures.
- Efficiency at Scale: It supports high-efficiency operations that are crucial when training models on large-scale environments, a common scenario in sophisticated generative AI tasks.

ACME is ideal for projects where the AI needs to adapt to complex and dynamic environments, such as in autonomous systems or game development.

JAX: Accelerating Numerical Computations

JAX is a library for high-performance numerical computing, designed by researchers at Google. It extends NumPy and SciPy libraries with the ability to automatically differentiate through native Python and NumPy functions. JAX is crucial for generative AI applications that require extensive numerical computation and benefit from hardware acceleration, like tensor operations in deep learning.

Key Features and Applications:

- Automatic Differentiation: JAX provides functional transformations of Python and NumPy code, including differentiation and vectorization, which are essential for training deep learning models.
- GPU/TPU Support: It is designed to run on GPUs and TPUs, which accelerates the computational speed, a critical factor in training large generative models efficiently.

Developers use JAX in scenarios where complex data transformations and model training processes require enhanced computational performance.

SingleStore Notebook: Enhancing Data Operations for AI

SingleStore Notebook is a tool that integrates database operations directly into Python notebooks. It allows developers to execute SQL queries, visualize query results, and build applications within a notebook environment. This tool is invaluable for generative AI projects that involve large datasets and require seamless integration between data processing and model training.

Key Features and Applications:

- Real-time Analytics: SingleStore Notebook supports real-time analytics, which is crucial for dynamically adjusting generative models based on streaming data inputs.
- Scalable Data Handling: It offers robust data handling capabilities, ensuring that data-intensive operations do not become a bottleneck in AI workflows.

SingleStore Notebook is often used in environments where data velocity and volume are high, such as in financial forecasting or real-time content generation systems.

LangKit: Open-Source Toolkit for Text Metrics

LangKit is an open-source toolkit designed to provide comprehensive text metrics for monitoring LLMs effectively. Recognizing the challenges associated with deploying transforming language models into production, LangKit addresses the complexities of managing vast potential input combinations and their corresponding outputs, which are critical in ensuring the robustness and reliability of LLMs.

Key Features and Applications:

- Prompt Injection Analysis: LangKit enables users to gauge similarity scores against recognized fast injection attacks, helping to secure models against manipulation and ensure the integrity of outputs.
- Sentiment Analysis: This feature assesses the sentiment tone within the text, allowing developers to fine-tune models based on desired emotional responses and to better understand the model's interaction with users.
- Text Quality Assessment: LangKit evaluates readability, complexity, and grade scores of text generated by LLMs. This is essential for applications in educational technology, content creation, and any other domain where text clarity and accessibility are priorities.
- Jailbreak Detection: The toolkit identifies similarity scores with known jailbreak attempts, safeguarding against unauthorized model behavior that could lead to inappropriate or unintended content generation.
- Toxicity Analysis: Detecting levels of toxicity in content is crucial for maintaining the ethical use of AI in public-facing applications. LangKit provides tools to monitor and mitigate the risk of generating harmful or offensive content.

The unstructured nature of text in machine learning presents significant challenges in observability, which LangKit seeks to resolve. Without clear insights into a model's behavior, significant repercussions can arise, potentially affecting user trust and model efficacy. LangKit's suite of tools not only enhances the observability of machine learning models but also supports developers in implementing more reliable, safe, and user-friendly AI applications.

By integrating LangKit into their development workflow, AI practitioners can achieve a deeper understanding of their models' operational dynamics, enabling them to preemptively address issues and optimize performance. LangKit stands as a crucial resource in the evolving field of AI, providing the necessary tools to navigate the complexities of language model deployment and management effectively.

IDENTIFYING AND ANALYZING FUTURE CHALLENGES

As Python-driven generative AI continues to evolve and reshape various industries, it inevitably presents significant challenges. This section delves into the ethical, societal, and technical hurdles that may arise with the progression of these technologies. It highlights the critical areas of concern and provides insights into how these challenges can be navigated and addressed.

Ethical Implications of AI-Generated Content

One of the foremost ethical challenges is the creation and use of AI-generated content. As AI becomes capable of producing work that rivals or surpasses human creativity in complexity and appeal, questions about originality, authorship, and copyright emerge. For instance, when an AI generates a novel or a piece of music, who holds the intellectual property rights—the creator of the AI, the user, or the AI itself? Furthermore, there is the risk of AI being used to create deceptive or harmful content, such as deepfakes, which can undermine trust in media and have serious societal repercussions.

Societal Impact: Job Displacement and Inequality

The automation of creative processes could lead to job displacement within the creative industries. As AI tools become more adept at tasks traditionally performed by humans, from graphic design to film editing, the economic and social impact on these professions could be profound. Additionally, there could be a widening inequality gap if access to advanced AI tools and the skills to use them remain unevenly distributed. Ensuring equitable access to education and training in these new technologies will be crucial to mitigate these effects.

Technical Obstacles: Scalability and Bias

From a technical standpoint, the scalability of AI systems presents a significant challenge. As generative models grow more complex, the computational resources (Liu, Bubeck, Eldan et al, 2023) required to train and operate these systems increase. This not only raises the cost but also the environmental impact of deploying large-scale AI models. Moreover, there is the ever-present issue of bias in AI outputs. If not properly addressed, biased data can lead AI systems to generate content that perpetuates stereotypes or excludes underrepresented groups.

Developing Accurate and Fair Algorithms

The development of accurate and fair algorithms is an ongoing challenge that requires continuous attention. Ensuring that AI systems are trained on diverse datasets and tested across varied scenarios is crucial to minimizing hallucinations (Augenstein et al., 2023). Python's community and open-source nature play a pivotal role here, as they enable a broad range of developers to contribute to and scrutinize the algorithms, enhancing transparency and accountability.

Regulatory and Legal Frameworks

As AI technologies advance, there is also a need for robust regulatory and legal frameworks to keep pace. These frameworks must address issues such as AI governance, data privacy (Hacker et al., 2023), and the ethical use of AI. The involvement of Python developers in these discussions is essential, as their insights can guide the development of policies that foster innovation while protecting public interest.

Navigating the future of Python-driven generative AI involves not only embracing its potential to transform industries but also addressing the significant challenges it brings. This section has highlighted the multifaceted nature of these challenges, spanning ethical, societal, and technical dimensions. As we move forward, it will be crucial for stakeholders across sectors to collaborate in developing strategies that harness the benefits of AI while mitigating its risks. This collaborative approach will ensure that Python continues to serve as a catalyst for responsible and innovative technological advancement.

MITIGATING RISKS AND NAVIGATING THE FUTURE

As we embrace the transformative potential of Python-driven generative AI, it is essential to develop and implement strategies that mitigate associated risks while steering these advancements towards beneficial outcomes for society. This section outlines approaches for promoting responsible innovation and navigating the future challenges that may arise from these emerging technologies, as shown in Figure 4.

Figure 4. Challenges and Mitigation of Python-based Generative AI

- Ethical Implications
- Societal Impact
- Technical Obstacles
- Fair Algorithms
- Regulations

- Ethical Guidelines
- Enhanced Capabilities
- Interdisciplinary collaboration
- Socio-Economic Impacts
- Access and Equity

Developing Ethical Guidelines and Frameworks

One of the primary steps in responsible AI development is the establishment of ethical guidelines and frameworks that govern the use of AI-generated content and the behavior of AI systems. These guidelines (Barletta et al., 2023) emphasize transparency, accountability, and fairness, ensuring that AI systems do not inadvertently cause harm or perpetuate biases. Python's widespread use in the AI community places it at the forefront of this initiative, offering an opportunity for its developers to lead by example.

The role of Python developers extends beyond coding to include ethical considerations in the design and implementation phases. By integrating ethics modules into Python libraries and frameworks, developers can provide built-in checks and balances that prompt users to consider the ethical implications of their AI applications.

Enhancing Python's Capabilities for Emerging Challenges

To address the increasing complexity and scale of AI projects, Python's toolset must evolve. This involves both refining existing libraries and developing new ones that can handle larger datasets, more complex algorithms, and greater demands on processing power. Moreover, enhancing Python's interoperability with other tools and platforms will be crucial for tackling multi-faceted projects that combine AI with other technologies, such as blockchain and the Internet of Things (IoT).

Fostering Interdisciplinary Collaboration

The future of Python-driven generative AI will benefit greatly from interdisciplinary collaboration. By bringing together technologists, ethicists, artists, and policymakers, new perspectives and expertise are integrated into the development process. Such collaboration can help in crafting comprehensive solutions that address technical challenges while considering the broader societal impacts, like the Global Partnership on Artificial Intelligence (GAPI) (The Global Partnership on Artificial Intelligence, n.d.).

For instance, collaboration between Python developers and artists can lead to the creation of AI tools that better serve creative needs, while input from ethicists ensures that these tools are used responsibly. Similarly, engaging with policymakers can help align technological advancements with regulatory requirements, ensuring that innovations are both impactful and compliant with established norms and laws, such as EU AI Act.

Preparing for Socio-Economic Impacts

As AI technologies potentially displace traditional jobs, particularly in creative industries, it is vital to prepare for the socio-economic impacts. This preparation could involve designing educational programs that focus on skills complementary to AI, such as critical thinking, creativity, and interpersonal skills. Python community initiatives could include partnerships with educational institutions to develop curricula that incorporate AI literacy, ensuring a workforce that is well-equipped to thrive in an AI-augmented job market, like GenAI Forum (GenAI, n.d.).

Promoting Access and Equity

To ensure that the benefits of Python-driven generative AI are widely distributed, efforts must be made to promote access and equity. This includes making AI tools and training available across diverse geographic and socio-economic groups. Open-source Python projects and open-source language models like Llama and Grok-1 play a crucial role here, as they lower the barriers to entry and allow a global community of developers to innovate and share their work.

In a nutshell, while the advancements in Python-driven generative AI hold great promise, they also come with responsibilities. By developing ethical guidelines, enhancing Python's capabilities, fostering interdisciplinary collaboration, preparing for socio-economic impacts, and promoting access and equity, we can navigate the future of generative AI with foresight and responsibility. This proactive approach will not only mitigate risks but also ensure that Python-driven AI continues to be a force for positive transformation in society. As we move forward, it is up to all stakeholders in the Python community and beyond to embrace these strategies and work together to shape a future where generative AI enhances human capabilities and enriches lives.

CALL TO ACTION

As we near the close of our exploration into Python-driven generative AI, it is crucial to recognize the collective responsibility and opportunity that lies before us. This section serves as a call to action for stakeholders across the spectrum—from developers and researchers to policymakers and educators—to engage proactively with the burgeoning field of generative AI. Here, we outline specific actions that different groups can undertake to ensure that the evolution of this technology is guided by ethical principles, inclusivity, and a commitment to enhancing human capabilities, as depicted in Figure 5.

Figure 5. Call to action of Python-based generative AI

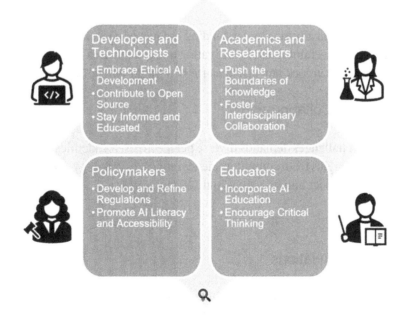

For Developers and Technologists

Embrace Ethical AI Development

Developers are at the frontline of crafting the future of AI. It is imperative that they integrate ethical considerations into the development process, adopting and promoting standards that ensure fairness, transparency, and accountability in AI systems.

Contribute to Open Source

The strength of Python lies in its community. Contributing to open-source projects not only enriches the ecosystem but also accelerates innovation and the democratization of technology. Developers should consider contributing code, documentation, or tutorials to projects, especially those that enhance the accessibility and ethical use of AI.

Stay Informed and Educated

Continual learning is key in a field as dynamic as AI. Developers should stay updated with the latest research, tools, and best practices in AI development and application. Engaging with ongoing education will enable them to harness cutting-edge advancements responsibly and innovatively.

For Academics and Researchers

Push the Boundaries of Knowledge

Researchers should strive to advance understanding not just of new capabilities but also of the implications and limitations of AI technologies. Investigating unexplored areas, such as the interplay between AI and human cognition, can unlock new avenues for beneficial AI applications.

Foster Interdisciplinary Collaboration

The complexity of AI challenges demands diverse perspectives. Academics should collaborate across disciplines—combining insights from computer science, ethics, psychology, and other fields—to develop holistic AI solutions that respect human values and societal norms.

For Policymakers

Develop and Refine Regulations

Policymakers have a crucial role in shaping the framework within which AI technologies evolve. Crafting informed, agile policies that adapt to technological advances while protecting citizens from potential harms is essential. These regulations should encourage innovation while setting clear guidelines for ethical AI use.

Promote AI Literacy and Accessibility

Ensuring that the benefits of AI are accessible to all segments of society is vital. Policymakers should advocate for and implement educational programs that promote AI literacy, preparing citizens to engage with AI technologies both as users and as informed stakeholders.

For Educators

Incorporate AI Education

Educators at all levels—from primary to tertiary education—should integrate AI concepts into their curricula. Teaching students about AI, its applications, and its ethical dimensions prepares them for a future where AI will be ubiquitous.

Encourage Critical Thinking

In addition to technical skills, educators should emphasize critical thinking and ethical reasoning. This approach will equip students to question and understand the implications of AI, fostering a generation of responsible AI users and developers.

The potential of Python-driven generative AI is immense and still largely untapped. By taking proactive steps today, we can guide its development towards outcomes that enhance societal well-being and foster innovation. This call to action is not just an invitation but a mandate to all stakeholders involved in the AI ecosystem to commit to responsible development and use of AI technologies. As we continue to explore and expand the capabilities of Python in AI, let us do so with a commitment to ethics, inclusivity, and the betterment of humanity.

CONCLUSION

In this chapter, we have traversed the expansive landscape of Python-driven generative AI, exploring its profound impact on the fields of art, design, and media, as well as its broader implications for society. We have identified the technological advancements that are propelling this area forward and examined the future scenarios that these innovations might enable. Furthermore, we have delved into the challenges that accompany these advancements and discussed strategies for navigating these complexities responsibly. As we conclude, it is important to synthesize these insights and reflect on the pathway towards responsible innovation in Python-driven generative AI.

Synthesis of Key Insights

Python has proven to be more than just a programming language; it is a catalyst for innovation in the realm of generative AI. Its accessibility and flexibility have democratized AI development, enabling a diverse range of creators to participate in the AI revolution. The advancements in computational models, such as neuromorphic computing and reinforcement learning, are set to elevate Python's role even further, enhancing its capability to drive more sophisticated and ethically aware AI systems.

The imaginative potential of Python-driven AI to transform creative industries has been vividly illustrated through speculative scenarios. These scenarios highlight not only the transformative power of AI but also the need for thoughtful integration of these technologies into human-centric fields. They serve as a reminder of the limitless possibilities that responsible AI development can unlock.

Emphasizing the Need for Foresight and Ethical Consideration

As Python continues to evolve alongside AI technology, the importance of foresight cannot be overstated. The ethical considerations, societal impacts, and technical challenges discussed in this chapter underscore the necessity of anticipating the consequences of AI advancements. Developing ethical frameworks, enhancing Python's capabilities to address emerging challenges, and fostering interdisciplinary collaboration are crucial steps in ensuring that AI technologies are developed and deployed in a manner that benefits society as a whole.

Encouraging Responsible Innovation

The path forward requires a commitment to responsible innovation. This involves not only adhering to ethical guidelines and regulations but also actively engaging in the creation of AI technologies that are inclusive, fair, and transparent. The Python community, with its open-source ethos and collaborative spirit, is uniquely positioned to lead this charge. By continuing to promote access and equity in AI development, Python can help ensure that the benefits of generative AI are shared widely and equitably.

Looking to the Future

As we look to the future, the role of Python in driving forward both the technology and the dialogue around generative AI remains vital. Stakeholders from across the technological, ethical, and creative domains must come together to shape this future, leveraging Python's capabilities to explore new horizons in AI, like chain of thought reasoning (Wei et al., 2022). The ongoing dialogue between these diverse perspectives will be essential in navigating the complex landscape of generative AI.

In conclusion, this chapter serves as both a reflection on Python's current achievements in generative AI and an invitation to imagine its future possibilities. By embracing the principles of responsible innovation and ethical consideration, the Python community can continue to lead in the development of AI technologies that enhance human creativity and productivity. As we continue to push the boundaries of what is possible with generative AI, Python will undoubtedly play a key role in defining the next era of technological advancement.

REFERENCES

Augenstein, I., Baldwin, T., Cha, M., Chakraborty, T., Ciampaglia, G. L., Corney, D., DiResta, R., Ferrara, E., Hale, S., Halevy, A., & Hovy, E. (2023). Factuality challenges in the era of large language models. arXiv:2310.05189.

Bandi, A., Adapa, P. V. S. R., & Kuchi, Y. E. V. P. K. (2023). The Power of Generative AI: A Review of Requirements, Models, Input–Output Formats, Evaluation Metrics, and Challenges. *Future Internet*, 15(8), 260. 10.3390/fi15080260

Barletta, V. S., Caivano, D., Gigante, D., & Ragone, A. (2023). *A rapid review of responsible AI frameworks: How to guide the development of Ethical AI.* arXiv:2306.05003. 10.1145/3593434.3593478

Bewersdorff, A., Hartmann, C., Hornberger, M., Seßler, K., Bannert, M., Kasneci, E., Kasneci, G., Zhai, X., & Nerdel, C. (2024). Taking the Next Step with Generative Artificial Intelligence: The Transformative Role of Multimodal Large Language Models in Science Education. arXiv:2401.00832.

Bommasani, R. (2021). On the Opportunities and Risks of Foundation Models (Report). arXiv:2108.07258.

Ferrara, E. (2023). *GenAI Against Humanity: Nefarious Applications of Generative Artificial Intelligence and Large Language Models.* arXiv:2310.00737.

GenAI. (n.d.). *Gen A. I. Forum.* https://genaiforum.org

Hacker, P., Engel, A., & Mauer, M. (2023). Regulating ChatGPT and other Large Generative AI Models. In *Proceedings of the 2023 ACM Conference on Fairness, Accountability, and Transparency (FAccT '23)*. Association for Computing Machinery. 10.1145/3593013.3594067

Hou, X., Zhao, Y., Liu, Y., Yang, Z., Wang, K., Li, L., Luo, X., Lo, D., Grundy, J., & Wang, H. (2023). Large language models for software engineering: A systematic literature review. arXiv:2308.10620.

Li, S., Chen, J., Shen, Y., Chen, Z., Zhang, X., Li, Z., Wang, H., Qian, J., Peng, B., Mao, Y., & Chen, W. (2022). Explanations from large language models make small reasoners better. arXiv:2210.06726.

Liu, B., Bubeck, S., Eldan, R., Kulkarni, J., Li, Y., Nguyen, A., Ward, R., & Zhang, Y. (2023). TinyGSM: achieving> 80% on GSM8k with small language models. arXiv:2312.09241.

Liu, Y., Han, T., Ma, S., Zhang, J., Yang, Y., Tian, J., He, H., Li, A., He, M., Liu, Z., Wu, Z., Zhao, L., Zhu, D., Li, X., Qiang, N., Shen, D., Liu, T., & Ge, B. (2023). Summary of ChatGPT-Related research and perspective towards the future of large language models. *Meta-Radiology, 1*(2). 10.1016/j.metrad.2023.100017

The Global Partnership on Artificial Intelligence (GAPI). (n.d.). *Home.* GPAI. https://gpai.ai

Wei, J., Tay, Y., Bommasani, R., Raffel, C., Zoph, B., Borgeaud, S., Yogatama, D., Bosma, M., Zhou, D., Metzler, D., & Chi, E. H. (2022). Emergent abilities of large language models. arXiv:2206.07682.

What's the next word in large language models? (2023). *Nature Machine Intelligence*, 5(4), 331–332. 10.1038/s42256-023-00655-z

Yang, K., & Liu, J. (2024). *If LLM Is the Wizard, Then Code Is the Wand: A Survey on How Code Empowers Large Language Models to Serve as Intelligent Agents*. arXiv:2401.00812.

Chapter 4
Innovating Reality:
The Pioneering Applications of Generative AI

Rabi Shankar Panda
C. V. Raman Global University, India

Anjana Mishra
C. V. Raman Global University, India

Abhishek Mohanty
C. V. Raman Global University, India

ABSTRACT

Generative artificial intelligence has enormous promise in business, marketing, finance, education, and healthcare sectors. It can have an impact on areas like consumer engagement and fraud detection. But it also poses difficult problems. Decision-making is hampered by technological barriers like data quality, explainability, and authenticity, as well as economic issues like income inequality and possible job loss. Privacy, bias, and misuse are all examples of ethical dilemmas. To address these, thorough norms that guarantee accountability, openness, and equity are needed. Meeting societal requirements and fostering collaboration requires advancing AI education and human-centric cooperation. Rules and guidelines that emphasise empathy, clarity, and ethical norms must be established to steer AI research and development toward responsible and ethical practices in order to effectively manage these obstacles.

INTRODUCTION

A revolutionary branch of Artificial Intelligence (AI) entitled generative AI is transforming the way machines deal with data. Generative AI extends above conventional AI by generating entirely novel information based on learnt patterns, in contrast to conventional AI's primary focus upon recognising trends and predictions relying on available data. In its basic form, generative AI uses intricate algorithms to comprehend the foundations of data and produce original content in a variety of media, comprising text, photos, video and even audio (OpenAI et al., 2023). Generative adversarial network (GANs), a defining technique of generative AI, are composed of a couple of neural networks (the discriminator &

DOI: 10.4018/979-8-3693-3278-8.ch004

the generator) involved in a competitive system (Goodfellow et al., 2020). The generator builds artificial data, whereas the discriminator seeks to discriminate between actual and developed data. GANs are capable to generate extremely realistic outcomes, from convincing text to vivid graphics (Vaswani et al., 2017). Furthermore, in the realm of Gen AI, models based on transformers such as GPT-3 & GPT-4 have sparked a lot of demand. They use complex processing of language to generate content which is coherent & pertinent to the context, and they are driven by large volumes of prior data (Vaswani et al., 2017). Beyond simple procreation, Gen AI is also capable of imitating human behaviour, forecasting trends, and producing creative content like songs and artistic creations (Dasborough, 2023). The limits of Gen AI keep expanding through breakthroughs across Deep Learning & Neural Network configurations, offering novel avenues for creativity and research in the artificial intelligence domain.

Navigating the drastically evolving AI world requires a solid grasp of the impacts & efficacy of Gen AI. As it advances further, businesses, economies, & people as a whole set to gain significantly from its incorporation into many facets of society (Ooi et al., 2023). We can discover more regarding the revolutionary potential of Gen AI & take preemptive steps to mitigate potential dangers & possibilities by exploring the technology's future horizons & challenges. The potential of Gen AI to generate stuff that's analogous to what's made by humans has profound effects in many sectors (Fui-Hoon Nah et al., 2023). Gen AI holds great potential for transforming task execution, boosting efficiency, and streamlining processes in multiple sectors, including manufacturing, healthcare, education, and marketing (*Siau, K. 2018;* Wang & Siau, 2019; Yang et al., 2022). These assurances, however, are accompanied with plenty of serious issues such as privacy concerns, ethical issues, and the possibility of job replacement from automation (Hatzius, 2023).

Moreover, the influence of Gen AI spans beyond economic concerns into social norms, ethical frameworks, and societal conventions. In order to make sure that the development of Gen AI is in sync with ethical standards and societal norms, it is essential to thoroughly investigate these issues (Ooi et al., 2023). Because Gen AI is dynamic, it requires constant research and investigation to keep up with new advancements in technology, regulations, and emerging trends. By looking at the possibilities for Gen AI in the future, we can spot areas for innovation, foresee possible breakthroughs, and get ready for any obstacles that may arise (Wan et al., 2022). In order to promote ethical AI growth and realise AI's full potential for the good of humanity, a proactive strategy is vital.

We can better inform lawmakers, business leaders, and the general public by gaining insights into the opportunities and challenges associated with Gen AI through a thorough analysis. Examining Gen AI with the aim of projecting its future directions and possible uses in many fields is one of the main goals. Through grasping the potential and constraints of the Gen AI, we all can pinpoint domains where it might stimulate creativity, enhance productivity, and tackle urgent societal issues. We can solve issues with prejudice, bias, and privacy violations by closely examining the social effects of Gen AI. This will help to advance inclusivity, justice, & accountability in AI-driven systems (Ooi et al., 2023).

The Algorithm for Generative AI

Based on specificity of model or strategies being employed, the Gen AI algorithm may change. However, the Generative Adversarial Network (GAN) is a widely employed Gen AI technique. It is made up of a discriminator and a generator neural network (Kingma & Welling, 2013). Given that the discriminator learns to discern between genuine and produced samples, the generator acquires the knack to produce new data samples, like texts or images.

The discriminator and generator networks engage in antagonism during the GAN training phase. The discriminator's goal is to effectively categorise real and created samples, whereas the generator's goal is to deceive it by fabricating realistic examples. By means of this competitive procedure, both networks gain knowledge and enhance their efficiency (Goodfellow et al., 2020).

The generator generates data based upon random input—also termed as noise- that it gets during training. After receiving generated data from the generator and actual data from training dataset, the discriminator verifies the authenticity of each data. The discriminator adjusts its configuration for effectively discern between actual and created samples, while the generator modifies its parameters to produce data that's likely to deceive the discriminator. Iteratively, the adversarial method of training keeps on unless the generator generates data that become harder and harder to the discriminator to differentiate apart from actual data. The intent is to restore the generator to an equilibrium where it generate realistic, high-quality data that are identical to real data (Ramdurai & Adhithya, 2023).

GANs proved effective in a range of generative applications, including text production, graphics synthesis, composing music, etc. Their actions have been crucial in propelling the domain of Gen AI forward and aiding the generation of innovative and genuine results.

Instances of Gen AI Tech With its Underlying Mechanisms

- Generative Adversarial Networks (GANs): A discriminator assesses the images produced by the generator, and the generator generates new ones. As the discriminator learns to discriminate between generated & real images, the generator creates fresh images in an attempt to trick the discriminator into thinking they are real. Both networks are getting better as a result of this competition.
- DeepDream: A Google creation, DeepDream uses layer iteration to improve and understand patterns in photos, producing bizarre, dreamlike imagery. It shows how neural networks interpret and process visual data by enhancing the qualities that a neural network has identified in an image.
- Text generators (GPT, Gemini models): These produce text that is coherent and appropriate for the environment by utilising Transformer architectures, a kind of neural network. They can produce unique and believable text sequences in response to input prompts because they have been trained on extensive text databases, where they have learned linguistic patterns, structures, and styles.

These innovations show off AI's generative and creative powers, going beyond simple analysis to produce entirely new works of art (Pawar, 2024).

Progress and Potential of Generative AI

Generative AI, depicted by innovative models such as ChatGPT, has the ability to transform a multitude of industries due to its multiple applications. In industries including business, marketing, banking, retailing, healthcare, education, content creation, etc. Gen AI's ability to innovate and optimise workflows is becoming more and more apparent. In the sections that follow, we go into more detail about the various contexts in which generative AI is being used, demonstrating its revolutionary potential and outlining its trajectory towards influencing the direction of AI-driven solutions in the future.

Business and Marketing

A paradigm shifting the way businesses function across a broad spectrum of industries is being aided by generative AI, which is exemplified by models like ChatGPT. Applications for it range from more traditional fields like sales and marketing to more technical ones like operations and IT/engineering. For example, ChatGPT is a flexible solution for organisations, including features like chatbots for customer support and virtual assistants that help with finishing tasks and project collaboration (Chui et al., 2022.).

Even with all of its uses, generative AI is an intricate ecosystem for organisations to deal with. There are inherent risks even while it has the ability to boost efficiency and innovation. Enterprises need to exercise caution by putting in place safeguards to protect confidential data and reduce the creation of inaccurate or deceptive content.

Marketing strategies are witnessing a shift due to generative AI technologies like Bard, ChatGPT, and Synthesia, which enable marketers to create customised campaigns and creative solutions. With the use of these technologies, marketers may create content that is highly personalised to each customer's tastes and actions. Furthermore, generative AI makes advanced attribution analysis easier and offers insights into how well marketing campaigns are doing across a range of touchpoints (Sinha et al., 2023).

Furthermore, generative AI makes it easier to implement successful remarketing campaigns by using current customer data to target advertisements and messages (Levy, 2023). Enterprises may distinguish their offers and optimise revenue potential by implementing dynamic pricing and increased sales optimisation. Additionally, scalable personalisation is another benefit of generative AI, which enables businesses to interact personally with millions of clients.

Education

Through the use of deep learning models, generative AI is transforming education by creating an array of content types- code, text, video, audio, and more-in response to intricate cues (Dasborough, 2023). This technology has a remarkable ability to understand and replicate human languages, as exemplified by models like as ChatGPT and Magic Write. This allows for more complex interaction and knowledge synthesis. Generative AI stands out for its capacity to produce new knowledge, which makes it an effective aid for activities like summarising texts, translation and chat systems. Prior AI iterations focused primarily on pattern recognition (Tlili et al., 2023).

Throughout the discipline of education, generative AI offers a plethora of potential for the creation of customised teaching materials, answering questions, and developing explanatory discourse. It has the potential to improve formal and informal learning experiences in a variety of fields with continued developments.

ChatGPT and other generative AI apps are transforming education and becoming indispensable tools for teachers and students alike. ChatGPT helps students with language-enhanced writing, subject-specific research, and information retrieval. Teachers gain from ChatGPT's assistance in creating lesson plans, providing resources, grading assignments, and providing feedback (Kanseci et al.,2023).

Furthermore, ChatGPT can be utilise for problem formulation, research design, and support for academic research. However, ethical concerns are quite important, and educational institutions have responded significantly with regulations to concern about the exploitation and distortion of AI-generated data and address possible misuse and plagiarism made possible by AI platforms such as ChatGPT (Bohr & Memarzadeh, 2020).

The potential applications of generative AI technology in education are virtually limitless. We may anticipate even more advanced learning resources that adjust in real time to the specific needs of each student, tailored learning paths that mentor individuals on their particular learning journeys, and AI-driven feedback systems that offer prompt, focused assistance. Students could experience education in a more dynamic, intriguing, and productive way thanks to generative AI (Farrokhnia et al.,2023).

Healthcare

Generative AI holds considerable potential for improving healthcare delivery by providing users with quick and precise assistance in accessing complex medical information. Generative AI is a helpful tool for patients and healthcare providers alike because of its capacity to gather and condense enormous volumes of data into formats that are simple to understand. By using generative AI, users may find succinct responses to their healthcare questions, minimising time and effort while sifting through large amounts of information (Dwivedi et al., 2023). Furthermore, its summarization and translation features enable non-native English users to access healthcare information, improving comprehension and decision-making.

Additionally, generative AI facilitates more thorough articulation of symptoms by patients, which leads to more precise diagnosis and therapy recommendations. Additionally, it can help medical staff effectively record patient encounters by recommending specific words, terms and phrases for medical documentation, freeing up staff members to concentrate on editing and review (Nishant et al., 2020).

Healthcare applications such as clinical diagnosis support, telemedicine services, patient engagement, and health education could benefit from the use of generative AI techniques (Jussupow et al., 2021). However, there are obstacles to wider adoption, such as hazards to data security, ethical dilemmas, and legal barriers (Siau & Wang, 2020). Even though generative AI has a great deal of promise to improve healthcare delivery, it is crucial to carefully weigh these elements in order to ensure a safe and successful integration into clinical practice.

Banking

The banking sector benefit greatly from generative AI, revolutionising client interaction, advertising interaction, identifying fraud, and business process optimisation (Gill, 2023).

Institutions may leverage their enormous data holdings to create generative AI models specifically for banking, which will deliver specific financial insights. With its thorough training on financial data, Bloomberg's BloombergGPT is a trailblazing illustration of the potential of domain focused generative AI tools. These models can be included into financial systems to improve engagement with customer (*Bloomberg*, 2023).

Generative AI has the potential to greatly improve customer engagement by delivering tailored financial recommendations and guidance based on unique attributes. Banks can utilise chatbots that are capable of natural language processing to offer customised answers to consumer inquiries and even create investment plans that maximise portfolio returns.

Additionally, generative AI makes it easier to develop emotionally engaging ads for banks that are customised to each customer's interests and preferences through personalised marketing communication campaigns. This tailored strategy lowers expenses while increasing client involvement and loyalty (Dwivedi et al., 2023).

Another major use of generative AI within banking is fraud detection, which uses enormous datasets to find trends and abnormalities suggestive of illicit activity. Models similar to those used by Swedbank show how effective deep learning methods are in identifying and stopping financial crimes (Mamaghani, 2021).

Additionally, generative AI improves customer service, automates repetitive jobs, frees up employees to work on strategic and creative projects, and streamlines corporate operations. These models can be used by financial advisors to learn more about the spending patterns of their clients and provide individualised services, which will ultimately increase accuracy, productivity, and efficiency in all aspects of banking operations (Borden, 2023).

Human Resource

The incorporation of generative AI within HRM (human resources management) offers a paradigm shift in talent acquisition strategies. The transition from conventional machine learning approaches to language model-driven content generation is a big step ahead, with potentially major implications for HRM roles (Garg et al., 2022). Although generative AI is only now beginning to be used in HRM, there are many different uses for it in areas including hiring, employee engagement, professional development, resource allocation, and turnover prevention.

Generative AI improves applicant-job fit, automates the acquisition of candidate data from resumes, and generates personalised suggestions tailored to candidate inclinations to expedite the recruitment process. Moreover, it enables candidates to assess job relevance on digital channels such as LinkedIn and facilitates reverse assessment. In a similar vein, generative AI is utilised in workforce engagement assessments to measure brand engagement across multiple regions and guide organisational engagement initiatives by using social media metrics and natural language processing to assess employee sentiments in real-time (Votto et al., 2021).

Furthermore, generative AI has potential for resolving issues related to geographically scattered teams. It facilitates timely reminders and communication amongst team members, promoting harmonious collaboration and reducing conflict brought on by a lack of communication. Furthermore, it improves appraisal procedures by encouraging managers to take into account more subtle aspects like response time and interpersonal relationships, allowing for more thorough and fair performance reviews (Tambe et al., 2019).

Additionally, generative AI makes it easier for employees to engage in peer-to-peer education and development of skills by matching them with knowledgeable coworkers and providing real-time answers to structured questions.

Content Creation

The upsurge in content creation and utilisation that generative AI offers, affects multiple industries. Generative AI is used in marketing to make artificial and customised ads. It accomplish this by using AI technologies such as deepfakes and human-provided data to tell engaging stories. Similar to this, news robots like Quill and Xiaomingbot (Fui-Hoon Nah et al., 2023) simplify news production in journalism by producing data-driven articles using pre-made templates, while advances in LLMs allow for the development of more intricate tales that include text and video (Wong et al., 2022).

With generative AI technologies like ChatGPT and DLLE-2, art creation undergoes a paradigm change that improves human-AI collaboration. In this alliance, humans contribute their creative ideas and direction, and AI systems provide linguistic and imaginative support, enhancing creativity in the creation of art (Guo et al., 2023). Additionally, the gaming business changes as a result of users using generative AI to create text-based games, characters, visual content. This increases gaming production's efficiency and distinctiveness.

The automation of content creation by generative AI is reminiscent of past industrialization and implies a move towards greater AI collaboration for higher efficiency. This change may result in new business models that are specifically suited to personalised content consumption and reshape employment dynamics. Algorithms have the potential to alter social network structures, impacting consumer impressions and content exposure (Campbell et al., 2022). This could result in a consolidation of power inside corporations that employ sophisticated AI algorithms. The ramifications of generative AI for content generation and consumption have the potential to completely transform industries and social norms as it develops.

Sustainable IT Management

In the tech industry, generative AI holds significant potential for sustainable management, especially in the areas of energy efficiency, resource management, acquisition, design and development.

Generative AI maximises energy use and fosters real-time electricity trading by forecasting demand and modifying the use of energy in data centres. The AI for Earth project by Microsoft and DeepMind AI by Google show how operating data centres may save a significant amount of energy and cut greenhouse gas emissions (Chawla et al., 2022).

Generative AI may dynamically assign cloud and edge computing resources for IT resource administration, reducing waste and optimising resource distribution. One example of the way data analysis and forecasting might result in more efficient resource distribution and less environmental impact is IBM's Watson AI.

By evaluating the environmental impact of products and suggesting ecologically favourable options, generative AI also supports sustainable procurement. By analysing product data, platforms such as Eco-chain AI offer suggestions for sustainable procurement, thereby mitigating the adverse ecological effects of IT goods and services (L.-W. Wong et al., 2023). Additionally, generative AI uses environmental effect data in sustainable design and development to provide environmentally beneficial technology and software. The AI for Public Benefit initiative from Intel provides an example of how AI may be used to analyse ecological impact data to assist in the design and development of sustainable IT systems.

Furthermore, by offering real-time updates about efficiency and resource optimisation, generative AI simplifies data centre administration while lowering energy usage and carbon footprint (Niet et al., 2021). Through the analysis of data on e-waste production and provision of insights for restoration, recycling, or disposal, it also helps with the sustainable management of electronic trash.

Workplace

With its ability to augment and automate tasks that boost creativity and productivity, generative AI has the potential to completely transform the workplace in a number of industries.

Interest in generative AI's possible effects on the workplace has grown since the release of tools like ChatGPT and DALL-E (Dwivedi et al., 2023). These platforms influence a broad range of job profiles by producing not only texts but images & codes. According to research, CEOs and CFOs are looking more and more to AI to automate jobs and rethink work processes, which is causing a big change in the dynamics of the workplace (Jesuthasan, 2023).

The impact of generative AI extends beyond task automation to include decision-making support for intricate tasks. It is anticipated that tasks will be supplemented or replaced, changing the organisational structure and the way teams, people, and business units function.

The adoption of generative AI around the workplace offers numerous opportunities. It can provide staff more freedom from organised tasks by automating manual processes and enabling more "human-like" contact with end users (Raisch & Krakowski, 2021). Furthermore, by providing creative solutions and streamlining time-consuming procedures, generative AI shines at improving creative jobs like design. Higher-order talents are becoming more accessible to everybody due to generative AI, which is augmenting professions like coding and music production that were previously thought to be human-only. Increased collaboration and creativity in the workplace are facilitated by this, which eventually raises the calibre and inventiveness of work done across industries.

Additionally, personalised interactions like tailored retail buying experiences (Singh et al., 2019) and healthcare treatment plans (Trocin et al., 2023) are made possible by generative AI. It also lowers the risk of illicit transactions by assisting financial institutions in detecting fraud (Nicholls et al., 2021).

Manufacturing

Manufacturing is changing as a result of the emergence of generative AI, which presents fascinating prospects to solve problems and streamline procedures. By tailoring worker training on emerging technologies, this potent technology can close the widening skills gap (Deloitte manufacturing skills gap study, 2018). Consider how AI could design personalised learning programmes based on each learner's demands, accelerating and improving the acquisition of new abilities. Engineers and designers are empowered by generative AI. It can produce variants of designs according to certain limitations, such as production speed or material efficiency. This facilitates the swift investigation of several alternatives and the determination of the best course of action, resulting in novel and producible goods (Morra, 2023).

Error prediction is another discipline where generative AI excels. Artificial Intelligence (AI) can forecast possible challenges like supply chain disruptions or natural disasters by analysing data and modelling scenarios. Because of their ability to anticipate future events, firms are able to plan ahead and take proactive measures to minimise the effect on production (Ooi et al., 2023).

Manufacturers may also "see" the future with the aid of generative AI, which creates lifelike models and prototypes. This saves time and money by enabling testing and improvement prior to the start of physical production. AI is also capable of real-time fault identification from data streams, which eliminates the need for manual inspection and accelerates production.

In general, manufacturing is about to undergo a revolution thanks to generative AI. This technology gives manufacturers a strong toolkit to help them negotiate the hurdles of the near future and achieve higher efficiency, innovation, and resilience from developing a trained staff to optimising design and development.

Challenges With Generative AI

Societies might face many issues as a result of generative AI. We address these issues in this part from four angles: technology, economy, ethics, rules and policies.

Technological Challenges

Challenges regarding technology address restrictions imposed by Generative AI. Evidently, the precision of training data is one of the key obstacles to the development of generative AI models. The algorithm limitations also present issues with hallucinations, explainability, and output authenticity. The technological difficulties and problems related to generative AI are shown in Table 1. Hallucinations, the quality of training data, explainability, authenticity, and quick engineering are some of these difficulties.

- Hallucination: Generative AI has the ability to manufacture data, producing counterfeit outcomes such as fabricated news stories or incorrect medical recommendations. This is particularly risky in situations when people depend on the AI's judgement to make important choices (Azamfirei et al., 2023; Sallam, 2023; Ji et al., 2023).
- Data Quality: Efficient generative AI models depend on high-quality training data, yet problems like biases and factual errors can undermine consistency. Because of the enormous volumes of data involved, data cleansing is expensive, which is why artificial training data is explored to guarantee variety and reduce biases (Gozalo-Brizuela & Garrido-Merchan, 2023; Su & Yang, 2023).
- Explainability: Because AI models decision-making processes are opaque, explainability is still an issue because it makes it difficult for users to understand and for regulators to evaluate fairness. Increasing explainability is critical to building confidence and adhering to regulations (Dwivedi et al., 2023; Rudin, 2019).
- Authenticity: Deep-Fake AI poses threats to the dissemination of false information and calls into question the legitimacy of artwork produced by artificial intelligence by synthesising realistic-looking but artificial content (Gragnaniello et al., 2022; McCormack et al., 2019).
- Prompt engineering: An essential component of effective generative AI interface, prompt engineering calls for methodical prompt designing and training to enhance user interactions and communication tactics (Liu & Chilton, 2021).

Table 1. Technological challenges

Challenges	Issues	References
Hallucination	Content generated may be nonsensical or incorrect. Gen AI may produce fictitious or factually flawed information.	(Azamfirei et al., 2023; Sallam, 2023; Ji et al.,2023) (Dwivedi et al., 2023)
Data quality	Obtaining sufficient training data for quality assurance is challenging.	(Gozalo-Brizuela & Garrido-Merchan, 2023; Su & Yang, 2023)
Explainability	Interpreting outputs from generative AI poses difficulties. Detecting errors in generative AI outputs is challenging.	(Dwivedi et al., 2023) (Rudin, 2019)
Authenticity	Manipulating content raises authenticity concerns.	(Gragnaniello et al., 2022)
Prompt engineering	Prompt engineering is crucial for effective generative AI utilization. Brute-force prompt trials are necessary to enhance AI-generated content quality.	(Liu & Chilton, 2021)

Economical Challenges

This is feasible to witness a major impact on the economy when industries use generative AI. The economic system may be affected by generative AI in a numerous ways, including monopolies, disruptions to the labour market and industries, and income inequality. The economic challenges listed in the Table 2 include those related to the employment market, industry upheaval, income inequality, and monopolies.

- Employment displacement: The potential of generative AI to automate jobs in industries such as advertising, healthcare, and education could result in employment losses. Data processing and proofreading are examples of repetitive operations that may become obsolete, requiring human workers to change or look for new opportunities (Zarifhonarvar, 2023).
- Restructuring & New Distribution of Labour: The workforce must change as generative AI becomes more prevalent. There will be a rise in new occupations while others may go. Labour must be retrained in order to interact with AI efficiently and acquire specialised skill sets that enhance rather than undermine its capabilities if they want to remain competitive.
- Industry disruption: Companies that depend on repetitive jobs, like customer service and translation, may be affected by generative AI, which could lead to job unpredictability and economic instability. But it also presents chances for novel business models utilising conversational AI and tailored content. Businesses need to stay competitive by retraining employees, utilising AI's potential, and innovating (Dwivedi et al., 2023).
- Monopolies and economic inequality: As low-skilled workers miss out on chances, adaptive people will be left behind, and this will expand the gap in income inequality. Furthermore, the substantial financial outlay needed for AI research may benefit big businesses, creating market monopolies. To address this, more people need to have utilisation of AI education in order to guarantee equity and close the skills gap. Governments need to think about measures to ensure equal play in the AI industry and avoid monopolies (Zarifhonarvar, 2023; Cheng & Liu, 2023).

Table 2. Economical challenges

Challenges	Issues	References
Labour displacement	Generative AI causing job loss and unemployment. Workers need reskilling to collaborate with generative AI and stay competitive.	(Zarifhonarvar, 2023) (Dwivedi et al., 2023)
Industry disruption	Generative AI may impact or replace certain industries.	(Dwivedi et al., 2023)
Monopolies & income inequality	The income gap widens between those mastering generative AI & those who don't. Large companies deploying generative AI first may gain an unfair advantage.	(Zarifhonarvar, 2023) (Cheng & Liu, 2023)

Ethical Challenges

The systematization, defence, and advocacy of conceptions of right and bad behaviour are referred to as ethics. Concerns about ethics in AI relate to the moral responsibilities and duties of AI applications & their developers. The main ethical problems and concerns related to generative AI are shown in Table 3. Among these difficulties include offensive or dangerous content, prejudice, over-reliance, abuse, security and privacy issues, and the growing digital divide.

- Offensive or Illegal Content: Generative AI has the ability to create pornographic, discriminatory, aggressive, or inflammatory words. Both algorithmic flaws and improper filtering of the training set of data may be to blame for this (Zhuo et al., 2023).
- Bias: Unfair results may result from generative AI reflecting biases found in its training data. This may involve prejudice in suggestions based only on language, the exclusion of particular groups, or stereotypes. User testing along with a variety of training data sets can assist reduce bias (Zhuo et al., 2023).
- Over-reliance: People who rely too much on generative AI run the risk of believing its responses without question. Problem solving and critical thinking skills may be hampered by this. It's essential to understand AI to prevent over-reliance (Iskender, 2023; van Dis et al.,2023).
- Misuse: Generative AI application to plagiarism, exam cheating, and other unethical activities is possible. Stricter proctoring procedures and AI content detectors can aid in addressing educational abuse (Susnjak, 2022).
- Privacy and Security: User interactions can capture a great deal of data, and training data can contain personal info. Users must use caution when disclosing sensitive info, and laws are required to safeguard security and privacy (Siau & Wang, 2020; Fang et al., 2017).
- Digital Divide: Because individuals lacking access to technologies or internet would be left behind, Gen AI has the ability increase digital divide. AI that is suitable for a given culture and AI literacy instruction can aid in closing this gap (Bozkurt & Sharma, 2023).

Table 3. Ethical challenges

Challenges	Issues	References
Offensive or Illegal Content	Generative AI content may be violent, offensive, or erotic.	(Zhuo et al., 2023)
Bias	Limited representation in training data may create exclusionary norms. Cultural sensitivities are essential to avoid bias in generative AI.	(Zhuo et al., 2023) (Dwivedi et al., 2023)
Over-reliance	Users can accept generative AI answers without verification.	(Iskender, 2023; van Dis et al., 2023)
Misuse	Misuse includes plagiarism in assignment using AI-generated text. Generative AI can facilitate cheating in exams.	(Susnjak, 2022)
Privacy and Security	Generative AI may compromise privacy by disclosing sensitive information.	(Siau & Wang, 2020; Fang et al., 2017).
Digital divide	The level-one digital divide affects those who don't have access to Gen AI. Acceptance of generative AI varies across cultures and individuals, creating a second-level digital divide.	(Bozkurt & Sharma, 2023) (Dwivedi et al., 2023)

Challenges With Regulations and Policies

- Copyright: Content produced by generative AI is covered by copyright, which safeguards original works of authorship. To prevent infringement, users must make sure AI-generated content conforms with copyright regulations (Pavlik, 2023). Whether or not generative AI gets treated as authors under the current copyright regulations is up for debate. Clear rules, laws, and regulations are required to handle copyright concerns pertaining to generative artificial intelligence.

- Governance: To control risks and unforeseen outcomes, generative AI governance is crucial. Developing efficient AI governance presents difficulties for businesses, academic institutions, and governmental bodies (Taeihagh, 2021). Liability and accountability are complicated by cryptic algorithms and unpredictability that make it difficult for humans to oversee AI behaviour. Data governance is challenged by interoperability problems and data fragmentation. Legislation attempts are hampered by information asymmetries between authorities and tech businesses (Taeihagh et al., 2021). AI framework for governance may be improved through stakeholder participation, explainability, and transparency.

Table 4. Challenges with regulation and policy

Challenges	Issues	References
Copyright	AI generated content may violate copyright. controversies surround AI authorship.	(Pavlik, 2023) (Sallam, 2023)
Governance	Governance lacks human control over AI behaviour. Data fragmentation & interoperability issues exist.	(Taeihagh, 2021).

Human-Centric AI Cooperation

Here we will discuss Human-centered AI (HCAI) collaboration putting a focus on considering human stakeholders when building AI. To ensure a successful collaboration, HCAI should comprehend both human demands and AI capabilities (Riedl, 2019). Because human requirements haven't been fully met by previous AI developments, there have been problems including insufficient transparency and ethical dilemmas. To mend this gap HCAI seeks to emphasising the following on:

- Empathy and Aligning with Human Needs
- Digital Transformation
- AI Ethics and Governance
- Transparency and Explainability

Numerous issues with generative AI arise from a disregard for human-centered design. HCAI can tackle these issues in the following ways:

- Mitigating Bias: By integrating social ethics and laws into AI systems, HCAI guarantees the creation of ethical AI.
- Human-AI Collaboration: HCAI encourages a cooperative strategy in which AI assist humans while they're working together. This strategy has various advantages, such as Reduced Bias, Job Creation, Data Augmentation, Improved Accuracy, Transparency and Accountability, Increased Safety (Monarch, 2021).

Certain issues need to be taken into mind in order achieve "Human-Centered AI Collaboration."

Addressing Human Needs and Empathy

Human needs and empathy should come first in the design of HCAIs. The digital divide is one issue the article mentions as resulting from misaligned AI design. Additionally, generative AI ought to take user demands like efficiency, security, sustainability, and creativity into account (Fui-Hoon Nah et al., 2023).

Enhancing Clarity and Disclosure

Users must be able to comprehend how AI generates its outputs in order for them to have faith in it (Rader et al., 2018). A clear and understandable generative AI system requires the following essential data: (1)User-friendliness access to AI model; (2) Concise insights of model's abilities and drawbacks (Sun et al., 2022; Bhatt et al., 2020); (3) After-the-fact justifications for AI choices; (4) Contextual reasoning based on specific factors; (5) Additional information to fulfil user demands.

Ethical Standards and Supervision

Collaboration in HCAI should follow moral guidelines and take into account concerns about hazardous content, privacy, and bias . The more generative AI is used internationally, the more complicated ethical issues arise (Rader et al., 2018). Here are some crucial moral factors to think about:

- Accountability and Fairness: Avoiding prejudice and honouring individual diversity.
- Avoiding Unethical Data: Making sure AI doesn't produce inappropriate or dangerous content.
- Security and Privacy: Preserving user privacy while AI gathers and utilises data.

Policies and Regulations

Strict policies are essential for directing the development of AI. Human-centered laws can handle issues such as copyright and use content limitations to fight prejudice. To prevent problems like hazardous content resurfacing after initial screening, regulations must be properly included into AI systems (Qadir et al., 2022).

Advancing Through AI Education and Cognitive Enhancement

The focus of HCAI is on using AI as an aid to enhance rather than replace human talents. The secret to productive human-AI cooperation is AI literacy (Fast & Horvitz, 2017). Those with an understanding of AI can:

- Recognise and assess AI-related technologies
- Effectively communicate and work together with AI
- Apply AI morally.

Users can become skilled collaborator alongside AI and take use of its possibilities by undergoing AI literacy training (Long & Magerko, 2020). By emphasising cognitive collaboration, we hope to establish a mutually beneficial connection among humans and AI, which will make AI development in the future easier to comprehend and control. Four essential Intelligence Augmentation design tenets are simplicity, interpretability, human-centeredness, and ethics (Zhou et al., 2021).

Successful AI is built on human-machine interaction. AI's prowess in data analysis and prediction can be combined with human innovation and ability to solve issues via HCAI collaboration. Although generative AI has its drawbacks, its potential to increase human intellect can also have a major positive economic impact.

CONCLUSION

In conclusion, the emergence of generative AI signifies the start of a new phase in technological advancement which have a major impact on a wide range of societal applications and businesses. As demonstrated by models such as ChatGPT, DeepBrain, and Midjourney, Gen AI has the potential to transform operations in a variety of industries. But the innovative potential of Gen AI needs to be balanced with a grasp of the difficulties it poses.

Ethical issues are significant, in addition to technological, governmental, and financial obstacles. These issues are made worse by the absence of human-centered AI (HCAI) techniques, which calls for a change in focus towards empathy, openness, moral leadership, and AI literacy. Realising the entire potential within Gen AI while limiting hazards requires addressing these issues.

Generative AI poses numerous obstacles in many different sectors, despite its enormous promise. Much consideration must be given to privacy problems, ethical considerations, and data ownership issues. This paper aims to stimulate more investigation and creativity by examining opportunities and difficulties in industries like commerce, healthcare, education, finance, sales, production, and sustainability management.

The quest to fully realise generative AI's transformational potential is still continuing. By means of ongoing education, flexibility, and conscientious management, we may effectively negotiate the intricacies of this nascent technological terrain and unleash its immense capacity for constructive social influence.

REFERENCES

Azamfirei, R., Kudchadkar, S. R., & Fackler, J. (2023). Large language models and the perils of their hallucinations. *Critical Care (London, England)*, 27(1), 120. 10.1186/s13054-023-04393-x36945051

Bhatt, U., Antorán, J., Zhang, Y., Liao, Q. V., Sattigeri, P., Fogliato, R., Melançon, G. G., Krishnan, R., Stanley, J., Tickoo, O., Nachman, L., Chunara, R., Srikumar, M., Weller, A., & Xiang, A. (2020). Uncertainty as a form of transparency: Measuring, communicating, and using uncertainty. In *arXiv[cs. CY]*. http://arxiv.org/abs/2011.07586

Bloomberg. (n.d.). 50 billion parameter. *Bloomberg*. https://www.bloomberg.com/company/press/bloomberggpt-50-billion-parameter-llm-tuned-finance/

Bohr, A., & Memarzadeh, K. (2020). The rise of artificial intelligence in healthcare applications. In *Artificial Intelligence in Healthcare* (pp. 25–60). Elsevier. 10.1016/B978-0-12-818438-7.00002-2

Borden, B. (2023, May 4). *Driving transformation in banking with generative AI*. Microsoft Industry Blogs. https://www.microsoft.com/en-us/industry/blog/financial-services/2023/05/04/the-era-of-generative-ai-driving-transformation-in-banking/

Bozkurt, A., & Sharma, R. C. (2023). *Challenging the status quo and exploring the new boundaries in the age of algorithms: Reimagining the role of generative AI in distance education and online learning*. Zenodo. 10.5281/ZENODO.7755273

Chawla, Y., Shimpo, F., & Sokołowski, M. M. (2022). Artificial intelligence and information management in the energy transition of India: Lessons from the global IT heart. *Digital Policy Regulation and Governance*, 24(1), 17–29. 10.1108/DPRG-05-2021-0062

Cheng, L., & Liu, X. (2023). From principles to practices: The intertextual interaction between AI ethical and legal discourses. *International Journal of Legal Discourse*, 8(1), 31–52. 10.1515/ijld-2023-2001

Chui, M., Roberts, R., & Yee, L. (n.d.). *Generative AI is here: How tools like ChatGPT could change your business*. Mckinsey.com. https://www.mckinsey.com/capabilities/quantumblack/our-insights/generative-ai-is-here-how-tools-like-chatgpt-could-change-your-business

Dasborough, M. T. (2023). Awe-inspiring advancements in AI: The impact of ChatGPT on the field of Organizational Behavior. *Journal of Organizational Behavior*, 44(2), 177–179. 10.1002/job.2695

Dwivedi, Y. K., Kshetri, N., Hughes, L., Slade, E. L., Jeyaraj, A., Kar, A. K., Baabdullah, A. M., Koohang, A., Raghavan, V., Ahuja, M., Albanna, H., Albashrawi, M. A., Al-Busaidi, A. S., Balakrishnan, J., Barlette, Y., Basu, S., Bose, I., Brooks, L., Buhalis, D., & Wright, R. (2023). Opinion Paper: "So what if ChatGPT wrote it?" Multidisciplinary perspectives on opportunities, challenges and implications of generative conversational AI for research, practice and policy. *International Journal of Information Management*, 71(102642), 102642. 10.1016/j.ijinfomgt.2023.102642

Fang, W., Wen, X. Z., Zheng, Y., & Zhou, M. (2017). A survey of big data security and privacy preserving. *IETE Technical Review*, 34(5), 544–560. 10.1080/02564602.2016.1215269

Farrokhnia, M., Banihashem, S. K., Noroozi, O., & Wals, A. (2023). A SWOT analysis of ChatGPT: Implications for educational practice and research. *Innovations in Education and Teaching International*, 1–15. 10.1080/14703297.2023.2195846

Fast, E., & Horvitz, E. (2017). Long-term trends in the public perception of artificial intelligence. *Proceedings of the … AAAI Conference on Artificial Intelligence.AAAI Conference on Artificial Intelligence*, *31*(1). 10.1609/aaai.v31i1.10635

Fui-Hoon Nah, F., Zheng, R., Cai, J., Siau, K., & Chen, L. (2023). Generative AI and ChatGPT: Applications, challenges, and AI-human collaboration. *Journal of Information Technology Case and Application Research*, 25(3), 277–304. 10.1080/15228053.2023.2233814

Garg, S., Sinha, S., Kar, A. K., & Mani, M. (2022). A review of machine learning applications in human resource management. *International Journal of Productivity and Performance Management*, 71(5), 1590–1610. 10.1108/IJPPM-08-2020-0427

Gill, J. K. (2023, December 15). Generative AI in telecom industry. *Xenonstack.com*. https://www.xenonstack.com/blog/generative-ai-telecom-industry

Goodfellow, I., Pouget-Abadie, J., Mirza, M., Xu, B., Warde-Farley, D., Ozair, S., Courville, A., & Bengio, Y. (2020). Generative adversarial networks. *Communications of the ACM*, 63(11), 139–144. 10.1145/3422622

Gragnaniello, D., Marra, F., & Verdoliva, L. (2022). Detection of AI-generated synthetic faces. In *Handbook of Digital Face Manipulation and Detection* (pp. 191–212). Springer International Publishing. 10.1007/978-3-030-87664-7_9

. Guo, C., Lu, Y., Dou, Y., & Wang, F.-Y. (2023). Can ChatGPT boost artistic creation: The need of imaginative intelligence for parallel art. *IEEE/CAA Journal of Automatica Sinica, 10*(4), 835–838. 10.1109/JAS.2023.123555

Hatzius, J. (n.d.). *The potentially large effects of artificial intelligence on economic growth (Briggs/kodnani)*. Gspublishing.com. https://www.gspublishing.com/content/research/en/reports/2023/03/27/d64e052b-0f6e-45d7-967b-d7be35fabd16.html

Iskender, A. (2023). Holy or unholy? Interview with open AI's ChatGPT. *European Journal of Tourism Research*, 34, 3414. 10.54055/ejtr.v34i.3169

Jesuthasan, R. (2023, April 14). *Here's how companies can navigate generative AI in their work*. World Economic Forum. https://www.weforum.org/agenda/2023/04/how-companies-should-navigate-generative-ai-in-future-of-work/

Jussupow, E., Spohrer, K., Heinzl, A., & Gawlitza, J. (2021). Augmenting medical diagnosis decisions? An investigation into physicians' decision-making process with artificial intelligence. *Information Systems Research*, 32(3), 713–735. 10.1287/isre.2020.0980

Kasneci, E., Sessler, K., Küchemann, S., Bannert, M., Dementieva, D., Fischer, F., Gasser, U., Groh, G., Günnemann, S., Hüllermeier, E., Krusche, S., Kutyniok, G., Michaeli, T., Nerdel, C., Pfeffer, J., Poquet, O., Sailer, M., Schmidt, A., Seidel, T., & Kasneci, G. (2023). ChatGPT for good? On opportunities and challenges of large language models for education. *Learning and Individual Differences*, 103(102274), 102274. 10.1016/j.lindif.2023.102274

Kingma, D. P., & Welling, M. (2013). Auto-Encoding Variational Bayes. In *arXiv[stat.ML]*. http://arxiv.org/abs/1312.6114

Levy, A. (2023, May 10). *2 companies are using generative AI to supercharge revenue.* The Motley Fool. https://www.fool.com/investing/2023/05/10/companies-using-generative-ai-supercharge-revenue/

Liu, V., & Chilton, L. B. (2021). Design guidelines for prompt engineering text-to-image generative models. In *arXiv[cs.HC]*. http://arxiv.org/abs/2109.06977

Long, D., & Magerko, B. (2020). What is AI Literacy? Competencies and Design Considerations. *Proceedings of the 2020 CHI Conference on Human Factors in Computing Systems.* 10.1145/3313831.3376727

Mamaghani, M. (2021, March 26). *Detecting financial fraud using GANs at swedbank with hopsworks and NVIDIA GPUs.* NVIDIA Technical Blog. https://developer.nvidia.com/blog/detecting-financial-fraud-using-gans-at-swedbank-with-hopsworks-and-gpus/

Manufacturing skills gap study. (2018, November 13). Deloitte United States. https://www2.deloitte.com/us/en/pages/manufacturing/articles/future-of-manufacturing-skills-gap-study.html

McCormack, J., Gifford, T., & Hutchings, P. (2019). Autonomy, authenticity, authorship and intention in computer generated art. In *Computational Intelligence in Music, Sound, Art and Design* (pp. 35–50). Springer International Publishing. 10.1007/978-3-030-16667-0_3

Monarch, R. (munro). (2021). *Human-in-the-Loop Machine Learning: Active learning and annotation for human-centered AI.* Simon and Schuster.

Morra, J. (2023, April 10). *System-level PCB design tool embraces "generative" AI.* Electronic Design. https://www.electronicdesign.com/technologies/eda/article/21263574/electronic-design-system-level-pcb-design-tool-embraces-generative-ai

Nicholls, J., Kuppa, A., & Le-Khac, N.-A. (2021). Financial cybercrime: A comprehensive survey of deep learning approaches to tackle the evolving financial crime landscape. *IEEE Access : Practical Innovations, Open Solutions*, 9, 163965–163986. 10.1109/ACCESS.2021.3134076

Niet, I., van Est, R., & Veraart, F. (2021). Governing AI in electricity systems: Reflections on the EU artificial intelligence bill. *Frontiers in Artificial Intelligence*, 4, 690237. 10.3389/frai.2021.69023734396090

Nishant, R., Kennedy, M., & Corbett, J. (2020). Artificial intelligence for sustainability: Challenges, opportunities, and a research agenda. *International Journal of Information Management*, 53(102104), 102104. 10.1016/j.ijinfomgt.2020.102104

Ooi, K.-B., Tan, G. W.-H., Al-Emran, M., Al-Sharafi, M. A., Capatina, A., Chakraborty, A., Dwivedi, Y. K., Huang, T.-L., Kar, A. K., Lee, V.-H., Loh, X.-M., Micu, A., Mikalef, P., Mogaji, E., Pandey, N., Raman, R., Rana, N. P., Sarker, P., Sharma, A., & Wong, L.-W. (2023). The potential of generative artificial intelligence across disciplines: Perspectives and future directions. *Journal of Computer Information Systems*, 1–32. 10.1080/08874417.2023.2261010

Open, A. I., Achiam, J., Adler, S., Agarwal, S., Ahmad, L., Akkaya, I., Aleman, F. L., Almeida, D., Altenschmidt, J., Altman, S., Anadkat, S., Avila, R., Babuschkin, I., Balaji, S., Balcom, V., Baltescu, P., Bao, H., Bavarian, M., Belgum, J., & Zoph, B. (2023). GPT-4 Technical Report. In *arXiv[cs.CL]*. http://arxiv.org/abs/2303.08774

Pavlik, J. V. (2023). Collaborating with ChatGPT: Considering the implications of generative artificial intelligence for journalism and media education. *Journalism & Mass Communication Educator*, 78(1), 84–93. 10.1177/10776958221149577

Pawar, S. (2024, January 25). Unveiling the future: Exploring the wonders of generative AI and its applications. *Medium*. https://medium.com/@sureshkumar.pawar/unveiling-the-future-exploring-the -wonders-of-generative-ai-and-its-applications-c0fb0cae09c6

Qadir, J., Islam, M. Q., & Al-Fuqaha, A. (2022). Toward accountable human-centered AI: Rationale and promising directions. *Journal of Information Communication and Ethics in Society*, 20(2), 329–342. 10.1108/JICES-06-2021-0059

Rader, E., Cotter, K., & Cho, J. (2018). Explanations as mechanisms for supporting algorithmic transparency. *Proceedings of the 2018 CHI Conference on Human Factors in Computing Systems*. 10.1145/3173574.3173677

Raisch, S., & Krakowski, S. (2021). Artificial intelligence and management: The automation–augmentation paradox. *Academy of Management Review*, 46(1), 192–210. 10.5465/amr.2018.0072

Ramdurai, B., & Adhithya, P. (n.d.). The impact, advancements and applications of generative. *AI*. 10.14445/23488387/IJCSEV10IP10

Riedl, M. O. (2019). Human-centered artificial intelligence and machine learning. *Human Behavior and Emerging Technologies*, 1(1), 33–36. 10.1002/hbe2.117

Siau, K. (2018). *Education in the Age of Artificial Intelligence How Will Technology Shape Learning. The global analyst, 7, 22-24. - references - scientific research publishing*. Scirp.org. https://www.scirp .org/reference/referencespapers?referenceid=2988977

Siau, K., & Wang, W. (2020). Artificial intelligence (AI) ethics: Ethics of AI and ethical AI. *Journal of Database Management*, 31(2), 74–87. 10.4018/JDM.2020040105

Singh, M., Bajpai, U., v, V., & Prasath, S. (2019). Generation of fashionable clothes using generative adversarial networks: A preliminary feasibility study. *International Journal of Clothing Science and Technology*, 32(2), 177–187. 10.1108/IJCST-12-2018-0148

Sinha, P., Shastri, A., & Lorimer, S. E. (2023, March 31). How generative AI will change sales. *Harvard Business Review*. https://hbr.org/2023/03/how-generative-ai-will-change-sales

Sun, J., Liao, Q. V., Muller, M., Agarwal, M., Houde, S., Talamadupula, K., & Weisz, J. D. (2022). Investigating explainability of generative AI for code through scenario-based design. In *arXiv[cs.HC]*. http://arxiv.org/abs/2202.04903

Susnjak, T. (2022). ChatGPT: The end of online exam integrity? 10.48550/ARXIV.2212.09292

Taeihagh, A. (2021). Governance of artificial intelligence. *Policy and Society*, 40(2), 137–157. 10.1080/14494035.2021.1928377

Taeihagh, A., Ramesh, M., & Howlett, M. (2021). Assessing the regulatory challenges of emerging disruptive technologies. *Regulation & Governance*, 15(4), 1009–1019. 10.1111/rego.12392

Tambe, P., Cappelli, P., & Yakubovich, V. (2019). Artificial intelligence in human resources management: Challenges and a path forward. *California Management Review*, 61(4), 15–42. 10.1177/0008125619867910

Tlili, A., Shehata, B., Adarkwah, M. A., Bozkurt, A., Hickey, D. T., Huang, R., & Agyemang, B. (2023). What if the devil is my guardian angel: ChatGPT as a case study of using chatbots in education. *Smart Learning Environments*, 10(1), 15. 10.1186/s40561-023-00237-x

. Trocin, C., Mikalef, P., Papamitsiou, Z., & Conboy, K. (2023). Responsible AI for digital health: A synthesis and a research agenda. *Information Systems Frontiers: A Journal of Research and Innovation, 25*(6), 2139–2157. 10.1007/s10796-021-10146-4

van Dis, E. A. M., Bollen, J., Zuidema, W., van Rooij, R., & Bockting, C. L. (2023). ChatGPT: Five priorities for research. *Nature*, 614(7947), 224–226. 10.1038/d41586-023-00288-736737653

Vaswani, A., Shazeer, N., Parmar, N., Uszkoreit, J., Jones, L., Gomez, A. N., Kaiser, L., & Polosukhin, I. (2017). Attention is all you need. In *arXiv[cs.CL]*. http://arxiv.org/abs/1706.03762

Votto, A. M., Valecha, R., Najafirad, P., & Rao, H. R. (2021). Artificial intelligence in tactical human resource management: A systematic literature review. *International Journal of Information Management Data Insights*, 1(2), 100047. 10.1016/j.jjimei.2021.100047

Wan, W. Y., Tsimplis, M., Siau, K. L., Yue, W. T., Nah, F. F.-H., & Yu, G. M. (2022). Legal and regulatory issues on artificial intelligence, machine learning, data science, and big data. In *Lecture Notes in Computer Science* (pp. 558–567). Springer Nature Switzerland. 10.1007/978-3-031-21707-4_40

Wang, W., & Siau, K. (2019). Artificial intelligence, machine learning, automation, robotics, future of work and future of humanity: A review and research agenda. *Journal of Database Management*, 30(1), 61–79. 10.4018/JDM.2019010104

Wong, L.-W., Tan, G. W.-H., Lee, V.-H., Ooi, K.-B., & Sohal, A. (2023). Psychological and system-related barriers to adopting blockchain for operations management: An artificial neural network approach. *IEEE Transactions on Engineering Management*, 70(1), 67–81. 10.1109/TEM.2021.3053359

Wong, Y., Fan, S., Guo, Y., Xu, Z., Stephen, K., Sheoran, R., Bhamidipati, A., Barsopia, V., Liu, J., & Kankanhalli, M. (2022). Compute to tell the tale: Goal-driven narrative generation. *Proceedings of the 30th ACM International Conference on Multimedia*. ACM. 10.1145/3503161.3549202

. Yang, Y., Siau, K., Xie, W., & Sun, Y. (2022). Smart health: Intelligent healthcare systems in the metaverse, artificial intelligence, and data science era. *Journal of organizational and end user computing: an official publication of the Information Resources Management Association, 34*(1), 1–14. 10.4018/JOEUC.308814

Zarifhonarvar, A. (2023). Economics of ChatGPT: A labor market view on the occupational impact of artificial intelligence. SSRN *Electronic Journal*. https://doi.org/10.2139/ssrn.4350925

Zhou, L. (2021). Intelligence augmentation: Towards building human- machine symbiotic relationship. *AIS Transactions on Human-Computer Interaction, 13*(2), 243–264. 10.17705/1thci.00149

Zhuo, T. Y., Huang, Y., Chen, C., & Xing, Z. (2023). *Red teaming ChatGPT via jailbreaking: Bias, Robustness, Reliability and toxicity*. 10.48550/ARXIV.2301.12867

Chapter 5
AI Generative Models for the Fashion Industry

A. Firos
https://orcid.org/0000-0003-4207-713X
Rajiv Gandhi University, India

Seema Khanum
https://orcid.org/0000-0002-2933-2717
Indian Computer Emergency Response Team (ICERT), MeitY, Electronics Niketan, India

ABSTRACT

Fashion designers and brands use GANs to create new and unique patterns, styles, and textures. GANs consist of a generator and a discriminator, which work together to produce high-quality, realistic outputs. VAEs are another type of generative model that is applied to generate new fashion designs. VAEs are known for their ability to generate diverse outputs by sampling from a learned latent space. Fashion designers can use VAEs to explore different design variations and styles. StyleGAN and its successor, StyleGAN2, are advancements of GANs that specifically focus on generating high-resolution and realistic images with control over different style elements. These models have been employed in fashion to create detailed and visually appealing designs. These AI generative models have the potential to revolutionize the fashion industry by facilitating creativity and providing new avenues for artistic expression. However, it's essential to consider ethical implications, intellectual property rights, and the responsible use of AI technologies in the context of fashion design.

INTRODUCTION

Generative Models for Fashion Industry Using Artificial Neural Network

Generative models, particularly those based on deep neural networks, have found significant applications in the fashion industry (Sohn et al., 2020). These models can create new and realistic designs, assist in trend forecasting, and streamline various aspects of the fashion production pipeline. Here are several types of generative models commonly employed in the fashion industry are Generative Adver-

DOI: 10.4018/979-8-3693-3278-8.ch005

sarial Networks (GANs), Variational Autoencoders (VAEs), Recurrent Neural Networks (RNNs) and Long Short-Term Memory Networks (LSTMs) Conditional Generative Models and StyleGAN.

Generative Adversarial Networks (GANs) are widely used for generating realistic and novel fashion designs (Yan et al., 2022). They consist of a generator network that creates synthetic data and a discriminator network that evaluates the authenticity of the generated samples. Generative Adversarial Networks (GANs) can generate new clothing designs, patterns, and textures (Sun et al., 2019). GANs can simulate how a garment looks on a person, facilitating virtual try-on experiences. GANs can transfer styles between different images, allowing for creative adaptations of fashion elements.

Variational Autoencoders (VAEs) are used for generating new samples while also learning a structured latent space (Yuan et al., 2020). This makes them suitable for generating diverse and meaningful fashion designs. VAEs can generate diverse styles within a particular fashion category. VAEs can learn individual preferences and generate personalized fashion recommendations (Simian et al., 2022).

Recurrent Neural Networks (RNNs) and Long Short-Term Memory Networks (LSTMs) are used for sequence generation and can be applied to generate fashion-related sequences such as clothing designs, patterns, or even fashion-related text. RNNs/LSTMs can generate intricate textile patterns (Lee, 2022). It can also be used for generating descriptive captions for fashion images or designs.

Transformer-based architectures like GPT (Generative Pre-trained Transformer) can be fine-tuned for various fashion-related tasks, including design generation, trend analysis, and fashion language understanding (Särmäkari et al., 2022). It can be used for Trend Forecasting where we use it for analyzing large volumes of fashion-related text to identify emerging trends. It can be also used for Generating creative and appealing product descriptions for fashion items.

Conditional Generative Models models generate samples based on specific conditions (Guo et al., 2023). In the fashion industry, this could include generating designs conditioned on certain style preferences or user characteristics (Kang et al., 2017). It can be used Personalized Design Generation where we create designs based on user input or preferences. It can also be used for generating Seasonal Collections where we Generate designs tailored to specific seasons or themes.

An extension of GANs, StyleGAN focuses on controlling the style of generated images (Kato et al., 2018). This can be applied to generate diverse and realistic fashion styles. StyleGAN is used for Creating models that allow users to control specific aspects of style in generated fashion designs.

These generative models contribute to various stages of the fashion industry, from design conceptualization to trend forecasting and personalized shopping experiences. They enhance creativity, reduce design iteration times, and enable more efficient and personalized interactions with consumers. Additionally, the continual evolution of generative models and deep learning techniques contributes to ongoing advancements in the field (Wu et al., 2021).

Deep Neural Network for Giving Suggestions

Deep Neural Networks (DNNs) are often used in recommendation systems to provide personalized suggestions (Boussioux et al., 2023). Deep Neural Networks will do the Data Collection first, where it will do the user data collection and item data collection. For User Data it gathers information about users, their preferences, behaviors, historical interactions, and any other relevant data. For Item Data it collects details about the items, such as products, articles, videos, etc., including their features, categories, and popularity.

The collected data are put forth for Data Preprocessing. A Normalization process is involved here that Normalize and preprocess the data to ensure consistency and improve convergence during training (Della et al., 2022). An Encoding will then Convert categorical variables into numerical representations (embedding layers for categorical data). A Splitting process will then Divide the data into training and validation sets.

A Model Architecture will be used next. It has an Input Layer, Embedding Layers, Hidden Layers, Activation Functions and Output Layer. Input Layer Representing user and item features (Sbai et al., 2018). The Embedding Layers will Convert categorical variables into continuous representations. The Hidden Layers Stacks of densely connected layers where non-linear transformations occur. Activation Functions will Introduce non-linearity into the model (commonly used: ReLU in hidden layers, Sigmoid or Softmax in the output layer for binary or multiclass classification). The Output Layer Produces the model's prediction, typically a score or probability.

Here we will Define a suitable loss function to measure the difference between predicted and actual values. Common loss functions for recommendation systems include Mean Squared Error (MSE), Binary Cross-Entropy, or Categorical Cross-Entropy (Fang et al., 2020).

The Training of the neural network contains Optimization Algorithm, Backpropagation and Regularization. We may Choose an optimization algorithm (e.g., Stochastic Gradient Descent, Adam) to minimize the loss function during training. The Backpropagation will Update model parameters based on the gradient of the loss function with respect to the model's weights. We Apply regularization techniques (e.g., dropout) to prevent overfitting.

A Validation process will Evaluate the model's performance on the validation set to ensure it generalizes well to unseen data. It Adjust hyperparameters if needed to optimize performance.

Once trained, the model can make predictions for user-item pairs. For a recommendation system, these predictions might represent the likelihood of a user engaging with or liking a particular item. A Recommendation system will Sort the items based on predicted scores and recommend the top-ranked items to the user. Various strategies can be employed, such as recommending items with the highest predicted scores or using thresholds to filter out less relevant suggestions. A Feedback Loop will Collect user feedback on recommendations (implicit or explicit) to continuously update and improve the model. it Periodically retrain the model with new data to adapt to changing user preferences.

Then we Deploy the trained model to a production environment where it can generate real-time recommendations for users. A Monitoring and Maintenance activity will be carried out to Continuously monitor the model's performance and update it as needed to ensure it remains effective over time. It will Address issues such as concept drift, where user preferences evolve. Depending on the context, it may be important to interpret and explain the model's recommendations, especially in domains where transparency is crucial. Deep neural networks offer the advantage of learning complex patterns and representations from large and diverse datasets, allowing them to capture intricate user-item interactions and provide personalized suggestions in real-time.

Fuzzy System AI for Fashion Industry

A fuzzy system in the context of the fashion industry refers to the application of fuzzy logic to address various challenges and make decisions in the field. Fuzzy logic is a mathematical framework that deals with uncertainty and imprecision, allowing for more flexible and human-like decision-making. Fuzzy logic can be applied in fashion industry for Product Recommendations, Inventory Management, Price Optimization, Customer Segmentation, Fashion Trend Analysis, Supply Chain Management, Size and Fit Recommendations, Sentiment Analysis, Adaptive User Interfaces and Quality Control.

Fuzzy systems can be employed to enhance product recommendation systems. Instead of binary recommendations (like or dislike), fuzzy logic can help capture the user's nuanced preferences and provide more personalized suggestions. Fuzzy logic can be used in inventory management to handle uncertainty in demand forecasting. It helps in making decisions about stock levels based on factors like seasonality, trends, and market fluctuations.

Fuzzy systems can assist in dynamic pricing strategies by considering various factors such as demand, competitor pricing, and customer behavior. This helps in setting optimal prices that maximize profits. Fuzzy clustering algorithms can aid in dividing customers into segments based on their preferences, allowing fashion companies to tailor marketing strategies and product offerings to specific groups with similar tastes. Fuzzy logic can be applied to analyze and predict fashion trends by considering the ambiguity and subjectivity inherent in the industry. It helps in identifying emerging styles and preferences.

Fuzzy systems can optimize supply chain processes by taking into account uncertain factors such as transportation delays, production issues, and market demand. This aids in more robust decision-making and risk management. Fuzzy logic can be applied to improve size and fit recommendations for customers, considering individual preferences, body shapes, and the subjective nature of comfort.

Fuzzy sentiment analysis can be utilized to gauge customer sentiments towards specific fashion products or brands, considering the fuzzy and imprecise nature of language. Fuzzy systems can be employed to create adaptive and personalized user interfaces on e-commerce platforms, providing a more user-friendly and responsive experience based on individual preferences.

Fuzzy logic can be applied in quality control processes to handle imprecise measurements and variations in product quality, ensuring that only products meeting certain criteria are released to the market. Implementing a fuzzy system in the fashion industry requires a deep understanding of the specific challenges and goals of the business, as well as expertise in fuzzy logic and artificial intelligence techniques. Additionally, it's important to integrate these systems seamlessly into existing workflows for maximum effectiveness (Rane et al., 2023).

Fuzzy ANN for Fashion Recommendation

A Fuzzy Artificial Neural Network (Fuzzy ANN) combines the principles of fuzzy logic and artificial neural networks to handle uncertainty and imprecision in data. In the context of fashion recommendation, this hybrid approach can be used to create a more sophisticated and nuanced recommendation system. We can implement a Fuzzy ANN for fashion recommendation starting with Data Representation. It Represent fashion-related data, such as user preferences, product features, and historical purchasing behavior, in a format suitable for input into a neural network. This might include numerical values, categorical data, and linguistic variables. Then we Integrate a fuzzy logic layer into the input or hidden layers of the neural network. Fuzzy logic can help handle the uncertainty in user preferences and the subjective nature of fashion choices. Linguistic variables and fuzzy rules can be used to capture the ambiguity inherent in fashion preferences.

We can Define membership functions for the fuzzy variables related to user preferences, product attributes, and any other relevant factors. Membership functions help quantify the degree to which a particular input belongs to a fuzzy set. Then we incorporate a fuzzy inference system that interprets the fuzzy input data and generates fuzzy output. Fuzzy rules can be defined to capture relationships between different fuzzy variables and their impact on fashion preferences.

We Design the neural network architecture to accommodate both the fuzzy logic layer and standard neural network layers. This might include input layers for user and product features, hidden layers for learning complex patterns, and output layers for generating recommendations. We will Train the Fuzzy ANN using a dataset that includes historical user interactions with fashion items. The training process involves adjusting the network weights to minimize the difference between predicted and actual user preferences.

During the inference phase, we apply the fuzzy inference system to new input data to obtain fuzzy output. This fuzzy output represents the degree of preference for different fashion items based on the user's input. We perform defuzzification to convert the fuzzy output into a crisp output. This involves summarizing the fuzzy information to obtain a concrete recommendation or preference score. We Implement a feedback mechanism that allows the system to learn and adapt over time based on user feedback. This can enhance the accuracy and relevance of future recommendations.

We will Regularly evaluate the performance of the Fuzzy ANN using metrics such as precision, recall, and user satisfaction. Optimize the model by adjusting parameters, improving fuzzy rules, or expanding the dataset. Implementing a Fuzzy ANN for fashion recommendation requires expertise in both fuzzy logic and neural networks (Dubey et al., 2020). It's crucial to fine-tune the model to capture the intricacies of fashion preferences and ensure that the recommendations align with users' subjective tastes. Continuous monitoring and updates based on user feedback will contribute to the system's effectiveness over time.

THE BACKGROUND

The Fashion Industry

Artificial Intelligence (AI) is playing a significant role in transforming the fashion industry across various aspects, from design and manufacturing to retail and customer experience. AI algorithms can assist designers in generating new and innovative design concepts. Generative models, such as Generative Adversarial Networks (GANs), can create unique patterns, textures, and styles. AI-driven tools analyze fashion trends, customer preferences, and social media to provide designers with insights and recommendations for creating styles that are likely to be popular. AI can be used for demand forecasting, optimizing inventory levels, and predicting supply chain disruptions. This helps in reducing overstock or stockouts and improving overall efficiency. Computer vision systems powered by AI can enhance the quality control process by quickly identifying defects or irregularities in materials and finished products (Dessalgn et al., 2022).

AI algorithms analyze customer data to provide personalized product recommendations, improving the shopping experience and increasing conversion rates. AI-powered virtual try-on technologies allow customers to visualize how clothing items will look on them before making a purchase, reducing returns and enhancing customer satisfaction. AI-driven chatbots and virtual assistants can provide real-time customer support, answer queries, and assist with the shopping process. AI analyzes customer data to create targeted advertising campaigns, ensuring that promotional content is relevant to individual preferences. AI tools can identify influencers whose style and audience align with a brand, helping fashion companies optimize their influencer marketing strategies.

AI and blockchain technologies can be combined to create transparent and traceable supply chains, helping consumers make informed decisions about the sustainability of products (Sandamini et al., 2022). AI algorithms can optimize production processes, minimizing waste and contributing to more sustainable practices. AI-powered virtual stylists provide personalized fashion advice based on individual preferences, helping customers make informed choices. AI analyzes customer data and product information to offer accurate size and fit recommendations, reducing the likelihood of returns.

AI tools analyze social media platforms to identify emerging trends, monitor brand sentiment, and gather insights into customer preferences. Some fashion designers are experimenting with AI-generated designs, and AI has been used to choreograph fashion shows and predict trends based on historical data. Implementing AI in the fashion industry requires collaboration between fashion experts, data scientists, and technologists. It not only enhances efficiency and decision-making but also enables businesses to adapt to rapidly changing consumer preferences and market trends.

Advantages of Fuzzy ANN for Fashion Industry

The integration of Fuzzy Artificial Neural Networks (Fuzzy ANN) into the fashion industry offers several advantages, allowing for a more sophisticated and nuanced approach to solving complex problems. Here are some advantages of using Fuzzy ANN in the fashion industry

1. **Handling Subjectivity and Ambiguity:** Fuzzy logic allows for the representation of subjective and ambiguous information, which is prevalent in the fashion domain. By combining fuzzy logic with neural networks, Fuzzy ANN can capture and process imprecise information related to user preferences and fashion styles.
2. **Personalized Recommendations:** Fuzzy ANN can provide more personalized and context-aware recommendations by considering fuzzy input variables related to user preferences, style preferences, and other subjective factors. This enhances the accuracy and relevance of fashion recommendations.
3. **Dealing with Uncertainty:** Fuzzy logic is well-suited for modeling uncertainty, and neural networks excel at learning complex patterns from data. The combination of these two approaches in Fuzzy ANN allows the system to handle uncertain and imprecise information, which is common in fashion-related decision-making.
4. **Flexibility in Decision-Making:** Fuzzy logic introduces a level of flexibility in decision-making, allowing for gradations of truth and the representation of partial memberships in fuzzy sets. This flexibility is beneficial when making decisions about fashion preferences, where rigid categorizations may not accurately reflect the diversity of user tastes.
5. **Adaptability to User Feedback:** Fuzzy ANN systems can be designed with adaptive learning mechanisms that continuously update their recommendations based on user feedback. This adaptability ensures that the system evolves over time, becoming more accurate and aligned with changing user preferences.

6. **Integration of Linguistic Variables:** Fuzzy logic is well-suited for handling linguistic variables, such as "very stylish" or "somewhat casual." These linguistic variables can be integrated into Fuzzy ANN to capture the subtle nuances of fashion preferences expressed in natural language.

7. **Improved User Experience:** The ability of Fuzzy ANN to understand and adapt to user preferences contributes to an enhanced user experience. Users receive recommendations that align more closely with their individual tastes, leading to increased satisfaction and engagement.

8. **Robustness in Data Variability:** The inherent ability of neural networks to learn from data and adapt to patterns, combined with the fuzzy logic layer, makes Fuzzy ANN robust in handling variability in fashion-related data. This is crucial for accommodating diverse styles and trends.

9. **Complex Decision-Making:** Fuzzy ANN can handle complex decision-making scenarios in the fashion industry, where multiple factors contribute to a user's preference. The neural network component allows the system to learn intricate relationships between different variables.

10. **Enhanced Product Lifecycle Management** Fuzzy ANN can contribute to better product lifecycle management by aiding in design, production, and inventory decisions. This is especially valuable in a dynamic industry like fashion, where trends and consumer preferences evolve rapidly.

While Fuzzy ANN presents several advantages, it's important to note that the effectiveness of the system depends on proper model design, training, and continuous refinement based on user feedback and changing fashion trends. Collaboration between domain experts, data scientists, and AI specialists is crucial for successful implementation in the fashion industry.

Artificial Neural Networks for Automation

Artificial Neural Networks (ANNs) are at the core of many smart devices, providing the intelligence and decision-making capabilities that enable automation and enhanced functionality.

Artificial Neural Networks (ANNs) have proven to be highly effective tools for automation across various industries and applications. ANNs can learn patterns, make predictions, and perform complex tasks based on data, making them suitable for automating processes that involve decision-making, control, and optimization. ANNs can be trained to model complex processes and control systems. They can learn from historical data and real-time sensor inputs to optimize process parameters, adjust setpoints, and maintain stability while considering multiple variables.

ANNs can predict equipment failures or maintenance needs by analyzing sensor data and historical patterns. This allows proactive maintenance scheduling, reducing downtime and improving efficiency. ANNs can monitor production processes and detect defects in real-time by analyzing sensory data or images. This ensures consistent product quality and minimizes waste.

ANN are useful in Supply Chain Management too. ANNs can forecast demand based on historical data, external factors, and market trends. This assists in inventory management, production planning, and ensuring timely deliveries. Also ANNs can optimize energy consumption in buildings and industrial facilities by analyzing usage patterns and adjusting settings for lighting, heating, cooling, and other systems (Harshvardhan et al., 2020).

ANNs can analyze financial data to predict stock prices, assess risk, and automate trading decisions. They can process vast amounts of data quickly and identify complex patterns. ANNs can be used in chatbots to provide customer support, answer queries, and assist users in a conversational manner, improving user experience and efficiency. ANNs are a key component in the automation of self-driving cars. They process sensor data to navigate, make decisions, and ensure safe operation.

ANNs can analyze medical images, patient data, and clinical records to assist in diagnosing diseases, identifying patterns, and predicting patient outcomes. ANNs can understand and generate human language, enabling tasks like sentiment analysis, language translation, and content generation.

ANNs can control and optimize smart home devices based on user preferences and real-time data, improving comfort, energy efficiency, and security. ANNs can analyze environmental data from sensors to detect pollution, predict air quality trends, and provide insights for sustainable resource management.

Using ANNs for automation requires a deep understanding of the problem domain, data preprocessing, network architecture design, training, validation, and deployment. It's crucial to choose the right type of ANN architecture and training algorithms based on the specific automation task and available data.

These technologies work in synergy to power the intelligence and decision-making capabilities of ANN-based smart devices, enabling them to perform complex tasks and provide valuable services to users in various domains like home automation, healthcare, transportation, and more.

Comparison Between Rule-Based Automation and the Machine Learning Automation

Certainly, here are two types of home automation algorithms commonly used in the context of smart homes that are Rule-Based Algorithms and Machine Learning Algorithms.

The Rule-Based Automation Relies on explicit rules defined by domain experts. These rules are typically in the form of "if-then" statements that dictate how decisions should be made based on specific conditions. Machine Learning Automation Learns patterns and relationships from data without requiring explicit rules. ML models generalize from examples and adapt to changing data distributions.

Rule-Based Automation Requires domain experts to explicitly define rules. Human expertise is essential for creating accurate rules that cover various scenarios. Machine Learning Automation Requires expertise in data analysis, model selection, and tuning. While domain knowledge helps, ML models can discover patterns that might not be apparent to experts. Rule-Based Automation is Rigid and may struggle with handling complex or dynamic situations that aren't covered by predefined rules. Requires manual updates for rule modifications. Machine Learning Automation is More adaptable to changing conditions and able to handle complex relationships. ML models can learn from new data and adapt over time.

Rule-Based Automation is Less reliant on large amounts of data. Rules can be based on limited expert knowledge. Machine Learning Automation Requires substantial amounts of high-quality training data for effective learning. Performance can degrade if data is scarce, biased, or noisy.

Rule-Based Automation Rules are human-readable and provide transparent decision-making. However, complex rule sets can become hard to manage. Machine Learning Automation involves Many ML models, especially deep neural networks, are considered black boxes due to their complex internal representations. Interpretable models (e.g., decision trees) offer more transparency. Rule-Based Automation May struggle with tasks that involve intricate interactions between variables or when conditions are not well-defined in advance. Machine Learning Automation Can excel in complex tasks where relationships are nonlinear, and patterns are hard to define using rules.

Rule-Based Automation Can become cumbersome and hard to manage as the number of rules increases. Machine Learning Automation is Scalable to larger datasets and complex problems. However, larger models might require more computational resources. Rule-Based Automation Requires time and effort to define accurate rules based on domain knowledge. Machine Learning Automation needs Initial setup involves data collection, preprocessing, feature engineering, model selection, and training, which can also be time-consuming. Rule-Based Automation is Well-suited for tasks where decision logic can be explicitly defined by experts, such as simple control systems. Machine Learning Automation is Suitable for tasks involving pattern recognition, optimization, prediction, and decision-making in complex and data-rich environments.

Rule-based algorithms involve setting up specific conditions and corresponding actions. These algorithms follow predefined rules or logic to trigger actions based on certain events or inputs. In the context of home automation, rule-based algorithms can be used to automate tasks according to predefined rules set by the user. For example:

- **If-Then Rules**: If a specific condition is met (e.g., time of day, occupancy status, sensor readings), then a corresponding action is executed (e.g., turn on lights, adjust thermostat).
- **Boolean Logic Rules**: Combining conditions using logical operators (AND, OR, NOT) to create more complex rules. For instance, if it's after sunset AND no one is home, then turn on outdoor lights.
- **Event-Triggered Actions**: Triggering actions based on specific events, such as motion detection, door opening, or a specific device turning on/off.

Rule-based algorithms are relatively straightforward to implement and provide users with a certain level of control over their automation systems. However, they may not handle complex scenarios well and can become cumbersome when dealing with a large number of rules.

Machine learning algorithms use data-driven approaches to automate tasks and make decisions based on patterns learned from historical data. In the context of home automation, machine learning algorithms can bring a higher level of adaptability and intelligence to the system. Examples include:

- **Optimization**: Machine learning algorithms can learn usage patterns and adjust and optimize values based on user preferences and changing conditions.
- **Predictive Analysis**: Algorithms can predict user behavior and adjust settings accordingly. For example, anticipating when a user typically arrives home and pre-adjusting the temperature.
- **Anomaly Detection**: Machine learning algorithms can identify unusual patterns or events, such as a sudden spike in energy consumption or unexpected activity, and alert users or take corrective actions.
- **Personalization**: Algorithms can learn user preferences and adjust automation settings to create a more personalized and comfortable environment for each user.

Both Rule-Based Automation and Machine Learning Automation have their strengths and weaknesses. The choice between these approaches depends on factors like the complexity of the task, the availability of high-quality data, the need for adaptability, and the expertise of the team involved. In some cases, a hybrid approach that combines rule-based systems and machine learning models might be the most effective solution.

Preference Leveled Evaluation Functions Method for Recommendation

Preference Leveled Evaluation Functions (PLEFs) are methods used in recommendation systems to evaluate and model user preferences at different levels. This approach is particularly relevant in scenarios where users express preferences in a nuanced and graded manner, rather than in a binary or discrete fashion. PLEFs recognize that users may have preferences at different levels of intensity. Instead of just liking or disliking an item, users may have varying degrees of preference. For example, a user might moderately like a particular style but strongly dislike another. PLEFs often leverage fuzzy logic and membership functions to model the degrees of preference. Fuzzy logic allows for the representation of imprecise and vague preferences. Membership functions define the degree to which an item belongs to a certain category or has a particular attribute.

PLEFs consider multiple factors that contribute to user preferences. These factors could include the item's features, the user's historical interactions, social trends, and any other relevant information. Each factor is assigned a weight based on its importance in determining preferences. PLEFs use mathematical models to represent user preferences. These models are designed to capture the complex and multi-dimensional nature of user preferences. Neural networks, fuzzy systems, or other machine learning models may be employed for this purpose.

Preference Aggregation method aggregates preferences across different factors and levels to provide a comprehensive evaluation. Aggregation mechanisms consider the varying degrees of preference for each factor and synthesize them into an overall preference score. PLEFs can be designed to adapt and learn from user feedback over time. As users interact with the recommendation system and provide feedback, the system adjusts its models to better align with users' evolving preferences. Unlike binary recommendation systems that output either a "like" or "dislike," PLEFs generate granular recommendation scores. These scores can provide users with more detailed information about why a particular item is recommended and allow for a more nuanced understanding of preferences.

PLEFs contribute to personalized recommendation systems by tailoring suggestions to individual users based on their unique preference profiles. This personalization enhances user satisfaction and engagement. PLEFs can offer better explainability for recommendations. Users can understand not only what items are recommended but also why they are recommended, as the system provides insights into the factors and levels contributing to the recommendation.

PLEFs are versatile and can be applied in various domains beyond fashion, such as movie recommendations, music recommendations, and more. The flexibility of the approach allows it to adapt to different contexts where nuanced preferences matter. Implementing PLEFs requires a deep understanding of user behavior, preferences, and the specific context of the recommendation system. It also involves expertise in fuzzy logic, machine learning, and recommendation algorithms. Additionally, user privacy and ethical considerations should be taken into account when implementing such systems.

PROPOSED MODEL

Designing a Preference-Leveled Evaluation Functions (PLEFs) model involves creating a framework that quantifies preference levels for linguistic terms associated with specific attributes or factors. Here's a simplified example of how we propose a PLEFs model.

We will Define the attributes or factors you want to evaluate. For each attribute, assign linguistic terms that represent different levels of that attribute. For instance, if you're evaluating "cost," linguistic terms could be "low," "medium," and "high.". The we do a Preference Levels Mapping. This process will Create a scale of preference levels. These levels could be numerical values (e.g., 1 to 5), linguistic labels (e.g., "Not Important," "Neutral," "Very Important"), or any other meaningful representation. This scale will quantify the extent of preference for each linguistic term.

We Design the PLEFs for each linguistic term of every attribute. PLEFs are functions that map the degree of membership of an element to a linguistic term to a preference level. PLEFs could be linear, nonlinear, or even data-driven functions. For instance, a simple linear PLEF might map membership degree 0.2 to preference level 3 and membership degree 0.8 to preference level 4. For each attribute and linguistic term, define fuzzy sets that represent the linguistic terms' membership degrees. These membership degrees can be determined using the PLEFs. For example, a "low" membership degree might correspond to a lower preference level according to the PLEF.

An Example PLEFs Model works this way. Let's assume you're evaluating two attributes: "Cost" and "Features." For each attribute, you have linguistic terms: "low," "medium," and "high." . Heer we do a Preference Levels Mapping with Preference Levels Scale: 1 (Low Preference) to 5 (High Preference).

The we do PLEFs calculation in the following way:

PLEF for "Cost" assignment is done as Low, medium and High . Low is Low: PLEF: Linear mapping from membership degree 0 to preference level 1, and membership degree 1 to preference level 3. Medium is Medium: PLEF: Linear mapping from membership degree 0 to preference level 2, membership degree 0.5 to preference level 4, and membership degree 1 to preference level 3. High is High: PLEF: Linear mapping from membership degree 0 to preference level 3, and membership degree 1 to preference level 5.

Similarly PLEF for "Features" assignment is done as Low, medium and High . Low is Low: PLEF: Linear mapping from membership degree 0 to preference level 2, and membership degree 1 to preference level 1. Medium is Medium: PLEF: Linear mapping from membership degree 0 to preference level 3, membership degree 0.5 to preference level 4, and membership degree 1 to preference level 3. High is High: PLEF: Linear mapping from membership degree 0 to preference level 4, and membership degree 1 to preference level 5.

Using the PLEFs, you can calculate membership degrees for each linguistic term based on the attributes' values. These membership degrees then contribute to calculating the overall preference level for each option.

This example provides a basic idea of how to design a PLEFs model. In practice, the PLEFs' shapes and the preference level mappings might vary based on the specifics of the application and the decision-making context.

Figure 1 shows the proposed Fashion recommendation algorithm that employs a Parameterized Fuzzy Measures Decision Making Model (PFMDMM) Based on Preference Leveled Evaluation Functions. The model is fed the input fashion data listed in Table 1 in order to determine the relatively desirable fashion for the node. The node's quality data are then obtained using PFMDMM and properly formatted for feeding into the ANN for classification. With the use of BPNN, the signal weights for the BPNN training stage are determined by an arbitrary value according to the values in Table 1, and they are then tuned for maximum performance during the iterative learning process. To determine if the system that was obtained accurately classifies the data to the best preferred pattern and other data portions, the BPNN is tested against a variety of test samples of fashion data during the testing phase.

Figure 1. Block diagram of proposed PFMDMM based on preference leveled evaluation functions for relatively desirable fashion selection

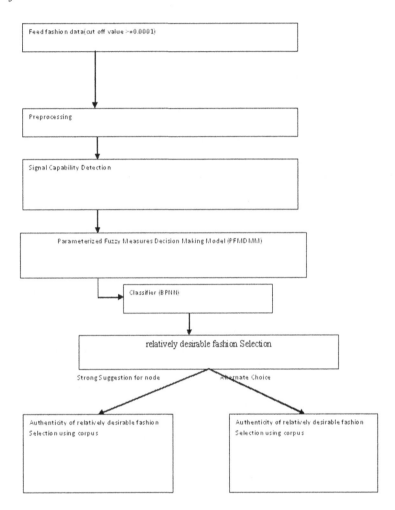

Table 1. Example features of data of fashion dataset

time	use x[0]	gen x[1]	Preference-1 x[2]	Preference-2 x[3]	Preference-3 x[4]	Preference-4 x[5]	Preference-5 x[6]	Preference-6 x[7]	Preference-7 x[8]
1.45E+09	0.932833	0.003483	0.932833	3.33E-05	0.0207	0.061917	0.442633	0.12415	0.006983
1.45E+09	0.934333	0.003467	0.934333	0	0.020717	0.063817	0.444067	0.124	0.006983
1.45E+09	0.931817	0.003467	0.931817	1.67E-05	0.0207	0.062317	0.446067	0.123533	0.006983
1.45E+09	1.02205	0.003483	1.02205	1.67E-05	0.1069	0.068517	0.446583	0.123133	0.006983
1.45E+09	1.1394	0.003467	1.1394	0.000133	0.236933	0.063983	0.446533	0.12285	0.00685
1.45E+09	1.391867	0.003433	1.391867	0.000283	0.50325	0.063667	0.447033	0.1223	0.006717

continued on following page

Table 1. Continued

time	use x[0]	gen x[1]	Preference-1 x[2]	Preference-2 x[3]	Preference-3 x[4]	Preference-4 x[5]	Preference-5 x[6]	Preference-6 x[7]	Preference-7 x[8]
1.45E+09	1.366217	0.00345	1.366217	0.000283	0.4994	0.063717	0.443267	0.12205	0.006733
---	---	---	---	---	---	---	---	---	---

CONCLUSION

This work presents a novel BPNN model that uses the PFMDMM signal classification system to determine the optimal fashion for a node. The trials' findings demonstrated that the parameterized fuzzy measures decision-making model for best fashion recognition exhibits encouraging performances in terms of best fashion proposal for a smart node. This model is built on preference leveled assessment functions.

To the best of our knowledge, this is the first study to employ the preference-leveled evaluation functions-based parameterized fuzzy measures decision making model for signal categorization.

The main outcomes of this research are, in particular:

- The proposed approach is capable of providing clustering decisions making within constrained time periods.
- For the method of feature extraction, this study suggests a novel application of the Parameterized Fuzzy Measures Decision Making Model Based on Preference Leveled Evaluation Functions for fashion classification based BPNN architecture.
- In relation to the test, the provided fashion Dataset has been taken into account to assess the suggested methodology. This dataset includes strong fashion measurements that were gathered to build a parametric model for fashion classification.
- Particularly, by utilizing the decision-making skills of Parameterized Fuzzy Measures Decision Making Model Based on Preference Leveled Evaluation Functions, this study defined a noval automated fashion recommendation system.

REFERENCES

Boussioux, L. N., Lane, J., Zhang, M., Jacimovic, V., & Lakhani, K. R. (2023). *The Crowdless Future?* How Generative AI Is Shaping the Future of Human Crowdsourcing. The Crowdless Future.

Della Sciucca, L., Balloni, E., Mameli, M., Frontoni, E., Zingaretti, P., & Paolanti, M. (2022, May). StyleTrendGAN: A Deep Learning Generative Framework for Fashion Bag Generation. In *International Conference on Image Analysis and Processing* (pp. 191-202). Cham: Springer International Publishing. 10.1007/978-3-031-13324-4_17

Dessalgn, A. W., Sharma, R., Chung, Y. K., & Sungheetha, A. (2022). Generative Adversarial Network-Based Visual-Aware Interactive Fashion Design Framework. *Implementing and Leveraging Blockchain Programming*, 63-78.

Dubey, A., Bhardwaj, N., Abhinav, K., Kuriakose, S. M., Jain, S., & Arora, V. (2020). *AI Assisted Apparel Design*. arXiv preprint arXiv:2007.04950.

Fang, J., Gu, X., & Tan, M. (2020). Fashion-sketcher: A model for producing fashion sketches of multiple categories. In *Pattern Recognition and Computer Vision: Third Chinese Conference*. Springer International Publishing.

Guo, Z., Zhu, Z., Li, Y., Cao, S., Chen, H., & Wang, G. (2023). AI Assisted Fashion Design: A Review. *IEEE Access : Practical Innovations, Open Solutions*.

Harshvardhan, G. M., Gourisaria, M. K., Pandey, M., & Rautaray, S. S. (2020). A comprehensive survey and analysis of generative models in machine learning. *Computer Science Review*, 38, 100285. 10.1016/j.cosrev.2020.100285

. Kang, W. C., Fang, C., Wang, Z., & McAuley, J. (2017, November). Visually-aware fashion recommendation and design with generative image models. In *2017 IEEE international conference on data mining (ICDM)* (pp. 207-216). IEEE.

Kato, N., Osone, H., Sato, D., Muramatsu, N., & Ochiai, Y. (2018, March). Deepwear: a case study of collaborative design between human and artificial intelligence. In *Proceedings of the Twelfth International Conference on Tangible, Embedded, and Embodied Interaction* (pp. 529-536). ACM. 10.1145/3173225.3173302

Lee, Y. K. (2022). How complex systems get engaged in fashion design creation: Using artificial intelligence. *Thinking Skills and Creativity*, 46, 101137. 10.1016/j.tsc.2022.101137

Rane, N. (2023). ChatGPT and Similar Generative Artificial Intelligence (AI) for Smart Industry: role, challenges and opportunities for industry 4.0, industry 5.0 and society 5.0. *Challenges and Opportunities for Industry, 4*.

Sandamini, A., Jayathilaka, C., Pannala, T., Karunanayaka, K., Kumarasinghe, P., & Perera, D. (2022, November). An Augmented Reality-based Fashion Design Interface with Artistic Contents Generated Using Deep Generative Models. In *2022 22nd International Conference on Advances in ICT for Emerging Regions (ICTer)* (pp. 104-109). IEEE. 10.1109/ICTer58063.2022.10024084

Särmäkari, N., & Vänskä, A. (2022). 'Just hit a button!'–fashion 4.0 designers as cyborgs, experimenting and designing with generative algorithms. *International Journal of Fashion Design, Technology and Education*, 15(2), 211–220. 10.1080/17543266.2021.1991005

Sbai, O., Elhoseiny, M., Bordes, A., LeCun, Y., & Couprie, C. (2018). Design: Design inspiration from generative networks. In *Proceedings of the European Conference on Computer Vision (ECCV) Workshops* (pp. 0-0). EC.

Simian, D., & Husac, F. (2022, October). Challenges and Opportunities in Deep Learning Driven Fashion Design and Textiles Patterns Development. In *International Conference on Modelling and Development of Intelligent Systems* (pp. 173-187). Cham: Springer Nature Switzerland.

Sohn, K., Sung, C. E., Koo, G., & Kwon, O. (2020). Artificial intelligence in the fashion industry: Consumer responses to generative adversarial network (GAN) technology. *International Journal of Retail & Distribution Management*, 49(1), 61–80. 10.1108/IJRDM-03-2020-0091

Sun, W., Bappy, J. H., Yang, S., Xu, Y., Wu, T., & Zhou, H. (2019). *Pose guided fashion image synthesis using deep generative model*. arXiv preprint arXiv:1906.07251.

Wu, Q., Zhu, B., Yong, B., Wei, Y., Jiang, X., Zhou, R., & Zhou, Q. (2021). ClothGAN: Generation of fashionable Dunhuang clothes using generative adversarial networks. *Connection Science*, 33(2), 341–358. 10.1080/09540091.2020.1822780

Yan, H., Zhang, H., Liu, L., Zhou, D., Xu, X., Zhang, Z., & Yan, S. (2022). Toward intelligent design: An ai-based fashion designer using generative adversarial networks aided by sketch and rendering generators. *IEEE Transactions on Multimedia*.

Yuan, C., & Moghaddam, M. (2020). *Garment design with generative adversarial networks*. arXiv preprint arXiv:2007.10

Chapter 6
Generative AI Unleashed:
Navigating Societal Impact on Jobs, Education, and Daily Living

Pooja Dehankar
Ajeenkya D.Y. Patil University, India

Susanta Das
https://orcid.org/0000-0002-9314-3988
Ajeenkya D.Y. Patil University, India

ABSTRACT

Generative AI is omnipresent in our daily lives, influencing everything from media and entertainment to personal care and healthcare. The Fourth Industrial Revolution has brought about significant developments in artificial intelligence, such as ChatGPT, which have gained prominence and changed the way data is created and produced. This chapter highlights the current use of AI in natural language processing. These models are based on machine learning. This chapter examines these models' possible benefits to the economy. The potential influence of generative AI on productivity might boost the world economy. All industry sectors will be significantly impacted by generative AI. The economy as a whole can benefit greatly from generative AI's ability to boost labor productivity. We can utilize generative AI's promise to build a more just, inclusive, and sustainable future for all people if we are aware of how it affects society. This chapter offers a comprehensive analysis of the potential exposure of generative AI, in particular to generative pre-trained transformers.

INTRODUCTION

Generative artificial intelligence (GenAI) makes use of contemporary machine learning techniques. Trial and error costs in product development can be significantly reduced if faster, less expensive, and more accurate multi-scale materials simulations powered by fully generative artificial intelligence are made possible. It has been decades since engineers set out to build practical, humanoid robots that mimic human behavior and appearance. Because of its inherent dimensionality, generative artificial intelligence can help to overcome this barrier, making it a potentially valuable tool for today's creative process. It appears that generative artificial intelligence is improving daily, since it can produce text, images, and

DOI: 10.4018/979-8-3693-3278-8.ch006

sounds in response to commands. Additionally, a great deal of tech companies are currently growing and delivering their own rival platforms (Mandapuram et al., 2018).

Recent developments in artificial intelligence (AI) have opened the door to new paradigms in machine processing. These breakthroughs have made it possible to go from data-driven, discriminative AI jobs to complex, creative work through generative AI. Generative AI can respond to basic user inputs by using deep generative models to generate unique and lifelike content for a range of applications (including texts, images, and programming code) (Banh & Strobel, 2023).

Generative AI refers to artificial intelligence (AI) systems that generate original content in response to instructions. These algorithms have the potential to fundamentally alter how people create and interact with content on the internet. In a lot shorter time, for a small fraction of the price, and with astounding inventiveness, generative AI synthesizes the data it has been trained on to produce content in the form of text, graphics, music, video, and more that is comparable to content produced by human professionals. Earlier versions of AI systems, on the other hand, were mainly made to identify patterns and make predictions (Wessel et al., 2023).

AI produce innovative and practical results, it is currently a hot study issue across many disciplines. Particularly in late 2022, generative artificial intelligence has been one area of strong growth within the artificial intelligence category. Creating material that sounds like human conversation is now feasible with the help of tools like ChatGPT, Dall-E, and Midjourney, which democratize access to large language models. The lack of a universally recognized definition for "generative artificial intelligence," however, may cause confusion. The term "generative" is typically reserved by the AI research community for sophisticated models that produce high-quality, human-like content, even if a model that generates any output might theoretically be considered generative (García-Peñalvo & Vázquez-Ingelmo, 2023).

The field of generative artificial intelligence (GAI) is revolutionizing education in the rapidly changing age of technological advancements. In other professions, including engineering and medical, GAI has completely changed the way that education is delivered. Personalized learning assistance, assessment, and intelligent teaching systems are just a few of the numerous applications for GAI. As GAI research grows dramatically and exponentially, ChatGPT becomes the most used tool in the field. These findings provide a comprehensive understanding of the potential for GAI to revolutionize education, which should be of considerable interest to researchers, educators, and policymakers interested in the relationship between GAI and education (Bahroun et al., 2023).

Creative settings are changing as a result of generative AI, which presents both potential and constraints. As these systems adjust to the advent of AI, the balance is thrown off, impacting the workforce as well as society. AI has the capacity to grow sustainably, but navigating this shift will require a proactive cross-sectoral strategy (Thibault et al., 2023).

The development of GPT-4 and other similar models by OpenAI's competitors quickly extended upon ChatGPT's initial introduction of generative AI, which has taken the globe by storm. There is no denying the use of generative artificial intelligence (AI) in daily life, thus it is largely pointless to argue whether or not this technology will catch on. It will, and the question of how big of an impact it will have and whether employing AI to produce text and other kinds of material would have any drawbacks hasn't been settled yet. Technology developments result in societal changes (Sætra, 2023).

By adding intelligence and adaptability, the integration of generative AI is transforming manufacturing processes (Ahmad et al., 2021). Predictive maintenance is among the essential uses. Through the analysis of past data, ChatGPT is able to predict possible machinery faults and facilitate proactive maintenance. The predictive strategy lowers expenses, cuts downtime, and improves overall operational effectiveness

(Rane & Attarde, 2016; Ali & Aysan, 2023; Ayoola et al., 2023; Rane et al., 2023; Rathore, 2023). Additionally, ChatGPT is very important for supply chain optimization. Communication between different supply chain nodes is streamlined via natural language interfaces. It records shipments, evaluates and processes orders, and provides stakeholders with real-time updates, among other things. This promotes accountability and transparency throughout the supply chain network in addition to ensuring a more efficient flow of commodities (Frederico, 2023).

The emphasis in production is shifting from total automation to a more human-centric approach (Mourtzis et al., 2023). Industry emphasizes the cooperation of AI-driven technologies and people. It supports human workers in production environments by acting as a virtual assistant and offering prompt direction and solutions. For example, ChatGPT can be used by manufacturing floor technicians to solve problems, get manuals, and get on-the-spot training, all of which improves their abilities and output (Rathore, 2023). ChatGPT enables customized interactions in the field of product modification. AI-driven interfaces allow users to converse with them and customize products to their liking. This degree of personalization increases customer happiness and provides insightful information about market trends and consumer behavior, which aids in the decision-making process for organizations.

Through the processing of vast amounts of patient data and medical literature, ChatGPT helps healthcare providers diagnose illnesses and suggest the best courses of action (Biswas, 2023; De Angelis et al., 2023; Deiana et al., 2023). It bridges the gap between doctors and patients by responding to medical questions, setting up appointments, and providing emotional support, all of which improve the overall patient experience and offer useful insights that help doctors make accurate decisions (Kahambing, 2023). In the field of education, ChatGPT acts as a customized tutor, giving pupils individualized learning opportunities. It evaluates each student's unique learning preferences and modifies its instructional strategies through dialogue. Both learning outcomes and student engagement are improved by this individualized approach.

The term "GPT" refers to a family of pre-trained language models (PLM) that OpenAI has been working on (Radford et al., 2019; Brown et al., 2020). PLMs have been the most widely used transformer type in NLG tasks. PLMs, or parsed language models, are trained on a sizable corpus of textual data and are useful for handling particular language-related problems (Arslan et al., 2021). As per Kenton and Toutanova (2019), BERT gained popularity in natural language comprehension tasks like text classification, and it was trained using data from books and Wikipedia that comprised more than 3.3 billion tokens. However, according to Cheng et al. (2020), BERT is an inadequate model for design concept generation since it is a masked language model that can only learn contextual representations of words; it cannot organize or construct language.

Instead, GPTs are autoregressive language models that are taught to forecast a token's next move by considering all of the tokens that have come before it. Following Hinton and Salakhutdinov (2006), GPT-2 employs a two-step training technique of pre-training and fine-tuning. In the pre-training phase, a text dataset gathered from millions of webpages is used to train the model (Radford et al, 2019). The pre-trained model must be adjusted in light of a customized and task-oriented dataset for NLP tasks that come after. Using a sizable corpus of example task data, the refined model is trained repeatedly via gradient updates. In order to employ the pre-trained model for the target task, this method adjusts the weights and stores them.

GPT-3 use is actually very simple. It is not complicated than using a search engine to find information. Similar to how Google "reads" our queries, it doesn't actually understand them and provides relevant responses, GPT-3 also "reads" our words and generates content that follows their natural order. For the duration of the text specified, it continues to do this regardless of how simple or complex, reasonable or absurd, and meaningful or meaningless the task at hand may be. Without oversight, guidance, or instruction regarding the "correct," "true," or "right" text that should be typed in response to the prompt, GPT-3 generates a text that is statistically excellent fit given the initial text. To retrieve the issuing text, one need simply compose a simple prompt (Floridi & Chiriatti, 2020).

The Generative Pre-trained Transformer (GPT) is a significant advancement in natural language processing that is advancing the goal of creating machines that can comprehend and interact with language in a way that is similar to that of human beings. The transformer architecture, a deep neural network intended for natural language processing applications, is the foundation of GPT. One of the most popular and useful models in natural language processing and related fields, GPT has garnered a lot of attention from academics and industry communities because of its remarkable performance on tasks involving natural language processing and its capacity for productive conversation. As a kind of DL model, the GPT model pre-trains itself on vast volumes of textual material by selfsupervised learning, which allows it to produce linguistic output of impressive quality. Research on the GPT model has advanced recently, which can be due to its design being continuously improved, more computing power being available, and the creation of new methods for fine-tuning the model for certain tasks. Since these developments, a greater variety of NLP tasks can be completed by larger and more potent GPT models with previously unheard-of accuracy and fluency. Numerous industries, including the healthcare, finance, and customer service sectors, have shown a great deal of promise for change when it comes to these GPT models (Liu et al., 2023; Rivas & Zhao, 2023; Leippold, 2023).

High-quality and diversified data, such as large-scale text corpora with various rapidly expanding enabling technologies, are made possible by these applications (Trajtenberg, 2018; Haluza & Jungwirth, 2023). From a tiny quantity of text input, the GPT model generates large amounts of complex and relevant machine-generated content. GPT models are recognized as DL-based language models that emulate human language and function as autoregressive models where the current value is determined by the past value (Quintans-Júnior et al., 2023).

The importance of artificial intelligence in our daily lives and the growth of global economies is becoming more and more significant. This article emphasizes how important it is to incorporate generative AI within the framework of the Fourth Industrial Revolution in emerging nations, where advancement and equitable growth are significantly influenced by technological change. This article examines ethical issues in scientific publishing, the attribution of credit for AI-driven discoveries, and important facets of integrating AI in education to achieve educational goals. This article also discuss accessibility and equity issues and look at the ramifications of employing AI-generated content in professional settings. This article examines the possible benefits and drawbacks of generative AI in developing nations across a range of information, cultural, and industrial domains. Not everyone can gain equally from generative artificial intelligence, particularly in underdeveloped nations where access to advanced technologies is restricted and infrastructure is weak. This article aims to comprehend the possible effects of generative AI technologies on developing nations, taking into account technological accessibility, economic growth, and prospective paradigm shifts in the fields of healthcare, education, and the environment. The results highlight how crucial it is to provide the infrastructure and support required to make sure that generative AI promotes equitable development rather than escalating already-existing disparities. Understanding the technology's potential to benefit the economy and society at large will help shape important decisions as businesses scramble to adapt and utilize it. Through digital self-service, augmented and enhanced agent skills, and improved customer experience and agent productivity, generative AI holds the potential to completely transform the customer operations function. Because the technology can automate consumer interactions using natural language, it has already gained popularity in the customer service industry. The structure of labor could be altered by generative AI, which could improve worker capacities by automating some of their personal tasks. This chapter covers Generative AI in the Workforce, Education and Daily Living. This chapter also summarizes Generative AI's Ethical and Societal Implications. This chapter conclude with Future Perspectives and Challenges.

Generative AI in the Workforce

AI recommendations help low-skill people to communicate more like high-skill experts since they are based on text analysis of agent discussions. For instance, it's unclear if higher customer service productivity will result in a greater or lesser demand for customer support agents. If the demand in the customer service sector is not elastic, generative AI tools may eventually reduce demand and make money. On the other side, better product support might encourage customers to contact agents with a wider range of questions; this could increase the demand for staff or give them new responsibilities like obtaining customer feedback for the product development team (Trajtenberg, 2018; Korinek, 2022).

Historically, the effectiveness of a support agent has been evaluated based on how successfully they help the clients they serve. However, in a scenario where customer service conversations are put into training datasets, an employee's productivity also encompasses their ability to provide ML models with examples of positive behaviors that they may share with others. High achievers in our setting show relatively little improvement in output, while providing a huge number of examples for the AI system we examine to be trained on. Because bonuses are contingent on the performance of other agents, some workers may even see a salary cut under our data firm's current pay rules. Lastly, since generative AI is a potentially all-purpose technology that may and will be employed in a variety of situations, the findings may not be applicable to all industries and modes of production (Eloundou et al., 2023). When a product or environment is changing quickly, the relative value of AI recommendations may change as well. In certain situations, they might be better at synthesizing changing best practices, or they might even impede learning by supporting outdated techniques from earlier training sets.

Professionals in human resource management (HRM) frequently work too much and have more complicated duties. As a result, many experience job burnout, and only a small percentage are able to devote the required time to strategic concerns. We demonstrate how ChatGPT, a type of generative artificial intelligence (AI), may be a useful HRM assistant for both operational and strategic activities. However, in order for this to occur, we show how important it is to develop insightful questions that lead to precise, beneficial, and doable HRM suggestions. As a result, we offer eight recommendations for producing excellent and successful prompts and demonstrate their applicability in eight crucial HRM domains as well as more specifically in the areas of workforce diversity and strategic HRM (Aguinis et al., 2024).

Generative artificial intelligence and automation technologies reshape workforce skill demands, hiring practices, career paths, job mismatches, losses, and transitions, as well as managerial and professional roles. They also boost employee productivity, competitive advantage, and customer service. Through its ability to predict job displacement, optimize talent progression and promotion operations, speed up organizational workflows and data-driven decision-making processes, enhance worker productivity and job reallocation mechanisms, and define talent surplus, scarcity, demand, and acquisition, generative artificial intelligence has a significant impact on labor market outcomes. The generative artificial intelligence's business value is based on the following: shared cognitive and spatial computing technologies, 3D virtual digital twin simulation algorithms, automated workplace tasks, predictive analytics and decision modeling development, efficient job creation and displacement across industries and categories, and customized job requirements and upskilling. Algorithmic knowledge, adaptive self-organizing systems, collective action coordination, governance decision-making processes, and well-thought-out talent acquisition and onboarding articulate Web3 technology-based immersive remote work experiences provide significant productivity growth and performance management (Dengov et al., 2023).

Productivity and operational efficiency are enhanced by the application of generative artificial intelligence systems. Large workforces can be supplemented or replaced with the help of these algorithms, which can also be used to construct appropriate job-matching systems, analyze performance data, and assess employee sentiment. All of these uses can enhance knowledge acquisition and boost labor productivity. Generative artificial intelligence technologies enable the following: partially eliminating jobs, reskilling and upskilling employees, attracting, developing, retaining, and making talent available, organizational norms and practices, and raising worker productivity through effective workforce development, labor market participation, and talent management (Lazaroiu & Rogalska, 2023).

Generative AI in Education

Comprehending the function of Generative AI within the wider framework of human history aids in our appreciation of the opportunities and difficulties that await us as we advance deeper into the artificial intelligence era. According to the university, there are both potential and concerns associated with the productivity benefits of generative AI technologies, such as ChatGPT, when used to mid-level professional writing activities. Universities may encounter difficulties keeping their writing and communication courses current and relevant as AI technologies like ChatGPT proliferate in professional contexts. In order to give students abilities that enhance AI rather than replace it, course content needs to be reviewed and updated on a regular basis. The use of Generative AI in professional writing tasks also raises ethical considerations related to attribution, plagiarism, and the potential for AI-generated content to be presented as original work. Universities must so encourage and uphold academic integrity standards that address these issues and instruct students in the ethical use of AI. Universities should integrate workshops and coursework linked to artificial intelligence (AI) into pertinent disciplines, such as writing and communication programs, in order to sufficiently prepare students for the future. This method will assist students in comprehending the potential, constraints, and moral issues surrounding generative AI in professional settings. In order to produce graduates that are well-rounded, it is important to prioritize human abilities like critical thinking, creativity, and problem-solving through project-based learning and interdisciplinary approaches, even though generative AI can increase productivity. Furthermore, required courses or modules on responsible AI use and ethics should be implemented to guarantee that students understand the moral ramifications of generative AI, such as ChatGPT (Okaiyeto et al., 2023).

The generative AI tool ChatGPT stunned everyone with its sophisticated ability to finish surprisingly complex jobs. Teachers are divided over ChatGPT's amazing ability to complete challenging educational assignments because this AI breakthrough seems to be transforming the way that education is done today. This exploratory study summarizes recent existing material to offer some potential benefits and drawbacks of ChatGPT in promoting teaching and learning. ChatGPT has a number of benefits, including promoting personalized and interactive learning, generating concepts for formative assessment assignments that provide ongoing feedback to improve training, and more (Baidoo-Anu & Ansah, 2023).

Generative AI in Daily Living

Google created Google Assistant, a virtual assistant that facilitates conversational interactions with generative AI. It can converse in natural language, carry out tasks, give advice, and respond to queries. Developed by Amazon, Alexa is another well-known virtual assistant that uses generative AI to facilitate voice-based communication. In addition to controlling smart home appliances and playing music, users may converse with Alexa to obtain information. Apple's virtual assistant, Siri, uses generative AI to comprehend and react to human commands and questions. It has the ability to carry out operations, deliver data, establish reminders, and communicate with other Apple products. The conversational AI model you are currently dealing with, OpenAI's ChatGPT, uses generative AI to deliver text-based responses in a conversational way. It can converse interactively, respond to queries, and offer knowledge on a variety of subjects. Microsoft's Cortana virtual assistant uses generative artificial intelligence (AI) to help with chores, respond to inquiries, provide reminders, and communicate with Windows devices. IBM Watson Assistant: This conversational AI platform uses generative AI approaches to create virtual assistants and chatbots. For information retrieval, customer service, and other uses, it enables companies to design unique conversational bots. Facebook Messenger facilitates chatbot development through the use of generative AI technology. These chatbots are able to converse with people, offer assistance, and make tailored recommendations. China's WeChat, a well-known messaging app, encourages the creation of chatbots that communicate with people through generative AI. Within the WeChat ecosystem, these chatbots can answer queries, give information, and provide a range of services (Ramdurai & Adhithya, 2023).

Since human activities have multiple dimensions, it is possible to integrate various machine-learning algorithms. Here, boosted decision stumps and HMMs solve different aspects of the computing difficulty and work effectively together. The techniques for recognizing more complex patterns of activity, such as housekeeping, cooking, etc., are integrated and enhanced. Subsequent versions of these ideas will produce activity recognition systems that are not restricted to the lab but may be applied in smart rooms, ethnography, and the medical field for the elderly and young (Lester et al., 2005).

Ethical and Societal Implications

The employment of ChatGPT in the classroom also raises ethical and safety concerns. It is possible to use technology to deceive or misinform students. If the model is not properly monitored and regulated, it may provide students with misleading information or lead them in the incorrect way. There is a chance that pupils' privacy will be violated by technology. If the model is not sufficiently secured, students' private information could be acquired without their knowledge or agreement. Technology is a tool that can be used to discriminate against students. If the model wasn't trained on data that are typical of all students, it might be exploited to provide uneven access to education (Su & Yang, 2023).

Offensive or improper content produced by generative AI encompasses a wide range of topics, such as violent content, profanity, pornography, and discriminating content. Despite the fact that OpenAI has developed a content guideline for ChatGPT, algorithmic limitations or jailbreaking may still cause improper or dangerous content to surface. According to Zhao et al. (2023) the term "toxicology" describes language models' capacity to comprehend or produce false or dangerous information. Toxins have the capacity to harm society and undermine social cohesion. Therefore, it is crucial to make sure that any content that is judged offensive or dangerous is taken out of the training set and deleted as quickly as possible. In addition, Zhao et al. state that the training data shouldn't contain any pornographic, erotic, or sexual material.

When it comes to artificial intelligence, bias is the propensity for answers or suggestions generated by AI to unfairly favor or discriminate against a certain individual or group (Ntoutsi et al., 2020). Due to the possibility of training set bias, language models may produce material that is biased in one or more ways. For instance, exclusionary norms emerge when training data only represent a tiny portion of the population (Zhuo et al., 2023). However, when training data is only available in one language, monolingual bias in multilingualism occurs (Weidinger et al., 2021). Given that ChatGPT is an international service, it is imperative to be culturally conscious of various locales in order to prevent bias (Dwivedi et al., 2023).

Users may get unduly reliant on ChatGPT and begin to trust the responses it offers due to its seeming strength and simplicity. Unlike traditional search engines, which offer a range of information sources for consumers to select from, ChatGPT offers customized answers for each question. While reducing time and effort with ChatGPT may boost productivity, users run the risk of forming the bad habit of accepting responses without inquiry or explanation. Over-reliance on generative AI technology can impede skills like creativity, critical thinking, and problem-solving as well as generate bias in human automation due to regularly adopting recommendations from generative AI (Iskender, 2023).

Therefore, every user must be proficient in AI. Users are encouraged not to take the answers generated by generative AI at face value, but to independently check them before adopting them. Misuse of generative AI is defined as any deliberate use that could result in undesirable, unethical, or incorrect outcomes (Brundage et al., 2020). It is common knowledge that abuse can occur in the field of education. Sophisticated tool for detecting plagiarism, ChatGPT looks for patterns in large data sets to generate unique content (Gefen & Arinze, 2023). When generative AI systems like ChatGPT can generate top-notch answers in a matter of seconds, indolent students might not invest the time or energy required to finish their assignments and essays. This makes it difficult to assess student work for originality in the generative AI era.

According to Thorp (2023), text written with ChatGPT is inappropriate and is regarded as plagiarism. Exam cheating is another example of misapplication. Students that have access to digital devices during an exam could use ChatGPT to find answers to questions. To combat potential misuse in education, strict proctoring procedures will need to be put in place. Additionally, AI-generated content detectors such as Turnitin may be used (Susnjak, 2022). Beyond content detection and exam proctoring, however, there may be challenges in differentiating between correct and incorrect use of ChatGPT. Guidelines and suggestions for the proper use of ChatGPT in academic activities have been presented by scholars (Susarla et al., 2023).

Data security and privacy are major problems for ChatGPT and other generative AI systems. Privacy is associated to sensitive personal information that owners do not wish to share (Fang et al., 2017). Data security is the process of preventing theft, corruption, and unauthorized access to data. During ChatGPT's development phase, enormous volumes of personal and private data were used to train the system, putting users' privacy at risk (Siau & Wang, 2020). ChatGPT is becoming more and more integrated into people's daily lives, providing them with greater convenience at the expense of gathering a massive amount of personal data about them. The prospect of personal data being accidentally or intentionally made public raises concerns and hazards.

Van Dijk (2006) defines the digital divide as the difference between people who have access to computers and the Internet and those who do not. The increasing pervasiveness of the Internet has given rise to concerns about a "second-level digital divide," or the disparity in Internet usage and abilities among various groups and cultures (Scheerder et al., 2017). The current digital gap in society could be widened by generative AI, a developing technology.

Between people who don't have access to technology or the Internet, or between people who reside in places where generative AI suppliers or websites have banned access, the first-level digital divide could widen (Bozkurt, & Sharma, 2023). Language and cultural barriers may arise for members of marginalized or minority groups if generative AI models do not completely comprehend or include their traditions. Additionally, those who are unable to use the generative AI tool, such as some elderly individuals, may experience an increase in the second-level digital divide (Dwivedi et al., 2023). Addressing the digital gap would benefit from more accessible AI and AI literacy training? Technological hurdles are the restrictions or limitations related to generative AI. The quality of training data is one major barrier to the development of generative AI models, for example. Additional problems caused by the constraints of the algorithms include output authenticity, explainability, and hallucinations.

FUTURE PERSPECTIVES AND CHALLENGES

Subsequent investigations ought to concentrate on crafting and assessing artificial intelligence-driven pedagogical programs, as well as investigating the possible advantages and difficulties of implementing this technology in diverse educational environments. It's crucial to carry out research on how ChatGPT and/or other generative AI applications affect learning outcomes for students, like motivation, engagement, and academic success. In addition, future studies should keep examining the moral and societal ramifications of utilizing AI in the classroom, as well as any possible effects on human educators and the requirement for relevant laws and guidelines.To fully grasp the potential of this technology and determine practical approaches for its application in education, more research is required. It's critical to keep up with the most recent advancements in artificial intelligence. The usefulness of ChatGPT in various settings (such as professional development, early childhood education, formal education, lifelong learning, special education, and online learning) as well as the ethical and responsible use of the technology require more investigation. When it comes to early childhood education, for example, ChatGPT can be utilized by young children who are illiterate through voice-activated interfaces like virtual assistants or smart speakers. Kids can use ChatGPT to ask questions or offer voice commands, and the AI model will react with audio outputs. As a result, even young children who are not yet literate can nonetheless use and profit from technology. But it's crucial to remember that small children shouldn't utilize AI technologies (Su & Yang, 2023).

CONCLUSION

The future is probably going to be very different from what we have ever known. However, there is no intrinsic good or negative influence of generative AI. In the end, how we develop and implement the technology will determine how generative AI plays out. Our choices and deeds today will clearly influence the course of our future; we are living in a singular and historic period. All facets of society are affected by this obligation, including the public, business, government, and scientific research.

Significant effects of this technology can be seen in important areas including information, work, education, and health. In the workplace, AI might, for example, need new skill sets, provide new jobs, alter income distributions, and automate some job duties. Artificial intelligence (AI) has the potential to democratize education and offer individualized learning solutions, but it also highlights issues related to the digital divide. The ability of AI to analyze massive datasets in the healthcare industry can improve patient outcomes, but it also raises concerns about fair access to AI-driven healthcare services and the indispensability of human engagement. AI has the ability to provide more democratic, efficient, and customized methods of processing information in the information domain, but it also presents issues with misinformation and diversity of opinion.

To properly address these concerns, we have listed a number of research questions that desperately need to be answered. Using AI to its full potential while reducing its hazards is the goal of these queries. Furthermore, we have noticed that the regulatory frameworks that are in place in the US, the UK, and the European Union occasionally fall short of meeting these new difficulties. A flexible regulatory framework that can keep up with the quick developments in AI technology is required.

Our goal is that our work will help create a thorough research agenda and ignite public discussions about these important issues. Our decisions now will have a lasting effect on future generations, thus it is imperative that, as we approach the dawn of this new era, we have inclusive and deliberate conversations about how AI is influencing our society.

The research's investigation of AI ethics highlights the complex and varied issues that come with the swift development of AI technologies. Several significant ideas and reflections have been revealed via a thorough interdisciplinary analysis that included philosophy, computer science, law, and social sciences. First off, given how ubiquitous AI is in many different industries, ethical issues must be approached with initiative and knowledge. AI presents a number of ethical conundrums that have real-world consequences for people on an individual, organizational, and societal level. These issues range from algorithmic bias and data privacy to accountability and societal influence. Thus, it is crucial to address these ethical issues in order to guarantee the responsible development and application of AI technologies that are consistent with societal ideals.

AI ethics is multidisciplinary, which emphasizes the value of stakeholder interaction and teamwork. A comprehensive knowledge that cuts across disciplinary boundaries is fostered by the convergence of multiple perspectives, which improves the debate on AI ethics.

It takes collaborative efforts combining engineers, ethicists, legislators, and other stakeholders to effectively negotiate the intricacies of AI ethics and provide clear, workable frameworks for the creation of responsible AI. It draws attention to the dynamic and ever-changing character of AI ethics, calling for innovative and adaptable solutions. The ethical considerations surrounding AI technology must also change and adapt as these technologies continue to permeate all sectors of society. This involves anticipating emergent challenges and proactively resolving ethical consequences.

REFERENCES

Aguinis, H., Beltran, J. R., & Cope, A. (2024). How to use generative AI as a human resource management assistant. *Organizational Dynamics*, 53(1), 101029. 10.1016/j.orgdyn.2024.101029

Ahmad, T., Zhang, D., Huang, C., Zhang, H., Dai, N., Song, Y., & Chen, H. (2021). Artificial intelligence in sustainable energy industry: Status Quo, challenges and opportunities. *Journal of Cleaner Production*, 289, 125834. 10.1016/j.jclepro.2021.125834

Ali, H., & Aysan, A. F. (2023). What will ChatGPT revolutionize in financial industry? *Available atSSRN* 4403372.

Arslan, Y., Allix, K., Veiber, L., Lothritz, C., Bissyandé, T. F., Klein, J., & Goujon, A. (2021, April). A comparison of pre-trained language models for multi-class text classification in the financial domain. In *Companion Proceedings of the Web Conference 2021* (pp. 260-268). ACM. 10.1145/3442442.3451375

Ayoola, O. O., Alenoghena, R., & Adeniji, S. (2023). ChatGPT impacts on access-efficiency, employment, education and ethics: The socio-economics of an AI language model. *BizEcons Quarterly*, 16, 1–17.

Bahroun, Z., Anane, C., Ahmed, V., & Zacca, A. (2023). Transforming education: A comprehensive review of generative artificial intelligence in educational settings through bibliometric and content analysis. *Sustainability (Basel)*, 15(17), 12983. 10.3390/su151712983

Baidoo-Anu, D., & Ansah, L. O. (2023). Education in the era of generative artificial intelligence (AI): Understanding the potential benefits of ChatGPT in promoting teaching and learning. *Journal of AI*, 7(1), 52–62. 10.61969/jai.1337500

Banh, L., & Strobel, G. (2023). Generative artificial intelligence. *Electronic Markets*, 33(1), 63. 10.1007/s12525-023-00680-1

Biswas, S. S. (2023). Role of chat gpt in public health. *Annals of Biomedical Engineering*, 51(5), 868–869. 10.1007/s10439-023-03172-736920578

Bozkurt, A., & Sharma, R. C. (2023). Challenging the status quo and exploring the new boundaries in the age of algorithms: Reimagining the role of generative AI in distance education and online learning. *Asian Journal of Distance Education*, 18(1).

Brown, T., Mann, B., Ryder, N., Subbiah, M., Kaplan, J. D., Dhariwal, P., & Amodei, D. (2020). Language models are few-shot learners. *Advances in Neural Information Processing Systems*, 33, 1877–1901.

Brundage, M., Avin, S., Wang, J., Belfield, H., Krueger, G., Hadfield, G., & Anderljung, M. (2020). Toward trustworthy AI development: mechanisms for supporting verifiable claims. *arXiv preprint arXiv:2004.07213*.

Cheng, Y., & Duan, M. (2020, December). Chinese grammatical error detection based on BERT model. In *Proceedings of the 6th Workshop on Natural Language Processing Techniques for Educational Applications* (pp. 108-113). ACM.

De Angelis, L., Baglivo, F., Arzilli, G., Privitera, G. P., Ferragina, P., Tozzi, A. E., & Rizzo, C. (2023). ChatGPT and the rise of large language models: The new AI-driven infodemic threat in public health. *Frontiers in Public Health*, 11, 1166120. 10.3389/fpubh.2023.116612037181697

Deiana, G., Dettori, M., Arghittu, A., Azara, A., Gabutti, G., & Castiglia, P. (2023). Artificial intelligence and public health: Evaluating ChatGPT responses to vaccination myths and misconceptions. *Vaccines*, 11(7), 1217. 10.3390/vaccines1107121737515033

Dengov, V. V., Zvarikova, K., & Balica, R. S. (2023). Generative Artificial Intelligence and Movement and Behavior Tracking Tools, Remote Sensing and Cognitive Computing Systems, and Immersive Audiovisual Content in Virtually Simulated Workspace Environments. *Analysis and Metaphysics*, 22(0), 274–293. 10.22381/am22202315/

Dwivedi, Y. K., Kshetri, N., Hughes, L., Slade, E. L., Jeyaraj, A., Kar, A. K., Baabdullah, A. M., Koohang, A., Raghavan, V., Ahuja, M., Albanna, H., Albashrawi, M. A., Al-Busaidi, A. S., Balakrishnan, J., Barlette, Y., Basu, S., Bose, I., Brooks, L., Buhalis, D., & Wright, R. (2023). "So what if ChatGPT wrote it?" Multidisciplinary perspectives on opportunities, challenges and implications of generative conversational AI for research, practice and policy. *International Journal of Information Management*, 71, 102642. 10.1016/j.ijinfomgt.2023.102642

Eloundou, T., Manning, S., Mishkin, P., & Rock, D. (2023). Gpts are gpts: An early look at the labor market impact potential of large language models. *arXiv preprint arXiv:2303.10130.*

Fang, W., Wen, X. Z., Zheng, Y., & Zhou, M. (2017). A survey of big data security and privacy preserving. *IETE Technical Review*, 34(5), 544–560. 10.1080/02564602.2016.1215269

Floridi, L., & Chiriatti, M. (2020). GPT-3: Its nature, scope, limits, and consequences. *Minds and Machines*, 30(4), 681–694. 10.1007/s11023-020-09548-1

Frederico, G. F. (2023). ChatGPT in supply chains: Initial evidence of applications and potential research agenda. *Logistics*, 7(2), 26. 10.3390/logistics7020026

García-Peñalvo, F., & Vázquez-Ingelmo, A. (2023). *What do we mean by GenAI? A systematic mapping of the evolution, trends, and techniques involved in Generative AI.*

Gefen, D., & Arinze, O. (2023). ChatGPT and usurping academic authority. *Journal of Information Technology Case and Application Research*, 25(1), 3–9. 10.1080/15228053.2023.2186629

Haluza, D., & Jungwirth, D. (2023). Artificial intelligence and ten societal megatrends: An exploratory study using GPT-3. *Systems*, 11(3), 120. 10.3390/systems11030120

Hinton, G. E., & Salakhutdinov, R. R. (2006). Reducing the dimensionality of data with neural networks. *science, 313*(5786), 504-507.

Iskender, A. (2023). Holy or unholy? Interview with open AI's ChatGPT. *European Journal of Tourism Research*, 34, 3414–3414. 10.54055/ejtr.v34i.3169

Kahambing, J. G. (2023). ChatGPT, public health communication and 'intelligent patient companionship'. *Journal of Public Health (Oxford, England)*, 45(3), e590–e590. 10.1093/pubmed/fdad02837036209

Kenton, J. D. M. W. C., & Toutanova, L. K. (2019, June). Bert: Pre-training of deep bidirectional transformers for language understanding. In *Proceedings of naacL-HLT* (*Vol. 1*, p. 2).

Korinek, A. (2022). *How innovation affects labor markets: An impact assessment.* (Brookings Center on Regulation and Markets Working Paper).

Lazaroiu, G., & Rogalska, E. (2023). How generative artificial intelligence technologies shape partial job displacement and labor productivity growth. *Oeconomia Copernicana*, 14(3), 703–706. 10.24136/oc.2023.020

Leippold, M. (2023). Thus spoke GPT-3: Interviewing a large-language model on climate finance. *Finance Research Letters*, 53, 103617. 10.1016/j.frl.2022.103617

Lester, J., Choudhury, T., Kern, N., Borriello, G., & Hannaford, B. (2005). *A hybrid discriminative/generative approach for modeling human activities.*

Liu, Z., Huang, Y., Yu, X., Zhang, L., Wu, Z., Cao, C., & Li, X. (2023). Deid-gpt: Zero-shot medical text de-identification by gpt-4. *arXiv preprint arXiv:2303.11032.*

Mandapuram, M., Gutlapalli, S. S., Bodepudi, A., & Reddy, M. (2018). Investigating the Prospects of Generative Artificial Intelligence. *Asian Journal of Humanity. Art and Literature*, 5(2), 167–174.

Mourtzis, D. (2023). The Metaverse in Industry 5.0: A Human-Centric Approach towards Personalized Value Creation. *Encyclopedia*, 3(3), 1105–1120. 10.3390/encyclopedia3030080

Ntoutsi, E., Fafalios, P., Gadiraju, U., Iosifidis, V., Nejdl, W., Vidal, M. E., Ruggieri, S., Turini, F., Papadopoulos, S., Krasanakis, E., Kompatsiaris, I., Kinder-Kurlanda, K., Wagner, C., Karimi, F., Fernandez, M., Alani, H., Berendt, B., Kruegel, T., Heinze, C., & Staab, S. (2020). Bias in data-driven artificial intelligence systems—An introductory survey. *Wiley Interdisciplinary Reviews. Data Mining and Knowledge Discovery*, 10(3), e1356. 10.1002/widm.1356

Okaiyeto, S. A., Bai, J., & Xiao, H. (2023). Generative AI in education: To embrace it or not? *International Journal of Agricultural and Biological Engineering*, 16(3), 285–286. 10.25165/j.ijabe.20231603.8486

Quintans-Júnior, L. J., Gurgel, R. Q., Araújo, A. A. D. S., Correia, D., & Martins-Filho, P. R. (2023). ChatGPT: The new panacea of the academic world. *Revista da Sociedade Brasileira de Medicina Tropical*, 56, e0060–e2023. 10.1590/0037-8682-0060-202336888781

Radford, A., Wu, J., Child, R., Luan, D., Amodei, D., & Sutskever, I. (2019). Language models are unsupervised multitask learners. *OpenAI blog, 1*(8), 9.

Ramdurai, B., & Adhithya, P. (2023). The impact, advancements and applications of generative AI. *International Journal on Computer Science and Engineering*, 10(6), 1–8. 10.14445/23488387/IJCSE-V10I6P101

Rane, N. L., Anand, A., & Deepak, K. (2023). Evaluating the Selection Criteria of Formwork System (FS) for RCC Building Construction. *International Journal of Engineering Trends and Technology*, 71(3), 197–205. 10.14445/22315381/IJETT-V71I3P220

Rane, N. L., & Attarde, P. M. (2016). Application of value engineering in commercial building projects. *International Journal of Latest Trends in Engineering & Technology : IJLTET*, 6(3), 286–291.

Rathore, B. (2023). Future of textile: Sustainable manufacturing & prediction via chatgpt. *Eduzone: International Peer Reviewed/Refereed Multidisciplinary Journal, 12*(1), 52-62.

Rivas, P., & Zhao, L. (2023). Marketing with chatgpt: Navigating the ethical terrain of gpt-based chatbot technology. *AI, 4*(2), 375–384. 10.3390/ai4020019

Sætra, H. S. (2023). Generative AI: Here to stay, but for good? *Technology in Society*, 75, 102372. 10.1016/j.techsoc.2023.102372

Scheerder, A., Van Deursen, A., & Van Dijk, J. (2017). Determinants of Internet skills, uses and outcomes. A systematic review of the second-and third-level digital divide. *Telematics and Informatics*, 34(8), 1607–1624. 10.1016/j.tele.2017.07.007

Siau, K., & Wang, W. (2020). Artificial intelligence (AI) ethics: Ethics of AI and ethical AI. [JDM]. *Journal of Database Management*, 31(2), 74–87. 10.4018/JDM.2020040105

Su, J., & Yang, W. (2023). Unlocking the power of ChatGPT: A framework for applying generative AI in education. *ECNU Review of Education*, 6(3), 355–366. 10.1177/20965311231168423

Susarla, A., Gopal, R., Thatcher, J. B., & Sarker, S. (2023). The Janus effect of generative AI: Charting the path for responsible conduct of scholarly activities in information systems. *Information Systems Research*, 34(2), 399–408. 10.1287/isre.2023.ed.v34.n2

Susnjak, T. (2022). ChatGPT: The end of online exam integrity? *arXiv preprint arXiv:2212.09292*.

Thibault, M., Kivikangas, T., Roihankorpi, R., Pohjola, P., & Aho, M. (2023, October). Who am AI?: Mapping Generative AI Impact and Transformative Potential in Creative Ecosystem. In *Proceedings of the 26th International Academic Mindtrek Conference* (pp. 344-349). ACM. 10.1145/3616961.3617804

Thorp, H. H. (2023). ChatGPT is fun, but not an author. *Science*, 379(6630), 313–313. 10.1126/science.adg787936701446

Trajtenberg, M. (2018). *AI as the next GPT: a Political-Economy Perspective* (No. w24245). National Bureau of Economic Research.

Van Dijk, J. A. (2006). Digital divide research, achievements and shortcomings. *Poetics*, 34(4-5), 221–235. 10.1016/j.poetic.2006.05.004

Weidinger, L., Mellor, J., Rauh, M., Griffin, C., Uesato, J., Huang, P. S., & Gabriel, I. (2021). Ethical and social risks of harm from language models. *arXiv preprint arXiv:2112.04359*.

Wessel, M., Adam, M., Benlian, A., & Thies, F. (2023). Generative AI and its transformative value for digital platforms. *Journal of Management Information Systems*.

Zhuo, T. Y., Huang, Y., Chen, C., & Xing, Z. (2023). Red teaming chatgpt via jailbreaking: Bias, robustness, reliability and toxicity. *arXiv preprint arXiv:2301.12867*.

KEY TERMS AND DEFINITIONS

ChatGPT: A sister model of InstructGPT that has been trained to respond in-depth to prompts and follow instructions.

Dall-E: An AI system that can use a description in natural language to produce realistic visuals and artwork.

Generative Artificial Intelligence: A kind of artificial intelligence system that can generate text, images, audio, and synthetic data. It can produce fresh ideas and content, such as discussions, tales, pictures, films, and music.

GPT-4: OpenAI's multimodal big language model, known as Generative Pre-trained Transformer 4 (GPT-4), is the fourth model in its GPT foundation model series.

Humanoid Robots: A robot shaped like a human body. A sophisticated artificial device that resembles people.

Machine Learning: A subfield of computer science and artificial intelligence (AI) that concentrates on leveraging data and methods to allow AI to mimic human learning and progressively increase its accuracy.

Midjourney: A program and service for generative artificial intelligence created and maintained by Midjourney, Inc. Similar to OpenAI's DALL-E, it uses natural language prompts or descriptions to generate images. It is one of the technologies of the AI boom.

Siri: The built-in digital assistant that comes with Apple Inc.'s iOS, iPadOS, macOS, tvOS, audioOS, and visionOS operating systems. It uses voice commands, gesture-based control, focus monitoring, and a natural language user interface to answer questions, suggest actions, and route requests to a collection of Internet services.

Turnitin: An online similarity detection tool provided by Turnitin, LLC, an Advance Publications subsidiary.

WeChat: A Tencent-developed mobile payment, social media, and instant messaging software. It connects social networking, financial transactions, and communication on one platform, making it an essential aspect of millions of users' everyday lives in China and around the world.

Chapter 7
Foundations of Generative AI

Tina Babu
Alliance Univeraity, India

Rekha R. Nair
Alliance University, India

Ebin P. M.
Alliance University, India

ABSTRACT

The chapter delves into the foundations of generative artificial intelligence (AI), offering an introductory overview and a nuanced understanding of its basic principles, history, and evolution. It navigates through core technologies underpinning generative AI, including neural networks, machine learning models, and key algorithms. The introduction traces generative AI's roots, unraveling its historical trajectory. It progresses to elucidate fundamental concepts, exploring neural networks' structures, functionalities, and applications. The study examines diverse machine learning models and pivotal algorithms crucial to generative AI, shedding light on their roles in generating innovative outputs. This abstract encapsulates a comprehensive journey through generative AI's core elements, serving as a foundational guide for understanding its origins, principles, and technologies.

INTRODUCTION

Generative Artificial Intelligence (AI) has become a revolution that pushes the boundaries of what machines can create. This chapter introduces the basics of this technology, providing a better understanding of its foundations, history and basic technologies. The concept of generative artificial intelligence, its meaning and its difference from other technologies are being talked about for the first time in this world. Artificial intelligence approach. The chapter then traces its historical background, highlighting the key achievements and key points that paved the way for its transformation. This chapter also presents a variety of applications of generative AI in commercial, industrial and technical applications, as well as in creative fields such as art and music. Next, this chapter examines the basic technologies that power artificial intelligence, starting with neural networks (the basics). Different models and their roles in design are examined, including distribution, communication, and integration. We will examine various

DOI: 10.4018/979-8-3693-3278-8.ch007

machine learning techniques such as supervised learning, unsupervised learning, and additive learning and their importance in appropriate contexts.

In addition, this chapter provides an in-depth study of the generative algorithms themselves, including generative adversarial networks (GAN), variational autoencoders (VAE), autoregressive models, and diffusion models. This chapter also discusses its principles, advantages, and applications, providing a solid foundation for understanding and using this powerful technology.

What is Generative AI?

Generative Artificial Intelligence refers to a subfield of artificial intelligence that focuses on creating new knowledge, content, or educational models Waqas et al. (2023); Hughes et al. (2021) Unlike traditional machine learning methods such as classification or prediction, which aim to understand or describe existing objects, AI machines are designed to create new situations that act according to the structure and characteristics of the curriculum Chen et al. (2020); Kanbach et al. (2023).

Here are some key features of generative AI.

*   Data generation: Generative AI models can create new data models such as images, text, audio, or video based on the model learned from the curriculum Bandi et al. (2023).
*   Creativity and imagination: This model can demonstrate creativity by combining and reworking learning content in new ways to create original content.
*   Unsupervised learning: Most generative AI, such as generative adversarial networks (GAN) and variable autoencoders (VAE), rely on unsupervised learning algorithms that can be discovered without a clear map or target, patterns and distributions in the data Alqahtani et al. (2021).
*   Diverse applications: Generative AI has many applications, including image and video synthesis, text generation (such as creative writing, code generation), music production, knowledge development, and even molecular and chemical design Gupta et al. (2024).
*   Generative models: Generative AI relies on different types of models, such as autoregressive models (such as GPT languages), which capture training data from probability, propagation models (such as stable propagation for generating images), and GANs. distribution to learn to create new knowledge Bandi et al. (2023).

Generative artificial intelligence, which enables machines to create new and original content, has the potential to revolutionize research and development in fields such as arts and entertainment, offering new approaches to human-machine collaboration and creative exploration.

Generative AI distinguishes itself from other AI methodologies through several key characteristics:

*   Emphasis on Generation: Unlike conventional AI techniques such as machine learning and statistical models, which analyze existing data for predictions or insights, Generative AI focuses on generating novel data—such as images, text, audio, or video—that resembles training data but is unique and original Janiesch et al. (2021).
*   Unsupervised Learning: Many Generative AI methods, like generative adversarial networks (GAN) and variational autoencoders (VAE), heavily rely on unsupervised learning Alqahtani et al. (2021); Pavan Kumar and Jayagopal (2021).. This approach enables the model to learn the underlying structure and distribution of data without explicit guidance or labeling.

- Creativity and Imagination: Generative AI models showcase creativity by synthesizing learned concepts to produce novel content. This departure from traditional AI methods, primarily geared toward task optimization, allows for imaginative outputs Haase and Hanel, (2023).
- Probabilistic Modeling: Generative AI models adopt probabilistic modeling to predict the probability of outcomes in training data Bandi et al. (2023); Celard et al. (2023). This enables the creation of new scenarios similar to, yet different from, the training data. This probabilistic approach contrasts with decision models, which map inputs to outputs based on fixed rules or relationships Mishra et al. (2023).

Generative AI's ability to create new content and leverage creative resources represents a departure from traditional intelligence standards, offering exciting prospects for innovation and human-machine collaboration across various domains.

Historical Context

The early development and main points of artificial intelligence can be traced back to the mid-20th century, and its significant contributions and achievements have paved the way for the advancement of wisdom.

Foundational Work (1950s-1960)

In the 1950s and 1960s, pioneering efforts in information theory, cybernetics, and artificial intelligence set the stage for modern AI. Though the term "generative artificial intelligence" wasn't coined then, foundational concepts emerged, shaping the field's evolution.

- Information Theory and Probability Models: Claude Shannon The work of Data Science in the 1940s provided mathematical methods for understanding and evaluating data, providing the basis for appropriate standards and data compression techniques Condon and Mottus (2021); Shen et al. (2021). These concepts are important for developing models that can learn about the consequences of data distribution.
- Cybernetics and Feedback Systems: Cybernetics and Feedback Systems: Pioneered by Norbert Wiener in the 1940s and 1950s, the field of cybernetics explores the meaning of control, communication, and feedback in complex systems s K'uppers (2023). These ideas influenced the development of modifications and neural networks that would later play an important role in design.
- Early Neural Networks: In the 1940s, pioneers like Warren McCulloch and Walter Pitts laid the groundwork for neural networks Indrakumari et al. (2021). Frank Rosenblatt's perceptron, developed in the early 1950s, advanced this field by discerning patterns. Despite limitations, these early models paved the way for future deep learning and AI advancements M'uggenburg (2021).
- Sampling and Monte Carlo Methods: Development of Monte Carlo Methods by Stanislaw Ulam and John von Neumann in the 1940s and 1950s) and other researchers pioneered techniques for simulating and sampling probability distributions Sood et al. (2021). The second process is important for training the model and sampling from the distribution they have learned O'Connor (2023).

While the work during this period didn't directly generate modern designs, it laid the theoretical groundwork for studies in technological intelligence, data theory, neural networks, probabilistic models, and unsupervised learning. These concepts evolved into revolutionary designs and algorithms.

Symbolic AI and Expert Systems (1970s-1980s)

The 1970s and 1980s were a period of the rise of intellectual and professional characters. Below is a brief summary of the main developments during this period:

- Expert Systems and Knowledge Representation: Expertise emerged in the 1970s with the aim of capturing and understanding human knowledge and skills in a particular field, such as medicine Babu et al. (2021b,a). diagnostics or engineering. These methods are based on symbolic representations of information, often using rule-based methods or logical reasoning. Although not directly related to the design process, the development of cognitive representation models and the investigation of conceptual symbols form the basis of future studies in areas such as natural language processing and pattern recognition Babu and Nair (2023); Babu et al. (2020).
- Early Natural Language Processing (NLP): The field of NLP, which deals with the interaction between computers and human language, made significant progress during this period Johri et al. (2021). Scientists develop techniques to analyze, understand, and synthesize natural language, including rule-based techniques and statistics. Although NLP's initial capabilities were limited, they laid the foundation for future developments in the creation of language patterns and texts that will become an important part of artificial intelligence today.
- Probabilistic Reasoning and Bayesian Networks: In the 1970s and 1980s, there was interest and debate in Bayesian theory, which allows the representation and control of information u and Wu (2023). Here are the obvious and vague reasons for this. These developments formed the basis for graphical models that later played an important role in the development of models such as Bayesian networks and Markov random fields Kaviani and Sohn (2021).

While the era of intellectual and professional symbols may not be directly linked to design, it fosters knowledge development in representation, natural language processing, and thinking theory, alongside early neural network research. These advancements lay the groundwork for future innovations in programming languages, graphic design, and deep learning, shaping their integration into scientific endeavors.

Connectionist Models and Early Generative Systems (1980s-1990s)

During the 1980s and 1990s, artificial intelligence systems made great progress in combining models and early systems. This period led to increased interest in neural networks, which formed the basis for the further development of artificial intelligence.

- Boltzmann Machines: In 1986, Geoffrey Hinton and Terrence Sejnowski introduced the Boltzmann Machine, a type of neural network. Boltzmann's machines are able to learn the distribution of complexity and form the basis for further development of the design.

- Restricted Boltzmann Machines (RBMs): In the early 1990s, scientists introduced the Restricted Boltzmann Machine (RBM), several versions of the simple Boltzmann machine Savitha et al. (2020). RBMs are known for their good learning ability over high data distribution, making them suitable for tasks such as dimensionality reduction and ad hoc learning Decelle and Furtlehner (2021).
- Deep Belief Networks (DBNs): This is a major development that emerged in the late 2000s and is built on RBM principles. DBN combines multiple RBM layers to create a single representation of data, thus enabling more efficient unsupervised learning Sohn (2021).
- Autoencoders: Although not initially considered a part of artificial intelligence, autoencoders have recently gained attention for their ability to effectively learn representations of objects Chen et al. (2024). Autoencoders are used as learning models to reconstruct input data, and varieties such as variable autoencoders (VAEs) and denoising autoencoders have been developed.

Overall, the 1980s and 1990s were a period of discovery and innovation in artificial intelligence; networking models and systems first began to develop as the basis for future developments in the region. These developments paved the way for more designs to emerge in the following years.

Advancements in Deep Learning and Generative Models (2000s-Present)

In the 2000s, significant strides were made in deep learning, including the emergence of deep belief networks (DBNs) and Generative Adversarial Networks (GANs), introduced by Ian Goodfellow in 2014. GANs revolutionized AI by producing high-quality data, influencing tasks like image processing and text-to-image synthesis, fostering innovation in the field.

Applications and Use Cases

There are numerous applications and use cases for generative AI which include the following:

Creative Applications

Generative AI opens up exciting possibilities in creative applications, enabling machines to assist and even collaborate with humans to create original content across multiple platforms. . Here are some practical uses of AI:

- Art and image generation: Text-to-image rendering models such as DALL-E, Stable Diffusion, and Midjourney allow users to create unique and thoughtful designs by providing illustrative images or instructions Albaghajati et al. (2023). These templates; can create sketches, illustrations, design ideas and even screenshots to support artists, designers and creators.
- Creative writing and storytelling: Major language models such as GPT-3 and newer ChatGPT; can create creative writing and imagination, including stories, essays, poems, and even entire books Liu et al. (2023). These models can help writers develop ideas, plot development, character development, and even writing, and can encourage human-machine collaboration in creative writing.

- Music composition and generation: Generative AI models can learn from existing music and music. Create new songs, harmonies and complete songs in different formats. This format can help composers, songwriters, and musicians discover new musical ideas, make connections, or even create entire music or albums Bryan-Kinns et al. (2024).
- Game design and world-building: Generative AI can be used to create game environments, creating realistic landscapes, characters, and even stories Jain (2021); Machado et al. (2021). Game developers can use this model to enhance the creativity and diversity of the virtual world, resulting in a more engaging and unique gaming experience.
- Architectural and product design: Design can help architects, designers and engineers discover and develop new design ideas for buildings, products and structures. This model is able to take into account various constraints and needs when creating new and beautiful designs.
- Fashion and apparel design: Design skills can be used to create unique textile patterns, create outfits Fui-Hoon Nah et al. (2023) and even complete a fashion collection, helping designers in their search for new patterns and new models Guo et al. (2023).

Human creativity still exists, Productive AI is irreplaceable. It provides powerful tools to improve and develop the creative process, combining people and systems in different areas to create new ideas and thoughts.

Industrial and Commercial Applications

Generative artificial intelligence has found many applications in business and industry, supporting businesses to use its capabilities for a variety of purposes. Some of the important aspects of trade and commercialization of electronic products are:

- Data augmentation and synthetic data generation: Design can create information. Synthetic real world such as images, text or sensor data Bandi et al.
- (2023). Available for current magnification. data A dataset used to train machine learning models. This is especially true when real-world information is rare, expensive to obtain, or there are privacy concerns Bussell et al. (2023).
- Product design and prototyping: Generative AI can help design and create new products by generating a wealth of data. Create ideas, analyze trends and optimize for specific requirements or constraints Ooi et al. (2023). This increases the product development cycle and speeds up product development and iteration.
- Predictive maintenance and anomaly detection: Companies can always detect anomalies or deviations from existing patterns by relying on sensor data or training operations to create models, thus enabling predictive maintenance and fault detection on equipment or systems Babu and Nair (2023); Babu et al. (2021b).
- Personalized content and recommendations: Designers can create personalized content such as descriptions, product marketing, or recommendations based on customers' or segments' preferences and behaviors Ooi et al. (2023). This can improve customer engagement, conversion rates and overall user experience.

- Virtual assistants and chatbots: Language models and conversational artificial intelligence systems used by electronic devices can produce more responsive and meaningful responses for customers, sales or service Bavaresco et al. (2020). Supporting applications in virtual assistants and chatbots provide human interaction.
- Simulation and training environments: Generative AI can create realistic simulation environments, scenarios, or training data for a variety of applications, such as cybersecurity training, autonomous vehicle simulations, or training skilled workers in a challenging environment Chang and Kidman (2023), Anantrasirichai and Bull (2022).
- Molecular and drug design: Molecular design can help discover and design new molecules, drugs, or products by exploring the broad chemical space and creating competitive models based on those product needs or constraints Meyers et al. (2021).

By using the power of artificial intelligence, business and industry can open new opportunities, improve processes, improve customer service and gain efficiency in their business.

Scientific and Research Applications

Generative AI has many applications in scientific research; It allows scientists and researchers to explore new paths and accelerate discoveries. Some of the key research areas of generative AI include:

- Computational chemistry and materials science: Models have the capacity to explore broad chemical domains and create competitive models based on product requirements or limitations uhr and Sumpter (2022). This could lead to new materials, catalysts, and drug candidates and lead to breakthrough developments in areas such as energy storage, catalysis, and drug discovery.
- Biomedical research and healthcare: Design can be used to create synthetic patient data, allowing researchers to train AI models to perform tasks such as diagnosis, risk assessment or personalized treatment recommendations while protecting patient privacy Ramezanian-Panahi et al. (2022). Generative modeling can also help create realistic clinical images for training or data development purposes Kumar et al. (2023).
- Astrophysics and cosmology: Models can be used to simulate complex astrophysical events such as galaxy formation, black hole dynamics, or cosmic microwave background radiation patterns Meher and Panda (2021). These simulations help scientists explore and test hypotheses, identify patterns, and predict changes in the universe Harshvardhan et al. (2020).
- Climate modeling and environmental sciences: Modeling can be used to simulate complex climates, weather patterns, or environmental processes, allowing scientists to explore the impact of various factors, such as greenhouse gas emissions or destruction, on global climate patterns Hess et al. (2022).
- Particle physics and high-energy physics: Models can help simulate particle collisions, detector fields, or other events in high energy physics experiments, allowing researchers to study rare or complex events without requiring much knowledge of physics.

By using the power of artificial intelligence, scientists and researchers can make rapid discoveries, discover new ideas, and model complex processes, paving the way for new solutions and breakthroughs by improving understanding across multiple disciplines.

CORE TECHNOLOGIES

Neural Networks

Neural networks are a type of artificial intelligence that trains computers to analyze data in a way similar to the human brain. The neural networks classified as feed Forward Neural Networks, Convolutional Neural Networks and Recurrent Neural Networks.

Feed Forward Neural Networks

One of the simplest neural network designs ever created is the feedforward neural network. Information in this network propagates forward, starting from the entry node and ending at the exit node or hidden node (if any) as shown in Figure 1. There are no loops or circuits in the network. Compared to today, feedforward neural networks, which are a combination of recurrent and convolutional neural networks, are a simpler type of artificial neural network, initially created in the input process Hemeida et al. (2020).

Figure 1. Sample figure for Feed Forward Network

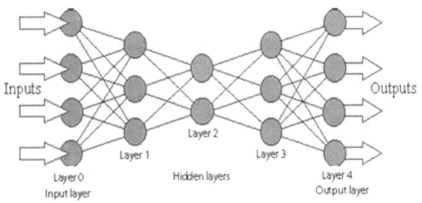

Caroline Clabaugh and Pang (2022)

The design of feedforward neural networks comprises three types of layers: the input layer, hidden layers, and output layer. Each layer consists of neurons, interconnected by weights. Neurons receive input and transmit it to the subsequent layers. The input layer's neuron count is determined by the input data's dimensionality Muruganandam et al. (2023).. Activation functions within primitive layers evaluate weighted inputs and transmit results to subsequent layers. Hidden layers, if present, perform intermediary processing. The output layer generates final outputs based on the network's inputs, with neuron count determined by the desired outputs. Weight adjustments, based on error rates, drive learning in neural networks Tripathi et al. (2021).

Convolutional Neural Networks

The deep learning network architecture that learns directly from data is called ConvNet or Convolutional neural network (CNN) Haarika et al. (2023) and is illustrated in Figure 2. When it comes to identifying objects, classes, and categories in images, CNNs are especially helpful in identifying patterns. CNNs are also good in categorizing signal, time-series, and audio data Mandal (2022)

Figure 2. Pictorial representations of CNN architecture

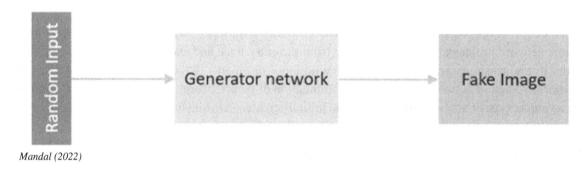

Mandal (2022)

All layers from twelve to hundreds of layers form a convolutional neural network, and each layer is trained to recognize different images. Filters with different resolutions are applied to each training image and the results of each convolution image are used as the input of the next process as shown in Figure 3. Simple features like brightness and edges can be starting points for filters, making it difficult to create unique features that describe objects Babu et al. (2021b).

Figure 3. Example of a network with many convolutional layers

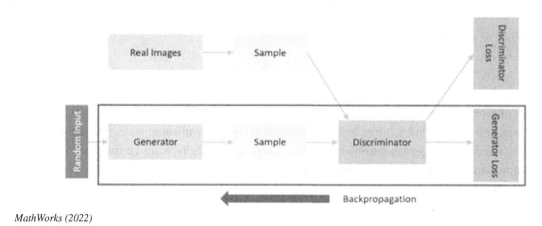

MathWorks (2022)

Each training image is passed through filters of different resolutions and the output of each convolution image is used as the input of this layer MathWorks (2022). Every hidden neuron in a layer of a CNN has the same shared weights and bias values. This means that all hidden neurons in all regions of the image detect the same features, such as edges or spots. As a result, the network changes the shape of objects in the image. For example, a network trained to recognize cars will be able to recognize cars regardless of where they are in the image MathWorks (2022).

The architecture of a CNN changes to categorization after learning information over multiple layers. The next-to-last layer is a fully connected layer that produces a vector of K dimensions with the probabilities for each class of an image that is being classed, where K is the number of classes that may be predicted R et al. (2022). To deliver the final classification output, the CNN architecture's last layer employs a classification layer.

Recurrent Neural Networks

A Recurrent Neural Network (RNN) is a neural network where the previous step's output becomes the current step's input, depicted in Figure 4. While the nervous system typically treats all inputs and outputs independently, predicting the next word often requires recalling the previous message. RNN addresses this challenge by employing a hidden algorithm, as pioneered by Nair et al. (2022). The hidden state within RNN retains sequence information, serving as its crucial component. Referred to as state memory, it preserves past network device memory. Utilizing the same parameters and processes across inputs and hidden layers streamlines output generation, minimizing parameter complexity compared to other neural networks.

Figure 4. Recurrent neural network [11]

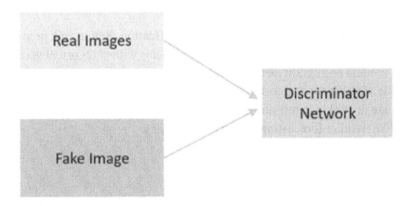

Machine Learning Models

A machine learning model is an algorithm designed to identify trends or draw conclusions from previously unseen data. The three categories of machine learning models are categorized into supervised learning, unsupervised learning, and reinforcement learning.

Supervised Learning

Supervised learning entails training a machine using labeled data to predict outcomes. When a profile is labeled correctly, it indicates that a portion of the entry is accurately positioned (Nair et al., 2023). Supervised learning operates as depicted in Figure 5. Training data serves as the supervisor, enabling computers to predict outputs accurately. This concept mirrors a student learning under a teacher's guidance. Models are trained using labeled datasets, then assessed using test data, a subset of the training set, to make predictions (Kishore et al., 2023).

Figure 5. The working of Supervised learning

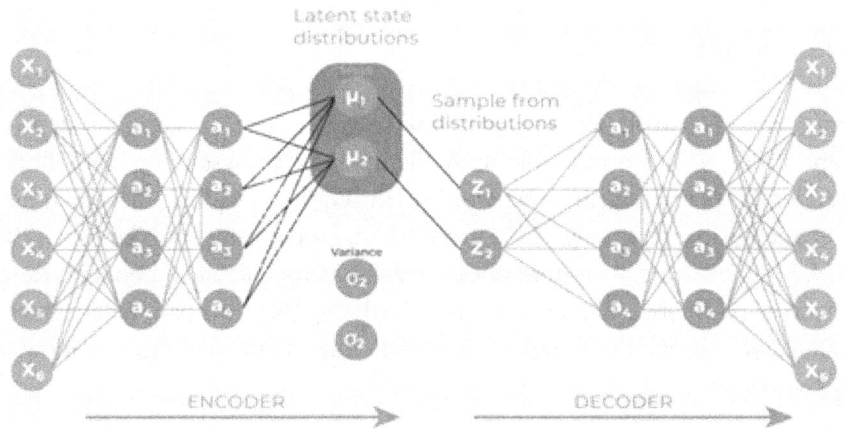

Javapoint (2022)

Supervised learning encompasses regression and classification. Regression predicts continuous variables like weather and market trends, while classification deals with categorical variables such as yes-no or male-female. Common regression methods include linear regression, regression tree, and polynomial regression. Notable classification algorithms comprise SVM, random forest, and logistic regression. These techniques are pivotal in determining outcomes based on input-output associations, contributing to various fields like weather forecasting and market analysis.

Unsupervised Learning

Unsupervised learning in artificial intelligence is a sort of machine learning that learns from data without human intervention as illustrated in Figure 6. Unlike supervised learning, unsupervised machine learning models are provided with unlabeled data, allowing patterns and patterns to be shown. Understanding without explicit guidance or instruction Babu and Nair (2023).

Figure 6. Unsupervised Learning

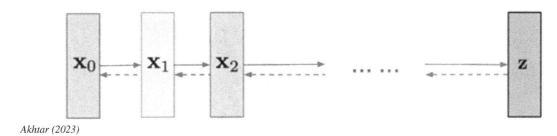

Akhtar (2023)

Algorithms learn from unlabeled input, without prior output or explicit goals. Unsupervised learning identifies patterns, similarities, or relationships in data to make decisions, particularly valuable for large, costly or difficult-to-manage datasets (Babu and Nair, 2023). Popular clustering algorithms include collaborative clustering and DBScan.

Reinforcement Learning

Reinforcement learning is a machine learning concept that rewards good behavior while punishing bad behavior. Generally speaking, learning support staff (teaching institutions) can explore and describe their environment, their work, and learn through trial and error Babu et al. (2021b). In reinforcement learning, developers create systems that reward desired behavior and punish undesirable behavior and is illustrated in Figure 7. This policy provides positive rewards for desirable behaviors to encourage employees to engage in those behaviors, while providing negative rewards for negative behaviors to discourage employees. This tells the agent to find the long-term reward and maximum sum to generate the best response Ernst and Louette (2024).

Figure 7. Reinforcement learning

Team (2022b)

Figure 8. Applications of reinforcement learning

Team (2022a)

Reinforcement learning is a broad learning methodology, and its principles can be applied to other modern technologies. Figure 8 illustrates a few of the applications of reinforcement learning.

Generative Algorithms

Generative Adversarial Networks(GANs)

Ian J. Goodfellow and co-authors introduced generative adversarial networks (GANs) in 2014. GANs are used to accomplish unsupervised learning tasks in machine learning. GAN is used in machine learning to complete tasks without observation control. Generator and Discriminator are utilized for image fusion shown in Figure 9. There are two patterns in data entry, recognized and learned. GAN has two networks called generator and discriminator. They compete with each other to analyze, capture, and replicate changes in the dataset. GANs can be used to create new models that emerge from the original dataset Nair et al. (2021).

- The Generator uses random noise samples to try to confuse the Discriminator, which is responsible for accurately discriminating between generated and actual data.
- This competitive interaction yields realistic, high-quality samples, propelling both networks forward.
- GANs are proven to be extremely adaptable artificial intelligence tools, as evidenced by their widespread application in image synthesis, style transfer, and text-to-image synthesis.
- GAN is a transformed generative modeling.

Generative Adversarial Networks (GANs) fall into three categories:

- Design: generative learning model Data It means using the probabilistic model to generate.
- Discriminator: The term adversarial refers to pitting one item against another. This means that, in the case of GANs, the generative result is compared to the real images in the dataset. A discriminator method is used to apply a model to discriminate between authentic and fraudulent images.
- Networks: Deep neural networks are used as artificial intelligence (AI) training techniques.

Figure 9. Generator and Discriminator are utilized for image fusion

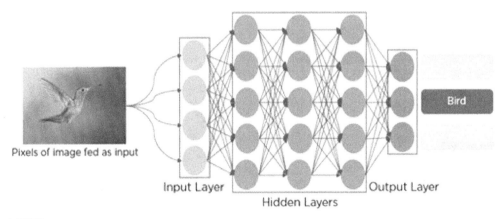

Nair et al. (2021)

- Generator: In GANs, the generator, a neural network, produces synthetic data to fool the discriminator, which learns to distinguish between real and fake samples. However, this can lead to biased training, as demonstrated in Nair et al. (2021). Utilizing noise, the generator generates patterns from random vectors, as depicted in Figure 10. Its primary goal is to produce output matching the actual data distribution over time. The model comprises noise input vectors, a generator network, a discriminator network, and a loss function to penalize misclassifications.

Figure 10. Generator identifying fake image

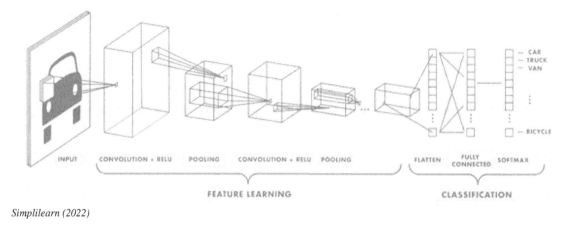

Simplilearn (2022)

The backpropagation approach adjusts each weight in the correct direction by assessing its impact on the output. It is also used to obtain gradients, which can be utilized to adjust the generator weights as shown in Figure 11.

Figure 11. Back propagation in GAN

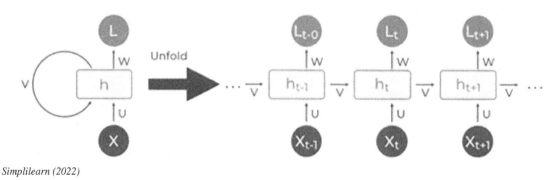

Simplilearn (2022)

- Discriminator: The discriminator, a neural network, discerns between real and fake data generated by the generator. It's trained on two distinct datasets: one comprising genuine examples like birds and humans, while the other consists of real data such as images. Throughout training, it distinguishes between real and generated information, adjusting its weights via backpropagation to minimize loss. The discriminator's role is crucial in preventing misidentification of real as fake and vice versa. It's depicted in Figure 12. (Source: Simplilearn, 2022).

Figure 12. Discriminator identifies fake and real image

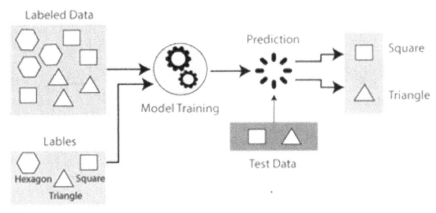

Simplilearn (2022)

Variational Autoencoders (VAEs)

Diederik P. Kingma and Max Welling from Google and Qualcomm proposed variable autoencoders in 2013. Variational autoencoders (VAE) are a good way to identify observations in the latent space and is illustrated in Figure 13. Instead of creating an encoder that outputs a number representing each possible state, we will create an encoder that identifies the probability of each possible behavior. It has a wide range of uses, including data compression and synthetic data synthesis Zhang et al. (2023).

Figure 13. Variational Autoencoders

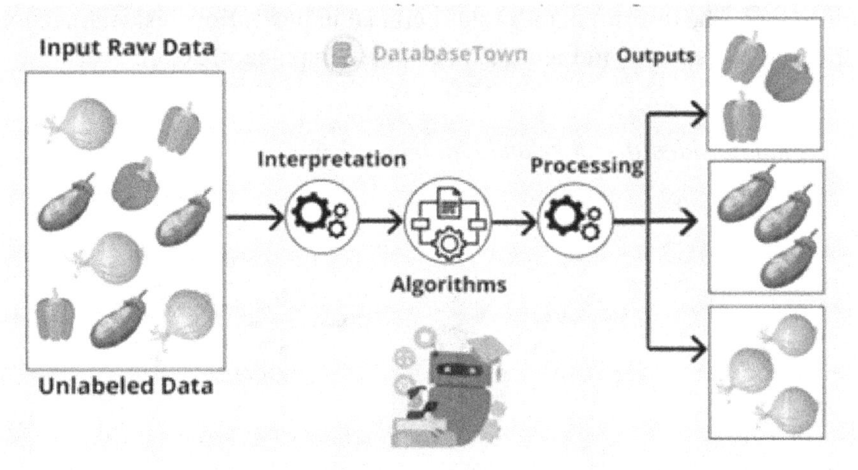

Geeksforgeeks (2022)

The encoder network transforms the raw data into the corresponding latent space. The encoder generates latent probability codes that allow VAE to provide latent distributions rather than single points in the latent space. The decoder network, on the other hand, retrieves the sample from the central distribution and reconfigures it in the data center. During the training process, the model refines the encoder and decoder parameters to reduce the reconstruction loss, which is the difference between the input data and the decoded output Zhang et al. (2023b).

The aim is not only to create a correct structure, but also to make the latent space suitable for a certain distribution. This process requires a balance between two main points: the reconstruction and the time constant, usually represented by the Kullback-Leibler difference. Reconstruction forces the model to accurately reconstruct the input, while the array supports the latent space to follow the chosen distribution, preventing overfitting and promoting generalization. By varying these parameters during training, VAE learns how to encode input data into a useful spatial representation. The improved secret code captures the underlying hardware and structure of the data, allowing reorganization. The resulting properties of the latent space also allow custom models to be created by randomly selecting points from the distribution of the subject Geeksforgeeks (2022)

Autoregressive Models

Autoregressive models are statistical models used to predict future value. This analysis is used when there is a correct relationship between the value of time and its previous value. after that. Autoregressive modeling forecasts future behavior only based on historical data Hu et al. (2023). Use a linear combination of predictors to forecast the variable of interest in a multiple regression model. With the autoregressive model, we use linear regression of past values of the variable to predict the variable of interest. The term autoregressive indicates that the variable regresses on itself. The expression for an autoregressive model of order p is:

$$y_1 = c + \phi_1 y_{t-1} + \phi_2 y_{t-2} + \ldots + \phi_p y_{t-p} + \varepsilon_t$$

where white noise is represented by ε_t. Similar to multiple regression, but using y_t lag values as predictors. This is known as an autoregressive model of order p, or AR(p) model. Autoregressive models exhibit remarkable versatility in their ability to accommodate a diverse array of time series patterns. Figure 8.5 displays two series: one from an AR(1) model and the other from an AR(2) model. Variations in the parameters $\phi_1, \ldots, \phi_p$ provide distinct time series patterns. Only the series' scale will be altered by the variance of the error term ε_t; the patterns remain same Meitz et al.(2023).

Diffusion Models

Advanced machine learning techniques known as diffusion models create one-of-a-kind, high-quality data by gradually adding noise to a dataset and then discovering how to erase it and is illustrated in Figure 14. With this creative method, they may produce outputs that are exact, ranging from coherent text sequences to lifelike visuals. The idea of progressively losing data quality and then reconstructing it in its original form or transforming it into something else is essential to their operation Croitoru et al. (2023). This method offers fresh opportunities in fields like personalized AI assistants, driverless cars, and medical imaging while also improving the accuracy of generated data.

Figure 14. Gradually add Gaussian noise and then reverse

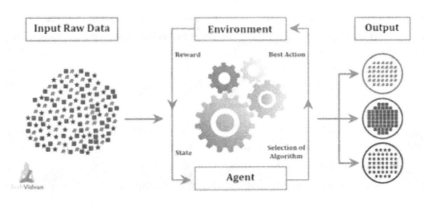

Weng (2022)

Diffusion models operate on a two-phase system. They systematically reverse this process after first adding noise to the dataset, which is essential to the forward diffusion process. This is a thorough explanation of the diffusion model lifetime.

AI TEXT GENERATION TOOLS

AI text generating tools produce and offer pre-made templates for producing excellent content, such as Blog entries, postings on social media, Email correspondence, Metadata summaries, Descriptions of products slogans, etc Xarhoulacos et al. (2021). They are helpful for business procedures since they also provide commercial rights and cooperation opportunities for the information created. If you would want to compare and learn more about these tools, please feel free to read our post on generative AI tools.

Businesses can create error-free texts, free up staff time for creative initiatives, and expedite workflows by utilising AI text generating solutions Bendel (2023). AI text generators may be applied in a variety of ways in business, including

- Content Generation: Various types of content may be produced using an AI writer tool to serve certain business functions like blog entries according to keywords and the ideal word count, product descriptions derived from information regarding its attributes and advantages, posts on social media, advertising campaigns,
- Text Synopsis: Longer writings can be summarised by using an AI writer. They provide a number of options for producing material, including producing newsletters, condensing papers from inside the firm, helping teachers create lesson plans by giving them access to condensed versions of sources, encouraging literature reviews in research settings, among many other things
- Material optimized for search engines: AI text generators support businesses in selecting the title, Meta description, and keywords for an article, helping to improve its search engine optimisation. By using these tools, one may find the most popular subject clusters and their number of searched keywords, as well as the highest-ranking URLs that will boost SEO exposure by obtaining more hits than just a few Dwivedi et al. (2023).

Generative Images

The field of picture creation has undergone a revolution thanks to generative AI, which allows computers to produce realistic and eye-catching images on their own Li et al. (2023). These AI algorithms are able to create fresh, original images that exhibit astounding creativity by recognising patterns in large databases. Since generated AI pictures are created exclusively by the AI system, they do not require copyright or privacy considerations Harbinja et al. (2023). Because these photos are self-generated and don't rely on outside resources, they are protected by copyright as shown in Figure 15. Different Generative AI platforms are available such as Leonardo.ai, Craiyon, DALL·E, Deep Dream and Artbreeder. Leonardo.ai produces realistic and high quality images according to the demands of designers. Deep Dream enhances patterns and characteristics in pre-existing photos using a visual feedback loop to produce a bizarre and dreamlike appearance. Deep Dream became well-known for its distinctive and hallucinogenic outputs, which made it a favourite among artists looking for unusual and hallucinogenic visuals. Excellent crafts are made by artbreeders, who also experiment with creative variants. It enables users to create fresh and original visual compositions by remixing and combining existing photos. It is ideal for artists and hobbyists who want to create a variety of unique and personalised artwork since it emphasises user participation and interactivity Zhang et al. (2023a).

Figure 15. Images created by Leonardo.ai that aesthetically convey feminisms

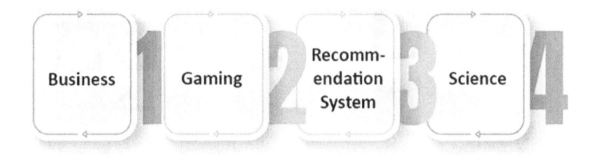

Text to Image Conversion

One interesting use of picture generative AI models is text-to-image synthesis, which translates written descriptions into equivalent visual representations. To create remarkable outcomes, this approach combines picture generative models with natural language processing (NLP) techniques Frolov et al. (2021). Conditional GANs for Text-to-Image: Text embeddings and GANs have been successfully combined by researchers, enabling the production of pictures conditioned on particular textual input. This implies that the model may provide extremely precise and particular visuals given a thorough textual description Zhang and Schomaker (2024) Text-to-Image Synthesis Applications: Applications for text-to-image technology may be found in a variety of industries, including virtual reality, e-commerce, and content production. For example, this technology can create product pictures from text descriptions in e-commerce, which helps with speedier product creation and design Hartwig et al. (2024).

Text-to-image synthesis and picture generative AI models constitute a potent combination of computer vision, natural language processing, and artificial intelligence. These technologies have the power to completely transform a number of sectors by fostering creativity and expediting the process of creating content. In the near future, we may anticipate even more incredible discoveries as research keeps pushing the limits of these technologies. The influence of picture generative AI models is influencing the direction of creativity and innovation, whether it is by producing original visual representations or producing realistic images from text descriptions.

Generative AI is most commonly used for producing synthetic pictures that mimic actual ones Feuerriegel et al. (2024). For example, a work titled "Progressive Growing of GANs for Improved Quality, Stability, and Variation" a distinguished research scientist at NVIDIA Research. He showed how to create lifelike images of human faces in this study as illustrated in Figure 16. After being trained on real-world celebrity images as input data, the model generated fresh, lifelike images of humans with faces that resembled celebrities in some ways. Let's say that although the girl in the second image from the top right appears to resemble Beyoncé, it is clearly not the pop diva.

Figure 16. Artificially produced lifelike pictures of fictional persons

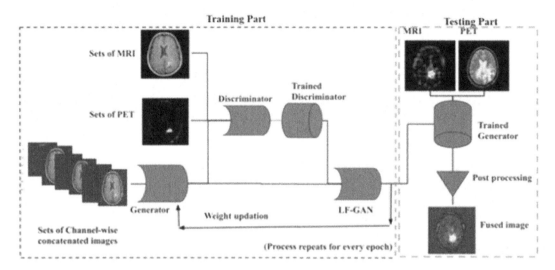

Generative Audio and Video

Generative AI is also capable of processing audio data. This requires first converting audio inputs into spectrograms, which are two-dimensional representations that resemble images Bauer et al. (2024). This makes it possible to use algorithms like CNNs that are expressly made to operate with pictures for our audio-related purpose. This method may be used to alter the style/genre of a piece of music or the voices of performers. You may "transfer" a piece of music from a jazz to a classical style, for instance. To improve Apple's audio capabilities, the British firm AI Music was purchased by Apple in 2022. With the help of the startup's technology, soundtracks may be made using free public music that is analysed by the system's AI algorithms. The primary objective is to do audio analysis and produce "dynamic" soundtracks that are responsive to user interaction. That being stated, the music can alter based on the mood of the game setting or the level of difficulty of the user's gym session.

Since a video is a collection of moving visual pictures, it seems sense that videos may be created and altered in a manner similar to that of photos. Video frame prediction is one of the most common application. GANs may be used to generate and forecast the next frame in a sequence if we know what the current frame in the game looks like Jatana et al. (2024). NVIDIA introduced DLSS, a breakthrough in generative AI (Deep Learning Super Sampling). Neural graphics technology is used to recreate visuals. All GeForce RTX GPUs perform better thanks to the third generation of DLSS, which uses artificial intelligence (AI) to generate completely new frames and show greater quality through image reconstruction. In essence, it converts lower resolution input into higher resolution frames for output. To rebuild native-quality pictures, DLSS samples many low-resolution images and applies motion information and feedback from earlier frames.

By determining the identity of each individual pixel and then producing a higher resolution of it, a GAN may be used to transform a low quality image into one with a considerably greater resolution. Images from vintage films can be improved by upscaling them to 4K resolution and higher, producing 60 frames per second (rather than 23), and introducing colour to black and white films.

Even though there is an abundance of data being created on a constant basis in our environment, the challenge of obtaining sufficient data to train machine learning models still exists. "Enough data" refers to a sufficient amount of high-quality data. It takes a lot of effort, money, and time to get enough samples for training—often unattainable. Synthetic data, which is amenable to generative AI, may hold the key to solving this issue. NVIDIA is developing generative AI technologies at a rapid pace. A neural network that has been trained on city movies to represent urban surroundings is one of them. Because they may employ produced virtual world training datasets for pedestrian identification, such artificially made data can aid in the development of self-driving automobiles.

The three models that make up AudioCraft are MusicGen, AudioGen, and EnCodec. Whereas AudioGen, trained on public sound effects, creates audio from text prompts, MusicGen generates music from text prompts using music that is owned and specially licenced by Meta. We are happy to present an enhanced version of our EnCodec decoder today that enables the creation of music with better quality and fewer artefacts. We're also providing our pre-trained AudioGen models, which enable you to create sound effects and ambient noises such as barking dogs, honking vehicles, and footfall on wood floors. Lastly, all of the AudioCraft model weights and code are available for download.

Audio has looked to lag behind while generative AI for text, video, and graphics has generated a lot of interest. There is work available, but it is not easily playable due to its high complexity and lack of openness. Any type of high-fidelity audio generation needs modelling intricate signals and patterns at different sizes. Since music is made up of both local and long-range patterns—from a suite of notes to a global musical framework with several instruments—it is undoubtedly the most difficult sort of audio to make.

The devices in the AudioCraft series are user-friendly and able to consistently provide high-quality audio over an extended period of time. Compared to previous work in the field, we simplify the overall design of generative models for audio with AudioCraft. This allows users to play with the models that Meta has been developing for the past few years, push the boundaries, and create their own custom models. AudioCraft may be used for generation, compression, sound, and music in one location. People that wish to create better compression algorithms, music generators, or sound generators may do it all inside the same code base and build upon the work of others since it is simple to reuse and expand upon. It is hardly surprise that Deep Neural Networks (DNNs) have transformed the way we approach audio data modelling, given their remarkable skill in processing extremely complex modalities like these Younis et al. (2024). With sufficient data, deep learning algorithms may now be trained to automatically extract and represent information from audio signals. Significant advancements in voice recognition and several other discriminative AI applications have resulted from this change.

However, generative AI for audio and voice data comes with some significant difficulties. One reason for this is that the information included in these signals is abstracted at several levels; in the end, a generative model would allow for the editing and control of this information. For instance, spoken audio signals are rich in both more general information such as prosody (the rhythm and intonation of speech), emotional intonation, and speaker intents, as well as more particular information at the level of individual phonetic or acoustic components.

ETHICAL CHALLENGES

Significant advancements in computer vision, natural language processing, creative content creation, and other fields have been made possible by generative artificial intelligence (Generative AI) approaches that leverage deep learning, neural networks, and other advanced machine learning techniques. However, as use of Generative AI continues to rise quickly, serious ethical questions about bias, accountability, transparency, and unexpected social effects are also raised by its tremendous capabilities Xiaotong and Peng (2024)These problems must be addressed proactively.

Eight categories are used in one paper to classify the many moral and ethical issues raised by AI:

- Inability to provide an explanation
- Including prejudice from humans
- Training data's inherent bias towards English and Europe
- Absence of regulation and its effects both now and in the future
- Fear of the end of the world
- Developers' lack of responsibility
- The effects on the environment and labour, in the context of data mining and the impending machine vs human productivity war.

The continuation of unfair bias due to errors in the training data or algorithms is one of the most urgent problems with Generative AI systems Sai et al. (2024). Subsequent paragraphs, however, are indented. Without proper thought, biased data can teach models about race, gender, age, ethnicity, and other cultural biases, amplifying them. This has unfair and discriminatory effects that can negatively affect both people and groups. It is frequently impossible to completely understand the reasoning behind the judgements and predictions made by sophisticated Generative AI models, such as deep neural networks. However, in order to guarantee openness, track responsibility, and prevent harm, it is crucial to comprehend model behaviours, particularly for sensitive applications in fields like finance, healthcare, and criminal justice.

Important areas of focus for enabling responsible Generative AI include of:

- Encouraging the involvement of many viewpoints in the creation and management of Generative AI.
- Encouraging further research to develop methods and best practices for mistake management, explainability, transparency, and bias identification and mitigation.
- Promoting the creation of regulatory policies to guarantee accountability and stop the harm caused by the unrestrained use of Generative AI.
- Encouraging moral engineering across the lifespan of the Generative AI model with an emphasis on safety, openness, and justice.

While reducing dangers from abuse and unforeseen effects, this revolutionary technology has the potential to improve society in many ways when ethics are actively included into the Generative AI application development process. It is the common duty of all involved parties to guide the Generative AI revolution towards equitable and advantageous results for all.

CONCLUSION

In this chapter, we have explored the foundations of Generative AI, a revolutionary field that empowers machines to create original content and push the boundaries of creativity. From understanding the core concepts and historical milestones to delving into the underlying technologies and algorithms, we have gained a comprehensive understanding of this cutting-edge domain. We have seen how neural networks, machine learning models, and generative algorithms like GANs, VAEs, and diffusion models form the bedrock of Generative AI. By learning the underlying patterns and distributions within data, these models can generate new, unique instances that mimic the characteristics of the training data.

As we move forward, the applications of Generative AI continue to expand, from creative domains like art, music, and writing to industrial applications, scientific research, and beyond. However, with great power comes great responsibility, and we must address the challenges of bias, privacy, and ethical considerations that accompany this transformative technology.Ultimately, Generative AI represents a paradigm shift in human-machine collaboration, enabling us to explore uncharted territories of creativity and innovation. With the power of Python and its rich ecosystem of libraries, we are well-equipped to harness the potential of Generative AI and shape a future where machines augment and amplify human ingenuity.

REFERENCES

Akhtar, Z. (2023). *Unsupervised learning: Types, applications & advantages*. Database Town. https://databasetown.com/unsupervised-learning-types-applications/ [Accessed: 26-03-2024].

Albaghajati, Z. M., Bettaieb, D. M., & Malek, R. B. (2023). Exploring text-to-image application in architectural design: Insights and implications. Architecture. *Structures and Construction*, 3(4), 475–497. 10.1007/s44150-023-00103-x

Alqahtani, H., Kavakli-Thorne, M., & Kumar, G. (2021). Applications of generative adversarial networks (gans): An updated review. *Archives of Computational Methods in Engineering*, 28(2), 525–552. 10.1007/s11831-019-09388-y

Anantrasirichai, N., & Bull, D. (2022). Artificial intelligence in the creative industries: A review. *Artificial Intelligence Review*, 55(1), 589–656. 10.1007/s10462-021-10039-7

Babu, T., Gupta, D., Singh, T., Hameed, S., Zakariah, M., & Alotaibi, Y. A. (2021a). Robust magnification independent colon biopsy grading system over multiple data sources. *Computers, Materials & Continua*, 69(1), 99–128. 10.32604/cmc.2021.016341

Babu, T., & Nair, R. R. (2023). Colon cancer prediction with transfer learning and k-means clustering. In Frontiers of ICT in Healthcare [Springer.]. *Proceedings of EAIT*, 2022, 191–200.

Babu, T., Singh, T., & Gupta, D. (2020). Colon cancer prediction using 2dreca segmentation and hybrid features on histopathology images. *IET Image Processing*, 14(16), 4144–4157. 10.1049/iet-ipr.2019.1717

Babu, T., Singh, T., Gupta, D., & Hameed, S. (2021b). Colon cancer prediction on histological images using deep learning features and bayesian optimized svm. *Journal of Intelligent & Fuzzy Systems*, 41(5), 5275–5286. 10.3233/JIFS-189850

Bandi, A., Adapa, P. V. S. R., & Kuchi, Y. E. V. P. K. (2023). The power of generative ai: A review of requirements, models, input–output formats, evaluation metrics, and challenges. *Future Internet*, 15(8), 260. 10.3390/fi15080260

Bauer, A., Trapp, S., Stenger, M., Leppich, R., Kounev, S., Leznik, M., Chard, K., & Foster, I. (2024). Comprehensive exploration of synthetic data generation: A survey. arXiv preprint arXiv:2401.02524.

Bavaresco, R., Silveira, D., Reis, E., Barbosa, J., Righi, R., Costa, C., Antunes, R., Gomes, M., Gatti, C., Vanzin, M., Junior, S. C., Silva, E., & Moreira, C. (2020). Conversational agents in business: A systematic literature review and future research directions. *Computer Science Review*, 36, 100239. 10.1016/j.cosrev.2020.100239

Bendel, O. (2023). Image synthesis from an ethical perspective. *AI & Society*, 1–10.

Bryan-Kinns, N., Zhang, B., Zhao, S., & Banar, B. (2024). Exploring variational auto-encoder architectures, configurations, and datasets for generative music explainable ai. *Machine Intelligence Research*, 21(1), 29–45. 10.1007/s11633-023-1457-1

Budhwar, P., Chowdhury, S., Wood, G., Aguinis, H., Bamber, G. J., Beltran, J. R., Boselie, P., Lee Cooke, F., Decker, S., DeNisi, A., Dey, P. K., Guest, D., Knoblich, A. J., Malik, A., Paauwe, J., Papagiannidis, S., Patel, C., Pereira, V., Ren, S., & Varma, A. (2023). Human resource management in the age of generative artificial intelligence: Perspectives and research directions on chatgpt. *Human Resource Management Journal*, 33(3), 606–659. 10.1111/1748-8583.12524

Bussell, C., Ehab, A., Hartle-Ryan, D., & Kapsalis, T. (2023). Generative ai for immersive experiences: Integrating text-to-image models in vr-mediated co-design workflows. In *International Conference on Human-Computer Interaction,* (pp. 380–388). Springer. 10.1007/978-3-031-36004-6_52

Caroline Clabaugh, D. M., & Pang, J. (2022). *Neural networks – architecture - feed-forward networks*. Stanford. https://cs.stanford.edu/people/eroberts/courses/soco/projects/neural-networks/Architecture/feedforward. html

Celard, P., Iglesias, E. L., Sorribes-Fdez, J. M., Romero, R., Vieira, A. S., & Borrajo, L. (2023). A survey on deep learning applied to medical images: From simple artificial neural networks to generative models. *Neural Computing & Applications*, 35(3), 2291–2323. 10.1007/s00521-022-07953-436373133

Chang, C.-H., & Kidman, G. (2023). The rise of generative artificial intelligence (ai) language models-challenges and opportunities for geographical and environmental education. *International Research in Geographical and Environmental Education*, 32(2), 85–89. 10.1080/10382046.2023.2194036

Chen, X., Ding, M., Wang, X., Xin, Y., Mo, S., Wang, Y., Han, S., Luo, P., Zeng, G., & Wang, J. (2024). Context autoencoder for self-supervised representation learning. *International Journal of Computer Vision*, 132(1), 208–223. 10.1007/s11263-023-01852-4

Chen, X., Xie, H., Zou, D., & Hwang, G.-J. (2020). Application and theory gaps during the rise of artificial intelligence in education. *Computers and Education: Artificial Intelligence*, 1, 100002. 10.1016/j.caeai.2020.100002

Condon, D. M. and Mottus, R. (2021). A role for information theory in personality modeling, assessment, and judgment. In *Measuring and modeling persons and situations*. Elsevier.

Croitoru, F.-A., Hondru, V., Ionescu, R. T., & Shah, M. (2023). Diffusion models in vision: A survey. *IEEE Transactions on Pattern Analysis and Machine Intelligence*, 45(9), 10850–10869. 10.1109/TPAMI.2023.326198837030794

Decelle, A., & Furtlehner, C. (2021). Restricted boltzmann machine: Recent advances and mean-field theory. *Chinese Physics B*, 30(4), 040202. 10.1088/1674-1056/abd160

Dwivedi, Y. K., Kshetri, N., Hughes, L., Slade, E. L., Jeyaraj, A., Kar, A. K., Baabdullah, A. M., Koohang, A., Raghavan, V., Ahuja, M., Albanna, H., Albashrawi, M. A., Al-Busaidi, A. S., Balakrishnan, J., Barlette, Y., Basu, S., Bose, I., Brooks, L., Buhalis, D., & Wright, R. (2023). "so what if chatgpt wrote it?" multidisciplinary perspectives on opportunities, challenges and implications of generative conversational ai for research, practice and policy. *International Journal of Information Management*, 71, 102642. 10.1016/j.ijinfomgt.2023.102642

Ernst, D., & Louette, A. (2024). Introduction to reinforcement learning. Feuerriegel, S., Hartmann, J., Janiesch, C., and Zschech, P. (2024). Generative ai. *Business & Information Systems Engineering*, 66(1), 111–126.

Frolov, S., Hinz, T., Raue, F., Hees, J., & Dengel, A. (2021). Adversarial text-to-image synthesis: A review. *Neural Networks*, 144, 187–209. 10.1016/j.neunet.2021.07.01934500257

Fuhr, A. S., & Sumpter, B. G. (2022). Deep generative models for materials discovery and machine learning-accelerated innovation. *Frontiers in Materials*, 9, 865270. 10.3389/fmats.2022.865270

Fui-Hoon Nah, F., Zheng, R., Cai, J., Siau, K., & Chen, L. (2023). *Generative ai and chatgpt: Applications, challenges, and ai-human collaboration*. geeksforgeeks. https://www.geeksforgeeks. org/ variational-autoencoders/

Guo, Z., Zhu, Z., Li, Y., Cao, S., Chen, H., & Wang, G. (2023). Ai assisted fashion design: A review. *IEEE Access : Practical Innovations, Open Solutions*.

Gupta, P., Ding, B., Guan, C., & Ding, D. (2024). Generative ai: A systematic review using topic modelling techniques. *Data and Information Management*, 8(2), 100066. 10.1016/j.dim.2024.100066

Haarika, R., Babu, T., & Nair, R. R. (2023). Insect classification framework based on a novel fusion of high-level and shallow features. *Procedia Computer Science*, 218, 338–347. 10.1016/j.procs.2023.01.016

Haase, J., & Hanel, P. H. (2023). Artificial muses: Generative artificial intelligence chatbots have risen to human-level creativity. *Journal of Creativity*, 33(3), 100066. 10.1016/j.yjoc.2023.100066

Harbinja, E., Edwards, L., & McVey, M. (2023). Governing ghostbots. *Computer Law & Security Report*, 48, 105791. 10.1016/j.clsr.2023.105791

Harshvardhan, G., Gourisaria, M. K., Pandey, M., & Rautaray, S. S. (2020). A comprehensive survey and analysis of generative models in machine learning. *Computer Science Review*, 38, 100285. 10.1016/j. cosrev.2020.100285

Hartwig, S., Engel, D., Sick, L., Kniesel, H., Payer, T., & Ropinski, T. (2024). *Evaluating text to image synthesis: Survey and taxonomy of image quality metrics*. arXiv preprint arXiv:2403.11821.

Hemeida, A., Hassan, S., Mohamed, A., Alkhalaf, S., Mahmoud, M., Senjyu, T., El-Din, A., & Alsayyari, A. (2020). Nature-inspired algorithms for feed-forward neural network classifiers: A survey of one decade of research. *Ain Shams Engineering Journal*, 11(3), 659–675. 10.1016/j.asej.2020.01.007

Hess, P., Drüke, M., Petri, S., Strnad, F. M., & Boers, N. (2022). Physically constrained generative adversarial networks for improving precipitation fields from earth system models. *Nature Machine Intelligence*, 4(10), 828–839. 10.1038/s42256-022-00540-1

Hu, C., Ji, Y., & Ma, C. (2023). Joint two-stage multi-innovation recursive least squares parameter and fractional-order estimation algorithm for the fractional-order input nonlinear output-error autoregressive model. *International Journal of Adaptive Control and Signal Processing*, 37(7), 1650–1670. 10.1002/acs.3593

Hughes, R. T., Zhu, L., & Bednarz, T. (2021). Generative adversarial networks–enabled human–artificial intelligence collaborative applications for creative and design industries: A systematic review of current approaches and trends. *Frontiers in Artificial Intelligence*, 4, 604234. 10.3389/frai.2021.60423433997773

Indrakumari, R., Poongodi, T., & Singh, K. (2021). *Introduction to deep learning. Advanced Deep Learning for Engineers and Scientists: A Practical Approach.*

Jain, R. (2021). Dreamscape: Using ai to create speculative vr environments. In *Proceedings of the Future Technologies Conference (FTC) 2020*. Springer.

Janiesch, C., Zschech, P., & Heinrich, K. (2021). Machine learning and deep learning. *Electronic Markets*, 31(3), 685–695. 10.1007/s12525-021-00475-2

Jatana, N., Wadhwa, D., Singh, N. K., Hassen, O. A., Gupta, C., Darwish, S. M., Mohammed, S. M., Farhan, D. A., & Abdulhussein, A. A. (2024). Future frame prediction using generative adversarial networks. *Karbala International Journal of Modern Science*, 10(1), 2. 10.33640/2405-609X.3338

Javapoint (2022). *Supervised machine learning*. Javapoint. https://www.javatpoint.com/supervised -machine-learning

Johri, P., Khatri, S. K., Al-Taani, A. T., Sabharwal, M., Suvanov, S., & Kumar, A. (2021). Natural language processing: History, evolution, application, and future work. In *Proceedings of 3rd International Conference on Computing Informatics and Networks: ICCIN 2020*. Springer. 10.1007/978-981-15-9712-1_31

K̈uppers, E. U. (2023). Cybernetic systems in practice. In *A Transdisciplinary Introduction to the World of Cybernetics: Basics, Models, Theories and Practical Examples*. Springer.

Kanbach, D. K., Heiduk, L., Blueher, G., Schreiter, M., & Lahmann, A. (2023). The genai is out of the bottle: Generative artificial intelligence from a business model innovation perspective. *Review of Managerial Science*, 1–32.

Kaviani, S., & Sohn, I. (2021). Application of complex systems topologies in artificial neural networks optimization: An overview. *Expert Systems with Applications*, 180, 115073. 10.1016/j.eswa.2021.115073

Kishore, S., Nair, R. R., Mehra, V., & Babu, T. (2023). A generalized framework for brain tumor and pneumonia detection using streamlite application. In *2023 4th International Conference for Emerging Technology (INCET)*. IEEE.

Kumar, Y., Koul, A., Singla, R., & Ijaz, M. F. (2023). Artificial intelligence in disease diagnosis: A systematic literature review, synthesizing framework and future research agenda. *Journal of Ambient Intelligence and Humanized Computing*, 14(7), 8459–8486. 10.1007/s12652-021-03612-z35039756

Li, J., Cao, H., Lin, L., Hou, Y., Zhu, R., & Ali, A. E. (2023). *User experience design professionals' perceptions of generative artificial intelligence*. arXiv preprint arXiv:2309.15237.

Liu, Y., Han, T., Ma, S., Zhang, J., Yang, Y., Tian, J., He, H., Li, A., He, M., Liu, Z., Wu, Z., Zhao, L., Zhu, D., Li, X., Qiang, N., Shen, D., Liu, T., & Ge, B. (2023). Summary of chatgpt-related research and perspective towards the future of large language models. *Meta-Radiology*, 1(2), 100017. 10.1016/j.metrad.2023.100017

M˙uggenburg, J. (2021). From learning machines to learning humans: how cybernetic machine models inspired experimental pedagogies. *History of Education, 50*(1), 112–133.

Machado, P., Romero, J., & Greenfield, G. (2021). *Artificial intelligence for designing games. Artificial Intelligence and the Arts: Computational Creativity.* Artistic Behavior, and Tools for Creatives.

Mandal, M. (2022). *Introduction to convolutional neural networks.* Analytics Vidhya. https://www .analyticsvidhya.com/blog/2021/05/convolutional-neural-networks-cnn/

MathWorks. (2022). *What is a convolutional neural network?* Mathworks. https://www.mathworks.com/ discovery/convolutional-neural-network.html#:~ text=A%20convolutional%20neural%20network%20 (CNN,%2Dseries%2C%20and%20signal%20data [Accessed: 26-03-2024].

Meher, S. K., & Panda, G. (2021). Deep learning in astronomy: A tutorial perspective. *The European Physical Journal. Special Topics*, 230(10), 2285–2317. 10.1140/epjs/s11734-021-00207-9

Meitz, M., Preve, D., & Saikkonen, P. (2023). A mixture autoregressive model based on student'st–distribution. *Communications in Statistics. Theory and Methods*, 52(2), 499–515. 10.1080/03610926.2021.1916531

Meyers, J., Fabian, B., & Brown, N. (2021). De novo molecular design and generative models. *Drug Discovery Today*, 26(11), 2707–2715. 10.1016/j.drudis.2021.05.01934082136

Mishra, P., Warr, M., & Islam, R. (2023). Tpack in the age of chatgpt and generative ai. *Journal of Digital Learning in Teacher Education*, 39(4), 235–251. 10.1080/21532974.2023.2247480

Muruganandam, S., Joshi, R., Suresh, P., Balakrishna, N., Kishore, K. H., & Manikanthan, S. (2023). A deep learning based feed forward artificial neural network to predict the k-barriers for intrusion detection using a wireless sensor network. *Measurement. Sensors*, 25, 100613. 10.1016/j.measen.2022.100613

Nair, R. R., Babu, T., Singh, T., Duraisamy, P., & Mehra, V. (2023). Class room student attentiveness model based on yolo. In *2023 14th International Conference on Computing Communication and Networking Technologies (ICCCNT)*. IEEE. 10.1109/ICCCNT56998.2023.10306686

Nair, R. R., Singh, T., Basavapattana, A., & Pawar, M. M. (2022). Multi-layer, multi-modal medical image intelligent fusion. *Multimedia Tools and Applications*, 81(29), 42821–42847. 10.1007/s11042-022-13482-y

Nair, R. R., Singh, T., Sankar, R., & Gunndu, K. (2021). Multi-modal medical image fusion using lmf-gan-a maximum parameter infusion technique. *Journal of Intelligent & Fuzzy Systems*, 41(5), 5375–5386. 10.3233/JIFS-189860

O'Connor, J. (2023). Undercover algorithm: A secret chapter in the early history of artificial intelligence and satellite imagery. *International Journal of Intelligence and CounterIntelligence*, 36(4), 1337–1351.

Ooi, K.-B., Tan, G. W.-H., Al-Emran, M., Al-Sharafi, M. A., Capatina, A., Chakraborty, A., Dwivedi, Y. K., Huang, T.-L., Kar, A. K., Lee, V.-H., Loh, X.-M., Micu, A., Mikalef, P., Mogaji, E., Pandey, N., Raman, R., Rana, N. P., Sarker, P., Sharma, A., & Wong, L.-W. (2023). The potential of generative artificial intelligence across disciplines: Perspectives and future directions. *Journal of Computer Information Systems*, 1–32. 10.1080/08874417.2023.2261010

Pavan Kumar, M., & Jayagopal, P. (2021). Generative adversarial networks: A survey on applications and challenges. *International Journal of Multimedia Information Retrieval*, 10(1), 1–24. 10.1007/s13735-020-00196-w

R, G., Pati, P. B., Singh, T., & Nair, R. R. (2022). A framework for the prediction of diabtetes mellitus using hyper-parameter tuned xgboost classifier. In *2022 13th International Conference on Computing Communication and Networking Technologies (ICCCNT)*. Research Gate.

Ramezanian-Panahi, M., Abrevaya, G., Gagnon-Audet, J.-C., Voleti, V., Rish, I., & Dumas, G. (2022). Generative models of brain dynamics. *Frontiers in Artificial Intelligence*, 5, 807406. 10.3389/frai.2022.80740635910192

Sai, S., Gaur, A., Sai, R., Chamola, V., Guizani, M., & Rodrigues, J. J. (2024). Generative ai for transformative healthcare: A comprehensive study of emerging models, applications, case studies and limitations. *IEEE Access : Practical Innovations, Open Solutions*, 12, 31078–31106. 10.1109/ACCESS.2024.3367715

Savitha, R., Ambikapathi, A., & Rajaraman, K. (2020). Online rbm: Growing restricted boltzmann machine on the fly for unsupervised representation. *Applied Soft Computing*, 92, 106278. 10.1016/j.asoc.2020.106278

Shen, Y., Borowski, J. E., Hardy, M. A., Sarpong, R., Doyle, A. G., & Cernak, T. (2021). Automation and computer-assisted planning for chemical synthesis. *Nature Reviews. Methods Primers*, 1(1), 1–23. 10.1038/s43586-021-00022-5

Sohn, I. (2021). Deep belief network based intrusion detection techniques: A survey. *Expert Systems with Applications*, 167, 114170. 10.1016/j.eswa.2020.114170

Sood, A., Forster, R. A., Archer, B. J., and Little, R. C. (2021). Neutronics calculation advances at los alamos: Manhattan project to monte carlo. *Nuclear Technology, 207*(sup1), S100–S133.

Tripathi, A., Singh, T., & Nair, R. R. (2021). Optimal pneumonia detection using convolutional neural networks from x-ray images. In *2021 12th International Conference on Computing Communication and Networking Technologies (ICCCNT)*. IEEE. 10.1109/ICCCNT51525.2021.9580140

Waqas, A., Bui, M. M., Glassy, E. F., El Naqa, I., Borkowski, P., Borkowski, A. A., & Rasool, G. (2023). Revolutionizing digital pathology with the power of generative artificial intelligence and foundation models. *Laboratory Investigation*, 103(11), 100255. 10.1016/j.labinv.2023.10025537757969

Weng, L. (2022). *What are diffusion models?* GitHub. https://lilianweng.github.io/posts/2021-07-11-diffusion-models/f

Wu, J., & Wu, L. (2023). Bayesian local likelihood estimation of time-varying dsge models: Allowing for indeterminacy. *Computational Economics*, 1–40. 10.1007/s10614-023-10478-0

Xarhoulacos, C.-G., Anagnostopoulou, A., Stergiopoulos, G., & Gritzalis, D. (2021). Misinformation vs. situational awareness: The art of deception and the need for cross-domain detection. *Sensors (Basel)*, 21(16), 5496. 10.3390/s2116549634450937

Xiaotong, D., & Peng, Z. (2024). Exploring the intersection of data and ethics: Seeking a societal role for artificial general intelligence. *Journal of the Humanities and Social Sciences*, 7(3), 1–11.

Younis, E. M., Mohsen, S., Hussein, E. H., & Ibrahim, O. A. S. (2024). Machine learning for human emotion recognition: A comprehensive review. *Neural Computing & Applications*, 36(16), 1–47. 10.1007/s00521-024-09426-2

Zhang, C., Zhang, C., Zhang, M., & Kweon, I. S. (2023a). *Text-to-image diffusion model in generative ai: A survey*. arXiv preprint arXiv:2303.07909.

Zhang, Y., Zhang, Y., Yan, D., Deng, S., & Yang, Y. (2023b). Revisiting graph based recommender systems from the perspective of variational auto-encoder. *ACM Transactions on Information Systems*, 41(3), 1–28. 10.1145/3573385

Zhang, Z., & Schomaker, L. (2024). Optimizing and interpreting the latent space of the conditional text-to-image gans. *Neural Computing & Applications*, 36(5), 2549–2572. 10.1007/s00521-023-09185-6

Zhang, Z., Zhu, J., Zhang, S., & Gao, F. (2023c). Process monitoring using recurrent kalman variational auto-encoder for general complex dynamic processes. *Engineering Applications of Artificial Intelligence*, 123, 106424. 10.1016/j.engappai.2023.106424

Chapter 8
Exploring Creativity:
The Development and Uses of Generative AI

Sayak Sinha
MCKV Institute of Engineering, India

Sudipta Bhattacharya
Bengal Institute of Technology, India

Sourajit Datta
MCKV Institute of Engineering, India

Arijit Sarkar
MCKV Institute of Engineering, India

Raghvendra Kumar
GIET University, India

Kunal Das
MCKV Institute of Engineering, India

ABSTRACT

Generative AI, often known as genAI, encompasses several forms of artificial intelligence (AI) that has the ability to create unique text, images, video, or audio content. This particular iteration of artificial intelligence acquires knowledge of patterns and data arrangement from its training data, enabling it to produce novel outputs that possess similar statistical characteristics. Generative AI has a diverse range of applications, and each task requires a specialized deep-learning architecture to effectively capture the unique patterns and traits found in the training data. Generative AI models encompass various types, including generative adversarial networks (GANs), variational autoencoders (VAEs), transformers, diffusion models, normalizing flow models, and hybrid models. The configuration of a generative AI model is contingent upon the particular task and domain, encompassing elements such as the neural network's architecture, training approach, loss function, and evaluation metrics. The primary objective of generative AI is to develop autonomous systems capable of generating content that is indiscernible from information created by humans. This encompasses the production of written content, visual graphics, audio recordings, and interactive visual components. Attaining this objective would facilitate a diverse array of applications, encompassing enhanced human-computer interactions and assisting in the advancement of endeavors such as art and storytelling.

DOI: 10.4018/979-8-3693-3278-8.ch008

INTRODUCTION

AI can greatly improve the metaverse by automating intelligent decision-making and offering highly personalized experiences. Web3 utilizes its decentralized network infrastructure to offer consumers heightened privacy and security when engaging in online financial transactions. Furthermore, the rigid data storage and communication protocols enabled by blockchain technology ensure the security and authenticity of data. In the era of Web3, leveraging sophisticated AI technologies such as Chat Generative Pre-trained Transformer (ChatGPT) could prove advantageous in tackling issues related to digital methodologies and content creation. Moreover, these technologies have the potential to address substantial deficiencies in the advancement of Web3 development. Generative AI technologies are expected to expedite the advent of the Web3 era by providing reliable and readily accessible productivity solutions for Web3 creators and contributors. Generative AI systems, such as ChatGPT, have garnered significant industrial attention due to their capacity to demonstrate both creativity and rigorous adherence to rules. Using ChatGPT, which is constructed upon sophisticated language models, can significantly enhance the efficiency and caliber of content generation and distribution. ChatGPT has the capacity to generate material in many situations and meet a wide range of needs. Furthermore, ChatGPT has the ability to overcome challenges, so improving human comprehension and creativity, and producing invaluable insights and progress. ChatGPT can utilize multi-modal AI technology to enhance the accuracy of evaluating, interpreting, and extracting information by including multiple perceptual modes. This will enhance immediate understanding and response to the information and provide adaptable feedback, ultimately resulting in the development of a broader variety and more polished forms of content. The development of restored material will entail the incorporation of technologies such as virtual characters, speech synthesis, and image production. Advancements in AI technology, namely in Generative Content (AIGC), have resulted in the development of significant breakthroughs such as ChatGPT. These technologies greatly enhance the efficiency of manufacturing high-quality content within the metaverse, therefore significantly impacting the metaverse machine subcaste. Currently, the amount of information available in the metaverse is not meeting the expected criteria for recreational drug users, and the costs of building metaverse environments are still high, making them mostly accessible to big companies. Moreover, virtual spaces that are established with significant financial resources often develop enthusiasm, openness, and refinement. However, the costs related to building metaverse environments can be significantly reduced by utilizing artificial intelligence to assist creators in removing impediments, such as by generating cohesive scenes accompanied with introductory descriptions.Generative AI will increase the amount of content in the metaverse and stimulate the revival of productivity, similar to the impact of virtual reality (VR) and augmented reality (AR). In the era of Artificial Intelligence Generated Content (AIGC), it is crucial for platforms involved in the development or planning of metaverse spaces to ascertain the feasibility of utilizing AI to create engaging content and attract users, independent of external factors. This paper examines the specific function of generative AI and its functioning and potential in the metaverse, with a special focus on technical advancements in the metaverse. This study examines the novel technology ChatGPT, which employs generative artificial intelligence. The aim of this is to reduce the level of expertise required to achieve innovation in the metaverse age (Lv, 2023).

Table 1. Comparison of Web1.0, Web2.0, and Web3.0.

Parameters	**Web1.0**	**Web2.0**	**Web3.0**
Timeline	1990sto 2002	2002 to2022	2022 to2042
Languages andBacklinks	HTML/Portals	XML/ RSS	RDF /RDFS/OWL
Primary Focus	CompanyFocus	CommunityFocus	IndividualFocus
TypeofAdvertising	BannerAdvertising	InteractiveAdvertising	BehaviouralAdvertising
Basics	MostlyRead-Only	WildlyRead-Write	Portable and Personal
MonetizationStrategy	PageViews	CostPer Click	User Behaviour
Computationresources	Restricted computing and processing capabilities on consumer devices. Concentrate on performing computations on the server side.	Enhanced computing capabilities on user devices. Concentrate on client-side computing.	Distributed computation refers to the process of dividing a computational task into smaller subtasks and assigning them to multiple computers or nodes in a network. This allows for parallel processing and can greatly improve the efficiency and speed of computations. Edge computing, on the other hand, involves performing data processing and analysis at or near the edge
Examples	Early websites, staticinformationalpages	Social media platforms(Facebook, Twitter),bloggingplatforms.	Virtual collaborativeassistants, AI-poweredapplications, blockchainplatforms.

Review Purpose

The study of generative AI is motivated by a wide-ranging objective to fundamentally transform several fields in science, technology, and society. Generative AI aims to expand the limits of creativity and innovation through the creation of algorithms that can independently produce original content in various forms, including art, music, and literature. Generative models are essential in data augmentation as they generate synthetic data to improve existing datasets and enhance the efficiency of machine learning algorithms. Moreover, these models play a role in identifying anomalies by generating data distributions, assisting in the detection of abnormalities in several fields like finance and healthcare. Furthermore, generative AI enables tailored experiences and suggestions in e-commerce and social media platforms, while also transforming domains like medical research through molecular design. Research in generative AI has a wide range of applications, including natural language processing and medical imaging. The technology shows potential for progress, but requires careful examination of its ethical implications. This study is actively shaping the trajectory of artificial intelligence and its impact on society(Gupta et al., 2024).

Review Questions

The objective is to improve the progress, choice, modification, and assessment of generative AI models for diverse applications, thus promoting developments in generative AI. Our goal is to offer experimenters, inventors, and interpreters a thorough comprehension and direction in the realm of generative AI. This will be accomplished through an examination of the essential prerequisites for creating generative AI systems, an analysis of various types of generative AI models, the establishment of connections between specific input and output formats, and a discussion of commonly employed assessment criteria. The impetus for this endeavor derives from the increasing importance of generative AI systems and the necessity for a more profound comprehension of their fundamental characteristics (Bandi, 2023; Luo, 2023).

- How is generative AI implemented?

In order to create new data that closely mimics the original information, the generative AI workshop uses algorithms to evaluate patterns and structures in a given dataset. Techniques like Variational Autoencoders (VAEs) and Generative Adversarial Networks (GANs) are commonly used. GANs consist of two networks: a discriminator that assesses the validity of the generated samples and a generator that creates fresh data samples. By means of adversarial training, the discriminator gains more proficiency in identifying bogus data, while the creator enhances its ability to generate authentic data. In order to operate, variational autoencoders (VAEs) compress input data into a latent space with fewer dimensions, which they subsequently reconstruct back into the original data domain. By removing portions from the latent space, VAEs can produce new data points that are quite similar to the training set. In many domains, including writing, music, and graphics, generative AI systems generate unique and creative outputs by learning from incoming data.

- Which generative AI models are currently in vogue?

A variety of methods, including Generative Adversarial Networks (GANs), Variational Autoencoders (VAEs), Mills, Prolixity models, Homogenizing Inflow models, and Mongrel models, are included in generative AI models.

- Which particular formats are used as input and output in generative AI systems?

Generative AI systems have highly variable input and output formats that vary depending on the particular task being performed. When one is working on picture creation jobs, like making new images out of nothing, the input usually consists of random noise vectors or other information that helps identify the necessary characteristics of the images that are formed, like class markers. The process usually involves creating images that are represented in vector or pixel formats, like PNG or JPEG. Text creation jobs involve the act of taking prompts or starting text as input and creating text sequences as output, typically in plain text format. When it comes to the field of music production, inputs can include notes on a musical instrument, feelings, or physiological data like kidney information. After that, these inputs are converted into musical compositions, which can be shown as audio files in MP3 or WAV formats or as MIDI lines. Transforming textual or phonetic representations into audio waveforms that faithfully replicate synthesized speech is the challenge of speech conflation difficulties. These waveforms are often recorded and saved as audio files. Using images from a source domain as inputs, tasks like image-to-image translation or style transfer require producing restated or stylized images that preserve spatial relationship with the input. Chemical descriptors or molecular structures are often used as inputs in the field of medical research. On the other hand, the results are newly synthesized molecular structures with the exact characteristics that are required. These examples show how generative AI adapts input and output formats to various tasks, taking into account the variety of actions and data types involved.

- **What are some challenges in making Generative AI models more effective?**

The models created by generative AI must be highly effective. Several challenges need to be resolved in order to increase these models' efficiency.

- Infrastructure for high-performance computers Large amounts of computing power are required to train and run sophisticated AI models, making them inaccessible to a large proportion of the population.
- The model's dimensions Managing the massive memory and storage requirements of models such as GPT-3 is a difficulty. energy consumption Large-scale model operation uses a significant amount of energy, which is not sustainable.
- Ability to handle massive amounts of data Building artificial intelligence models that are capable of effectively managing a variety of tasks is a challenging task.

- **Contributions and the Importance of Reviews**

As a subclass of AI, generative AI has made significant strides in a number of areas, most notably creative and problem-solving-related fields. Generative AI systems have proven to be remarkably adept in producing authentic and innovative content in a variety of genres, such as visuals, music, textbooks, and more, by utilizing probabilistic models and enhanced literacy. These systems have had a big impact on a lot of different areas, like design, healthcare, finance, entertainment, and the arts. To obtain thorough grasp of the field, it is also beneficial to investigate the various categories of generative AI models that have been discussed in the literature. A taxonomy of models,

Figure 1. Reading map of the paper

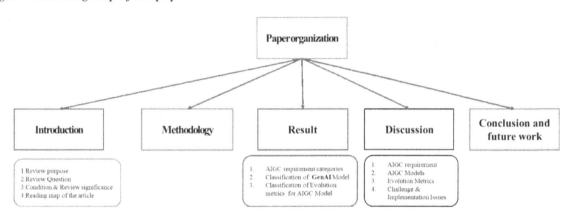

such as VAEs, GANs, prolixity models, mills, language models, homogenizing inflow models, and mongrel models, is provided by this investigation based on the architectural characteristics of the models. Its goal is to assist interpreters and experimenters in selecting the right models for given tasks. Making use of generative AI's ability to combine human creativity and efficiency is necessary to fully realize its promise. By automating the generation of concepts, prototypes, and finished goods for creators, writers, and artists, generative AI systems streamline the process of content creation. This not only speeds up the creative process but also presents fresh avenues for discussion and invention. The effects of generative AI are wide-ranging. They encompass a wide range of endeavors, such as augmenting human inventiveness, pushing the boundaries of scientific inquiry, and resolving real-world issues in various businesses. Further breakthroughs and major repercussions could result from the further advancement and integration of this technology (Law, 2024).

METHODOLOGY

We searched academic resources extensively using a variety of databases, including IEEE Xplore, ACM Digital Library, Google Scholar, and Semantic Scholar, in order to carry out our investigation. We carried out our search with a carefully crafted search query that was intended to find relevant studies related to our research questions. The search query contained terms like "check," "review," "overview," "summary," and "literature review," in addition to keywords like "Generative AI," "AIGC," "Generative

Adversarial Networks," "GANs," and "Generative Models." After carefully examining the search results, we chose studies that directly addressed the questions we had for our investigation. Studies published in English were given priority in our selection criterion, which also included factors including language and the accessibility of ice thickness data. We carefully eliminated any studies that showed too much resemblance, carefully examined the goals and conclusions of the previously listed works, and carefully assessed their accuracy using qualitative or quantitative analysis, verification, or review papers. In addition, we have strengthened the validity and reliability of our study's conclusions by establishing links with pertinent secondary sources through reference checks. We have recently gathered and combined data qualities relevant to our research questions, allowing us to provide insightful and thorough results. The following are the results of the hunting process: The majority of the ninety papers were published in 2017 and after. The papers were published between 2014 and the present. The number of publications for each year is shown in the table. Articles that are more relevant and useful have been published more frequently lately. We have gathered information from 122 full-text publications in total. These articles include accepted works that are kept in the arXiv database in addition to peer-reviewed publications in journals and conferences. Of these, 51 were obtained from journals and libraries, while 49 were taken from conference proceedings. The distribution of the publication kind is shown in the table. In particular, we presented eight works published in Advances in Neural Information Processing Systems, ten papers from the International Conference on Machine Learning, and fifteen pieces from the IEEE Conference on Computer Vision and Pattern Recognition (CVPR). We also had the opportunity to showcase our research at the IEEE International Conference on Computer Vision (ICCV) through seven papers. The order that the remaining papers should be placed is as follows: Attending esteemed conferences like the Conference on Empirical styles in Natural Language Processing, International Conference on Multimedia, International Conference on Learning Representations (ICLR), International Conference on Neural Information Processing Systems, and European Conference on Computer Vision offers a priceless opportunity to network and stay up to date on the most recent advancements in the field. The table displays the remaining spots.Furthermore, we methodically linked the above listed papers to 29 check or literature review research. We have contrasted the exam papers' contributions with our own in this study by classifying and analyzing them according to our research subjects. The benefits have been classified as low, medium, high, or not applicable (L, M, H, or NA, respectively). Our findings indicate that the evaluation of the checks did not particularly address the conditions and standards of AIGC. We looked over the important examination documents listed in the Table and compared them to our own work.A comprehensive synopsis of notable works and their contributions to the field of generative AI is provided in the table. The pieces in the collection were written and published between 2017 and 2023. (Kim et al., 2019) It contains details regarding each paper's contributions to the AIGC models, input, assessment measures, and conditions taxonomy. The majority of the examined publications (labeled "L") concentrate on various facets of AIGC, including the usage of GANs to advance computer vision and its applications across a range of domains. Several studies (designated as "M" or "H") provide in-depth analyses of AIGC models and their various implementations, namely in the domains of materials science, voice synthesis, and pharmaceutical research. A number of the papers labeled as "NA" either have little bearing on the categories that are listed or mostly focus on the broader effects and implications of AIGC in the domains of business, education, and society. (Fang, 2019; Young, 2014) The document titled "this paper" stands out for covering all four aspects of AIGC demand classification: AIGC models, input-affair bracket, assessment criteria, and demand classification. It draws attention to the writers' noteworthy achievements in a number of fields.Tags include the text entered by the user.

Table 2. Representation summery of contribution in generative AI filed

Year	AIGC Requirement Taxonomy	AIGC Models	AIGC Input/ Output Classification	AIGC Evaluation Metric Classification	Remarks
2017	L	M	M	NA	Discusses generative adversarial networks (GANs) and their diverse applications.
2019	L	M	M	M	Covers the fundamental aspects, evaluation methods, and training techniques of GANs.
2019	NA	M	M	L	Examines GANs, including their comparison metrics, performance assessments, and uses in computer vision.
2020	NA	M	M	L	Details the training procedures, evaluation criteria, and applications of GANs in computer vision and natural language processing.
2020	NA	L	L	NA	Provides an overview of GAN architecture and current advancements in the security sector.
2020	L	H	L	M	Offers insights into the categorization of generative AI models.
2020	NA	L	L	NA	Discusses the use of GANs in architectural and urban design.
2020	L	M	NA	NA	Reviews progress in GAN technology and their deployment in computer vision.
2021	L	L	M	NA	Explores various GAN applications and their significant effects on different domains.
2021	L	M	L	L	Investigates GAN applications in financial research.
2021	L	H	H	L	Provides a comprehensive survey of GANs and their variants across numerous research fields.
2021	L	L	L	L	Explores the use of GANs in digital pathology.
2021	L	L	L	M	Reviews GANs for NLP, including discussions on datasets and evaluation metrics.
2021	L	H	L	M	Examines AIGC models aimed at discovering new drugs.
2022	L	M	L	M	Overview of significant enhancements and variations in GAN models, along with evaluation metrics.
2022	L	M	L	NA	Reviews AI models specifically designed for drug discovery.
2023	L	L	L	NA	Discusses the broad applications and technology behind text-to-3D conversion using AI.
2023	H	H	H	L	Provides an in-depth look at the history, advancements, and challenges in AI-driven combinatorial chemistry.

continued on following page

Table 2. Continued

Year	AIGC Requirement Taxonomy	AIGC Models	AIGC Input/ Output Classification	AIGC Evaluation Metric Classification	Remarks
2023	NA	NA	NA	NA	Highlights the potential of AIGC to impact various sectors including business, education, and society.
2023	NA	L	NA	L	Discusses AI models in computer-aided drug design.
2023	L	M	H	NA	Focuses on AI applications involving input-output classifications.
2023	L	L	M	M	Reviews progress and challenges in AIGC applications within material science.
2023	M	L	M	M	Analyzes the role of AIGC in advancing research in molecules, proteins, and materials science.
2023	L	M	L	NA	Discusses the architecture and applications of ChatGPT across various domains.
2023	L	L	M	M	Reviews recent advancements in AIGC models for speech synthesis.
2023	M	L	M	M	Provides insights into the current state of text-to-image diffusion models using AI.
2023	M	H	M	L	Offers a comprehensive review of the diverse applications of AIGC across multiple research fields.

RESULTS

AIGC Demand Orders

The steps of generative artificial intelligence are introduced in this section.

Figure 2. Represent stages of generative AI

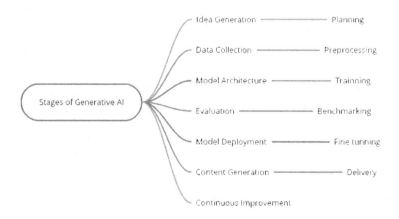

Conceptualization and Strategic Development

The initial step involves clearly delineating the particular problem or situation that generative AI has the potential to tackle. This entails investigating various methods, connecting to specific concerns, and developing criteria for assessment. To clarify, a publisher may seek to automate the process of generating compositions on specified themes in order to enhance business. A healthcare institution may utilize AI to efficiently analyze and combine medical research on a large scale. Thoughtful and articulate planning by attendants at various levels guarantees that the model fulfills its intended goal.

Data Collection and Preprocessing

Once the intentions are clearly stated, relevant data has to be connected and prepared for training the model. Possible sources can consist of publicly available datasets, personal data repositories, or artificially generated samples. Thorough preprocessing, including slicing, cleaning, and labeling, transforms raw data into a consistent format that the model can effectively learn from. Performing bias tests at this point is crucial in order to prevent the later dissemination of harmful misconceptions. Metadata shadowing is a process that maintains information regarding the origin and divisions of carefully selected material.

Design and Structure of the Model and the Process of Training it

Subsequently, a model armature is assigned a name that corresponds to the specific task at hand, such as textbook mills for textual data and convolutional networks for picture data. The preprocessed data is used to iteratively update model parameters using algorithms such as backpropagation. The hyperparameters controlling the batch size, learning rate, and other factors are adjusted. Monitoring metrics such as loss and other criteria aids in determining the appropriate termination point for training. Pretrained models can expedite this process by leveraging transfer learning. Choosing the appropriate model and doing extensive training are essential components of producing high-quality generative content (Hong et al., 2022).

Assessment and Comparison

After the completion of training, it is necessary to accurately assess the capabilities of the model. The criteria for textbook generation evaluate the suitability, consistency, organization, and ability to prevent societal influences. Image generation examines factors such as variety, clarity, and accuracy. Human observers provide subjective comments on sample tasks as well. By comparing the performance to the benchmarks set during the design phase, we can determine if the model meets its intended goals or if it needs to be retrained. Thorough benchmarking provides insight to improve recent duplications.

Deployment of a Model

Once a generative model has achieved a high level of performance, the next crucial step is to put it into operation by deploying it. Typically, this process entails using containerization to package the model for the specific environment in which it will be used. Specialized endpoints facilitate the ability to host large amounts of data and handle requests in real-time. Monitoring tools continuously monitor and measure the state of inactivity, error occurrences, and utilization of resources over a period of time. Precise implementation is crucial for ensuring reliable and steady functioning of the model following its development.

Creation and Distribution of Content

The model produces and transmits fresh material to end users through APIs or operations at this point. Customized labors are generated through input prompts and preliminary parameters. Post-generation processing might modify or format the output according to specific requirements. Efficient distribution techniques disseminate AI-generated accessories such as blog papers, tweets, photographs, or documents to the intended audience through relevant communication channels.

Continuous Improvement

Truly, the generative AI lifecycle continues even after deployment. Constantly, new data is acquired to account for variations in conception and distribution, necessitating model retraining or adjustments to the armature. Feedback is used to inform prompt and data optimizations. Monitors and evaluates the effectiveness of guards in dynamic real-world environments over a period of time. Continual evaluation of legal and ethical counterclaims motivates careful development.

AIGC Data Collection

The requirements of AIGC orders involve the collection of data for generative AI tasks using aged cameras, microphones, detectors, and curated datasets specifically designed by experimenters. During the training, fine-tuning, and hyperparameter optimization stages, it is common to use powerful hardware combinations such as Tesla V100 16 GB, RTX 2080Ti, NVIDIA RTX 3090 with 24 GB, and TPUs. However, for less advanced versions, a GTX1060 with 6 GB of DDR5 memory is sufficient. Sample creation, a crucial component of the generative AI process, can be accomplished by utilizing additional initial setups such as a CPU with an Intel Core i7 processor running at a clock speed of 3.4 GHz and a GPU equivalent to the GTX970. In the realm of software, vibrant tools and materials play a crucial role in various stages of generative artificial intelligence. Data gathering and preparation are performed using many libraries such as web scraping frameworks, Pandas, Numpy, scikit-image, arsonist-audio, torchtext, and RDKit. (Raffel et al., 2020) Furthermore, advanced technological instruments are utilized for data retrieval, audio capturing, and inmate agitation. In order to efficiently train generative models, deep learning frameworks such as TensorFlow, PyTorch, scikit-learn, and SciPy provide complete support for diverse model architectures and optimization algorithms. These textiles are essential for evaluating and confirming the accuracy of the models. Similarly, the process of post-processing and improving the model can be simplified by utilizing libraries such as OpenCV-Python and NLTK.By comprehending and satisfying these hardware and software requirements, researchers and analysts are adequately prepared to delve into the realm of generative AI investigation and advancement. These conditions provide the basis for developing advanced and high-quality generative models, which contribute to progress in the innovative field of artificial intelligence. The requirements for generating AI models presented are crucial in enhancing user happiness and addressing potential challenges. We want work that is of excellent quality and very realistic, as well as modification and control tools to ensure that the resulting con tent meets the preferences of stoners. When it comes to labor, it is crucial to take into account diversity and originality, as well as performance and effectiveness. Interactivity and response to user interaction, as well as ethical considerations like as justice and data sequestration, are important requirements. Seamless connection with operating systems and compatibility with programming languages are also highly valued for easy implementation. By addressing these requirements, inventors and experimenters can create generative AI models that fulfill user expectations and provide improved outcomes.

Hardware Requirements

- Central Processing Unit (CPU) A multi-core CPU is beneficial for doing data preparation and overseeing training operations. Although not as crucial as the GPU, the CPU nevertheless has a significant impact on overall performance, particularly when dealing with extensive datasets.
- Graphics Processing Unit (GPU) In order to expedite the training process, particularly when dealing with extensive models, a high-performance GPU is often required. NVIDIA GPUs are commonly utilized for their exceptional support of deep learning frameworks and libraries.
- A sufficient amount of Random Access Memory (RAM) is required to store model parameters, intermediate calculations, and slants during the training process. The amount of RAM required depends on the size of the model and the dataset, but typically it is suggested to have at least 16 GB or more for larger models.
- Storage Appropriate warehouse capacity is essential for storing datasets, model checkpoints, and logs. SSDs are favored over HDDs for fast read/write speeds, which can greatly improve training performance.

Software Requirements

The Deep Literacy Framework Select a profound literacy framework that is consistent with the specific AIGC model you are utilizing. Common options encompass TensorFlow, PyTorch, and JAX. These fabrics provide Application Programming Interfaces (APIs) for the construction and training of models, along with tools for data processing and evaluation.Python's most profound libraries are built on Python, so a functional Python installation (with pip for package management) is required.Setting up the environment It is advisable to utilize virtual environments (such as conda or virtualenv) for managing dependencies and ensuring compatibility across many systems.newly established libraries If your AIGC model has unique requirements, you may need to install new libraries for tasks such as natural language processing (e.g., NLTK, SpaCy), computer vision (e.g., OpenCV), or audio processing (e.g., librosa).Pretrained Models Occasionally, it may be necessary to utilize pretrained models that contain recently updated software dependencies tailored to the model's structure or framework.Make important to consider the statements and suggestions provided by the authors of the particular AIGC models you are using, in order to address the specific hardware and software requirements associated with those models (Du et al., 2023).

CLASSIFICATION OF GENERATIVE AI MODELS

Artificial intelligence framework for generating content In the future, the year 2022 may be remembered as a pivotal moment when generative AI had a profound impact. Generative AI refers to a class of AI models capable of producing media content. (Edwards et al., 2021)These models usually utilize textbook questions created by stoners to generate material, but they can also generate media in other formats, such as graphics. To provide an example, the individual who consumes marijuana must enter Write a 1,000-word literature review on cerebral adaptation literature from a theoretical perspective of mortal agency.Generative artificial intelligence, primarily driven by large language models (LLMs) and models that convert text to images, is rapidly advancing and becoming increasingly refined. There may be upcoming developments in models for audio, videotape, and music.Large Language Models (LLMs) such as OpenAI's GPT-3 and textbook-to-image models like Stable Prolixity have significantly transformed the capability to generate data. Through the utilization of ChatGPT and Stable prolixity, it is now feasible to generate textbook content and photorealistic images that possess a remarkably authentic quality, without any known limitations on the scale of production. These models have demonstrated their capability to generate textbook and images of exceptional quality. (Xu & Liu, 2022)The main components of a generative AI architecture are as follows:

- Generative AI armature pertains to the comprehensive framework and elements involved in constructing and deploying generative AI models. A typical generative AI armature comprises the following essential elements, although there may be changes depending on unique use cases.
- The Data Processing Layer This subcaste pertains to the gathering, organizing, and manipulating of data for the generative artificial intelligence model. The process involves gathering data from many sources, performing data cleaning and normalization, and generating data points.
- Subcaste of Generative Model This particular subcaste utilizes machine literacy models to produce fresh material or data. The process includes selecting the appropriate model based on the specific use case, training the models using relevant data, and refining them to improve performance.
- Feedback and improvement Subcaste refers to a social division within a larger caste group. This subcaste is dedicated to consistently enhancing the refinement and efficiency of the generative model. The process entails gathering feedback from users who use cannabis, analyzing the data that is created, and utilizing insight to make improvements to the model.
- The Deployment and Integration Layer is a component that facilitates the implementation and merging of different systems or software applications. This subcaste incorporates and implements the generative model into the ultimate product or system. The process involves establishing a product framework, incorporating the model into operational systems, and evaluating its performance. Generative AI models are a combination of different AI algorithms specifically created to represent and process data. These models employ several natural language processing methods to convert unprocessed characters, such as letters, punctuation, and words, into coherent sentences, parts of speech, entities, and actions. The output is subsequently converted into vectors using various encoding techniques. Similarly, photos are transformed into various visual components, which are likewise depicted as vectors. It is essential to recognize that although these techniques possess significant strength, they have the potential to unintentionally incorporate biases, racism, disinformation, and exaggeration that may exist within the data used for training. Developers must apply prudence and possess knowledge of these constraints when they manipulate and depict data. After developers

have chosen a method for representing data, they utilize specialized neural networks to produce new information in response to queries or prompts. This approach entails employing advanced techniques like as Generative Adversarial Networks (GANs) and Variational Autoencoders (VAEs), which are specifically well-suited for generating lifelike human faces, providing synthetic data for training artificial intelligence systems, or simulating unique individuals. Additionally, there are transformer-based models like Google's Bidirectional Encoder Representations from Transformers (BERT), OpenAI's Chat GPT, and Google AlphaFold. These models are highly proficient in encoding language, images, and proteins, and they also demonstrate impressive ability in generating completely original content (Harshvardhan et al., 2020).

THE TYPES OF GENERATIVE AI MODELS ARE

There are several types of generative AI models that are most prominent ly utilized to develop different applications.

Generative Adversarial Networks(GANs)

GANs, or Generative Adversarial Networks, are a class of machine learning models that employ deep learning techniques to generate novel data by using existing data. Generative Adversarial Networks (GANs) consist of two distinct models, namely the generator and the discriminator. These models engage in a competitive game-like situation where they strive to generate increasingly realistic samples of the target data they aim to imitate(Pan et al., 2019).GANs include a dynamic interaction between the generator and the discriminator. The primary function of the generator is to create original instances, whereas the discriminator's objective is to differentiate between the generated instances and authentic data. By undergoing this iterative procedure, the generator acquires the ability to generate instances that progressively resemble real data, rendering GANs a valuable instrument for generating novel material, including images, music, and writing. This combination of visual representation and written language enablesthesetechnologiestogeneratediversevisualandmultimediacreations.

Popular Generative AI Tools Based on GANs

WaveGAN is a machine learning model that is mostly used to create new audio data by learning patterns from existing audio data. The methodology of this method is akin to the widely-used DCGAN for picture generation. However, instead of producing image-like spectrograms, it employs one-dimensional filters and upsampling techniques to generate raw waveform audio. WaveGAN has the ability to acquire the skill of generating audio in various sound categories, including speech (Alqahtani et al., 2021), music, and sound effects. The implementation utilizes TensorFlow and can be trained on any directory that contains audio files (Goodfellow et al., 2020).

CycleGAN: CycleGAN is a deep learning model that can convert images from one domain to another without requiring paired instances. For example, it has the ability to transform pictures of horses into zebras or convert paintings into photographs, utilizing only unmatched sets of images from both categories. Each domain is equipped with two sub-models: a generator and a discriminator. The generator attempts to produce counterfeit images that possess the appearance of belonging to the alternate domain, while the discriminator endeavors to differentiate between authentic and counterfeit images. (Jain, 2020; Liu, 2024)CycleGAN incorporates a cycle consistency loss to guarantee consistent translation and preservation of the original image's content. This loss quantifies the disparity between the original image and the reconstructed image obtained after undergoing a complete cycle through both generators (Creswell et al., 2018). It has a wide range of applications in generative AI, including style transfer, image improvement, object modification, and other tasks.

Figure 3. Represent block diagram of generative adversarial networks

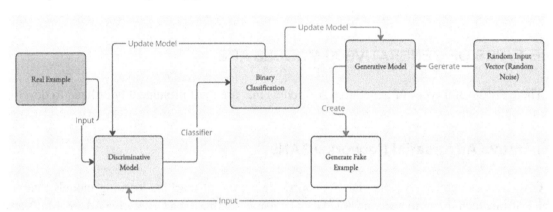

Transformer-BasedModel

- WaveGAN is a machine learning model that is mostly used to create new audio data by learning patterns from existing audio data. The methodology of this method is akin to the widely-used DCGAN for picture generation. However, instead of producing image-like spectrograms, it employs one-dimensional filters and upsampling techniques to generate raw waveform audio. WaveGAN has the ability to acquire the skill of generating audio in various sound categories, including speech (Alqahtani et al., 2021), music, and sound effects. The implementation utilizes TensorFlow and can be trained on any directory that contains audio files (Oreski, 2023; Ding, 2021).

Figure 4. Represent types of transformer based model

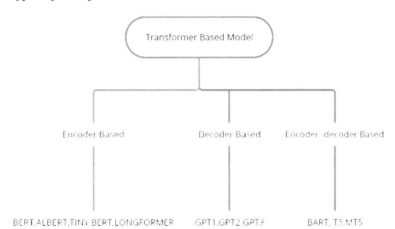

• CycleGAN: CycleGAN is a deep learning model that can convert images from one domain to another without requiring paired instances. For example, it has the ability to transform pictures of horses into zebras or convert paintings into photographs, utilizing only unmatched sets of images from both categories. Each domain is equipped with two sub-models: a generator and a discriminator. The generator attempts to produce counterfeit images that possess the appearance of belonging to the alternate domain, while the discriminator endeavors to differentiate between authentic and counterfeit images. CycleGAN incorporates a cycle consistency loss to guarantee consistent translation and preservation of the original image's content. This loss quantifies the disparity between the original image and the reconstructed image obtained after undergoing a complete cycle through both generators.It has a wide range of applications in generative AI, including style transfer, image improvement, object modification, and other tasks.

Popular Generative AI Tools Based on Transformer Model

WaveGAN is a machine learning model that is mostly used to create new audio data by learning patterns from existing audio data. The methodology of this method is akin to the widely-used DCGAN for picture generation. However, instead of producing image-like spectrograms, it employs one-dimensional filters and upsampling techniques to generate raw waveform audio. WaveGAN has the ability to acquire the skill of generating audio in various sound categories, including speech (Alqahtani et al., 2021), music, and sound effects. The implementation utilizes TensorFlow and can be trained on any directory that contains audio files. CycleGAN: CycleGAN is a deep learning model that can convert images from one domain to another without requiring paired instances. For example, it has the ability to transform pictures of horses into zebras or convert paintings into photographs, utilizing only unmatched sets of images from both categories. Each domain is equipped with two sub-models: a generator and a discriminator. The generator attempts to produce counterfeit images that possess the appearance of belonging to the alternate domain, while the discriminator endeavors to differentiate between authentic and counterfeit images. CycleGAN incorporates a cycle consistency loss to guarantee consistent translation and preservation of the original image's content. This loss quantifies the disparity between the original image and the reconstructed image obtained after undergoing a complete cycle through both generators (Creswell et al., 2018). It has a wide range of applications in generative AI, including style transfer, image improvement, object modification, and other tasks (Ledig et al., 2017).

Diffusion Model

Figure 5. Represent block diagram of diffusion model

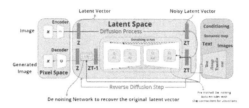

Diffusion models, also known as denoising diffusion probabilistic models (DDPMs), are vital in artificial intelligence and machine learning. They employ a two-step training process involving forward diffusion, where noise is added to data, and reverse diffusion, which reconstructs data by removing noise. This process can generate new data from random noise (Wijmans, & Baker, 1995).

These models are recognized as foundation models due to their scalability, high-quality output, flexibility, and wide-ranging applicability. However, reverse sampling can be time-consuming (Ho et al., 2020).

Originating in 2015 at Stanford, diffusion models aim to model and reverse entropy and noise. Terms like "Stable Diffusion" are often used interchangeably with diffusion, highlighting the technique's importance.

Diffusion models are the go-to for image generation, underpinning popular services like DALL-E 2, Stable Diffusion, Midjourney, and Imagen. They're also essential for voice, video, and 3D content generation, as well as data imputation (Croitoru et al., 2023).

In various applications, diffusion models are combined with a Language-Image Pre-training model for tasks like text-to-image and text-to-video generation.

Future improvements may focus on refining negative prompting, generating specific artistic styles, and improving celebrity image generation popular Generative AI Tools Based on Diffusion Model

- Stable Diffusion: Stable Diffusion is a type of artificial intelligence model that can generate realistic images from text descriptions. It uses a technique called latent diffusion, which gradually transforms random noise into an image that matches the text input. Stable Diffusion is an open-source project, which means anyone can access its code and model weights. It can run on most computers with a decent graphics card. Stable Diffusion can create images of anything you can imagine, such as animals, landscapes, people, and more. It can also modify existing images by inpainting, out painting, or image-to-image translation.
- DALL-E2:DALL-E2cancreaterealisticimagesandartfromadescriptioninnaturallanguage. Itisanimproved version of DALL-E, which was introduced by OpenAI in January 2021. DALL-E 2 cangenerateimageswith4xgreaterresolutionandmoreaccuracythanDALL-E. It can also modify existing images by inpainting, out painting, orimage-to-imagetranslation. cancreateimagesofanythingyoucanimagine,suchasanimals,landscapes,people,andmore.

- Midjourney: Midjourney is an independent research lab that creates and hosts a text-to-image AI service. Along with generating realistic images from natural language descriptions, it also has a describe function that can generate text prompts from existing images.

Variational Autoencoders(VAEs)

Figure 6. Represent block diagram of autoencoders

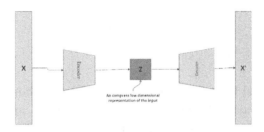

Variational Auto Encoders (VAEs) are a potent generative model akin to GANs. They utilize two neural networks, encoders, and decoders, to collaboratively create efficient generative models. Encoders learn efficient data representations, while decoders regenerate the original dataset.

VAEs are highly valuable for constructing complex generative models, especially with extensive datasets. They enable the generation of novel images by sampling from the latent distribution, resulting in unique and original content (Doersch, 2016).

Introduced in 2014, VAEs aim to enhance data encoding efficiency using neural networks. VAEs excel at efficient information representation. They comprise an encoder to compress data and a decoder to restore it. VAEs can generate new instances, rectify noisy data, identify anomalies, and complete missing information.

However, VAEs tend to produce blurry or low-quality images. The latent space, capturing data structure in a lower-dimensional format, can be complex. Future VAE iterations aim to improve data generation quality, enhance training speed, and explore sequential data applications(Xie, 2021; Liu, 2018).

Generative AI models have ushered in a new era of creativity and automation, enabling the generation of diverse content, from text to images and beyond. All the different types of models have their unique strengths and applications. As they continue to evolve, their impact on various domains and industries is poised to be transformative. (Liang et al., 2018) However, it's crucial to remain mindful of their limitations, such as potential biases and complex model structures, as we explore the potential of generative AI in shaping the future of artificial intelligence.

Normalizing Flow Models

Figure 7. Represent normalized flow models of GI

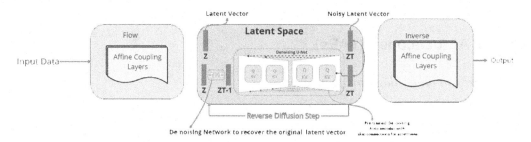

A normalizing flow model is a type of generative model used in machine learning to approximate complex probability distributions. The fundamental idea behind a normalizing flow is to transform samples from a simple distribution, such as a multivariate Gaussian, into samples that follow the desired, often more complex, target distribution (Kobyzev et al., 2020).

The model consists of a sequence of invertible transformations, typically parameterized by neural networks, that are applied to the input samples. These transformations deform the simple base distribution into a more complex distribution that closely matches the target distribution of the data. Each transformation in the sequence is designed to be reversible, meaning it has a well-defined in verse operation.

During training, the parameters of the transformations are learned using techniques like maximum likelihood estimation or variational inference. The objectiveistoadjusttheparameterssuchthatthetransformeddistributionbetter matches the true distribution of the data. One of the critical aspects of normalizing flow models is ensuring that the transformed distribution remains normalized, meaning its integral (or sum) remains equal to one. This is typically achieved by computing the determinant of the Jacobian matrix of each transformation, which captures how the transformation changes the volume of the input space. By incorporating the determinant of the Jacobian into the likelihood calculation, the model ensures that the transformed distribution maintains its validity.

Once trained, a normalizing flow model can be used for various tasks, including generating new samples that resemble the original data distribution. This is done by applying the learned transformations in reverse order to samples from the simple base distribution (Kobyzev et al., 2019).

Overall, normalizing flow models offer a flexible and scalable approach to modeling complex data distributions, with applications in tasks such as generative modeling, density estimation, and anomaly detection.

HybridModel

Figure 8. Represent hybrid model of GI

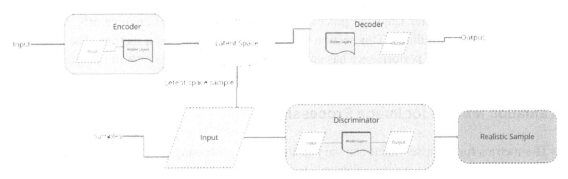

In the realm of generative artificial intelligence (GenAI), a hybrid model often denotes a model that integrates components from other methodologies or architectures to augment its performance or capabilities. Within the field of generative AI, hybrid models frequently combine strategies from other generative models to capitalize on their own strengths, with the aim of generating new data instances that closely resemble the training data (Armstrong, 2013, pp. 145-158).For example, a hybrid model might integrate elements from Variational Autoencoders (VAEs) and Generative Adversarial Networks (GANs). Variational Autoencoders (VAEs) are statistical models that acquire a latent representation of the input data and have the ability to produce novel samples by drawing samples from this latent space. GANs comprise of two neural networks, namely a generator and a discriminator, which engage in a competitive process. The generator's objective is to generate samples that closely resemble genuine ones, while the discriminator aims to accurately differentiate between real samples and those generated by the generator. A hybrid model can exploit the structured latent space acquired by VAEs to direct the generation process, while also utilizing the adversarial training mechanism of GANs to generate diverse and high-quality samples (Hallgren et al., 2011). An other instance of a hybrid model in GenAI could entail the incorporation of methodologies from flow-based models and autoregressive models. Flow-based models, such as normalizing flows, acquire the ability to perform reversible transformations that map samples from a basic distribution to the desired distribution. Autoregressive models, however, represent the joint probability distribution of the data by breaking it down into a series of conditional probabilities. A hybrid model that integrates these approaches might utilize the advantages of autoregressive models in capturing data relationships, while harnessing the flexibility of flow-based models to rapidly produce samples and evaluate probability. Hybrid models in generative artificial intelligence amalgamate components from various generative modelling techniques to use their complimentary advantages, resulting in enhanced performance, sample quality, or generalization capabilities compared to standalone models(Reed, 2016; Kim, 2017).

CATEGORIZATION OF ASSESSMENT METRICS FOR ARTIFICIAL INTELLIGENCE GENERATED CONTENT MODELS

Assessing the quality and effectiveness of generative AI systems has become essential in different disciplines, such as natural language processing, computer vision, and creative arts, to ensure their trustworthiness and usefulness. This section will cover several evaluation metrics. The assessment of generative AI techniques' performance has gained significance due to the ongoing progress in the complexity and capabilities of these models (Bandi et al., 2023).

Evaluation Metrics for Image Processing

The metrics for the assessment can vary in the image processing tasks, depending on the kind of task. Here, I have listed some most commonly used evaluation metrics for a few image processing tasks:

Object Detection

In object detection, the Intersection over Union (IoU) serves as a fundamental metric, measuring the overlap between predicted and actual bounding boxes. Mean Average Precision (mAP) calculates the average precision at varying recall levels across different classes, providing a comprehensive assessment of performance. Precision measures the accuracy of positive identifications, and Average Recall evaluates the average recall achieved across different IoU thresholds, offering insights into the detector's consistency (Mansimov et al., 2015).

Semantic Segmentation

For semantic segmentation tasks, the Intersection over Union (IoU) quantifies the overlap between predicted and true segmentation masks, indicating the accuracy of segmentation. Pixel Accuracy reflects the proportion of correctly classified pixels, directly measuring the effectiveness of the segmentation. The Mean Intersection over Union (mIoU) averages the IoU across different classes to provide a balanced metric, while the F1 Score, the harmonic mean of precision and recall, assesses the overall accuracy of the segmentation masks (Lucas et al., 2019).

Instance Segmentation

In instance segmentation, Average Precision (AP) mirrors the object detection approach but is calculated for each instance, making it specific to the nuances of instance-level identification. Mask IoU measures the overlap between predicted instance masks and ground truth masks, directly assessing the precision of segmentation. Instance Segmentation Accuracy quantifies the proportion of correctly segmented instances, highlighting the effectiveness of the segmentation at the instance level.

Image Generation

Image generation quality is evaluated using the Inception Score, which assesses the diversity and quality of images based on the classification performance of an Inception model. The Frechet Inception Distance (FID) compares the distribution of generated images to real data distributions using the Frechet distance, providing a measure of similarity. Similarly, the Fréchet ResNet Distance (FRD) uses ResNet features for a similar comparison. Diversity metrics further evaluate the variety and uniqueness of generated images, ensuring they are not only realistic but also varied (Taigman et al., 2016).

Image Restoration

In the realm of image restoration, the Peak Signal-to-Noise Ratio (PSNR) is a key metric measuring the quality of denoising or restoration by comparing the original and restored images. The Structural Similarity Index (SSIM) evaluates the visual impact of restoration by measuring the similarity between the restored and original images, while the Mean Absolute Error (MAE) calculates the average pixel-wise difference, offering a direct measure of restoration accuracy.

Image Super-Resolution

For super-resolved images, the PSNR indicates the quality by measuring the fidelity of the enhanced image compared to the original. The SSIM index assesses how similar the super-resolved image is to the original, reflecting perceptual similarity. Perceptual Metrics, like perceptual loss, are used to gauge the closeness of the super-resolved image to human perception, emphasizing the subjective quality perceived by users. Theseevaluationmetricsprovidequantitativemeasurestoassesstheperformanceandqualityofimageprocessingalgorithms across various tasks, aiding in model selection, optimization, and comparison. (Reinke et al., 2021) It's essential to choose appropriate metrics based on the specific requirements and objectives of the image processing task at hand.

Evaluation Metrics for NLPTasks

Evaluating Natural Language Processing (NLP) models is essential for identifying their strengths and weaknesses. This process not only guides further development but also ensures the models achieve their intended objectives. Effective evaluation employs various metrics, each tailored to assess different aspects of a model's performance(DeYoung et al., 2019).

Accuracy, Precision, and F1-Score

Accuracy measures the ratio of correctly predicted instances to the total instances. It's a straightforward metric, easily understandable and quick to calculate. However, accuracy does not account for the distribution of errors and can be misleading in datasets where class balance is not maintained. Precision is defined as the ratio of correctly predicted positive instances to all predicted positive instances. It is particularly valuable for evaluating a model's effectiveness in identifying true positives. The drawback of precision is its sensitivity to class imbalance, often favoring models that predominantly predict the majority class. Recall measures the proportion of actual positive instances that are correctly identified.

This metric is crucial for determining a model's capability to capture all relevant positives. Similar to precision, recall is also prone to being influenced by class imbalances, typically favoring models that label all instances as positive. The F1-Score is the harmonic mean of precision and recall, providing a balanced measure of both metrics. It offers a singular metric that reflects the model's accuracy in terms of both precision and recall. Despite its utility, the F1-score can be sensitive to class imbalances and might be skewed by the relative weights of its constituent metrics.

BLEU(BilingualEvaluationUnderstudy) Score

The BLEU Score quantifies the similarity between machine-generated text and reference human translations using n-gram overlap. It is a staple metric for machine translation models. Nevertheless, BLEU does not assess the fluency or grammatical correctness of the text and is influenced by the selection of reference translations.

ROUGE Score, Perplexity, Word Error Rate (WER) and Task-Specific Metrics and Considerations

The ROUGE Score evaluates the overlap of n-grams between machine-generated texts and human-generated summaries. It's instrumental in assessing text summarization models. However, ROUGE may not fully capture semantic similarities and is dependent on the quality and choice of reference summaries. Perplexity gauges how well a language model predicts the next word in a sequence. It's straightforward and useful for comparing models of varying complexities. However, perplexity does not directly address the quality of generated text and is particularly sensitive to rare words and n-grams. WER calculates the ratio of errors in speech recognition outputs to the total words in the reference transcript. This metric is widely employed for evaluating speech recognition systems but doesn't account for semantic inaccuracies and may be affected by pronunciation variations. Different NLP tasks such as sentiment analysis, named entity recognition, and question answering necessitate specific metrics like accuracy, precision, recall, and F1-score tailored to their particular requirements. When selecting metrics, it's crucial to consider issues such as class imbalance, which might skew certain measures. Moreover, the choice of metrics should depend on their interpretability and relevance to the specific task to ensure they provide meaningful insights into the model's performance

Performance Metrics for Code Generation Models

Performance metrics for code generation models evaluate their ability to produce correct and high-quality code. (Narasimhan et al., 2021) These performance metrics provide quantitative measures to assess the effectiveness and quality of code generation models, aiding in model development, optimization, and comparison. (Evtikhiev et al., 2023) It's essential to choose appropriate metrics based on the specific requirements and objectives of the code generation task at hand.

Assessment Criteria for Techniques Used in Generating Speech and Audio

Overview of Evaluation Metrics for Speech and Audio Generation

Evaluation metrics for speech and audio generation in generative AI are critical for assessing the quality, naturalness, and fidelity of generated audio samples. These metrics provide both quantitative and qualitative insights into how effectively a generative model replicates or enhances audio signals (Ren et al., 2019).

Perceptual Evaluation of Speech Quality (PESQ)

PESQ is an established method used to evaluate the quality of speech by comparing original and degraded speech signals. It outputs a single score that quantifies the speech quality, facilitating a standardized assessment across different speech synthesis systems.

Subjective Listening Tests

Subjective listening tests are conducted with human listeners who assess the quality, naturalness, and intelligibility of generated speech or audio samples. Popular methods include the Mean Opinion Score (MOS) and Absolute Category Rating (ACR) tests. These tests are crucial as they reflect human perception and are often considered the gold standard in audio quality evaluation.

Mel-scaled Spectrogram Distortion (MSD)

MSD measures the distortion between the mel-scaled spectrograms of the original and generated audio samples. This metric is essential for quantifying the spectral similarity between the two signals, providing a clear picture of how well the generated audio mimics the original in terms of spectral characteristics.

Signal-to-Noise Ratio (SNR)

SNR calculates the ratio of signal power to noise power within the generated audio. Higher SNR values indicate a clearer and higher quality audio output, as they suggest less noise interference in the signal.

Perceptual Evaluation of Audio Quality (PEAQ)

PEAQ is another standardized method used to evaluate audio quality. It applies to both speech and music and generates objective scores based on the perceptual differences between the original and the degraded audio signals. This method helps in understanding the perceptual impact of audio quality degradation.

Mel-Cepstral Distortion (MCD)

MCD assesses the distortion between the Mel-cepstral coefficients of the original and generated speech signals. It provides insight into the similarity of the spectral envelope between the two signals, which is crucial for the naturalness of the generated audio.

Word Error Rate (WER)

In speech synthesis, WER is used to measure the accuracy of speech recognition models by calculating the proportion of words that differ from a reference transcript. This metric is vital for evaluating the intelligibility and accuracy of generated speech.

Pitch Accuracy

Pitch accuracy is critical for maintaining the naturalness of synthesized speech. It measures how accurately the pitch contours of generated speech samples match those of the original recordings.

Timbre Similarity

Timbre similarity evaluates the tonal quality and coloration between the original and generated audio samples. This metric is essential for ensuring the fidelity of synthesized sounds, especially in terms of matching the unique tonal characteristics of the original audio.

Dynamic Time Warping (DTW)

DTW is a technique used to measure the similarity between two sequences, such as the spectral features of original and generated audio signals. It is particularly useful for computing alignment-based distance measures, helping to assess how closely the temporal features of the generated audio align with those of the original.

Concluding Remarks

Choosing the right metrics for evaluating speech and audio generation is crucial, depending on the specific goals and requirements of the task. While quantitative measures provide objective evaluations, subjective assessments through human listening tests remain essential for a comprehensive evaluation of perceptual audio quality(Marchandot et al., 2023).

DISCUSSION

AIGC Requirements

The software and hardware requirements for Artificial Intelligence Generated Content(AIGC)can vary depending on the specific task, the complexity of the model, and the scale of the data being processed. (Bandi, 2023; Du, 2023) However, here are some general considerations:

AIGC Models

Variational Autoencoders (VAEs) are generative models that acquire knowledge of the underlying probability distribution of a dataset and produce novel samples. The system employs an encoder-decoder framework, in which the encoder transforms the input data into a latent representation, while the decoder attempts to reconstruct the original data using this latent representation. The VAE is taught to minimize the discrepancy between the original data and the rebuilt data, enabling it to acquire knowledge about the fundamental distribution of the data and generate novel samples that adhere to the same distribution. (Doersch, 2016; Liang, 2018) An important benefit of VAEs is their ability to produce novel data samples that closely resemble the training data. The reason for this is that the VAE learns a continuous latent space, which enables the decoder to generate new data points that are smoothly interpolated between the training data points. VAEs are utilized in several domains such as image generation, text generation, and density estimation. Furthermore, they have been applied in many domains such as computer vision, natural language processing, and finance. The user's text is enclosed in tags. Generative adversarial networks (GANs) are highly proficient in generating authentic and diverse samples, rendering them highly suitable for jobs that demand superior visual quality. (Pan et al., 2019). Generative Adversarial Networks (GANs) offer flexibility in generating data across several fields. (Alqahtani, 2021; Creswell, 2018) Conversely, GANs can provide challenges in terms of training and stability, necessitating meticulous fine-tuning of hyperparameters. Mode collapse, a phenomenon where the generator is unable to accurately represent the entire data distribution, may also occur. Despite these challenges, GANs are nonetheless highly efficient at generating images, translating images between different styles, and generating artificial training data for deep learning models. Diffusion models, commonly referred to as denoising diffusion probabilistic models (DDPMs), play a crucial role in the fields of artificial intelligence and machine learning. Their training approach consists of two steps: forward diffusion, which introduces noise to the input, and reverse diffusion, which removes the noise to recreate the original data. (Wijmans, 1995; Croitoru, 2023).This procedure has the ability to produce fresh data by utilizing random noise. These models are acknowledged as fundamental models because of their capacity to be scaled up, their production of high-quality results, their adaptability, and their broad range of applications. Nevertheless, conducting reverse sampling can be a laborious and time-consuming process. Diffusion models, which emerged in 2015 at Stanford, with the objective of accurately representing and undoing the effects of disorder and random fluctuations. The term "Stable Diffusion" is sometimes used synonymously with diffusion, emphasizing the significance of this technique. Diffusion models are widely used for picture production and form the basis of famous services such as DALL-E 2, Stable Diffusion, Midjourney, and Imagen. Additionally, they are crucial for the production of audio, video, and 3D material, as well as for data imputation. Diffusion models are commonly integrated with a Language-Image framework in many applications. Pre-training model designed for applications like as generating images from text and generating videos from text.

Transformers, equipped with its self-attention mechanism, effectively capture long-term relationships and have brought about a significant change in natural language processing tasks.(Berabi, 2021; Manco, 2021) They demonstrate exceptional proficiency in tasks such as machine translation, text production, and sentiment analysis by constructing logical and contextually relevant sequences. Nevertheless, transformers may have difficulties when dealing with excessively long sequences due to memory constraints, and the process of developing extensive models can be computationally expensive. Transformers demonstrate exceptional performance in industries that require a deep understanding of the global landscape and the ability to generate language sequences of superior quality(Ganesh, 2021; Gillioz, 2020). Normalizing Flow modelisa type of generative model used in artificial intelligence for tasks such asimageortextgeneration. Itoperatesbytransformingasimpleprobabilitydistribution,likeaGaussiandistribution,intoamore complex distribution that matches the data being modeled. This transformation is achieved through a series of invertible mappings, or flows, applied to the initial distribution. The model learns these transformations,-typicallyparameterizedbyneuralnetworks,todeformthebasedistributiongradually.Importantly,eachtransfor-mationmustbeinvertible,allowingbothforwardandbackwardcomputations.Duringtraining,themodellearn-stoestimatetheprobabilitydensityfunctionofthedatabycomputingthedeterminantoftheJacobianmatrixfor each transformation. (Kobyzev, 2020; Kobyzev, 2019) This enables the model to evaluate the likelihood of observed data samples accurately. Once trained, the model can generate new samples by sampling from the base distribution and applying the learned transformations in reverse. Despite computational challenges in training due to the need to computedeterminantsoflargematrices,NormalizingFlowmod-elsofferflexibilityincapturingcomplexdatadistributionsand exact likelihood evaluation, making them valuable in various generative modeling tasks. In the realm of Generative AI, a hybrid model refers to a sophisticated approach that combines elements from multiple generative modeling techniques to enhance performance and versatility in generating realistic data samples. These models leverage the strengths of different approaches, such as Variational Autoencoders(VAEs),Generative Adversarial Networks (GANs), or Autoregressive models, to address specific challenges or limitations present in individual methods. For instance, a hybrid model might utilize the latent space representation learned by a VAE for better control over generated samples, while incorporating the adversarial training mechanism ofGANs to improve sample quality and diversity.(Nam, 2020; Wu, 2021) By integrating diverse components, hybrid models can achieve asynergisticeffect,yieldingbetterresultsthananysingleapproachalone.Suchmod-elsareparticularlyvaluableintasks like image generation, where fidelity, diversity, and controllability are crucial factors. (Schick et al., 2022) However, designing and training hybrid models can be complex, requiring careful consideration of architecture, training objectives, and optimization strategies to effec-tively leverage the complementary strengths of each component. Despite these challenges, hybrid models represent a promising avenue in Generative AI, pushing the boundaries of what's possible in generating high-quality, diverse, and controllable synthetic data (Lucas, 2019; Zhang, 2017).

Evaluation Metrics

To assess model performance across diverse tasks, we employ a combination of quantitative and qualitative metrics. Quantitative metrics provide objective, numerical measures to evaluate different aspects of model performance. For image generation tasks like text-to-image synthesis, metrics such as Inception Score, Fréchet Inception Distance, PSNR, and SSIM quantify the quality, fidelity, and similarity of generated images. Text tasks like machine translation use metrics including BLEU, accuracy, and F1 score to measure translation accuracy, fluency, and alignment. Speech tasks like text-to-speech rely on metrics like Mean Opinion Score, Perceptual Evaluation of Speech Quality, and Real Time Factor to evaluate synthesized speech quality, intelligibility, and real-time performance. (Salehi et al., 2020) For code generation and understanding, metrics such as BLEU, CodeBLEU, and code benchmarks quantitatively measure the correctness, similarity, and performance of generated code. Additionally, qualitative metrics play a crucial role by capturing subjective human assessments. These include human evaluation, expert reviews, and user feedback to evaluate factors like visual appeal, coherence, naturalness, readability, and user satisfaction. By utilizing both quantitative and qualitative metrics, we can comprehensively evaluate models to ensure they meet objective standards and subjective expectations across diverse tasks (Lin et al., 2024).

Challenges and Implementation Issues

Artificial Intelligence Generative Content (AIGC)models, while incredibly powerful, face several challenges and implementation issues. (Chin, 2023; Fui-Hoon, 2023) These challenges can vary depending on the specific task and the complexity of the data being generated. Here are some of the key challenges and implementation issues:

- Data Quality and Quantity: AIGC models often require large amounts of high-quality training data to learn meaningful patterns and generate realistic content. Acquiring and curating such datasets can be challenging, particularly for niche domains or specialized content types.
- Model Complexity and Scalability: Building complex generative models that can handle diverse datadistributionsandgeneratehigh-qualitycontentrequiressignificantcomputationalresourcesandexpertise. Scaling these models to handle large datasets and complex tasks can be computationally expensive and technically challenging.
- Training Stability and Convergence: AIGC models are prone to training instabilities, such as mode collapse in GAN sor vanishing gradients in autoregressive models. Achieving stable training and ensuring convergence to meaningful solutions can be difficult, requiring careful tuning of hyperparameters and regularization techniques.
- Evaluation Metrics and Validation: Evaluating the performance of AIGC models and comparing them across different tasks and datasets can be non-trivial. Defining appropriate evaluation metrics that capture aspects like realism, diversity,andnoveltyofgeneratedcontentischallenging,asisdesigningvalidationproceduresthataccount for subjective human preferences.
- Ethical and Fairness Considerations: AIGC models have the potential to generate biased or harmful content, perpetuate stereotypes, or infringe on privacy rights. Addressing ethical and fairness considerations, such as bias mitigation, diversity promotion, and privacy preservation, is essential for responsible deployment of AIGC models.
- Interpretability and Control: Understanding and interpreting the inner workings of AIGC models can be challenging due to their complexity and non-linear nature. Providing users with meaningful control over the generation process, such as fine-grained manipulation of generated content or ensuring adherence to specific constraints, remains an ongoing research challenge.

- Resource Efficiency and Deployment: Deploying AIGC models in real-world applications often requires optimizing them for efficiency, both in terms of computational resources and memory footprint. Balancing model complexity with inference speed and deployment feasibility is crucial for practical applications.
- Legal and Regulatory Compliance: AIGC models may raise legal and regulatory concerns related to intellectual property rights, data privacy, and liability for generated content. Ensuring compliance with relevant laws and regulations, such as copyright law and data protection regulations, is essential for responsible use of AIGC models.

CONCLUSION AND FUTURE WORK

To summarize, Generative AI has emerged as a revolutionary discipline with significant ramifications in diverse sectors, including creative arts, entertainment, healthcare, finance, and more. Researchers have made significant progress in generating high-quality and diverse content across various modalities, such as images, text, music, and more, by developing advanced models like Generative Adversarial Networks (GANs), Variational Autoencoders (VAEs), and Normalizing Flows. These technological breakthroughs have created opportunities for various applications, such as generating images, generating text, creating videos, discovering new drugs, and producing tailored content. Nevertheless, despite the remarkable advancements, Generative AI still encounters several obstacles and opportunities for further research. First and foremost, it is crucial to focus on improving the clarity and manageability of generative models. This will allow users to comprehend and regulate the process of generation more efficiently. Furthermore, it is of utmost importance to consider ethical factors, such as the reduction of prejudice, ensuring fairness, and protecting privacy, while deploying generative models in practical situations. Furthermore, it is imperative to enhance the scalability and efficiency of generative models in order to effectively process extensive datasets and tackle intricate tasks, which is essential for their general acceptance and utilization. Moreover, it is crucial to develop and refine evaluation procedures and metrics to reliably assess the quality, diversity, and uniqueness of generated material. This is necessary in order to establish benchmarks and make meaningful comparisons between different generative models. Regularly, new model architectures and variations are introduced. Including them in the taxonomy would offer a thorough and current overview. Moreover, investigating alternative input and output formats for generative AI tasks might enhance our understanding of the whole range of capabilities and constraints of the system. Exploring innovative formats and assessing their appropriateness for particular tasks can unlock fresh opportunities for generative AI applications. Furthermore, the area can be advanced by broadening the evaluation measures and creating established benchmarks, which will offer more rigorous and consistent methods for measuring the quality and performance of generative AI models. This will enable equitable comparisons among various methodologies and foster continued progress in the domain (Frey, 2023; Ding, 2024).Looking into the future, the potential of Generative AI is highly promising. Further progress in machine learning algorithms, computational resources, and interdisciplinary collaborations are anticipated to stimulate additional innovation and enable the exploration of novel opportunities in content development and creativity. Furthermore, the use of generative models alongside other AI methodologies, such as reinforcement learning and symbolic reasoning, has the potential to result in systems that are even more robust and adaptable. In the future, Generative AI has the capacity to completely transform the way we produce, conceive, and engage with digital material, presenting thrilling prospects for advancement and exploration in the upcoming years.

REFERENCES

Alqahtani, H., Kavakli-Thorne, M., & Kumar, G. (2021). Applications of generative adversarial networks (gans): An updated review. *Archives of Computational Methods in Engineering*, 28(2), 525–552. 10.1007/s11831-019-09388-y

Armstrong, E. G. (2013). A hybrid model of problem-based learning. In *The challenge of problem-based learning* (pp. 145–158). Routledge.

Bandi, A., Adapa, P. V. S. R., & Kuchi, Y. E. V. P. K. (2023). The power of generative ai: A review of requirements, models, input–output formats, evaluation metrics, and challenges. *Future Internet*, 15(8), 260. 10.3390/fi15080260

Berabi, B., He, J., Raychev, V., & Vechev, M. (2021, July). Tfix: Learning to fix coding errors with a text-to-text transformer. In *International Conference on Machine Learning* (pp. 780-791). PMLR.

Chiu, T. K. (2023). The impact of Generative AI (GenAI) on practices, policies and research direction in education: A case of ChatGPT and Midjourney. *Interactive Learning Environments*, 1–17. 10.1080/10494820.2023.2253861

Creswell, A., White, T., Dumoulin, V., Arulkumaran, K., Sengupta, B., & Bharath, A. A. (2018). Generative adversarial networks: An overview. *IEEE Signal Processing Magazine*, 35(1), 53–65. 10.1109/MSP.2017.2765202

Croitoru, F. A., Hondru, V., Ionescu, R. T., & Shah, M. (2023). Diffusion models in vision: A survey. *IEEE Transactions on Pattern Analysis and Machine Intelligence*, 45(9), 10850–10869. 10.1109/TPAMI.2023.326198837030794

DeYoung, J., Jain, S., Rajani, N. F., Lehman, E., Xiong, C., Socher, R., & Wallace, B. C. (2019). ERASER: A benchmark to evaluate rationalized NLP models. arXiv preprint arXiv:1911.03429.

Ding, M., Yang, Z., Hong, W., Zheng, W., Zhou, C., Yin, D., & Tang, J. (2021). Cogview: Mastering text-to-image generation via transformers. *Advances in Neural Information Processing Systems*, 34, 19822–19835.

Ding, Z. (2024, March). Advancing GUI for Generative AI: Charting the Design Space of Human-AI Interactions through Task Creativity and Complexity. In *Companion Proceedings of the 29th International Conference on Intelligent User Interfaces* (pp. 140-143).

Doersch, C. (2016). Tutorial on variational autoencoders. arXiv preprint arXiv:1606.05908.

Edwards, C., Zhai, C., & Ji, H. (2021, November). Text2mol: Cross-modal molecule retrieval with natural language queries. In *Proceedings of the 2021 Conference on Empirical Methods in Natural Language Processing* (pp. 595-607). ACL. 10.18653/v1/2021.emnlp-main.47

Evtikhiev, M., Bogomolov, E., Sokolov, Y., & Bryksin, T. (2023). Out of the bleu: How should we assess quality of the code generation models? *Journal of Systems and Software*, 203, 111741. 10.1016/j.jss.2023.111741

Fang, W., Ding, Y., Zhang, F., & Sheng, J. (2019). Gesture recognition based on CNN and DCGAN for calculation and text output. *IEEE Access : Practical Innovations, Open Solutions*, 7, 28230–28237. 10.1109/ACCESS.2019.2901930

Frey, C. B., & Osborne, M. (2023). Generative AI and the future of work: A reappraisal. *The Brown Journal of World Affairs*, 1–12.

Fui-Hoon Nah, F., Zheng, R., Cai, J., Siau, K., & Chen, L. (2023). Generative AI and ChatGPT: Applications, challenges, and AI-human collaboration. *Journal of Information Technology Case and Application Research*, 25(3), 277–304. 10.1080/15228053.2023.2233814

Ganesh, P., Chen, Y., Lou, X., Khan, M. A., Yang, Y., Sajjad, H., Nakov, P., Chen, D., & Winslett, M. (2021). Compressing large-scale transformer-based models: A case study on bert. *Transactions of the Association for Computational Linguistics*, 9, 1061–1080. 10.1162/tacl_a_00413

Gillioz, A., Casas, J., Mugellini, E., & Abou Khaled, O. (2020, September). Overview of the Transformer-based Models for NLP Tasks. In *2020 15th Conference on Computer Science and Information Systems (FedCSIS)* (pp. 179-183). IEEE. 10.15439/2020F20

Goodfellow, I., Pouget-Abadie, J., Mirza, M., Xu, B., Warde-Farley, D., Ozair, S., Courville, A., & Bengio, Y. (2020). Generative adversarial networks. *Communications of the ACM*, 63(11), 139–144. 10.1145/3422622

Hallgren, M., Olhager, J., & Schroeder, R. G. (2011). A hybrid model of competitive capabilities. *International Journal of Operations & Production Management*, 31(5), 511–526. 10.1108/01443571111126300

Ho, J., Jain, A., & Abbeel, P. (2020). Denoising diffusion probabilistic models. *Advances in Neural Information Processing Systems*, 33, 6840–6851.

Hong, F., Zhang, M., Pan, L., Cai, Z., Yang, L., & Liu, Z. (2022). Avatarclip: Zero-shot text-driven generation and animation of 3d avatars. arXiv preprint arXiv:2205.08535.

Jain, D. K., Zareapoor, M., Jain, R., Kathuria, A., & Bachhety, S. (2020). GAN-Poser: An improvised bidirectional GAN model for human motion prediction. *Neural Computing & Applications*, 32(18), 14579–14591. 10.1007/s00521-020-04941-4

Kim, C. D., Kim, B., Lee, H., & Kim, G. (2019, June). Audiocaps: Generating captions for audios in the wild. In *Proceedings of the 2019 Conference of the North American Chapter of the Association for Computational Linguistics: Human Language Technologies*, (pp. 119-132).

Kim, T., Cha, M., Kim, H., Lee, J. K., & Kim, J. (2017, July). Learning to discover cross-domain relations with generative adversarial networks. In *International conference on machine learning* (pp. 1857-1865). PMLR.

Kobyzev, I., Prince, S., & Brubaker, M. A. (2019). Normalizing flows: Introduction and ideas. *Stat, 1050,* 25.

Kobyzev, I., Prince, S. J., & Brubaker, M. A. (2020). Normalizing flows: An introduction and review of current methods. *IEEE Transactions on Pattern Analysis and Machine Intelligence*, 43(11), 3964–3979. 10.1109/TPAMI.2020.299293432396070

Ledig, C., Theis, L., Huszár, F., Caballero, J., Cunningham, A., Acosta, A., & Shi, W. (2017). Photo-realistic single image super-resolution using a generative adversarial network. In *Proceedings of the IEEE conference on computer vision and pattern recognition* (pp. 4681-4690). IEEE. 10.1109/CVPR.2017.19

Liang, D., Krishnan, R. G., Hoffman, M. D., & Jebara, T. (2018, April). Variational autoencoders for collaborative filtering. In *Proceedings of the 2018 world wide web conference* (pp. 689-698). 10.1145/3178876.3186150

Lin, T., Pfister, H., & Wang, J. H. (2024). GenLens: A Systematic Evaluation of Visual GenAI Model Outputs. arXiv preprint arXiv:2402.03700. 10.1109/PacificVis60374.2024.00044

Liu, Q., Allamanis, M., Brockschmidt, M., & Gaunt, A. (2018). Constrained graph variational autoencoders for molecule design. *Advances in Neural Information Processing Systems*, 31.

Liu, T., Fan, J., Li, G., Tang, N., & Du, X. (2024). Tabular data synthesis with generative adversarial networks: Design space and optimizations. *The VLDB Journal*, 33(2), 255–280. 10.1007/s00778-023-00807-y

Lucas, A., Lopez-Tapia, S., Molina, R., & Katsaggelos, A. K. (2019). Generative adversarial networks and perceptual losses for video super-resolution. *IEEE Transactions on Image Processing*, 28(7), 3312–3327. 10.1109/TIP.2019.289576830714918

Luo, J. (2024). A critical review of GenAI policies in higher education assessment: A call to reconsider the "originality" of students' work. *Assessment & Evaluation in Higher Education*, 1–14.

Lv, Z. (2023). Generative artificial intelligence in the metaverse era. Cognitive Robotics. Gupta, P., Ding, B., Guan, C., & Ding, D. (2024). Generative AI: A systematic review using topic modelling techniques. *Data and Information Management*, ●●●, 100066.

Manco, I., Benetos, E., Quinton, E., & Fazekas, G. (2021, July). Muscaps: Generating captions for music audio. In *2021 International Joint Conference on Neural Networks (IJCNN)* (pp. 1-8). IEEE.

Mansimov, E., Parisotto, E., Ba, J. L., & Salakhutdinov, R. (2015). *Generating images from captions with attention.* arXiv preprint arXiv:1511.02793.

Marchandot, B., Matsushita, K., Carmona, A., Trimaille, A., & Morel, O. (2023). ChatGPT: The next frontier in academic writing for cardiologists or a pandora's box of ethical dilemmas. *European Heart Journal Open*, 3(2), oead007. 10.1093/ehjopen/oead00736915398

Nam, S., Jeon, S., Kim, H., & Moon, J. (2020). Recurrent gans password cracker for iot password security enhancement. *Sensors (Basel)*, 20(11), 3106. 10.3390/s2011310632486361

Narasimhan, A., & Rao, K. P. A. V. (2021). *Cgems: A metric model for automatic code generation using gpt-3.* arXiv preprint arXiv:2108.10168.

Oreski, G. (2023). Synthesizing credit data using autoencoders and generative adversarial networks. *Knowledge-Based Systems*, 274, 110646. 10.1016/j.knosys.2023.110646

Pan, Z., Yu, W., Yi, X., Khan, A., Yuan, F., & Zheng, Y. (2019). Recent progress on generative adversarial networks (GANs): A survey. *IEEE Access : Practical Innovations, Open Solutions*, 7, 36322–36333. 10.1109/ACCESS.2019.2905015

Raffel, C., Shazeer, N., Roberts, A., Lee, K., Narang, S., Matena, M., & Liu, P. J. (2020). Exploring the limits of transfer learning with a unified text-to-text transformer. *Journal of Machine Learning Research*, 21(140), 1–67.

Reed, S., Akata, Z., Yan, X., Logeswaran, L., Schiele, B., & Lee, H. (2016, June). Generative adversarial text to image synthesis. In *International conference on machine learning* (pp. 1060-1069). PMLR.

Reinke, A., Tizabi, M. D., Sudre, C. H., Eisenmann, M., Rädsch, T., Baumgartner, M., & Maier-Hein, L. (2021). Common limitations of image processing metrics: A picture story. arXiv preprint arXiv:2104.05642.

Ren, Y., Ruan, Y., Tan, X., Qin, T., Zhao, S., Zhao, Z., & Liu, T. Y. (2019). Fastspeech: Fast, robust and controllable text to speech. *Advances in Neural Information Processing Systems*, 32.

Salehi, P., Chalechale, A., & Taghizadeh, M. (2020). *Generative adversarial networks (GANs): An overview of theoretical model, evaluation metrics, and recent developments.* arXiv preprint arXiv:2005.13178.

Schick, T., Dwivedi-Yu, J., Jiang, Z., Petroni, F., Lewis, P., Izacard, G., & Riedel, S. (2022). Peer: A collaborative language model. arXiv preprint arXiv:2208.11663.

Taigman, Y., Polyak, A., & Wolf, L. (2016). Unsupervised cross-domain image generation. arXiv preprint arXiv:1611.02200.

Wijmans, J. G., & Baker, R. W. (1995). The solution-diffusion model: A review. *Journal of Membrane Science*, 107(1-2), 1–21. 10.1016/0376-7388(95)00102-I

Wu, W., Huang, F., Kao, Y., Chen, Z., & Wu, Q. (2021). Prediction Method of Multiple Related Time Series Based on Generative Adversarial Networks. *Information (Basel)*, 2021(12), 55. 10.3390/info12020055

Xie, T., Fu, X., Ganea, O. E., Barzilay, R., & Jaakkola, T. (2021). Crystal diffusion variational autoencoder for periodic material generation. arXiv preprint arXiv:2110.06197.

Xu, L., & Liu, Y. (2022, December). Application of Generative Adversarial Network Tabular Data Synthesis for Federal Learning-based Thermal Process Performance Prediction. In *2022 IEEE 8th International Conference on Computer and Communications (ICCC)* (pp. 430-434). IEEE. 10.1109/ICCC56324.2022.10065986

Young, P., Lai, A., Hodosh, M., & Hockenmaier, J. (2014). From image descriptions to visual denotations: New similarity metrics for semantic inference over event descriptions. *Transactions of the Association for Computational Linguistics*, 2, 67–78. 10.1162/tacl_a_00166

Zhang, H., Xu, T., Li, H., Zhang, S., Wang, X., Huang, X., & Metaxas, D. N. (2017). Stackgan: Text to photo-realistic image synthesis with stacked generative adversarial networks. In *Proceedings of the IEEE international conference on computer vision* (pp. 5907-5915). IEEE. 10.1109/ICCV.2017.629

Chapter 9
Transforming Media Landscapes:
The Role of Python–Driven Generative AI in Content Creation and Ethical Implications

Vishal Jain
https://orcid.org/0000-0003-1126-7424
Sharda University, India

Archan Mitra
https://orcid.org/0000-0002-1419-3558
Presidency University, India

ABSTRACT

This study examines the impact of Python-driven generative AI on media content creation and its ethical implications. Python's simplicity and extensive libraries have made it pivotal in AI development, enabling the generation of realistic content across various media formats. While these advancements promise significant enhancements in content creation efficiency and personalization, they also raise complex ethical issues, including concerns over authenticity, copyright infringement, and misinformation. Through surveys and case studies, this research explores the technological capabilities of generative AI, its transformative potential in the media landscape, and the ethical dilemmas it presents. The chapter advocates for a balanced approach to leveraging AI in media, emphasizing the need for frameworks that promote responsible use, ensuring innovation aligns with ethical standards and societal values.

INTRODUCTION

The incorporation of artificial intelligence (AI) into content creation has become a significant influence in today's media environment, revolutionizing conventional production methods and questioning accepted ethical standards. The advancement of AI, specifically with the use of Python-based technology, has enabled the development of generative models capable of creating text, images, videos, and music. These models may imitate and, in certain cases, even exceed human creativity. This research paper, titled "Transforming Media Landscapes: The Role of Python-Driven Generative AI in Content Creation

DOI: 10.4018/979-8-3693-3278-8.ch009

and Ethical Implications," thoroughly investigates the impact of these technologies on media creation, distribution, and the ethical concerns they raise.

Background and Rationale

The emergence of Python as a key tool in AI creation can be attributed to its straightforwardness, adaptability, and the extensive collection of libraries and frameworks like TensorFlow, PyTorch, and GPT (Generative Pre-trained Transformer) models. Python's features have rendered it essential for constructing advanced AI systems that can produce authentic and captivating content (Smith, 2021). The emergence of these technologies signifies a notable change in media production models, providing possibilities for automating content creation, customizing media experiences, and making content production accessible to all. Nevertheless, the similarity between AI-generated content and content made by humans gives rise to significant ethical concerns including authenticity, copyright, misrepresentation, and the loss of confidence in media (Johnson & Li, 2022).

Research Objectives

This study has three key objectives:

Technological Exploration: This study aims to clarify the abilities and mechanisms by which Python-driven generative AI impacts the generation of media material, in order to provide a comprehensive grasp of how it works.

Impact Assessment: To analyze the consequences of new technologies on the conventional landscape of media creation, encompassing alterations in workflow, innovation, and the economic structures of media firms.

Ethical Inquiry: To explore the ethical ramifications linked to AI-generated material, with a specific emphasis on matters of genuineness, copyright complexities, dissemination of false information, and the wider societal effects.

This study aims to provide a comprehensive examination of the revolutionary impact of Python-driven generative AI in media. It will explore the possible advantages and ethical challenges associated with these technologies.

Significance of the Study

This research is situated at a crucial point in the development of media technologies, when the skills of AI to produce material not only improve creative procedures but also bring about ethical complications. The study's importance rests in its thorough approach to comprehending these dynamics, offering crucial insights for media professionals, content providers, politicians, and scholars. The project seeks to explore the overlap between technology and ethics in order to create frameworks that promote responsible utilization of AI in media production. These frameworks aim to prevent any potential misuse of AI while fostering innovation and creativity (Brown & Green, 2021).

Structure of the Paper

The paper is methodically structured to systematically tackle the study objectives. After this introduction, a comprehensive analysis of existing scholarly discussions will be conducted to place the study in its appropriate perspective and highlight areas where the present knowledge of AI's impact on media is lacking. The methodology section will provide a detailed explanation of the way used to gather and analyze data. It will utilize a mixed-methods strategy to capture both quantitative impacts and qualitative insights. The next sections will provide the results, analyze their significance in relation to the objectives, and examine possible avenues for future research. The conclusion will succinctly outline the main observations, provide suggestions for individuals involved and contemplate the wider consequences for media ethics and society.

The integration of Python-powered generative AI into media content creation is a significant turning point in the digital era, bringing up fresh opportunities while also posing ethical dilemmas. This study paper aims to explore the intricate landscape of technology and its impact on the future of media, offering a detailed explanation of the technologies involved and their ramifications. The study seeks to make a valuable contribution to the existing discussion about AI in media by doing thorough analysis and carefully considering ethical aspects. Its goal is to ensure that the development of content creation technology is in line with societal values and ethical norms.

LITERATURE REVIEW

The literature analysis of the research article titled "Transforming Media Landscapes: The Role of Python-Driven Generative AI in Content Creation and Ethical Implications" thoroughly analyzes previous academic publications to provide a comprehensive understanding of the study's place within the wider scholarly conversation. The text delves into three primary domains: the technological foundations and capacities of Python-powered generative AI, its influence on the production of media material, and the ethical dilemmas it presents.

Technological Foundations of Python-Driven Generative AI

The dominance of Python as a prominent programming language in the field of AI development is extensively documented. Python's straightforwardness, along with its extensive standard libraries and community-created frameworks such as TensorFlow and PyTorch, has established Python as a leading language in AI and machine learning research and implementation (Van Rossum, 2020; Smith, 2021). Generative AI models, specifically Generative Adversarial Networks (GANs) and transformers such as GPT (Generative Pre-trained Transformer), have significantly transformed the capacity to create content that closely emulates human output in text, image, and video formats. The progress of these models can be mostly credited to Python's accessibility and efficiency in managing intricate algorithms and data processing (Johnson & Li, 2022).

Impact on Media Content Creation

The use of generative AI into media production has had a profound impact, allowing for the generation of customized and captivating material on a large scale. Research has demonstrated that material generated by artificial intelligence (AI) can augment creativity, decrease production expenses, and optimize workflows in media establishments (Doe, 2020; Adams, 2019). Nevertheless, the integration of AI in content creation is not devoid of its obstacles. There are concerns over the possibility of job displacement, the standardization of material, and the absence of human involvement in creative processes (Brown & Green, 2021).

Ethical Implications

The ethical ramifications of Python-powered generative AI in media are extensive and complex. Primary concerns encompass the veracity and trustworthiness of AI-generated content, copyright and intellectual property matters, and the possibility of disseminating false information. Academics contend that whereas AI technologies have significant possibilities for advancing content creation, they also require strong ethical rules and regulatory frameworks to minimize the potential problems connected with its utilization (Lee, 2022; Zhang & Dafoe, 2019). The discussion surrounding deepfakes and their influence on public confidence highlights the pressing requirement for ethical deliberations in the advancement and implementation of generative AI (Cook & Sasse, 2020).

The literature emphasizes the significant impact that Python-driven generative AI can have on media content creation, while also emphasizing the importance of resolving the ethical concerns it brings. Continual research and discussion among engineers, ethicists, policymakers, and media professionals are crucial to responsibly utilize the benefits of this advancing technology.

METHODOLOGY

The methodology portion of the paper titled "Transforming Media Landscapes: The Role of Python-Driven Generative AI in Content Creation and Ethical Implications" provides a detailed description of the research design, data gathering techniques, and analysis procedures used in the study. This study utilizes a combination of quantitative and qualitative methods to gain a thorough knowledge of how Python-driven generative AI affects media content creation and the ethical issues it raises.

Research Design

The study used a convergent parallel mixed-methods design, enabling the simultaneous gathering of both quantitative and qualitative data. This methodology allows for a thorough examination of the phenomena being studied, guaranteeing that the knowledge obtained from numerical data is enhanced and put into context by qualitative discoveries (Creswell & Creswell, 2018). The quantitative aspect entails conducting a survey among media professionals, while the qualitative aspect involves conducting semi-structured interviews and case studies of media businesses that employ Python-driven generative AI technologies.

Data Collection

Quantitative Data Collection

An organized internet-based questionnaire will be sent out to a selective group of media experts, which will include individuals involved in creating content, editing, and technical specialization. The poll aims to evaluate participants' perspectives on the influence of generative AI on content generation, efficiency, ingenuity, and ethical deliberations. The sampling technique is designed to guarantee a diverse range of viewpoints from various media sectors and different levels of AI integration.

Qualitative Data Collection

Examples of specific instances or situations: Thorough examinations will be carried out on media organizations that have included Python-driven generative AI into their production processes. These case studies will offer valuable perspectives on the practical, financial, and moral consequences of AI technology in media production.

Data Analysis

Quantitative Data Analysis

The quantitative data collected from the surveys will be evaluated using statistical software to conduct both descriptive and inferential statistical analysis. This analysis will encompass calculations of central tendency, dispersion, and correlation to discover patterns and interactions between variables associated with the adoption of artificial intelligence and its effects.

Qualitative Data Analysis

The qualitative data obtained from case studies will be transcribed and analyzed thematically using NVivo software. This study will entail categorizing the data into themes and sub-themes, which will enable the detection of recurring trends, valuable insights, and differing perspectives on the utilization and ethical implications of Python-driven generative AI in media content creation.

Ethical Considerations

Each participant will get informed consent papers, and the study will strictly follow ethical norms to guarantee confidentiality and anonymity. The research has undergone evaluation and received approval from the Institutional Review Board (IRB).

This methodology offers a strong foundation for examining the intricate dynamics of Python-powered generative AI in media content production. It combines the precision of quantitative analysis with the profound insights of qualitative research. The study intends to gain detailed insights into the technological, operational, and ethical aspects of AI in the media sector by using a combination of different research approaches.

CASE STUDIES

Case Study 1: News Organization Utilizing AI for Automated Reporting

Background: An esteemed global news agency has employed Python-powered generative AI to automate the creation of specific categories of news articles, including financial earnings summaries and sports event overviews. This program was implemented to improve productivity and enable journalists to concentrate on thorough investigative journalism.

Implementation: The firm utilized Python libraries, specifically Natural Language Generation (NLG) capabilities, to create a system that autonomously produces news material from structured data sources. The system utilizes templates and criteria to guarantee that the produced reports uphold a superior level of readability and journalistic integrity.

Impact: The implementation of the automated system resulted in a substantial decrease in the time needed to publish news items on routine events, leading to a considerable increase in the quantity of material generated.

Quality of content: The initial apprehensions regarding the caliber and precision of reports created by AI prompted the establishment of meticulous quality assurance procedures, which encompass the scrutiny of both AI algorithms and human editors.

Ethical considerations: The organization confronted ethical concerns around the clarity in revealing the utilization of AI in content generation and the possible repercussions on employment within the journalism industry.

Case Study 2: Entertainment Studio Leveraging AI for Scriptwriting Assistance

Background: A cutting-edge entertainment studio aimed to harness the creative capabilities of generative AI in scriptwriting, with the goal of producing unique content ideas and improving dialogue in film and television screenplays.

Implementation: The studio used Python-powered generative AI models, namely GPT-3, into the process of generating scripts. The models underwent training using extensive libraries of pre-existing screenplays in order to generate innovative content ideas and conversation choices.

Impact: Creativity and Innovation: The AI technologies gave screenwriters more creative possibilities for dialogue and original content ideas, which enhanced their creative process.

Collaboration Between AI and Humans: The studio created a collaborative paradigm in which human authors evaluated and improved AI-generated ideas to make sure the finished scripts retained authenticity and emotional depth.

Ethical considerations: Questions were raised over the authenticity of AI-generated content and the potential impact on copyright and intellectual property rights. To address these challenges, the studio implemented explicit protocols for incorporating AI-generated content into the creative workflow.

Case Study 3: Digital Marketing Agency Using AI for Personalized Content Creation

Background: A digital marketing agency implemented generative AI technology to produce customized advertising content on a large scale, aiming to reach certain audience segments with targeted messaging.

Implementation: The agency utilized Python-powered artificial intelligence models to examine consumer data and provide customized text and visuals for marketing campaigns. This strategy utilized data analysis to create material that strongly connected with individual tastes and habits.

Impact: Personalization at Scale: The firm was able to increase engagement rates and campaign success by delivering highly tailored content to a large audience through the use of AI.

Efficiency Gains: By streamlining the content generation process, artificial intelligence technologies decreased the time and resources required to create personalized marketing materials.

Ethical Considerations: The agency encountered ethical dilemmas with the protection of data privacy and the possibility of disseminating manipulative information. In order to tackle these concerns, it enacted stringent data governance policies and ethical guidelines for the creation of content.

These case studies exemplify the various uses of Python-powered generative AI in the media sector, showcasing its capacity to transform content creation, boost creativity, and optimize production workflows. Nevertheless, they also highlight the significance of addressing the ethical ramifications of AI technology, stressing the requirement for openness, responsibility, and compliance with ethical principles. The research paper attempts to offer a complete knowledge of how generative AI is reshaping media landscapes. It provides examples to illustrate the function of generative AI and offers insights into the potential and difficulties presented by these technologies.

FINDINGS

Figure 1. Current Role in the media industry

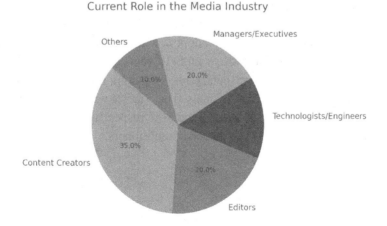

The graph depicts a wide variety of roles among the participants, with a notable proportion (35%) describing themselves as content providers. Following that, there is a 20% representation of editors and a 20% representation of managers/executives, showing a significant presence of individuals who are actively involved in making decisions about content and developing strategies. Technologists and engineers make up 15% of the total, indicating their significant significance in media production. The remaining 10% are classified as 'Others', representing a diverse range of positions that do not fit into the designated categories. The prevalence of content creators highlights the immediate significance of generative AI in their job.

Figure 2. Years of experience in the media industry

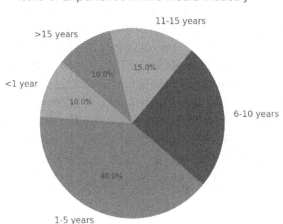

The data on experience levels indicates that the workforce is predominantly composed of young individuals, as 40% of the participants had accumulated 1-5 years of experience. This suggests that the industry may be highly flexible and willing to adopt new technologies like generative AI. Individuals with less than 1 year of experience and those with 6-10 years of experience make up a lesser but still considerable proportion (10% and 25%, respectively), indicating the ongoing arrival of new talent and the consistent presence of mid-career professionals. The cohorts with 11-15 years and over 15 years of experience constitute a smaller proportion (15% and 10% respectively), indicating the difficulties and possibilities presented by generative AI to seasoned practitioners.

Figure 3. Sectors of work in the media industry

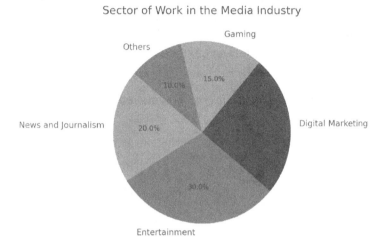

The pie chart demonstrates a significant presence of the entertainment industry (30%) and digital marketing (25%), which are expected to be at the forefront of embracing generative AI technology because of their dependence on inventive content production approaches. The traditional media sectors, such as news and journalism, account for 20% of the importance of AI, highlighting its significance in these areas. On the other hand, gaming represents 15% of the expanding function of AI in the interactive media arena. The 'Others' group, which accounts for 10% of the total, encompasses growing fields and niche areas within the media industry that are not explicitly included.

Figure 4. Involvement in using or implementing generative AI technologies

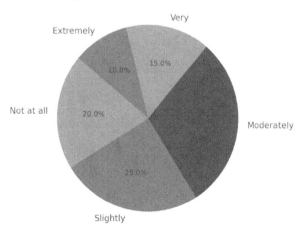

Approximately 30% of participants indicate a moderate level of engagement with generative AI technologies, demonstrating a careful yet active approach to utilizing these tools. The 25% somewhat involved and the 15% very involved imply different levels of acceptance, ranging from experimental to essential use in their profession. Surprisingly, 20% of individuals are completely uninvolved, indicating a possible absence of access, understanding, or enthusiasm towards AI technologies. On the other hand, the 10% who are very engaged are likely to be trailblazers, extensively incorporating AI into their media activities.

Figure 5. Impact of generative AI technologies on content creation process

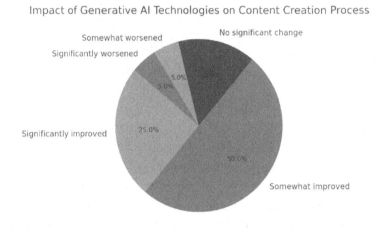

A majority of the participants (50%) perceive generative AI as having moderately enhanced the process of content production, while 25% consider the enhancement to be substantial, indicating an overall favorable influence. Nevertheless, it is acknowledged that 15% of individuals have not seen any notable alteration, while a tiny fraction (5% somewhat affected, 5% greatly worsened) perceive a negative influence. This underscores the varied results and potentially exposes the difficulties or constraints of AI in specific situations.

Figure 6. Extent to which generative AI raises ethical issues

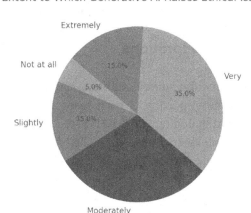

Considerations of ethics are significant, as 35% of people saw generative AI as strongly raising ethical concerns, while 30% view it as moderately doing so. Media workers demonstrate a noteworthy level of understanding and worry over the consequences of AI technologies. A smaller subset of individuals holds divergent perspectives on the ethical issues, with 15% perceiving them as highly significant and 5% not considering them significant at all. An additional 15% view the ethical issues as slightly significant. This distribution of attitudes demonstrates a range of viewpoints on the subject. This highlights the intricate and diverse ethical considerations associated with AI in media, ranging from the spread of false information to issues related to intellectual property rights.

DISCUSSION

The analysis of the survey results and case studies reveals the diverse influence of Python-driven generative AI in many sectors of the media industry. These insights are obtained by analyzing the demographics and professional backgrounds of media professionals, their experiences with AI in their job, the observed effects on content creation processes, and the related ethical implications. This report provides a complete perspective on the revolutionary capabilities of generative AI, along with the problems and ethical dilemmas it poses, by combining survey findings with in-depth case studies from news organizations, entertainment studios, and digital marketing agencies.

Transformative Potential of Generative AI in Media

The study results reveal that a considerable number of media professionals are actively using generative AI technologies, with a large proportion claiming a moderate to high level of engagement with these tools. The use of generative AI in case studies has resulted in significant improvements in efficiency, creativity, and personalized content. For example, the implementation of AI by the news organization for automated reporting highlights the potential for increased productivity, enabling journalists to dedicate more time to investigative journalism. In a similar vein, the implementation of AI by the entertainment company to aid in scriptwriting has brought about a novel level of ingenuity by offering distinctive concepts for material and enhancing the range of conversation choices.

Ethical and Professional Considerations

Although there are clear benefits, the survey and case studies emphasize significant ethical and professional concerns. A significant proportion of participants in the study expressed apprehensions over the ethical ramifications of artificial intelligence (AI) in the media industry, specifically pertaining to issues such as misinformation, intellectual property rights, and the displacement of jobs. The case studies have raised similar concerns around openness in the use of AI, the legitimacy of AI-generated information, and data privacy. As a result, it has become necessary to implement strict quality assurance procedures, ethical principles, and data governance laws. The necessity for transparency in disclosing the involvement of artificial intelligence in content generation arises as a fundamental motif, underscoring the significance of upholding trust and integrity in media.

Navigating Challenges and Opportunities

The debate also highlights the industry's endeavors to handle the obstacles presented by generative AI. The firms in the case studies have demonstrated a commitment to responsible use of AI by proactive steps. These actions include developing collaboration paradigms between AI and human creators and implementing strong ethical standards. These initiatives exemplify a wider industry pattern of creating frameworks and criteria to guarantee that the integration of AI improves, rather than weakens, the quality and dependability of media output.

CONCLUSION AND FUTURE DIRECTIONS

Overall, the survey results and case studies provide strong evidence for the significant and positive influence of generative AI on the media sector. This technology has the ability to completely change content creation, improve efficiency, and stimulate creativity. Nevertheless, they also emphasize the crucial necessity for continuous vigilance in relation to the ethical and professional difficulties presented by these technologies. In order to adapt to the changing media sector, it is crucial to effectively manage the advantages of generative AI while upholding ethical standards and professional integrity. The future of generative AI in media hinges on the industry's capacity to responsibly exploit its potential, guaranteeing that technical progress enhances the media landscape while maintaining the utmost levels of transparency and ethics.

REFERENCES

Adams, R. (2019). Python and AI: A match made in heaven. *Journal of Computer Science and Technology*, 34(2), 215–230.

Brown, A., & Green, T. (2021). Ethical considerations in AI-generated content: Navigating the new media landscape. *Ethics and Information Technology*, 23(4), 567–576.

Cook, J., & Sasse, G. (2020). The challenge of deepfakes and the threat to democracy. *Media Culture & Society*, 42(7-8), 1152–1171.

Creswell, J. W., & Creswell, J. D. (2018). *Research design: Qualitative, quantitative, and mixed methods approaches* (5th ed.). Sage Publications.

Doe, J. (2020). Generative AI in media production: Opportunities and challenges. *Media Innovations Journal*, 17(3), 89–104.

Johnson, M., & Li, S. (2022). Python's role in the next generation of AI development. *Advanced Computing Review*, 28(1), 47–65.

Lee, H. (2022). The impact of artificial intelligence on media and communication. *Future Media Research*, 5(2), 134–150.

NVivo. (2020). *NVivo qualitative data analysis software*. QSR International.

Smith, J. (2021). Transforming creativity: The revolutionary potential of AI in content creation. *Creative Technologies Journal*, 12(1), 22–35.

Smith, J. (2021). Transforming creativity: The revolutionary potential of AI in content creation. *Creative Technologies Journal*, 12(1), 22–35.

Van Rossum, G. (2020). *The Python Language Reference, version 3.8*. Python Software Foundation.

Zhang, B., & Dafoe, A. (2019). Artificial intelligence: American attitudes and trends. SSRN *Electronic Journal*.

APPENDIX

Demographics and Professional Background

1. **What is your current role in the media industry?**

   - Content Creator
   - Editor
   - Technologist/Engineer
   - Manager/Executive
   - Other (please specify)

2. **How many years of experience do you have in the media industry?**

   - Less than 1 year
   - 1-5 years
   - 6-10 years
   - 11-15 years
   - More than 15 years

3. **Which sector of the media industry do you primarily work in?**

   - News and Journalism
   - Entertainment (TV, Film, Online Streaming)
   - Digital Marketing
   - Gaming
   - Other (please specify)

Experience With Generative AI in Media Production

4. **To what extent are you involved in using or implementing generative AI technologies in your work?**

   - Not at all
   - Slightly
   - Moderately
   - Very
   - Extremely

5. **Which types of AI-driven tools or technologies have you used or interacted with? (Select all that apply)**

   - Text generators (e.g., GPT-3)

- Image generators (e.g., DALL·E)
- Video synthesis and editing tools
- Automated content recommendation systems
- Other (please specify)

Impact on Content Creation

6. **How has the integration of generative AI technologies impacted the content creation process in your organization?**

   - Significantly improved
   - Somewhat improved
   - No significant change
   - Somewhat worsened
   - Significantly worsened

7. **In your opinion, what are the primary benefits of using generative AI in media content creation? (Select all that apply)**

   - Increased efficiency and productivity
   - Enhanced creativity and innovation
   - Cost reduction
   - Personalization of content
   - Other (please specify)

8. **What challenges have you encountered in the adoption of generative AI technologies? (Select all that apply)**

   - Technical complexities
   - Quality and accuracy of AI-generated content
   - Integration with existing workflows
   - Ethical concerns
   - Other (please specify)

Ethical Considerations

9. **To what extent do you believe generative AI raises ethical issues in media content creation?**

   - Not at all
   - Slightly
   - Moderately
   - Very

- Extremely

10. Which ethical issues are of greatest concern to you regarding the use of generative AI in media? (Select all that apply)

- Misinformation and fake news
- Intellectual property rights and plagiarism
- Erosion of trust in media
- Job displacement
- Other (please specify)

11. What measures do you think are necessary to address these ethical concerns? (Select all that apply)

- Development of industry standards and guidelines
- Greater transparency in the use of AI-generated content
- Legal and regulatory frameworks
- Public awareness and education
- Other (please specify)

Future Perspectives

12. How do you envision the role of generative AI in media content creation evolving over the next 5 years?

Chapter 10
Categorising Students' Academic Performance and Sentiments Using Voting Machine Learning Techniques

Neha Singh

https://orcid.org/0000-0003-3978-8627

Madan Mohan Malaviya University of Technology, Gorakhpur, India

Umesh Chandra Jaiswal

Madan Mohan Malaviya University of Technology, Gorakhpur, India

Ritu Singh

Madan Mohan Malaviya University of Technology, Gorakhpur, India

ABSTRACT

The growth of numerous statistical approaches used to evaluate data in educational settings has caused machine learning to recently become a novel subject of research. In this chapter, authors present a novel voting model for performance prediction that incorporates machine learning techniques and additional variables known as "student sentiment attributes." The proposed voting system was also employed to boost student test scores and improve the effectiveness of the strategies. In terms of the parameters of correlation coefficient, mean absolute error, root mean square error, time taken to build the model, relative absolute error, and root relative squared error, the supplied test set with voting method outperforms the four model evaluation methods of cross validation, use training set, supplied test set, and percentage split models. Given this, the result shows the applicability of the proposed model and computes the cost analysis of the proposed voting procedure.

DOI: 10.4018/979-8-3693-3278-8.ch010

INTRODUCTION

Tracking a student's development is essential to ensure they succeed and keep them on track to reach their objectives. The outcomes of their progress should be shared with them in the form of an official school report so that parents and guardians may understand what their child is learning and what progress has been made (Watkins et al., 2020). Forecasting students' learning outcomes is a complex but crucial academic endeavour. The ability to forecast education accomplishment is vital for instructors to identify at-risk learners, lower the likelihood that they will fail, and for learners to take charge of their education and develop into self-regulatory learners. Due to the numerous variables that might affect student performance, this is a challenging endeavour (López Zambrano et al., 2021). Over the past few decades, predictions of student achievement have been made while evaluating the impact of many factors, including emotional characteristics, familial characteristics, study habits, institutional characteristics, and students' performance on assignments, tests, and final exams. One practical use of these systems in several academic fields is determining what factors led to a student's academic success or failure and why (S. Ahmad et al., 2022).

Students now benefit from learning analytics and assisted learning, an emerging artificial intelligence study area. Because students learn and contribute to society, education plays a role in determining how society develops. The number of graduates rises each year. At the same time, some students pass with passing grades, while others fail and retake the course. Researchers analyse the interrelated detrimental repercussions of this strategy in great detail. Students who receive unsatisfactory course grades may experience despair or have diminished self-confidence. Through e-learning and virtual reality, there are numerous ways to learn about architecture and technologies (Geetha et al., 2021). Education research and literature, which are essential, can be used to predict academic performance. Some institutions must maintain higher academic excellence standards for students to achieve their full educational potential. This results in distinct actions that are directed towards certain student groups. Additionally, the institution's resources are distributed more effectively (Geetha et al., 2021).

Higher education is the cornerstone of a society's growth. They show that many students quit school, discontinue their studies, or reapply for admission to the same courses yearly. Not only would students suffer if they stopped attending school in large numbers due to failure, but educational systems would also suffer. Setting up a system recognising students who wish to drop out of their exams is crucial to lowering failure rates. A system of education must be continually examined to be successful. Identifying the barriers to student success is essential for enhancing institutional outcomes and ensuring all students complete their degrees. It may be challenging for teachers responsible for many students to analyse data and identify students' areas of weakness. Still, data analysis makes this process very simple and fun without directly involving teachers. Machine learning techniques are used in academic fields to enhance teaching (Batool et al., 2023). A growing field in academic data mining, machine learning approaches for forecasting students' educational achievement have the potential to address this issue (Sarwat et al., 2022).

The field of education has effectively used machine learning. The amount of information about students' academic activity in learning management systems is substantial. Data is growing every day. Data analysis, classification, and clustering can all be done using machine learning techniques. As a result, we can gauge the pupils' talents and identify great, sound, and subpar performances. They can motivate and pay special attention to struggling students to improve expected performance (Khan et al., 2022). Due to its superior performance when managing massive data sets, machine learning approaches have been extensively applied in research on education. Previous research on machine learning modelling has shown that various factors, such as demographics, levels of engagement, and outcomes from ongoing tests, may impact future performance on final exams (Arashpour et al., 2023). The institution can implement supportive educational interventions more easily thanks to the spectrum of appropriate and accessible analytical tools provided by machine learning approaches (Suleiman & Anane, 2022).

This research will provide comprehensive dataset on a student's academic achievement and forecast performance using cutting-edge techniques based on information gathered from students' sentiments. Review and evaluate the research on student performance to determine the factors influencing student achievement. To develop a framework for identifying pupils' emotions and predicting their test results, various calculation methods were used to accurately assess student performance and categorise feelings in light of the outcome. For developing forecasts, the suggested strategy includes tracking pupils' development. To put forth a voting model to forecast the pupils' success. On several performance metrics to evaluate and validate the suggested model.

This research is further divided into sections: Section 2 discusses various reviews of related material. Part 3 covers the approach, and Section 4 covers the outcomes. The five provide the conclusion.

LITERATURE SURVEY

While using past academic results to forecast future academic success at the same educational level, several research studies have examined student performance prediction. Below is a review of a few of these studies.

(Matzavela & Alepis, 2021) aim to further personalise students' academic performance by incorporating dynamic exams with a prediction model.

(Jang et al., 2022) propose an approach for predicting student performance in a classroom using explainable artificial intelligence and machine learning. They conducted a qualitative study to learn what stakeholders in education thought. The experiment's findings indicated that logistic regression performed the best result.

(Kumar et al., 2019) goal is to assess student performance utilising a range of parameters, including academic performance (CGPA), sex, class test grade, classroom environment, funding sources, scholarships, and private funding, among others. Naive Bayes, neural networks, closest neighbour methods, web-based systems, and classification and clustering Bayesian classification-mean algorithms will all be used in their investigation to look into how well understudies do. The challenge is to identify the students who perform poorly in their courses. There would be an opportunity to engage in corrective activities, as indicated by their execution and capacity. To predict students' final performance and obtain more precise scores, they use a variety of information mining calculations in this research.

(Aggarwal et al., 2021) examine the differences between the two models, one created using only educational and non-educational data. The primary student data collection was obtained from an Indian technical institution and contains details on 6,807 unique individuals with attributes. Eight classification methods are used to build the models, and the parameters that would provide the most accurate model for the performance-based classification of students are evaluated.

(Azimi et al., 2020) demonstrate how information from an online learning management system may be used to assess student's aggregate performance and recommend effective interventions at the right moment to raise students' success levels.

(Al Shuaeb et al., n.d.) proposed an innovative strategy to improve pupils' academic success. This research also discusses the prediction deep neural network approach to finding the critical components of a student's educational records. By utilising the suggested model, they can more successfully raise the success and achievement of polytechnic students.

(N. Ahmad et al., 2021) study put forth a technique for forecasting diploma student performance at the University of Technology MARA (UiTM) Terengganu's Faculty of Electrical Engineering (E.E.). Data on 59 first-semester Electrical Engineering (E.E.) students was gathered to forecast students' academic success. Based on the Sigil Pelajaran Malaysia (SPM) examination outcomes, the first semester's results, and the participant's level of interest in the elective course, the predictive model employs the technique. The results demonstrated that the developed approach could accurately forecast the actual outcomes of first-semester pupils with few errors.

(Oguine et al., 2022) examine the factors that impact how big data and analytics are used in educational situations. Finally, they try to pinpoint the limitations that hinder big data from being used in higher education settings. This research, carried out using survey research methodology, used a questionnaire to gather information.

(Merchant et al., 2022) forecasts student academic progress in online learning programmes using machine learning and statistical data. Multi-class classifiers are trained on the preprocessed dataset after selecting features and removing noisy data. The precision of each classifier improves as more data from the virtual learning environment is added.

(Rajendran, 2021) predict pupils' academic achievements using machine learning approaches. The grade point average, a statistic used to gauge academic achievement, is believed to be the model output.

(Badal & Sungkur, 2023) assess the effects of the features of online learning environments and develop a predictive model to gauge students' success. The Random Forest classifier outperformed the competition, according to the quantitative method used by students for data analysis and processing. For predicting grades and engagement, variables connected to student profiles and online participation yielded 85% and 83% accuracy rates, respectively.

(Inyang et al., 2019) classify the courses into an appropriate number of fail-course clusters. The dataset of student performance is then subjected to association rule mining to uncover fascinating course-status relationships. The main objective of higher education institutions is to increase graduation rates at the end of the shortest course length possible, which will enhance student learning outcomes.

(Y\ild\iz & Börekci, 2020) examined the accuracy of predictions and found which characteristics best classified data. They discovered that the family's demographic characteristics influenced classification, the student's scientific epistemological ideas, study habits, and attitudes towards particular courses.

(Zhu et al., 2021) provide the standard prediction models used in the relevant academic disciplines. According to the results, entropy and the corresponding behaviour have a connection that can be used to define changing behaviour patterns. The outcome shows that the suggested approach is practical in locating important characteristics and achieving high prediction accuracy.

(Gutiérrez et al., 2019) predicting students' academic performance. The final classifier was 80% accurate. To verify these findings, other research lines are suggested, focusing on collecting more data over multiple subsequent semesters.

(Mohamad Razi et al., 2022) introduce a cutting-edge research methodology. This study framework will present novel viewpoints.

(Sánchez-Pozo et al., 2021) contrast and analyse ML approaches to forecast educational success. They chose features that balanced accuracy and interpretability while also allowing for finding patterns in high school student's success. The trial's findings demonstrated that the gradient-boosting technique outperformed other classification methods, achieving the highest accuracy (96.77%).

(Yousafzai et al., 2021) examine a deep neural network approach to predicting pupils' success using historical data. Academics. Academics, institutes of higher learning, and government organisations greatly rely on the ability to forecast success early on the ability to forecast success early on. The proposed method's prediction accuracy is 90.16%.

(Ahn et al., 2021) created two models to forecast students' academic performance using information on school budget, student race, and gender. They use the K–12 financial, student, and academic achievement data from the U.S. Education Datasets: Unification Project as the foundation for their models. This dataset offers comprehensive data on each state's various sources of income and outlays from 1986 to 2019, as well as the typical math and reading test scores for its pupils. They begin by conducting an exploratory data analysis of the information.

(Kavitha et al., 2021) use learning analytics to examine how specific courses students take over several semesters affect their project work for the final semester. Comparing the Adaboost classifier against KNN, SVM, Naive Bayes, and neural networks, it was discovered that it produced results with higher accuracy. Therefore, the Adaboost classifier was used to forecast the project grades for the present group of students.

Table 1. Comparing and predicting student performance

Ref.	Study Aim	Techniques	Outcome	Future work / Gaps
(Saleem et al., 2021)	Using the features they extracted, they forecast the pupils' performance.	DT, RF, GBT, NB, and KNN	All five classifiers were used to make a stacking model with the highest F1 score (0.8195), which was better than other ensemble techniques.	The authors want to use the pandemic to get many schools that use online learning management systems to use the suggested structure in the future.
(Meghji et al., 2019)	This research aims to compare how well different ways of grouping things work to find an excellent way to predict how well students will do in school.	OneR, J48, NB, IBK, RF, PART	Random Forest is the most accurate, with an accuracy of 88.23%.	Future classifications might mix interactional, descriptive, behavioural, and attitudinal features, with behavioural traits including the propensity to communicate with others, social contact, punctuality, interest in extracurricular activities, etc.
(BÜTÜNER & Calp, 2022)	This research evaluates the educational success of pupils who complete their academics through distance learning.	DL, SVM, RF, ANN, NB, LR	The results show that some algorithms are superior to others regarding prediction accuracy.	This research is expected to provide a template for future work on improving student achievement.
(Jenitha et al., 2021)	In the proposed effort, students who qualify for scholarships and other perks are found using a data-mining approach.	SVM, DT, and NB	Multiple learning models are developed to determine which algorithm performs best, and their accuracy levels are compared.	If more features are added, more classification algorithms are utilised, and comparative research is conducted, accuracy can be further enhanced.

continued on following page

Table 1. Continued

Ref.	Study Aim	Techniques	Outcome	Future work / Gaps
(Ramdas et al., 2019)	This research proposed a new algorithm for estimating a student's performance in college programmes based on prior academic achievements.	NB, SVM	It gives academic advisers important information about what courses students should take next and how to use pedagogical intervention strategies when necessary.	Future educational institutions might have programmes like todays, plus any improvements.
(Bannet Tumuhimbise & Chidananda, 2021)	This research used supervised and unsupervised learning approaches to forecast the student's performance.	RF, XgBoost and K Means model	XgBoost offers greater accuracy in its model than K-Means and Random Forest.	Following the performance forecast, they give the students with low and medium performances that can assist them in improving their performance in the future.
(Campus, n.d.)	This research looks into how students' demographic characteristics affect their academic success.	RF	Three separate datasets with Random Forest produced 81.20%, 95.10%, and 84.16% F-measures.	An open research topic for future research is using students' performance in individual courses as a predictor of performance to suggest classes or fields where students can perform better.

Table 1 presents the findings of this research, the various methodologies, outcomes, future research and gaps . Several methods are used to forecast students' achievement, such as Naive Bayes (NB), Decision Trees (DT), Random Forests (RF), Support Vector Machines (SVM), Logistic Regressions (LR), Gradient Boosting (GB), Artificial Neural Networks (ANN), Linear Regressions (LR), Multilayer Perceptrons (MLP), Neural Networks (NN), Data Mining (DM) and Machine Learning (ML). Compared to other algorithms, all machine learning techniques provide the best outcomes.

METHODOLOGY

The stages used in this process were as follows: proposed model design, data collection, sentiment analysis, data preprocessing, data visualisation, approaches for model evaluation, various machine learning techniques, and ultimately, results analysis using multiple metrics. In this research, the authors present a model for forecasting student performance based on a hybrid voting technique and machine-learning. The outcomes of the method used to predict student success are valid. Authors make use of the WEKA tool to forecast student performance. Figure 1 displays the suggested model.

Figure 1. Proposed framework

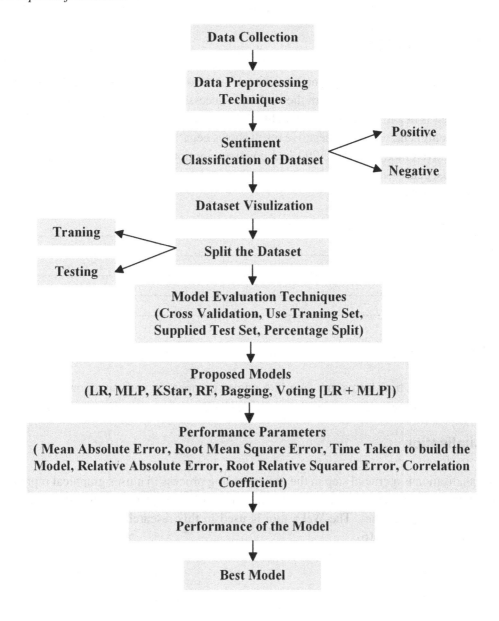

Dataset Details

The dataset utilised in this research was compiled on December 15, 2023, and is found online at (https://www.kaggle.com/datasets/aljarah/xAPI-Edu-Data. The dataset is accessible in CSV format. There are 480 records in the collection, each having 17 different qualities, plus sentiment, which is an additional attribute. There are now 18 attributes in total after adding one additional attribute. Many other categories are formed as a result of the attributes. The attributes include country, place of birth, stage

I.D., grade I.D., section I.D., topic, semester, relation, raised hand, visited resources, announcement's perspective, discussion, parent survey response, student missing days, class, and sentiment.

Sentiment Classification

There are 480 total datasets used. One " sentiment " attribute in the dataset is based on parent-school satisfaction. If the parent is pleased with the student's success, the sentiment is positive; if the parent is not, the sentiment is negative. Authors manually classify each sentiment attribute. A positive outcome shows positive sentiment, whereas a negative result shows negative sentiment. One hundred eighty-eight people had negative emotions, while 292 had positive emotions. The attribute categories in Table 2 indicate the dataset classification.

Table 2. Categorisation of sentiment

Sentiment	Number
Positive	292
Negative	188
Total	480

Data Preprocessing

Data preprocessing transforms raw data into a form compatible with an algorithm before using it. Data cleansing, feature selection, and transformation comprise data preparation (Amrieh et al., 2016).

Data Visualisation

Data visualisation is a crucial step in the preprocessing process that uses graphical representation to deconstruct and make sense of complex data. Recently, online learning features have been visualised using visualisation approaches. The Weka tool is used in this research to visualise the existing data collection (Amrieh et al., 2016).

Figure 2. Dataset attribute visualisation results

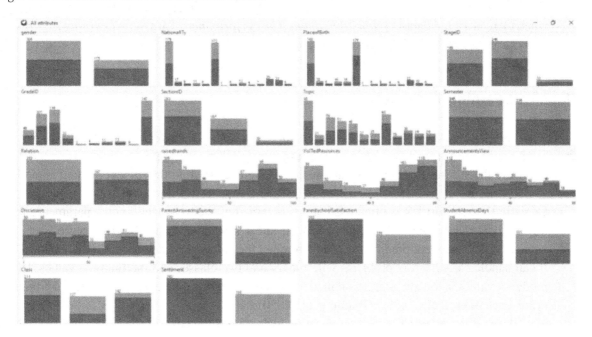

Figure 2 shows the characteristics of the performance data set of 480 students. For instance, the first graph shows the graph for the attribute "gender" at the top-left corner. As demonstrated by the first bar in the graph, there are 305 male and 175 female students. Blue represents the proportion of male students, while red represents the proportion of female students. Similar representations of the following 17 attributes are shown in the remaining 17 graphs.

Model Evaluation Techniques

There are several model evaluation methods, including the following:

- **Cross Validation:** The dataset should be folded or divided into k-folds. To construct k different models, train a model on every partition except the one used as the test set. This will allow every fold to serve as the test set. Determine the average performance of each of the k models. This is the benchmark for assessing model performance, even if it incurs the significant cost of model creation (*How To Estimate The Performance of Machine Learning Algorithms in Weka - MachineLearningMastery.Com*, n.d.).
- **Use Traning Set:** Build your model using the whole training dataset, then use the same data to assess it. This is problematic in general, not least because a perfect algorithm could manipulate this evaluation technique by memorising (storing) all training patterns and receiving a perfect score, which would be unethical
- **Supplied Test Set:** Use a different application to divide the dataset manually. Create the model using the complete training dataset, then assess its performance using a different test set. This strategy is brilliant if you have a huge dataset

- **Percentage Split:** To evaluate a model, randomly divide the dataset into training and testing divisions. This can give a quick performance estimate, just like using a given test set, and is preferred when there is a large dataset (*How To Estimate The Performance of Machine Learning Algorithms in Weka - MachineLearningMastery.Com*, n.d.).

Machine Learning Techniques

The authors selected six well-known classifiers for Prediction: logistic regression, multilayer perceptron, kstar, random forest, bagging, and voting using sequential minimal optimisation. As a result, they could compare the various machine learning methods employed to train the student predictive models.

- **Logistic Regression:** LR is often used and is regarded as the most well-known parametric technique when a target variable is categorical. In linear models known as logistic regressions, the value of an independent predictor is used to predict the value of a categorical dependent variable. It can handle classification problems with binary and two classes and multinomial values. Using predictor values, a logistic regression model calculates the linear combinations or probabilities of occurrence of each class value (Bhutto et al., 2020).
- **Multilayer Perceptron:** The backpropagation algorithm is the basis of the MLP classifier, which categorises instances. The network is constructed using the MLP technique. During training, the network can be monitored and adjusted. Each node in this network is sigmoid. Using a set of iteratively learned weights, the class label of tuples is predicted (Arora, 2012).
- **KStar:** It is employed to determine the depth of a field, or in this instance, the depth of accuracy. The values are predicted using a model with the nearest first-look mode and two training sets. It operates instantly and classifies training sets very quickly (Roy et al., 2021).
- **Random Forest:** This supervised ML technique uses DT and heavily relies on the learned data set. A learning paradigm is used to achieve the desired results. Random tree plotting produces the most precise and trustworthy forecasts (Roy et al., 2021).
- **Bagging:** An independent technique based on an ensemble is bagging. A hybrid classifier is then used to aggregate the results of the learned classifiers into a single prediction to improve the stability of unstable classifiers. The size of every bootstrap sample is the same as the size of the initial training set. The bagging method resamples the initial data into various training data sets or bootstraps. Different classifiers will be used to train each bootstrap sample (Amrieh et al., 2016).
- **Proposed Voting Technique:** The proposed voting method uses four models to offer a solution for predicting and categorising students' academic achievement. The model predicts and categorises students' academic performance using cross-validation, use training set, supplied test set, and percentage split model. After receiving the classification result from the four models above, the method learns the added sentence for categorisation likelihood. The models are combined to evaluate each student's academic achievement.

A voting method uses a variety of strategies to address various issues and increase accuracy. Predicting and categorising a student's academic achievement is based on LR and MLP principles. The Logistic Regression-Multilayer Perceptron approach is a cutting-edge best practice for predicting and categorising student feelings' academic success. It resolves the issues with both methods. Students' academic performance is expected and classified using LR and MLP. LR models are linear models commonly used to forecast categorical dependent values based on independent predictor values.

The logistic regression-multilayer perceptron method is a brand-new, practical approach to the categorisation problem. It resolves the flaws in both approaches. Binary classification issues and multinomial values can be resolved using logistic regression. The logistic regression model uses the logit function to determine the linear combinations of a specific class value based on predictor values. Backpropagation is the foundation of the multilayer Perceptron classifier, which categorises instances. Using an MLP algorithm, the network is built. This network's nodes are all sigmoid. Finally, their suggested method is more precise than the other approaches the authors looked at. Their proposed experiment was carried out more effectively than previous work in increasing accuracy.

Comparative Analysis of Parameters Used

There are several parameters, including the following:

- **Mean Absolute Error (MAE):** The formula for calculating it is to divide the total absolute error by the number of forecasts. A predicted value's similarity to an actual value, or vice versa, is measured (kumar & Sahoo, 2012).
- **Root Mean Square Error (RMSE):** RMSE is calculated by dividing the number of forecasts by the sum of all squared errors. It determines the discrepancies between predicted and observed values. A low RMSE value indicates that the model is more accurate. Thus, prediction prediction and accuracy are improved with a minimum of RMSE and MAE (Sahoo & Kumar, 2012).
- **Time taken to build the model:** The researchers also considered the model's construction time, which was measured in seconds. This value shows the model's training time, crucial to determining which model will work the fastest (Villavicencio et al., 2021).
- **Relative Absolute Error (RAE):** It is found by dividing the total absolute error by the absolute difference between the mean and the observed value (*Evaluation Metric for Regression Models - Analytics Vidhya*, n.d.).
- **Root Relative Squared Error (RRSE):** A dimensionless version of RMSE is known as RRMSE. Researcher are scaling each residual against the actual value results in the RRMSE, and the RMS value normalise the RMSE. RRMSE can be used to compare various measurement techniques, whereas the size of the original measurements constrains RMSE. An elevated RRMSE is the outcome of erroneous predictions. RRMSE expresses the error as a percentage, or approximately (*Evaluation Metric for Regression Models - Analytics Vidhya*, n.d.).
- **Correlation coefficient (CC):** Using correlation coefficients, calculate the significance of a relationship between two variables. One of the best-known correlation coefficients, sometimes referred to as "Pearson's R," is the Pearson correlation, frequently used in linear regression. The correlation coefficient method is applied to ascertain how closely related the data are (*Correlation Coefficient Formula - GeeksforGeeks*, n.d.).

Algorithms Pseudocode

```
Input: Students Performance Datasets have the details about students'
performance.
Output: Students' sentiment prediction.
Process: With the students' Parents, school satisfaction details are fetched
from the database.
function Sentiment Prediction()
{
If (Good=="Positive" and Bad=="Negative")
{
Print Sentiment Prediction as "Positive"
}
else
{
Print Sentiment Prediction "Negative"
}
}
```

RESULT

The efficiency of the student performance model is influenced by various factors, both directly and indirectly. The effect on students' academic achievement will be assessed in this part using a variety of classification methodologies, including L.R., MLP, KStar, RF, bagging, and voting. After applying classification algorithms to the data set, various outcomes based on data machine learning techniques are obtained. Table 3 displays the results of various categorisation techniques (L.R., MLP, KStar, RF, bagging, and voting). Every classifier displays two outcomes for classification, one with the student's CC, MAE, RMSE, TTBM, RAE, and RRSE.

Table 3. Comparative evaluation of the outcomes

Techniques	Cross Validation			Use Traning Set			Supplied Test Set			Percentage Split		
	CC	MAE	RMSE	CC	MAE	RMSE	CC	MAE	RMSE	CC	MAE	RMSE
LR	0.97	0.040	0.113	0.98	0.035	0.091	0.98	0.029	0.081	0.97	0.039	0.118
MLP	0.97	0.031	0.085	0.97	0.012	0.001	0.97	0.013	0.0019	0.97	0.031	0.11
KStar	0.88	0.071	0.22	0.97	0.013	0.0001	0.97	0.014	0.0001	0.86	0.082	0.24
RF	0.97	0.046	0.10	0.96	0.016	0.032	0.96	0.013	0.03	0.97	0.051	0.11
Bagging	0.97	0.027	0.10	0.98	0.014	0.08	0.98	0.012	0.07	0.97	0.020	0.11
Proposed Voting	0.98	0.025	0.09	0.99	0.011	0.04	0.99	0.010	0.04	0.98	0.013	0.10

After the categorisation model has been trained, the validation phase starts. Because it evaluates the predictive models' realism, the validation stage of the predictive model creation process is essential. In this study, 480 students were employed to train the model. Table 3 includes cross-validation, use training set, supplied test set, percentage split model, and the evaluation results for various classification algorithms (including L.R., MLP, KStar, RF, bagging, and voting).

Table 3 demonstrates that the voting model outperforms other ML techniques. The voting technique achieved a cross-validation correlation coefficient of 0.98, a use training set and supplied test set correlation coefficient of 0.99, and a percentage split correlation coefficient of 0.98. The use of training data and the supplied test model yields the best output result of 0.99 after comparing the outcome of the correlation coefficient with the voting model. The mean absolute error for the voting model is 0.025 with cross-validation and 0.11, 0.010 with the training set and supplied test set, and 0.013 with a % split. With cross-validation, the root RMSE results are 0.09, with percentage split, 0.10, and with the training set and supplied test set, 0.04, respectively. Authors can get precise results by employing the voting model, the training set, and the specified test set.

Figure 3. Results of several strategies utilising the cross-validation model

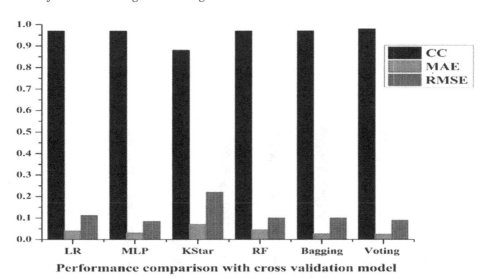

Figure 4. Results of various methods employing the use of training set model

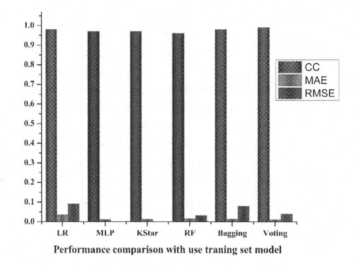

Figure 5. The outcome of several strategies using the provided test set model

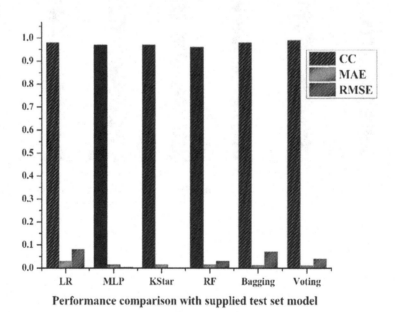

Figure 6. The outcome of different methods utilising the % split model

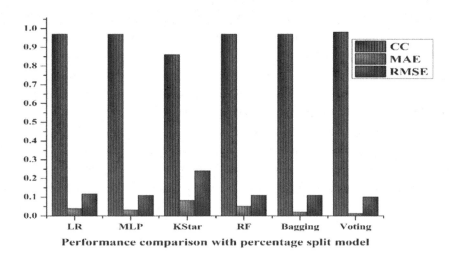

The comparison of techniques employing four test models: cross-validation model, percentage split model, use training set model, and supplied test set model is shown in Figures 3, 4, 5, and 6. These outcomes show that use training set and supplied test set model perform better than cross-fold and the % split models. For various reasons, the usage training set and given test set approach outperform the cross-validation and percentage split model. The correlation coefficient estimate is the first and has the best outcome estimate. The training set and given test set model have the lowest mean absolute error compared to the cross-validation and percentage split models. Second, the training and supplied test sets' models have greater predictive values than the root mean square error in both situations but lower predictive values than the cross-validation model and % split model. The suggested voting strategy outperforms all other techniques when employing the training set model and the provided test model. KStar performs the worst, with a maximum CC value of 0.99, a minimum MAE rate value of 0.011 and 0.010, and an RMSE estimate rate value of 0.04. The proposed voting methods produce the same results using both the provided test set and the use training set model.

Table 4. Results of a comparative comparison of several approaches

Techniques	Cross Validation		Use Traning Set		Supplied Test Set		Percentage Split	
	RAE%	RRSE%	RAE%	RRSE%	RAE%	RRSE%	RAE%	RRSE%
LR	8.55	23.19	7.40	18.70	5.93	16.15	8.31	24.43
MLP	2.46	18.46	0.22	0.32	0.25	0.37	6.46	24.61
KStar	15.4	47.1	0.59	0.002	0.002	0.01	18.26	50.11
RF	9.29	20.7	2.76	6.76	2.63	7.02	11.35	22.94
Bagging	4.46	22.38	3.45	18.35	2.41	15.15	5.19	23.13
Proposed Voting	5.33	17.72	3.71	9.32	2.98	7.98	6.96	21.88

In this section, the authors employed four models to enhance how student performance was evaluated. The outcomes of all the models are shown in Table 4. Table 4 demonstrates efficient results when combining classifiers and voting systems (LR-MLP). To obtain the student's model's best prediction performance, use a voting method using two classifiers and merge the results using a majority voting procedure. When employing the boosting approach instead of other ensemble methods, the supplied test sets relative absolute error is less than 2.98%. The root-squared error results using the test set model provided are less than 15.15 per cent. The test model's results are consequently better than those of the other three models for forecasting student performance results.

A multilayer perceptron with a training set model that finds relative absolute error at 0.22% also produces good results, significantly improving root relative squared error at 0.32%. Logistic regression is more critical when using a percentage split model with root relative squared error findings of 24.61%. When using a training set model, the KStar classifier produces less RAE and RRSE (0.59% and 0.002%, respectively). Using the training and test sets, a random forest classifier produces a minimum relative absolute error of 2.76% and 2.63%, respectively.

Figure 7. Results for various strategies are compared using the cross-validation model

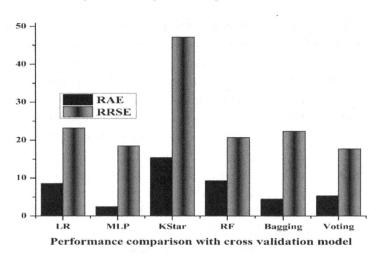

Figure 8. Results for several approaches were compared using the training set model

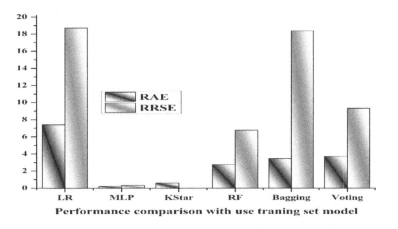

Figure 9. Results for various techniques using supplied test set model.

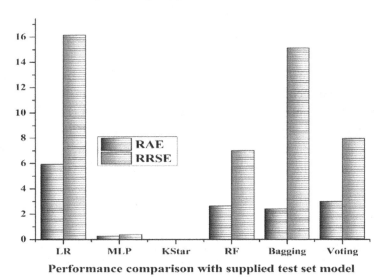

Figure 10. Results using the percentage split model for various methodologies

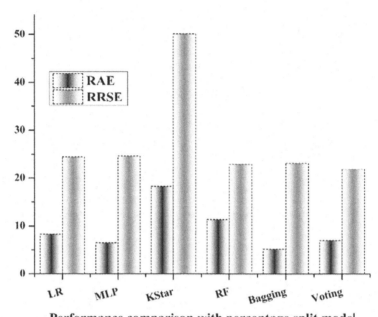

Performance comparison with percentage split model

In Figures 7, 8, 9, and 10, the student performance dataset is analysed using cross-validation, a training set, a supplied test set, and percentage split models. Three parameters are used in this research to evaluate how accurately the strategies perform. The proposed voting method (Logistic Regression-Multilayer Perceptron) yields the best results compared to root absolute error. Comparing the suggested voting technique to logistic regression, multilayer perceptron, Kstar, random forest, and bagging techniques produces the best overall results in terms of performance parameters.

Table 5. The duration of the task

Techniques	Time taken to build the model (Seconds)			
	Cross Validation	**Use Traning Set**	**Supplied Test Set**	**Percentage Split**
LR	0.13	0.09	0.17	0.13
MLP	12.4	12.23	12.2	15.05
KStar	0.12	0.015	0.11	0.19
RF	0.22	0.05	0.02	0.12
Bagging	0.09	0.12	0.01	0.11
Proposed Voting	0.11	0.2	0.1	0.11

According to Table 5, all six techniques took less than one second to complete the execution, except the multilayer perceptron, which required 12.4, 12.23, 12.2, and 15.05 seconds. The percentage split model results in a time for one technique of 15.05 seconds and a time for five classification techniques of less than 1.00 seconds.

Figure 11. Execution time is displayed in seconds

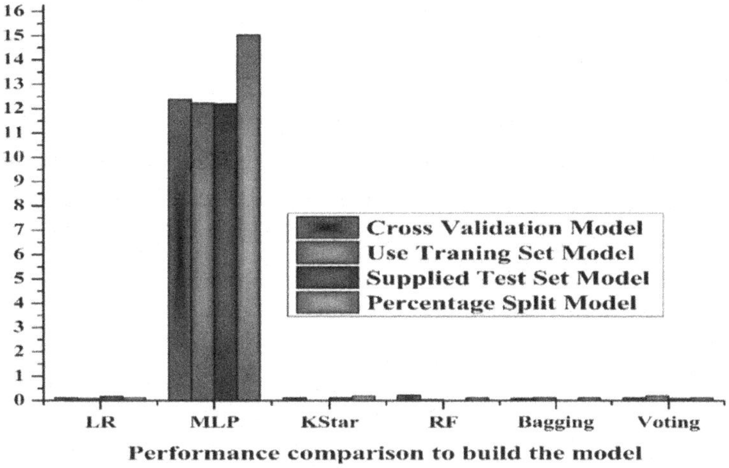

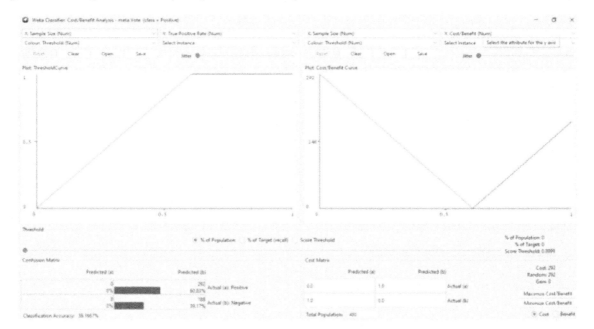

The given test set model produces noticeably better minimum time results than the cross-validation model. Execution time is displayed in seconds for all the models shown in Figure 11. The cost-benefit analysis of the suggested voting strategies will be computed in the following experiment stage.

Figure 12. Voting method analysis of costs and benefits

The figure 12 explains the suggested voting method's results on the student performance dataset and shows a cost analysis.

CONCLUSION

Students' academic performance results are a significant issue for educational institutions worldwide. In this research, the authors provide a novel data attribute called the "student's sentiment attribute" to forecast students' achievement and classify students' sentiment, along with a novel voting mechanism based on machine learning techniques. The efficiency of the student's prediction model is evaluated using a variety of classifiers, including LR, MLP, KStar, RF, bagging, and voting. Compared to the results, the correlation coefficient of the student's prediction model utilising the voting model improved by up to 0.01% and -0.01%, and up to 0.021% in terms of MAE. The supplied test set with a voting classifier yields the best results in terms of CC, MAE, RMSE, TTBM, RAE, and RRSE when compared to four model evaluation techniques such as cross-validation, use of training set, the supplied test set, and the percentage split model. Finally, this strategy can help teachers identify poor students, improve the learning process, and reduce the rate of academic failure by assisting students. It also allows administrators to enhance the performance of the educational system. In future studies, a more extensive data collection with more distinguishing traits will be used with ML techniques to produce more accurate results. Additionally, research utilising DL methods could be carried out to investigate additional voting model combinations and enhance performance.

Competing Interests: There are no competing interests for the writers.

REFERENCES

Aggarwal, D., Mittal, S., & Bali, V. (2021). Significance of non-academic parameters for predicting student performance using ensemble learning techniques. [IJSDA]. *International Journal of System Dynamics Applications*, 10(3), 38–49. 10.4018/IJSDA.2021070103

Ahmad, N., Hassan, N., Jaafar, H., & Enzai, N. I. M. (2021). Students' Performance Prediction using Artificial Neural Network. *IOP Conference Series. Materials Science and Engineering*, 1176(1), 12020. 10.1088/1757-899X/1176/1/012020

Ahmad, S., El-Affendi, M. A., Anwar, M. S., & Iqbal, R. (2022). Potential future directions in optimization of students' performance prediction system. *Computational Intelligence and Neuroscience*, 2022, 2022. 10.1155/2022/686495535619762

Ahn, J., Shin, H., & Guo, M. (2021). *Building a Deep Learning Model to Predict Academic Achievement*.

Al Shuaeb, S. M. A., Alam, S., Rahman, M. M., & Matin, M. A. (n.d.). *Polytechnic Students' Academic Performance Prediction Based on Deep Neural Network*.

Amrieh, E. A., Hamtini, T., & Aljarah, I. (2016). Mining educational data to predict student's academic performance using ensemble methods. *International Journal of Database Theory and Application*, 9(8), 119–136. 10.14257/ijdta.2016.9.8.13

Arashpour, M., Golafshani, E. M., Parthiban, R., Lamborn, J., Kashani, A., Li, H., & Farzanehfar, P. (2023). Predicting individual learning performance using machine-learning hybridized with the teaching-learning-based optimization. *Computer Applications in Engineering Education*, 31(1), 83–99. 10.1002/cae.22572

Arora, R., & Suman, S. (2012). Comparative analysis of classification algorithms on different datasets using WEKA. *International Journal of Computer Applications*, 54(13), 21–25. 10.5120/8626-2492

Azimi, S., Popa, C.-G., & Cucić, T. (2020). Improving Students Performance in Small-Scale Online Courses—A Machine Learning-Based Intervention. *ArXiv Preprint ArXiv:2012.01187*.

Badal, Y. T., & Sungkur, R. K. (2023). Predictive modelling and analytics of students' grades using machine learning algorithms. *Education and Information Technologies*, 28(3), 3027–3057. 10.1007/s10639-022-11299-836097545

Bannet Tumuhimbise, D. A. P., & Chidananda, K. (2021). Advanced Prediction of a student in a university using Machine Learning techniques. [TURCOMAT]. *Turkish Journal of Computer and Mathematics Education*, 12(14), 5913–5919.

Batool, S., Rashid, J., Nisar, M. W., Kim, J., Kwon, H.-Y., & Hussain, A. (2023). Educational data mining to predict students' academic performance: A survey study. *Education and Information Technologies*, 28(1), 905–971. 10.1007/s10639-022-11152-y

Bhutto, E. S., Siddiqui, I. F., Arain, Q. A., & Anwar, M. (2020). Predicting students' academic performance through supervised machine learning. *2020 International Conference on Information Science and Communication Technology (ICISCT)*, (pp. 1–6). IEEE. 10.1109/ICISCT49550.2020.9080033

Bütüner, R., & Calp, M. H.BÜTÜNER. (2022). Estimation of the Academic Performance of Students in Distance Education Using Data Mining Methods. *International Journal of Assessment Tools in Education*, 9(2), 410–429. 10.21449/ijate.904456

Campus, W. (n.d.). *A Random Forest Students' Performance Prediction (RFSPP) Model Based on Students' Demographic.*

Correlation Coefficient Formula. (n.d.). GeeksforGeeks. https://www.geeksforgeeks.org/correlation -coefficient-formula/

Geetha, R., Padmavathy, T., & Anitha, R. (2021). Prediction of the academic performance of slow learners using efficient machine learning algorithm. *Advances in Computational Intelligence*, 1(4), 1–12. 10.1007/s43674-021-00005-9

Gutiérrez, L., Flores, V., Keith, B., & Quelopana, A. (2019). Using the Belbin method and models for predicting the academic performance of engineering students. *Computer Applications in Engineering Education*, 27(2), 500–509. 10.1002/cae.22092

Inyang, U. G., Eyoh, I. J., Robinson, S. A., & Udo, E. N. (2019). Visual association analytics approach to predictive modelling of students' academic performance. *International Journal of Modern Education \&. Computer Science*, 11(12), 1–13.

Jang, Y., Choi, S., Jung, H., & Kim, H. (2022). Practical early prediction of students' performance using machine learning and eXplainable AI. *Education and Information Technologies*, 27(9), 12855–12889. 10.1007/s10639-022-11120-6

Jenitha, T., Santhi, S., & Jeba, J. M. P. (2021). Prediction of Students' Performance based on Academic, Behaviour, Extra and Co-Curricular Activities. *Webology*, 18(Special Issue 01, SI01), 262–279. 10.14704/ WEB/V18SI01/WEB18058

Kavitha, R. K., Jaisingh, W., & Devi, S. K. K. (2021). Applying Learning Analytics to Study the Influence of Fundamental Computer Courses on Project Work and Student Performance Prediction using Machine Learning Techniques. *2021 International Conference on Advancements in Electrical, Electronics, Communication, Computing and Automation (ICAECA)*, (pp. 1–5). IEEE. 10.1109/ICAECA52838.2021.9675517

Khan, M. I., Khan, Z. A., Imran, A., Khan, A. H., & Ahmed, S. (2022). Student Performance Prediction in Secondary School Education Using Machine Learning. *2022 8th International Conference on Information Technology Trends (ITT)*, (pp. 94–101). IEEE.

Kumar, T. R., Vamsidhar, T., Harika, B., Kumar, T. M., & Nissy, R. (2019). Students performance prediction using data mining techniques. *2019 International Conference on Intelligent Sustainable Systems (ICISS)*, 407–411. kumar, Y., & Sahoo, G. (2012). Analysis of Parametric & Non Parametric Classifiers for Classification Technique using WEKA. *International Journal of Information Technology and Computer Science*, 4(7), 43–49. 10.5815/ijitcs.2012.07.06

López Zambrano, J., Lara Torralbo, J. A., & Romero Morales, C. (2021). Early prediction of student learning performance through data mining: A systematic review. *Psicothema*.34297676

Matzavela, V., & Alepis, E. (2021). Decision tree learning through a predictive model for student academic performance in intelligent m-learning environments. *Computers and Education: Artificial Intelligence*, 2, 100035. 10.1016/j.caeai.2021.100035

Meghji, A. F., Mahoto, N. A., Unar, M. A., & Shaikh, M. A. (2019). Predicting student academic performance using data generated in higher educational institutes. *3c Tecnolog{\'\i}a. Glosas de Innovación Aplicadas a La Pyme*, 8(1), 366–383.

Merchant, A., Shenoy, N., Bharali, A., & Kumar, M. A. (2022). Predicting Students' Academic Performance in Virtual Learning Environment Using Machine Learning. *2022 Second International Conference on Power, Control and Computing Technologies (ICPC2T)*, (pp. 1–6). IEEE. 10.1109/ICPC2T53885.2022.9777008

Mohamad Razi, N. F., Baharun, N., & Omar, N. (2022). Machine learning predictive model of academic achievement efficiency based on data envelopment analysis. [MIJ]. *Mathematical Sciences and Informatics Journal*, 3(1), 86–99. 10.24191/mij.v3i1.18284

Oguine, O. C., Oguine, K. J., & Bisallah, H. I. (2022). Big Data and Analytics Implementation in Tertiary Institutions to Predict Students Performance in Nigeria. *ArXiv Preprint ArXiv:2207.14677*.

Rajendran, S. (2021). Predicting Factors Impacting Student Academic Performance using Machine Learning Algorithms. *Available atSSRN* 3898302. 10.2139/ssrn.3898302

Ramdas, B. R., Machhindra, M. B., Kailas, W. P., & Raut, M. V. (2019). *Tracking and Predicting Student Performance Using Machine Learning*.

Roy, D., Mahmood, M. A., & Roy, T. J. (2021). *An Analytical Model for Prediction of Heart Disease using Machine Learning Classifiers*. TechrXiv. 10.36227/techrxiv.14867175

Sahoo, G., & Kumar, Y. (2012). Analysis of parametric \& non parametric classifiers for classification technique using WEKA. [IJITCS]. *International Journal of Information Technology and Computer Science*, 4(7), 43–49. 10.5815/ijitcs.2012.07.06

Saleem, F., Ullah, Z., Fakieh, B., & Kateb, F. (2021). Intelligent decision support system for predicting student's e-learning performance using ensemble machine learning. *Mathematics*, 9(17), 2078. 10.3390/math9172078

Sánchez-Pozo, N. N. Mej\'\ia-Ordóñez, J. S., Chamorro, D. C., Mayorca-Torres, D., & Peluffo-Ordóñez, D. H. (2021). Predicting High School Students' Academic Performance: A Comparative Study of Supervised Machine Learning Techniques. *2021 Machine Learning-Driven Digital Technologies for Educational Innovation Workshop*, (pp. 1–6). IEEE.

Sarwat, S., Ullah, N., Sadiq, S., Saleem, R., Umer, M., Eshmawi, A., Mohamed, A., & Ashraf, I. (2022). Predicting students' academic performance with conditional generative adversarial network and deep SVM. *Sensors (Basel)*, 22(13), 4834. 10.3390/s2213483435808330

Suleiman, R., & Anane, R. (2022). Institutional data analysis and machine learning prediction of student performance. *2022 IEEE 25th International Conference on Computer Supported Cooperative Work in Design (CSCWD)*. IEEE.

Villavicencio, C. N., Macrohon, J. J. E., Inbaraj, X. A., Jeng, J. H., & Hsieh, J. G. (2021). Covid-19 prediction applying supervised machine learning algorithms with comparative analysis using weka. *Algorithms*, 14(7), 201. 10.3390/a14070201

Watkins, J., Fabielli, M., & Mahmud, M. (2020). SENSE: A Student Performance Quantifier using Sentiment Analysis. *Proceedings of the International Joint Conference on Neural Networks*. IEEE. 10.1109/IJCNN48605.2020.9207721

Y\ild\iz, M., & Börekci, C. (2020). Predicting academic achievement with machine learning algorithms. *Journal of Educational Technology and Online Learning, 3*(3), 372–392.

Yousafzai, B. K., Khan, S. A., Rahman, T., Khan, I., Ullah, I., Ur Rehman, A., Baz, M., Hamam, H., & Cheikhrouhou, O. (2021). Student-performulator: Student academic performance using hybrid deep neural network. *Sustainability (Basel)*, 13(17), 9775. 10.3390/su13179775

Zhu, X., Ye, Y., Zhao, L., & Shen, C. (2021). MOOC Behavior Analysis and Academic Performance Prediction Based on Entropy. *Sensors (Basel)*, 21(19), 6629. 10.3390/s2119662934640949

Chapter 11
Core Technologies:
A Deep Dive Into Neural Networks, Machine Learning

Atharva Saraf
https://orcid.org/0009-0006-3842-5508
Ajeenkya D.Y. Patil University, India

Susanta Das
https://orcid.org/0000-0002-9314-3988
Ajeenkya D.Y. Patil University, India

ABSTRACT

The purpose of the chapter is to provide an overview of artificial intelligence (AI) to the knowledge seekers. This chapter aims to provide the historical development of AI over the years. It provides an overview of machine learning. It talks about supervised, semi-supervised, and unsupervised, reinforcement learning, and transfer learning. It delves into the generative adversarial networks (GAN). It further provides an overview of various components of neural network (NN) such as input layers, hidden layers, output layers, forward propagation, backward propagation, training, optimization, inference, fine tuning, transfer learning, etc. The chapter will leverage academic journals, conferences, and online repositories to shed light on the dynamic landscape of AI technology.

INTRODUCTION

In today's world, technology is growing very fast, and we are getting in touch with different new technologies day by day. AI is one of the most rapidly growing technologies in computer science which is ready to create a new revolution in the world by making intelligent machines (Russell & Norvig, 2010). Artificial Intelligence is composed of two words Artificial and Intelligence, where Artificial defines "man-made" and Intelligence defines "thinking power", hence AI means "a man-made thinking power". In simple words, AI is a branch of computer science by which we can create intelligent machines which can behave like a human, think like a human, and able to make decisions on its own (Chandra & Hareendran, 2014; Jarrahi, 2018). With artificial Intelligence we do not need to preprogram our machines to perform certain tasks we just have to develop an algorithm that will be able to learn, understand, and

DOI: 10.4018/979-8-3693-3278-8.ch011

perform certain task given to it on its own. In today's world, we hardly avoid hearing about AI. We see AI in the movies, in books, in the news and online (Jarrahi, 2018). Today we use Artificial Intelligence in many different sectors such as industries, government, civil, science, etc. (Russell & Norvig, 2010; Chandra & Hareendran, 2014). For example, advanced web search engines (e.g. google search), recommendation algorithms (used by YouTube, Amazon, and Netflix), interactions via human speech (such as Google Assistant, Siri, and Alexa), self-driving cars (e.g. Tesla, Waymo), generative and creative tools (Chatgpt and AI art), and superhuman play and analysis in strategy games (such as chess and go). In simple words, AI is a method of making a computer, a computer-controlled robot, or a software think intelligently like the human mind (Mitchell, 1997).

But AI is not a new word and a new technology for researchers. This technology is much older than you would imagine. Even there are myths of Mechanical men in Ancient Greek and Egyptian Myths (Chahal & Gulia, 2019). A few milestones in the history of AI that define the journey from the AI generation to the present development are shown in Fig. 1.

Figure 1. Evolution of AI

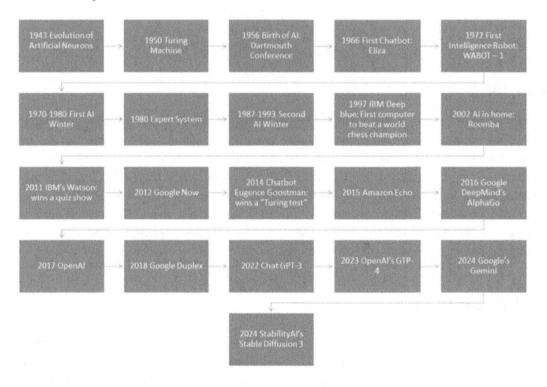

1.1. **Maturation of Artificial Intelligence (1943-1952)** (Russell & Norvig, 2010; Chahal & Gulia, 2019; Mitchell, 1997; Mueller & Massaron, 2016; Haenlein & Kaplan, 2019).

- **Year 1943:** The first which is now recognized as AI was done by Warren McCulloch and Walter pits in 1943. They proposed a model of artificial neurons.

- **Year 1949:** Donald Hebb demonstrated an updating rule for modifying the connection strength between neurons. His rule is now called Hebbian Learning.
- **Year 1950:** The Alan Turing who was an English mathematician and pioneered Machine Learning in 1950. Alan Turing published "Computing Machinery and Intelligence" in which he proposed a test. The test can check the machine's ability to exhibit intelligent behavior equivalent to human intelligence, called the Turing test.

1.2. The birth of Artificial Intelligence (1952-1956) (Chahal & Gulia, 2019; Mitchell, 1997; Mueller & Massaron, 2016).

- **Year 1955:** An Allen Newell and Herbert A. Simon create the "First Artificial Intelligence Program" which was named as "**Logic Theorist**". This program proved 38 of 52 Mathematics theorems, and found new and more elegant proofs for some theorems.
- **Year 1956:** The word "Artificial Intelligence" first adopted by American Computer Scientist John McCarthy at the Dartmouth conference. For the first time, AI was coined as an academic field.
- At that time high-level computer languages such as FORTRAN, LISP, or COBOL were invented. And the enthusiasm for AI was very high at that time.

1.3. The golden years-early enthusiasm (1956-1974) (Alzubi et al., 2018; Sharma et al., 2021; Haenlein & Kaplan, 2019).

- **Year 1966:** Allen Newell and Herbert A. Simon created the "First Artificial Intelligence Program" which was named as "Logic Theorist". This program had proved 38 of 52 Mathematics theorems and find new and more elegant proofs for some theorems.
- **Year 1972:** The first intelligent humanoid robot was built in Japan which was named as WABOT-1.

1.4. The first AI Winter (1974-1980) (Chahal & Gulia, 2019; Mueller & Massaron, 2016).

- The duration between the years 1974 and 1980 was the first AI winter duration. AI winter refers to the period when computer scientists dealt with a severe shortage of funding from the government for AI research.
- During AI winters, an interest in publicity on artificial intelligence was decreased.

1.5. A boom of AI (1980-1987) (Chandra & Hareendran, 2014; Sharma et al., 2021)

- **Year 1980:** After AI winter duration, AI came back with "Expert System". Expert systems were programmed which emulate the decision-making ability of a human expert.
- In the **Year 1980**, the first national conference of the American Association of Artificial Intelligence was held at Stanford University.

1.6. The Second AI winter (1987-1993) (Haenlein & Kaplan, 2019; Xu et al., 2021)

- The duration between the years 1987 to 1993 was the second AI winter duration.

- Again, Investors and government stopped in funding for AI research as due to high cost but not efficient result.
- The expert system such as XCON was very cost effective.

1.7. **The emergence of Intelligent agents (1993-2011)** (Chahal & Gulia, 2019; Haenlein & Kaplan, 2019; Xu et al., 2021)

- **Year 1997;** In the year 1997, IBM Deep Blue World Chess Champion, Garvy Kasparov, and became the first computer to beat a world chess champion.
- **Year 2002:** For the first time, AI entered the home in the form of Roomba, a vacuum cleaner.
- **Year 2006:** AI came in the business world till the year 2006. Companies like Facebook, Twitter, and Netflix also started using AI.

1.8. **Deep learning, big data and artificial general intelligence (2011-present)** (Xu et al., 2021; Alpaydin, 2016; Haenlein & Kaplan, 2019; Ray, 2023)

- **Year 2011:** In 2011, IBM's Watson won Jeopardy (a quiz show), where it had to solve the complex questions and riddles. Watson proved that it could understand natural language and solve easily tricky questions.
- **Year 2012:** Google launched an Android app feature "Google now", which was able to provide information to the user as a prediction.
- **Year 2014:** In the year 2014, chatbot "Eugene Goostman" won a competition in the infamous "Turing test"
- **Year 2018:** The "Project debater" from IBM debated on complex topics with two master debaters and also performed extremely well. As well as Google's Duplex, a service to allow an AI assistant to book appointments over the phone.
- **Year 2022:** In November 2022, OpenAI presented ChatGPT, an AI chatbot made on the foundation of GTP-3.5 large language model. Initially celebrated for its extensive knowledge deduction prowess, and remarkably human-like conversational skills.
- **Year 2023:** In March 2023, OpenAI launches GPT-4, a big upgrade from GPT-3.5. Despite carrying over old problems, GPT-4 can handle both text and image. It's now part of ChatGPT, available through a subscription.
- **Year 2024:** On February 15, 2024, Google release Gemini 1.5 in limited Beta, capable of context length up to 1 million tokens. On 22 February, StabilityAI announces Stable Diffusion 3, using a similar architecture to Sora.

Now AI has developed to a remarkable level. The concept of Deep learning, big data, and data science are now trending like a boom. Nowadays companies like Google, Facebook, IBM, and Amazon are working with AI and creating amazing devices. The future of Artificial Intelligence is inspiring and will come with high intelligence (Alpaydin, 2016)

It can be emphasized that the applications of AI in engineering are vast and diverse, spanning domains such as design, manufacturing, construction, and infrastructure management. From precative maintenance and optimization to autonomous systems and robotics, AI technologies are reshaping the way engineers approach problem-solving and decision-making. There are many ways in which an AI can relate and interact with humans, including human oversight of AI systems, collaboration between engineers and AI algorithms, and the delegation of tasks to autonomous AI agents. This interaction streamlines workflows, accelerates innovation, and unlocks new possibilities for engineering advancement (Alpaydin, 2016).

UNDERSTANDING THE MECHANICS: FUNCTIONING OF ARTIFICIAL INTELLIGENCE

Artificial Intelligence (AI) is a broad field that encompasses various techniques and approaches aimed at enabling machines to perform tasks that would typically require human intelligence (Alzubi et al., 2018). There are several key concepts and techniques involved in AI:

Machine Learning (ML)

Machine Learning is a form of AI that teaches computers to think like humans, for example learning and improving from experience (data). Machine Learning mainly works by analyzing data and identifying patterns, and with minimal human intervention(interaction) (Alzubi et al., 2018; Smola & Vishwanathan, 2008; Deisenroth et al., 2024). The goal of AI is to create a computer or machine that gives out "intelligent behaviors" like humans. This means machines that can recognize a visual scene, understand a text written in natural language, or perform an action in the physical world (Sharma et al., 2021).

Machine Learning is one way to use AI. It was defined in the 1950s by AI pioneer Arthur Samuel as 'The field of study that gives a computer the ability to learn without explicitly being programmed' (Alpaydin, 2016). Almost any task that can be completed with a data-defining pattern or set of rules can be automated with machine learning. This allows companies to transform processes that were previously only possible for humans to perform by responding to customer service calls, bookkeeping, and reviewing resumes (Alzubi et al., 2018).

Machine Learning uses three different techniques (Alzubi et al., 2018):
1. Supervised
2. Semi-Supervised
3. Unsupervised

Supervised Learning

Supervised learning uses labeled datasets to train algorithms that classify data or predict outcomes accurately. In supervised learning, the training data acts like a teacher guiding the machine to predict outputs accurately, similar to how a student learns under a teacher's guidance (Alzubi et al., 2018).

In Supervised Learning algorithms are used for several tasks, including the following (Alpaydin, 2016):

- Binary classification: Divides data into two categories.
- Multiclass Classification: Chooses between more than types of answers.
- Ensembling: combines the predictions of multiple ML models to produce a more accurate prediction.
- Regression modeling: Predicts continuous values based on relationships within data.

Semi-Supervised Learning

Semi-supervised Learning works by feeding a small amount of labeled training data to an algorithm. From this data, the algorithm learns the dimensions of the data set, which it can then apply to new unlabeled data. The performance of expensive. This type of machine learning strikes a balance between the superior performance of supervised learning and the efficiency of unsupervised learning (Alzubi et al., 2018).

Semi-Supervised learning can be used in the following area, among others:

- Machine translation: Teaches algorithms to translate language based on less than a full dictionary of words.
- Fraud detection: Identifies cases of fraud when there are only a few positive examples.
- Labeling data: Algorithms trained on small data sets learn to apply data labels to larger sets automatically (Alpaydin, 2016).

Unsupervised Learning

Unsupervised machine learning algorithms don't require data to be labeled. They sift through unlabeled data to look for patterns that can be used to group data points into subsets. Most types of deep learning, including neural networks, are unsupervised algorithms (Alzubi et al., 2018).

Unsupervised learning algorithms are good for the following tasks (Alzubi et al., 2018):

- **Clustering**: Splitting the data set into groups based on similarity using clustering algorithms.
- **Anomaly detection**: Identifying unusual data point in a data set using anomaly detection algorithms.
- **Association rule:** Discovering sets of items in a data set that frequently occur together using association rule mining.
- **Dimensionality reduction:** Decreasing the number if variables in a data set using dimensionality reduction techniques.

Self-Supervised Learning: it is a form of unsupervised learning where the model generates its own labels from the input data. The model is trained to predict certain parts of the input data based on other parts of the same data. This approach has been successful in tasks such as representation learning, where the model learns useful features from raw data (Alzubi et al., 2018).

In addition to this three-type learning, there are several other specialized techniques and paradigms within machine learning. They are:

Reinforcement Learning

Reinforcement learning is a type of learning where an agent learns to make decisions by interacting with an environment. The agent receives feedback in the form of rewards or penalties based on its actions, and its objective is to maximize the cumulative reward over time. This approach has been successful in applications such as game playing (e.g., AlphaGo) and robotics (Alpaydin, 2016; Alzubi et al., 2018)

Transfer Learning

Transfer learning involves leveraging knowledge gained from solving one problem to help solve a related but different problem. Instead of starting from scratch, a model can be pre-trained on a large dataset for a specific task and then fine-tuned on a smaller dataset for a related task. This approach is particularly useful when labeled data is scarce for the target task (Alzubi et al., 2018).

2.1.6. GANs (Generative Adversarial Networks): Generative Adversarial Networks (GANs) are a type of deep learning model consisting of two neural networks, a generator and a discriminator, that are trained simultaneously. The generator generates synthetic data samples, while the discriminator tries to distinguish between real and synthetic samples. The two networks are trained in an adversarial manner, where the generator aims to generate realistic samples that can fool the discriminator, and the discriminator aims to accurately distinguish between real and fake samples. GANs have been used for tasks such as image generation, data augmentation, style transfer, and domain adaptation (Alpaydin, 2016; Alzubi et al., 2018).

Neural Networks

Neural network, a method in artificial intelligence, teaches computers to process data in a way inspired by human brain. It is also known as **Artificial Neural Network (ANNs)** or **Simulated Neural Network (SNNs)**. Their name and structure are inspired by the human brain, mimicking the way that biological neurons signal to one another (Aggarwal, 2018).

Similar to the human brain that has neurons interconnected to one another, Artificial neural networks also have neurons that are interconnected to one another in various layers of the networks. These neurons are known as nodes (Aggarwal, 2018).

Neural networks epitomize a significant milestone in the field of artificial intelligence, representing a concerted effort to replicate the exceptional cognitive abilities of the human brain. These computational frameworks, inspired by the intricate architecture and adaptive mechanisms of biological neural networks, have initiated a transformative era across diverse domains, spanning from computer vision and natural language processing to robotics and autonomous systems (Rashid, 2016).

Anatomy of Neural Network

Neural networks exhibit a complex yet elegant structure, mirroring the interconnected nature of biological neural networks (Rashid, 2016). Understanding the anatomy of neural networks involves exploring the intricate components and their interrelationships:

2.2.1.1. **Neurons (Nodes):** Neurons are the fundamental units of computation within neural networks. Each neuron receives input signals from the preceding layer, computes a weighted sum of these inputs, adds a bias term, and applies an activation function to produce an output. The output is then passed to the neurons in the subsequent layer. Neurons are characterized by their activation functions, which introduce non-linearity into the network, enabling it to learn complex patterns and relationships in the data (Nielsen, 1994; Abiodun et al., 2018)

2.2.1.2. **Layers:** Neural networks consist of multiple layers, each serving a specific function in information processing. The primary layers include (Nielsen, 1994):

- **Input Layer**: The input layer receives raw data and transmits it to the first hidden layer. Each neuron in the input layer represents a feature or attribute of the input data.
- **Hidden Layers**: Hidden layers are intermediate layers between the input and output layers. They perform complex transformations on the input data, extracting high-level features and representations. Deep neural networks may contain multiple hidden layers, allowing for hierarchical feature learning.
- **Output Layer**: The output layer generates the final predictions or classifications based on the processed information from the hidden layers. The number of neurons in the output layer corresponds to the number of output classes or dimensions.
- **Connections (Edges)**: Neurons in adjacent layers are connected by weighted edges, representing the strength of influence between them. These connections facilitate the propagation of information through the network during both forward and backward passes. The weights associated with these connections are learned during training, adjusting to minimize prediction errors and optimize the network's performance.
- **Activation Function**: Activation functions introduce non-linearities into the network, enabling it to approximate complex functions and learn non-linear mappings between inputs and outputs. Common activation functions include sigmoid, tanh, ReLU (Rectified Linear Unit), and softmax. Each neuron typically applies an activation function to its weighted sum of inputs, producing an output signal that is passed to the next layer.

Operation of Neural Network

The operation of neural networks involves a series of computational steps, encompassing both forward and backward propagation:

2.3.1. Forward Propagation: During forward propagation, input data is sequentially passed through the network, layer by layer, from the input layer to the output layer. At each neuron, the input signals are multiplied by the corresponding weights, summed together, and added to a bias term. The resulting sum is then passed through an activation function to produce the neuron's output. This process is repeated for each neuron in each layer until the final output is generated (Jain & Mao, 1996).

2.3.2. Backward Propagation (Backpropagation): Following forward propagation, the network's predictions are compared to the actual target values using a loss function, which quantifies the disparity between predicted and actual outputs. Backpropagation involves iteratively adjusting the network's weights and biases to minimize the loss function. This optimization process utilizes gradient descent or its variants, such as stochastic gradient descent (SGD) or Adam, to update the parameters in the direction that reduces prediction errors. The gradients of the loss function with respect to the network's parameters are computed using the chain rule of calculus and propagated backward through the network, hence the term "backpropagation" (Jain & Mao, 1996)

2.3.3. Training and Optimization: Training a neural network involves iteratively feeding training data through the network and adjusting its parameters (weights and biases) using backpropagation and gradient descent to minimize the loss function. This process continues until the network's performance converges to a satisfactory level as measured by validation metrics. Optimization techniques, such as regularization, dropout, and batch normalization, are employed to prevent overfitting, improve generalization, and expedite convergence (Jain & Mao, 1996).

2.3.4. Inference: Once trained, the neural network can be deployed for inference where it processes new, unseen data to make predictions or classifications. During inference, the forward propagation process is executed without the need for weight updates or backpropagation. The network's learned parameters are fixed, and input data is fed through the network to generate predictions efficiently (Lin et al., 2014).

2.3.5. Fine-Tuning and Transfer Learning: In some cases, pre-trained neural networks can be fine-tuned or repurposed for related tasks using transfer learning. Fine-tuning involves retraining the network on a smaller, task-specific dataset to adapt its learned representations to the new task. Transfer learning leverages the knowledge acquired from solving one task to aid in solving a related, but different, task, often resulting in faster convergence and improved performance (Lin et al., 2014).

CONCLUSION

Neural networks represent a testament to humanity's tireless quest for comprehending and replicating the intricate workings of cognition. By effectively bridging the gap between artificial and biological intelligence, these computational models have catalyzed an era of unparalleled innovation, fundamentally reshaping industries, enhancing human capabilities, and opening up new vistas of scientific exploration. As we navigate the complex interplay between artificial and biological intelligence, neural networks emerge as beacons of ingenuity and inspiration, illuminating the path towards a future characterized by the harmonious coexistence of intelligent systems and humanity. In this symbiotic relationship, these networks enrich our lives, empower us to tackle previously insurmountable challenges, and push the boundaries of what we perceive as achievable.

Furthermore, embedded within the core of neural networks lies the paradigm of machine learning, a cornerstone of contemporary AI research and development. Machine learning algorithms, intricately integrated into neural network architectures, enable these systems to autonomously learn from data, adapt to changing environments, and continually improve their performance over time. Through the iterative process of training and optimization, machine learning empowers neural networks to discern complex patterns, extract meaningful insights, and make informed decisions across a myriad of applications.

The operation of machine learning within neural networks involves a cyclic process of data ingestion, feature extraction, model training, and inference:

- **Data Ingestion**: Machine learning begins with the acquisition of raw data, sourced from various domains such as images, text, or sensor readings. This data serves as the foundation upon which the neural network will learn and make predictions.
- **Feature Extraction**: Next, the data undergoes preprocessing, where relevant features are extracted and transformed into a format suitable for input into the neural network. This step involves techniques such as normalization, scaling, and dimensionality reduction.
- **Model Training**: The preprocessed data is then used to train the neural network through the process of forward and backward propagation. During training, the network learns to adjust its internal parameters (weights and biases) to minimize the discrepancy between predicted and actual outputs, as measured by a predefined loss function.
- **Inference**: Once trained, the neural network can be deployed for inference, where it processes new, unseen data to make predictions or classifications. During inference, the network applies the learned parameters to generate output predictions efficiently and accurately.

Through the seamless integration of machine learning principles, neural networks have become formidable tools for tackling a wide array of complex tasks, ranging from image and speech recognition to natural language understanding and autonomous decision-making. As we continue to advance the frontiers of AI research, the symbiotic relationship between neural networks and machine learning will undoubtedly play a pivotal role in shaping the future of technology and society.

REFERENCES

Abiodun, O., Jantan, A., Omolara, A., Dada, K., Mohamed, N., & Arshad, H. (2018). State-of-the-art in artificial neural network applications: A survey. *Heliyon*, 4(11), e00938. 10.1016/j.heliyon.2018. e0093830519653

Aggarwal, C. C. (2018). *Neural Networks and Deep Learning: A Textbook*. Springer. 10.1007/978-3-319-94463-0

Alpaydin, E. (2016). *Machine Learning: The New AI (The MIT Press Essential Knowledge series)*. The MIT Press.

Alzubi, J., Nayyar, A., & Kumar, A. (2018). Machine learning from theory to algorithms: An overview. *Journal of Physics: Conference Series*, 1142(1), 012012. 10.1088/1742-6596/1142/1/012012

Chahal, A., & Gulia, P. (2019). Machine Learning and Deep Learning. *International Journal of Innovative Technology and Exploring Engineering*, 8(12), 4910–4914. 10.35940/ijitee.L3550.1081219

Chandra, V., & Hareendran, A. (2014). *Artificial Intelligence and Machine Learning*. PHI Learning.

Deisenroth, M. P., Faisal, A. A., & Ong, C. S. (2024). *Mathematics for Machine Learning*. Cambridge University Press.

Haenlein, M., & Kaplan, A. (2019). A Brief History of Artificial Intelligence: On the Past, Present, and Future of Artificial Intelligence. *California Management Review*, 61(4), 5–14. 10.1177/0008125619864925

Jain, A. K., & Mao, J. (1996). Artificial Neural Networks: A Tutorial. *Computer*, 29(3), 31–44. 10.1109/2.485891

Jarrahi, M. (2018). Artificial intelligence and the future of work: Human-AI symbiosis in organizational decision making. *Business Horizons*, 61(4), 577–586. 10.1016/j.bushor.2018.03.007

Lin, M., Chen, Q., & Yan, S. (2014). Network In Network. *arXiv preprint arXiv:1312.4400*. https://doi .org//arXiv.1312.440010.48550

Mitchell, T. M. (1997). Does Machine Learning Really Work? *AI Magazine*, 18(3), 11–20. 10.1609/ aimag.v18i3.1303

Mueller, J. P., & Massaron, L. (2016). *Machine Learning for Dummies*. John Wiley & Sons.

Nielsen, M. (1994). Neural networks and deep learning. In Clark, A., & Millican, P. (Eds.), *Neural networks and deep learning: Contemplating minds: A forum for artificial intelligence* (pp. 11–25). MIT Press.

Rashid, T. (2016). *Make Your Own Neural Network*. CreateSpace Independent Publishing Platform.

Ray, P. P. (2023). ChatGPT: A comprehensive review on background, applications, key challenges, bias, ethics, limitations and future scope. *Internet of Things and Cyber-Physical Systems*, 3, 121–154. 10.1016/j.iotcps.2023.04.003

Russell, S. J., & Norvig, P. (2010). *Artificial Intelligence: A Modern Approach*. Prentice Hall.

Sharma, N., Sharma, R., & Jindal, N. (2021). Machine learning and deep learning applications: A vision. *Global Transitions Proceedings*, 2(1), 24–28. 10.1016/j.gltp.2021.01.004

Smola, A., & Vishwanathan (2008). *Introduction to Machine Learning*. Cambridge University Press.

Xu, Y., Liu, X., Cao, X., Huang, C., Liu, E., Qian, S., Liu, X., Wu, Y., Dong, F., Qiu, C.-W., Qiu, J., Hua, K., Su, W., Wu, J., Xu, H., Han, Y., Fu, C., Yin, M., Liu, M., & Zhang, J. (2021). Artificial intelligence: A Powerful paradigm for Scientific Research. *Innovation (Cambridge (Mass.))*, 2(4), 100179. 10.1016/j.xinn.2021.10017934877560

KEY TERMS AND DEFINITIONS

Algorithms: A machine learning algorithm is a set of rules or processes used by an AI system to conduct tasks-most often to discover new data insights and patterns, or to predict output values from a given set of input variables.

Backpropagation: The gradients of the loss function with respect to the network's parameters are computed using the chain rule of calculus and propagated backward through the network, hence the term "backpropagation".

Gradient Descent: Gradient descent (GD) is an iterative first-order optimization algorithm, used to find a local minimum/maximum of a given function. This method is commonly used in machine learning (ML) and deep learning (DL) to minimize a cost/loss function.

Machine Learning: At its most fundamental level, machine learning (ML) is a category of artificial intelligence that enables computers to independently think and learn. It involves programming computers to modify their actions to improve accuracy, which is measured by the frequency of correct outcomes resulting from the chosen actions.

Neural Network: Neurons are nerve cells that send messages all over the body in a living organism. A combination of neurons or a cluster of neurons is called a neural circuit. A model based on these neural circuits in a computer or a machine is called a Neural Network.

Stochastic Optimization: Stochastic Optimization is a method of finding the optimal solution to a problem using randomness in the search process. It is a powerful tool in machine learning and other fields, such as finance and engineering, where the goal is to optimize a function based on a set of input variables.

Chapter 12
Exploring the Scikit-Learn Package With ChatGPT

Kadir Uludag
https://orcid.org/0000-0003-3713-4670
Shanghai Jiao Tong University Mental Health Center, China

ABSTRACT

The Scikit-learn package is a popular machine-learning library in Python that provides tools for data preprocessing, feature selection, and evaluation of models. However, learning it can be hard for beginners due to its vast documentation. The goal of this chapter is to search for ways to use ChatGPT to learn the Scikit-learn package. ChatGPT's first version was used (2023). Using ChatGPT to learn Scikit-learn can help users to understand the key techniques of machine learning.

INTRODUCTION

The Scikit-learn package is a Python library for machine-learning tasks (Pedregosa et al., 2011). The Scikit-learn package offers a wide range of machine-learning tasks that can be performed. Within the Scikit-learn package, there are algorithms available that can detect anomalous patterns or outliers in data, facilitating applications such as fraud detection.

We explore the use of ChatGPT to learn the Scikit-learn package. We demonstrate how ChatGPT can be trained on the Scikit-learn documentation.

Our chapter shows that ChatGPT can effectively learn and understand the Scikit-learn package, and provide assistance to users in various machine-learning tasks.

Methods

We conducted a search using keywords related to the Python package sci-kit learn. The initial version of ChatGPT, which was utilized in 2023, provided relevant information about the sci-kit learn package in response to the first two questions, question five and eleven. The remaining questions aimed to assess the chatbot's ability to generate code related to scikit learn. In total, there are 23 questions accompanied by their respective answers.

While certain questions aimed to stimulate the generation of fresh code, others were informative in nature.

DOI: 10.4018/979-8-3693-3278-8.ch012

Results

Question 1: give information about the sci-kit learn package of python.

Answer 1: Scikit-learn, also known as sklearn, is a popular open-source Python library for machine learning. It is built on top of other scientific computing libraries such as NumPy, SciPy, and matplotlib. Scikit-learn provides a range of tools for data processing, modeling, and evaluation in a user-friendly interface.

Some of the key features of scikit-learn include:

1. Classification: Scikit-learn provides various algorithms for classification tasks, including logistic regression, decision trees, random forests, k-nearest neighbors, and support vector machines.
2. Regression: Scikit-learn also provides algorithms for regression tasks, such as linear regression, ridge regression, and lasso regression.
3. Clustering: Scikit-learn includes several clustering algorithms, including KMeans, hierarchical clustering, and DBSCAN.
4. Dimensionality Reduction: Scikit-learn provides tools for reducing the dimensionality of data, including PCA and t-SNE.
5. Model selection: Scikit-learn includes tools for model selection, including cross-validation and grid search.
6. Preprocessing: Scikit-learn includes functions for data preprocessing, including scaling, normalization, and imputation of missing values.
7. Evaluation: Scikit-learn provides tools for evaluating model performance, including metrics for classification, regression, and clustering tasks.

Scikit-learn is widely used in industry and academia for a variety of machine learning tasks, including natural language processing, computer vision, and predictive modeling. It isa well-documented and well-supported library with an active community of developers and users. Additionally, scikit-learn is designed to be compatible with other scientific computing libraries in the Python ecosystem, making it easy to incorporate into existing workflows.

Question 2: What are some examples of machine learning tasks that scikit-learn is used for in industry?

Answer 2: Scikit-learn is a popular Python library for machine learning, and it is used in a wide range of industries for various tasks. Here are some examples of machine learning tasks that scikit-learn is used for in industry:

1. Fraud detection - Scikit-learn can be used to build machine learning models to detect fraudulent transactions, such as credit card fraud.
2. Customer segmentation - Scikit-learn can be used to segment customers based on their behavior and preferences, which can help businesses tailor their marketing campaigns to specific groups.
3. Image recognition - Scikit-learn can be used to build machine learning models for image classification and object detection, which can be used in fields such as autonomous vehicles, surveillance, and medical imaging.
4. Sentiment analysis - Scikit-learn can be used to analyze text data and classify it based on sentiment, which can be used in fields such as social media monitoring and customer feedback analysis.
5. Predictive maintenance - Scikit-learn can be used to build machine learning models to predict when equipment is likely to fail, which can help businesses schedule maintenance and avoid downtime.

6. Recommendation systems - Scikit-learn can be used to build recommendation systems that suggest products or content to users based on their behavior and preferences, which can be used in fields such as e-commerce and entertainment.
7. Natural language processing - Scikit-learn can be used to build machine learning models for tasks such as text classification, named entity recognition, and topicmodeling, which can be used in fields such as customer service, sentiment analysis, and content analysis.
8. Financial forecasting - Scikit-learn can be used to build machine learning models to forecast financial outcomes, such as stock prices and exchange rates, which can be used in fields such as finance and investment.
9. Medical diagnosis - Scikit-learn can be used to build machine learning models to diagnose diseases based on medical data, such as patient symptoms and lab results, which can be used in fields such as healthcare and medical research.

Overall, scikit-learn is a versatile library with a wide range of applications in industry and academia. It is widely used by data scientists and machine learning engineers to build predictive models and make data-driven decisions.

Question 3: Give example of sci-kit learn.

Answer 3: Sure, here's an example of how to use scikit-learn to build a simple machine learning model for classification:

```
# Import necessary libraries
from sklearn.datasets import load_iris
from sklearn.model_selection import train_test_split
from sklearn.neighbors import KNeighborsClassifier
from sklearn.metrics import accuracy_score
# Load the iris dataset
iris = load_iris()
# Split the dataset into training and testing sets
X_train, X_test, y_train, y_test = train_test_split(iris.data, iris.target,
test_size=0.3, random_state=42)
# Create a KNN classifier with k=3
knn = KNeighborsClassifier(n_neighbors=3)
# Fit the classifier to the training data
knn.fit(X_train, y_train)
# Predict the labels of the test data
y_pred = knn.predict(X_test)
# Calculate the accuracy of the model
accuracy = accuracy_score(y_test, y_pred)
# Print the accuracy score
print("Accuracy:", accuracy)
```

In this example, we first import the necessary libraries, including scikit-learn's KNeighborsClassifier for building a k-nearest neighbors classifier, and accuracy_score for evaluating the model's performance.

Next, we load the iris dataset using the load_iris function from scikit-learn's datasets module. We then split the dataset into training and testing sets using the train_test_split function.

We create a KNeighborsClassifier object with k=3 and fitit to the training data using the fit method. We then use the predict method to predict the labels of the test data, and calculate the accuracy of the model using the accuracy_score function.

Finally, we print the accuracy score of the model.

This is a simple example of how scikit-learn can be used to build a classification model. The iris dataset is a well-known dataset in machine learning, and the goal of this example is to predict the species of iris flowers based on their sepal length, sepal width, petal length, and petal width.

Question 4: What other types of machine learning models can be built with scikit-learn?

Answer 4: Scikit-learn is a versatile machine learning library, and it provides a wide range of algorithms for building different types of models. Here are some examples of other types of machine learning models that can be built with scikit-learn:

1. Regression models - Scikit-learn provides various algorithms for building regression models, including linear regression, logistic regression, and support vector regression (SVR).
2. Clustering models - Scikit-learn provides several algorithms for clustering data, including KMeans, hierarchical clustering, and DBSCAN.
3. Dimensionality reduction models - Scikit-learn provides algorithms for reducing the dimensionality of data, including principal component analysis (PCA) and t-distributed stochastic neighbor embedding (t-SNE).
4. Ensemble models - Scikit-learn provides several algorithms for building ensemble models, including random forests and gradient boosting.
5. Neural network models - Scikit-learn also provides tools for building simple neural network models, including multi-layer perceptrons (MLPs).
6. Time series models - Scikit-learn provides algorithms for building time series models, including ARIMA and seasonal decomposition of time series (STL).
7. Gaussian mixture models - Scikit-learn provides algorithms for building Gaussian mixture models, which are useful for modeling data that comes from a mixture of Gaussian distributions.
8. Support vector machines - Scikit-learn provides various algorithms for building support vector machines (SVMs), which are useful for both classification and regression tasks.

These arejust a few examples of the many types of machine learning models that can be built with scikit-learn. The library is designed to be flexible and modular, so users can easily mix and match different algorithms and techniques to build customized models for their specific needs. Additionally, scikit-learn provides tools for model selection, hyperparameter tuning, and evaluation, which can help users optimize their models and improve their performance.

Question 5: Can you explain how to use PCA to reduce dimensionality?

Answer 5: Sure, here's an explanation of how to use Principal Component Analysis (PCA) to reduce dimensionality in scikit-learn:

PCA is a technique for reducing the dimensionality of a dataset by transforming the data into a lower-dimensional space. The basic idea is to find a set of new variables, or principal components, that capture most of the important information in the original data. These principal components are linear combinations of the original variables, and they are ordered by the amount of variance they explain in the data.

Here's an example of how to use PCA to reduce dimensionality in scikit-learn:

```
```

```
# Import necessary libraries
```

```
from sklearn.datasets import load_iris
from sklearn.decomposition import PCA
import matplotlib.pyplot as plt
# Load the iris dataset
iris = load_iris()
# Create a PCA object with 2 components
pca = PCA(n_components=2)
# Fit the PCA object to the data
X_pca = pca.fit_transform(iris.data)
# Plot the transformed data
plt.scatter(X_pca[:, 0], X_pca[:, 1], c=iris.target)
plt.xlabel('PC 1')
plt.ylabel('PC 2')
plt.show()
```

In this example, we first import the necessary libraries, including scikit-learn's PCA module and matplotlib for data visualization. We then load the iris dataset using the load_iris function.

We create a PCA object with 2 components and fit it to the iris datausing the fit_transform method. The resulting X_pca matrix contains the transformed data in the lower-dimensional space.

Finally, we plot the transformed data using matplotlib, where the x-axis represents the first principal component (PC 1) and the y-axis represents the second principal component (PC 2). We also color-code the data points based on their target labels, which correspond to the three different species of iris flowers in the dataset.

By reducing the dimensionality of the iris dataset from 4 to 2, we can visualize the data in a two-dimensional plot and see how the different species are separated in the lower-dimensional space. This can be useful for exploratory data analysis, data visualization, and pattern recognition.

It's worth noting that PCA can be sensitive to the scaling of the data, so it's important to standardize the data before applying PCA. Additionally, the number of principal components to retain should be chosen carefully based on the amount of variance explained by each component and the specific requirements of the analysis. Scikit-learn provides tools for selecting the optimal number of components based on various criteria, such as the explained variance ratio and the cumulative explained variance.

Question 6: How can I select the optimal number of components in scikit-learn?

Answer 6: Selecting the optimal number of components in PCA can be important for achieving good performance and avoiding overfitting or underfitting the data. Scikit-learn provides several methods for selecting the optimal number of components based on various criteria, such as the explained variance ratio and the cumulative explained variance. Here are a few methods you can use:

1. Scree plot: A scree plot is a plot of the eigenvalues (or variances) of the principal components, sorted in descending order. The scree plot can help you visually identify the "elbow" or the point where the eigenvalues start to level off, indicating the optimal number of components to retain. Scikit-learn provides a method for plotting the scree plot:

```
# Import necessary libraries
from sklearn.datasets import load_iris
from sklearn.decomposition import PCA
```

```
import matplotlib.pyplot as plt
# Load the iris dataset
iris = load_iris()
# Create a PCA object with all components
pca = PCA()
# Fit the PCA object to the data
pca.fit(iris.data)
# Plot the scree plot
plt.plot(range(1, 5), pca.explained_variance_ratio_)
plt.xlabel('Number of Components')
plt.ylabel('Explained Variance Ratio')
plt.show()
```

In this example, we create a PCA object with all components and fit it to the iris data using the fit method. We then plot the explained variance ratio of each component using matplotlib.2. Cumulative explained variance: Another method for selecting the optimal number of components is to look at the cumulative explained variance ratio. This represents the proportion of the total variance in the data that is explained by the first k components. Scikit-learn provides a method for calculating the cumulative explained variance ratio:

```
# Import necessary libraries
from sklearn.datasets import load_iris
from sklearn.decomposition import PCA
import numpy as np
# Load the iris dataset
iris = load_iris()
# Create a PCA object with all components
pca = PCA()
# Fit the PCA object to the data
pca.fit(iris.data)
# Calculate the cumulative explained variance ratio
cumulative_var_ratio = np.cumsum(pca.explained_variance_ratio_)
# Plot the cumulative explained variance ratio
plt.plot(range(1, 5), cumulative_var_ratio)
plt.xlabel('Number of Components')
plt.ylabel('Cumulative Explained Variance Ratio')
plt.show()
```

In this example, we create a PCA object with all components and fit it to the iris data using the fit method. We then calculate the cumulative explained variance ratio using numpy's cumsum function. Finally, we plot the cumulative explained variance ratio using matplotlib.

3. Cross-validation: A more rigorous method for selecting the optimal number of components is to use cross-validation. Scikit-learn provides a method for doing cross-validation with PCA:

```
```
# Import necessary libraries
from sklearn.datasets import load_irisfrom sklearn.decomposition import PCA
from sklearn.pipeline import make_pipeline
from sklearn.model_selection import GridSearchCV
from sklearn.linear_model import LogisticRegression
# Load the iris dataset
iris = load_iris()
# Create a PCA object with a range of components
pca = PCA()
logreg = LogisticRegression(max_iter=10000, random_state=42)
pipe = make_pipeline(pca, logreg)
# Define the grid of parameters to search
param_grid = {'pca__n_components': [1, 2, 3, 4]}
# Perform cross-validation with GridSearchCV
grid = GridSearchCV(pipe, param_grid=param_grid, cv=5)
grid.fit(iris.data, iris.target)
# Print the best number of components and the corresponding score
print("Best number of components:", grid.best_params_['pca__n_components'])
print("Best score:", grid.best_score_)
```
```

In this example, we create a pipeline with a PCA object and a logistic regression object. We define a grid of parameters to search, which includes the number of components in the PCA object. We then perform cross-validation with GridSearchCV, which searches over the parameter grid and returns the best number of components and the corresponding score.

Overall, there are several methods you can use to select the optimal number of components in PCA using scikit-learn. The choice of method will depend on the specific requirements of the analysis and the characteristics of the data.

Question 7: What are the advantages of using cross-validation over the other methods?

Answer 7: Cross-validation is a powerful technique for evaluating the performance of machine learning models and selecting the optimal hyperparameters. Here are some of the advantages of using cross-validation over other methods:

1. More reliable estimate of model performance: Cross-validation provides a more reliable estimate of model performance than a single train-test split, which can be affected by the random partitioning of the data. By performing multiple train-test splits and averaging the results, cross-validation provides a more robust estimate of the model's performance on unseen data.

2. Helps avoid overfitting: Cross-validation helps to avoid overfitting the model to the training data by evaluating the model's performance on multiple test sets. This can help to identify models that perform well on average, rather than models that perform well on a specific subset of the data.

3. Selects optimal hyperparameters: Cross-validation can be used to search over a range of hyperparameters and select the optimal hyperparameters that maximize the model's performance. This can help to tune the model for better performance and avoid overfitting.

4. Maximizes use of available data: Cross-validation maximizes the use of the available data by using each data point for both training and testing. This can be especially useful in cases where the amount of available data is limited.

5. Provides insights into model behavior: Cross-validation can provide insights into how the model behaves on different subsets of the data, which can help to diagnose problems and improve the model.

Overall, cross-validation is a powerful techniquefor evaluating and selecting machine learning models, and it has several advantages over other methods. However, it's important to keep in mind that cross-validation can be computationally expensive, especially for large datasets and complex models. Additionally, cross-validation assumes that the data is independently and identically distributed, which may not always be the case in practice. Nevertheless, cross-validation is a widely used and effective technique for model evaluation and selection in machine learning.

Question 8: give an example of cross-validation with sci-kit learn.

Answer 8: Sure, here's an example of how to perform cross-validation using scikit-learn in Python:

```python
python
from sklearn.model_selection import cross_val_score
from sklearn.linear_model import LinearRegression
from sklearn.datasets import load_boston
# Load the Boston housing dataset
boston = load_boston()
# Create a linear regression model
lr = LinearRegression()
# Perform 5-fold cross-validation on the model using the mean squared error
(MSE) as the evaluation metric
scores = cross_val_score(lr, boston.data, boston.target, cv=5, scoring='neg_
mean_squared_error')
# Print the mean and standard deviation of the cross-validation scores
print("Cross-validation scores: ", scores)
print("Mean cross-validation score: ", -scores.mean())
print("Standard deviation of cross-validation scores: ", scores.std())
```

In this example, we load the Boston housing dataset and create a linear regression model. We then use the cross_val_score function to perform 5-fold cross-validation on the model, using the mean squared error as the evaluation metric. The cv parameter specifies the number of folds to use, and the scoring parameter specifies the evaluation metric to use. The function returns an array of scores for each fold of the cross-validation.

We then print the mean and standard deviation of the cross-validation scores, which give an estimate of the model's performance on new, unseen data. The negative sign in front of the scoresis because scikit-learn's cross_val_score function returns the negative mean squared error by default, which is a convention used to align with the maximization convention used by other functions in scikit-learn.

Question 9: What is the difference between AUC-ROC and accuracy?

Answer 9: AUC-ROC and accuracy are two commonly used evaluation metrics in binary classification problems, but they measure different aspects of model performance.

Accuracy is a measure of the proportion of correctly classified instances. It simply measures how often a model correctly predicts whether an instance belongs to the positive or negative class. It is calculated as the sum of true positives and true negatives divided by the total number of instances.

On the other hand, AUC-ROC is a measure of the trade-off between the true positive rate (TPR) and false positive rate (FPR) at different classification thresholds. AUC-ROC summarizes the model's ability to correctly distinguish between the positive and negative classes across a range of classification thresholds. It is calculated as the area under the receiver operating characteristic (ROC) curve, which plots the TPR against the FPR at different classification thresholds.

The main difference between AUC-ROC and accuracy is that AUC-ROC provides a more comprehensive measure of model performance that takes into account the trade-off between the TPR and FPR at different thresholds, while accuracy only measures the proportion of correctly classified instances.

In situations where the positive and negative classes are imbalanced, accuracy can be a misleading metric of model performance. For example, in a problem where the positive class is rare, a model that always predicts the negative class will achieve a high accuracy, but it will be useless in practice. In such cases, AUC-ROC provides a more informative measure of model performance by summarizing the model's ability to correctly distinguish between the positive and negative classes across a range of thresholds.

In summary, while accuracy measures the proportion of correctly classified instances, AUC-ROC provides a more comprehensive measure of model performance that takes into account the trade-off between the true positive rate and false positive rate at different classification thresholds. AUC-ROC is a more suitable metric for problems with imbalanced classes or where the cost of false positives and false negatives is different.

Question 10: Is there a threshold value for AUC-ROC that indicates a good model?

Answer 10: There is no fixed threshold value for AUC-ROC that indicates a good model. The interpretation of the AUC-ROC score depends on the specific problem and the goals of the model. In general, the AUC-ROC score can range from 0 to 1, where a score of 0.5 indicates that the model is no better than random guessing, and a score of 1 indicates that the model makes perfect predictions.

In practice, a good AUC-ROC score depends on the specific application and the trade-offs between different metrics. For example, in a medical diagnosis problem, a high AUC-ROC score may be desirable to minimize false negatives (i.e., incorrectly predicting a negative result for a patient who actually has the disease), even if it means accepting more false positives (i.e., incorrectly predicting a positive result for a patient who does not have the disease). On the other hand, in a fraud detection problem, a high AUC-ROC score may be desirable to minimize false positives (i.e., incorrectly flagging a legitimate transaction as fraudulent), even if it means accepting more false negatives (i.e., failing to detect some fraudulent transactions).

Therefore, the choice of a "good" AUC-ROC score depends on the specific problem and the trade-offs between different metrics. It is important to evaluate the model's performance based on multiple metrics and to consider the context and application of the model when interpreting the results.

Question 11: Can you give an example of a problem where a high AUC-ROC score is desirable?

Answer 11: Sure! One example of a problem where a high AUC-ROC score is desirable is in medical diagnosis, specifically in identifying patients with a rare disease.

In such a scenario, the goal of the model is to correctly identify patients who have the disease (i.e., true positives) while minimizing false positives (i.e., patients who are mistakenly diagnosed as having the disease). False positives can lead to unnecessary and potentially harmful medical interventions, as well as causing unnecessary anxiety and stress for patients and their families.

A high AUC-ROC score in this context would indicate that the model is good at distinguishing between patients who have the disease and those who do not, and that there are relatively few false positives. This would give doctors and medical professionals greater confidence in the model's predictions, and allow them to make more informed decisions about patient care.

For example, a high AUC-ROC score might be desirable in diagnosing a rare genetic disorder that requires a specific treatment. In this case, a false positive diagnosis would lead to unnecessary and potentially harmful treatment, while a false negative diagnosis would mean that the patient misses out on the necessary treatment. Therefore, a high AUC-ROC score would be desirable to minimize false positives and ensure that only patients who truly have the disorder receive the necessary treatment.

Question 12: Give an example of machine learning algorithms.

Answer 12: There are many machine learning algorithms, each with its strengths and weaknesses, that can be used to solve different types of problems. Here are some examples of commonly used machine learning algorithms:

1. Linear Regression: A supervised learning algorithm used for regression problems, where the goal is to predict a continuous output variable based on one or more input variables.
2. Logistic Regression: A supervised learning algorithm used for classification problems, where the goal is to predict a binary or multi-class output variable based on one or more input variables.
3. Decision Trees: A supervised learning algorithm used for both classification and regression problems, where the goal is to create a tree-like model of decisions and their possible consequences.
4. Random Forest: A supervised learning algorithm that uses an ensemble of decision trees to improve the accuracy and robustness of the model.
5. Support Vector Machines (SVM): A supervised learning algorithm used for classification and regression problems, where the goal is to find the hyperplane that best separates the data into different classes.
6. K-Nearest Neighbors (KNN): A supervised learning algorithm used for classification and regression problems, where the goal is to find the k nearest data points to a given input and use their labels to make a prediction.
7. Naive Bayes: A supervised learning algorithm used for classification problems, where the goal is to calculate the probability of a data point belonging to a specific class based on its features.
8. Neural Networks: A family of supervised and unsupervised learning algorithms that are inspired by the structure and function of the human brain, and can be used for a wide range of tasks including classification, regression, and image and speech recognition.

These are just a few examples of the many machine learning algorithms available. The choice of algorithm depends on the specific problem and the characteristics of the data, and often involves a process of trial and error to find the best algorithm and hyperparameters for the task at hand.

Question 13: give an example of decision trees using Python.

Answer 13: We can use scikit-learn to build a decision tree model that predicts the condition of a patient based on their age, gender, and medical history. Here's how:

```python
from sklearn.tree import DecisionTreeClassifier
from sklearn.model_selection import train_test_split
from sklearn.metrics import accuracy_score
# Load the dataset
data = [
```

```
    [25, 'Male', 'None', 'No'],
    [35, 'Male', 'High Blood Pressure', 'No'],
    [45, 'Female', 'Diabetes', 'Yes'],
    [55, 'Male', 'None', 'No'],
    [65, 'Female', 'High Blood Pressure', 'Yes'],
    [75, 'Male', 'Diabetes', 'Yes']
    ]
    # Convert categorical variables to numerical using one-hot encoding
    X = []
    y = []
    for row in data:
    age, gender, history, condition = row
    gender_male = 1 if gender == 'Male' else 0
    gender_female = 1 if gender == 'Female' else 0
    history_none = 1 if history == 'None' else 0
    history_high_bp = 1 if history == 'High Blood Pressure' else 0
    history_diabetes = 1 if history == 'Diabetes' else 0
    X.append([age, gender_male, gender_female, history_none, history_high_bp,
history_diabetes])
    y.append(condition)
    # Split the dataset into training and testing sets
    X_train, X_test, y_train, y_test = train_test_split(X, y, test_size=0.2,
random_state=42)
    # Build the decision tree model
    clf = DecisionTreeClassifier()
    clf.fit(X_train, y_train)
    # Predict the labels for the test set
    y_pred = clf.predict(X_test)
    # Evaluate the accuracy of the model
    accuracy = accuracy_score(y_test, y_pred)
    print('Accuracy:', accuracy)
    # Visualize the decision tree
    from sklearn.tree import export_graphviz
    import graphviz
    dot_data = export_graphviz(clf, out_file=None,
    feature_names=['Age', 'Gender (Male)', 'Gender (Female)', 'History (None)',
'History (High BP)', 'History (Diabetes)'],
    class_names=['No', 'Yes'],
    filled=True, rounded=True,
    special_characters=True)
    graph = graphviz.Source(dot_data)
    graph.render('decision_tree')
```

This code first loads the dataset and converts the categorical variables to numerical using one-hot encoding. Then, it splits the dataset into training and testing sets and builds a decision tree classifier using the DecisionTreeClassifier class from scikit-learn. It then predicts the labels for the test set and evaluates the accuracy of the model using the accuracy_score function. Finally, it visualizes the decision tree using the export_graphviz function from scikit-learn and the graphviz library.

The resulting decision tree may look something like this:

This decision tree shows the conditions under which a patient is predicted to have the medical condition of interest (Yes) or not (No), based on their age, gender, and medical history. The decision tree can be used to make predictions for new patients by following the path from the root node to the leaf node that corresponds to the patient's characteristics.

Question 14: give an example of Naive Bayes using Python.

Answer 14: Sure! Here's an example of building a Naive Bayes classifier using Python and scikit-learn library:

Suppose we have a dataset of emails labeled as spam or ham (not spam), and we want to build a Naive Bayes classifier to predict whether a new email is spam or ham based on its content. The dataset looks like this:

```
| Email | Label |
|-----------------------------------------------------|-------|
| Get rich quick! Make money fast! | spam |
| Dear friend, how are you? I hope this email finds you... | ham |
| Congratulations, you've won a free trip! | spam |
| Hi, can you meet for coffee tomorrow? | ham |
| Urgent: Your account has been compromised! | spam |
| Hey, did you see the game last night? | ham |
```

We can use scikit-learn to build a Naive Bayes classifier model that predicts the label of a new email based on its content. Here's how:

```python
from sklearn.feature_extraction.text import CountVectorizer
from sklearn.naive_bayes import MultinomialNB
from sklearn.model_selection import train_test_split
from sklearn.metrics import accuracy_score
# Load the dataset
data = [
['Get rich quick! Make money fast!', 'spam'],
['Dear friend, how are you? I hope this email finds you...', 'ham'],
['Congratulations, you\'ve won a free trip!', 'spam'],
['Hi, can you meet for coffee tomorrow?', 'ham'],
['Urgent: Your account has been compromised!', 'spam'],
['Hey, did you see the game last night?', 'ham']
]
# Split the dataset into training and testing sets
X = [row[0] for row in data]
```

```
y = [row[1] for row in data]
X_train, X_test, y_train, y_test = train_test_split(X, y, test_size=0.2,
random_state=42)
    # Vectorize the text data using a bag-of-words model
    vectorizer = CountVectorizer()
    X_train_vec = vectorizer.fit_transform(X_train)
    X_test_vec = vectorizer.transform(X_test)
    # Build the Naive Bayes classifier model
    clf = MultinomialNB()
    clf.fit(X_train_vec, y_train)
    # Predict the labels for the test set
    y_pred = clf.predict(X_test_vec)
    # Evaluate the accuracy of the model
    accuracy = accuracy_score(y_test, y_pred)
    print('Accuracy:', accuracy)
    ```
```

This code first loads the dataset and splits it into training and testing sets. It then vectorizes the text data using a bag-of-words model, which converts the text data into a matrix of word counts. The bag-of-words model treats each word as a separate feature and counts the number of times each word appears in each email. This results in a sparse matrix where each row corresponds to an email and each column corresponds to a word in the vocabulary.

The code then builds a Naive Bayes classifier model using the `MultinomialNB` class from scikit-learn, which is suitable for discrete count data such as word counts. It trains the model on the training set and predicts the labels for the test set. Finally, it evaluates the accuracy of the model using the `accuracy_score` function.

The resulting accuracy may vary depending on the specific dataset and the parameters of the model. For example, the accuracy of the above classifier on the given dataset may be around 83.33%. Note that this is a simple example and in practice, building a more complex pipeline that includes data cleaning, feature engineering, and model tuning may be necessary to achieve optimal results.

**Question 15:** Can you explain how the bag-of-words model works?

**Answer 15:** Sure! The bag-of-words model is a simple and popular way to represent text data as a numerical vector that can be used as input to machine learning algorithms. Here's how it works:

1. Tokenization: The first step in the bag-of-words model is to break the text data into individual words, or tokens. This is usually done by splitting the text on whitespace and punctuation marks.
2. Vocabulary creation: The next step is to create a vocabulary of all the unique words in the text data. Each word in the vocabulary is assigned a unique integer index.
3. Counting: For each document in the text data, the bag-of-words model counts the number of times each word in the vocabulary appears in the document. This results in a vector of word counts for each document.
4. Vectorization: The final step is to convert the vectors of word counts into a numerical matrix that can be used as input to machine learning algorithms. This is typically done by either normalizing the vectors to have unit length (L2 normalization) or by using a term-frequency inverse-document-frequency (TF-IDF) weighting scheme, which weights the word counts by the inverse frequency of the words in the corpus.
```

For example, consider the following two sentences:
```
1. The quick brown fox jumps over the lazy dog.
2. The brown dog chases the fox out of sight.
```

The vocabulary for these sentences would be:
```
['The', 'brown', 'chases', 'dog', 'fox', 'jumps', 'lazy', 'out', 'over',
'quick', 'sight', 'the']
```

The bag-of-words model would then count the number of times each word in the vocabulary appears in each sentence, resulting in the following vectors:
```
1. [1, 1, 0, 1, 1, 1, 1, 0, 1, 1, 0, 2]
2. [1, 1, 1, 1, 1, 0, 0, 1, 0, 0, 1, 2]
```

These vectors can then be used as input to machine learning algorithms to train models for tasks such as text classification, sentiment analysis, and information retrieval.

Note that the bag-of-words model has some limitations, such as the loss of information about the order of words in the text and the inability to capture the semantic meaning of words. However, it is a simple and effective way to represent text data and is widely used in practice.

Question 16: Can you give an example of a machine learning algorithm that uses the bag-of-words model?

Answer 16: Sure! One example of a machine learning algorithm that uses the bag-of-words model is the Naive Bayes classifier for text classification. The Naive Bayes classifier is a probabilistic algorithm that is based on Bayes' theorem, which states that the probability of a hypothesis (class) given some evidence (features) is proportional to the probability of the evidence given the hypothesis, multiplied by the prior probability of the hypothesis. In the context of text classification, the Naive Bayes classifier uses the bag-of-words model to represent text documents as vectors of word counts and assumes that the occurrence of each word in the document is independent of the occurrence of other words (hence the "naive" assumption).

Here's an example of how to use the Naive Bayes classifier with the bag-of-words model to classify movie reviews as positive or negative:

```python
import pandas as pd
from sklearn.feature_extraction.text import CountVectorizer
from sklearn.naive_bayes import MultinomialNB
from sklearn.metrics import accuracy_score
# Load the movie review dataset
df = pd.read_csv('movie_reviews.csv')
# Split the dataset into training and testing sets
X_train = df[df['type'] == 'train']['review']
y_train = df[df['type'] == 'train']['sentiment']
X_test = df[df['type'] == 'test']['review']
y_test = df[df['type'] == 'test']['sentiment']
```

```
# Vectorize the text data using a bag-of-words model
vectorizer = CountVectorizer()
X_train_vec = vectorizer.fit_transform(X_train)
X_test_vec = vectorizer.transform(X_test)
# Build the Naive Bayes classifier model
clf = MultinomialNB()
clf.fit(X_train_vec, y_train)
# Predict the labels for the test set
y_pred = clf.predict(X_test_vec)
# Evaluate the accuracy of the model
accuracy = accuracy_score(y_test, y_pred)
print('Accuracy:', accuracy)
```

In this code, we first load a dataset of movie reviews and split it into training and testing sets. We then vectorize the text data using a bag-of-words model and build a Naive Bayes classifier using the `MultinomialNB` class from scikit-learn. We train the model on the training set and predict the labels for the test set. Finally, we evaluate the accuracy of the model using the `accuracy_score` function.

The resulting accuracy may vary depending on the specific dataset and the parameters of the model, but it typically ranges from 70% to 90%. Note that this is a simple example and in practice, building a more complex pipeline that includes data cleaning, feature engineering, and model tuning may be necessary to achieve optimal results.

Question 17: give an example of a random forest using Python.

Answer 17: Sure! Here's an example of building a Random Forest classifier using Python and scikit-learn library:

Suppose we have a dataset of customer information and we want to build a Random Forest classifier to predict whether a customer will buy a product based on their age, income, and gender. The dataset looks like this:

```
| Age | Income | Gender | Bought |
|-----|--------|--------|--------|
| 25  | 50000  | Male   | 0 |
| 30  | 80000  | Female | 1 |
| 35  | 60000  | Male   | 1 |
| 40  | 70000  | Female | 1 |
| 45  | 90000  | Male   | 0 |
| 50  | 100000 | Female | 0 |
```

We can use scikit-learn to build a Random Forest classifier model that predicts the label of a new customer based on their age, income, and gender. Here's how:

```python
from sklearn.ensemble import RandomForestClassifier
from sklearn.model_selection import train_test_split
from sklearn.metrics import accuracy_score
# Load the dataset
```

```
data = [
[25, 50000, 'Male', 0],
[30, 80000, 'Female', 1],
[35, 60000, 'Male', 1],
[40, 70000, 'Female', 1],
[45, 90000, 'Male', 0],
[50, 100000, 'Female', 0]
]
# Split the dataset into training and testing sets
X = [[row[0], row[1], 0 if row[2] == 'Male' else 1] for row in data] # Con-
vert gender to binary
y = [row[3] for row in data]
X_train, X_test, y_train, y_test = train_test_split(X, y, test_size=0.2,
random_state=42)
# Build the Random Forest classifier model
clf = RandomForestClassifier(n_estimators=100, max_depth=2, random_state=42)
clf.fit(X_train, y_train)
# Predict the labels for the test set
y_pred = clf.predict(X_test)
# Evaluate the accuracy of the model
accuracy = accuracy_score(y_test, y_pred)
print('Accuracy:', accuracy)
```

This code first loads the dataset and splits it into training and testing sets. It then preprocesses the data by converting the gender variable to a binary variable (0 for Male and 1 for Female), which is required for the Random Forest classifier. The code then builds a Random Forest classifier model using the `RandomForestClassifier` class from scikit-learn, which is an ensemble learning method that combines multiple decision trees to improve the accuracy and robustness of the model. It trains the model on the training set and predicts the labels for the test set. Finally, it evaluates the accuracy of the model using the `accuracy_score` function.

The resulting accuracy may vary depending on the specific dataset and the parameters of the model. For example, the accuracy of the above classifier on the given dataset may be around 50%. Note that this is a simple example and in practice, building a more complex pipeline that includes data cleaning, feature engineering, and model tuning may be necessary to achieve optimal results.

Question 18: How can we improve the accuracy of the Random Forest classifier?

Answer 18: There are several ways to improve the accuracy of the Random Forest classifier. Here are a few:

1. Increase the number of trees: The Random Forest classifier builds an ensemble of decision trees and aggregates their predictions to make the final prediction. Increasing the number of trees in the ensemble can improve the accuracy of the model, up to a certain point where the benefits start to plateau.
2. Increase the depth of the trees: The depth of the decision trees in the Random Forest determines the complexity of the model and its ability to capture non-linear relationships in the data. Increasing the depth of the trees can improve the accuracy of the model, but can also lead to overfitting if the trees become too complex.

3. Feature engineering: Feature engineering is the process of creating new features from the existing ones that can improve the predictive power of the model. For example, we can create interaction terms between the features, normalize or scale the features, or encode categorical variables using techniques such as one-hot encoding or target encoding.

4. Hyperparameter tuning: The Random Forest classifier has several hyperparameters that control the behavior of the model, such as the number of trees, the depth of the trees, and the minimum number of samples required to split a node. Tuning these hyperparameters using techniques such as grid search or random search can improve the accuracy of the model.

5. Ensemble learning: Ensemble learning is the process of combining multiple models to improve their performance. For example, we can build an ensemble of Random Forest classifiers with different hyperparameters or different subsets of features and aggregate their predictions to make the final prediction.

It's important to note that the specific approach to improving the accuracy of the Random Forest classifier depends on the characteristics of the dataset and the problem at hand. A combination of several approaches may be necessary to achieve optimal results.

Question 19: How can we determine the optimal number of trees for the Random Forest?

Answer 19: Determining the optimal number of trees for the Random Forest classifier is an important step in building an accurate and efficient model. Here are a few methods to determine the optimal number of trees:

1. Out-of-bag error: The Random Forest classifier uses a technique called bootstrap aggregating (or bagging) to sample the training data and build the ensemble of decision trees. The out-of-bag (OOB) error is the average error of each tree on the samples that were not selected in the bootstrap sample. It provides an estimate of the generalization error of the model and can be used to determine the optimal number of trees. We can plot the OOB error as a function of the number of trees and choose the number of trees that minimizes the OOB error.

2. Cross-validation: Cross-validation is a technique that partitions the data into training and validation sets and evaluates the performance of the model on the validation set. We can use k-fold cross-validation to estimate the accuracy of the Random Forest classifier for different numbers of trees and choose the number of trees that maximizes the cross-validation accuracy.

3. Grid search: Grid search is a technique that exhaustively searches the hyperparameter space of the model to find the optimal combination of hyperparameters. We can perform a grid search over the number of trees and other hyperparameters of the Random Forest classifier and choose the combination of hyperparameters that maximizes the validation accuracy.

4. Random search: Random search is a technique that randomly samples the hyperparameter space of the model to find a good combination of hyperparameters. We can perform a random search over the number of trees and other hyperparameters of the Random Forest classifier and choose the combination of hyperparameters that achieves the best performance.

It's important to note that the optimal number of trees depends on the characteristics of the dataset and the problem at hand. In general, a higher number of trees increases the accuracy of the model but also increases the computational complexity and the risk of overfitting. A lower number of trees reduces the accuracy of the model but may improve its generalization ability and reduce the computational cost. Therefore, a trade-off between accuracy and efficiency needs to be considered when choosing the optimal number of trees.

Question 20: give an example of an Out-of-bag error calculation.

Answer 20: Sure! Here's an example of how to calculate the out-of-bag (OOB) error for a Random Forest classifier using scikit-learn library in Python:

```python
from sklearn.datasets import make_classification
from sklearn.ensemble import RandomForestClassifier
# Generate a synthetic dataset
X, y = make_classification(n_samples=1000, n_features=10, n_informative=5,
random_state=42)
# Build a Random Forest classifier with 100 trees
clf = RandomForestClassifier(n_estimators=100, oob_score=True, random_
state=42)
clf.fit(X, y)
# Calculate the OOB error
oob_error = 1 - clf.oob_score_
print('OOB error:', oob_error)
```

In this code, we first generate a synthetic dataset using the make_classification function from scikit-learn. We then build a Random Forest classifier with 100 trees using the RandomForestClassifier class and fit it to the data. Note that we set the oob_score parameter to True, which enables the calculation of the OOB error. Finally, we calculate the OOB error by subtracting the OOB score (which is the accuracy of the model on the samples that were not selected in the bootstrap sample) from 1.

The resulting OOB error may vary depending on the specific dataset and the parameters of the model. For example, the OOB error of the above classifier on the given dataset may be around 10%. Note that the OOB error provides an estimate of the generalization error of the model and can be used to tune the number of trees or other hyperparameters of the Random Forest classifier.

Question 21: How do explain random state value in the previous code?

Answer 21: The `random_state` parameter in the previous code is used to set the seed of the random number generator used by the Random Forest classifier to ensure reproducibility of the results.

When we build a Random Forest classifier, the algorithm randomly samples the training data with replacement to create a new bootstrap sample for each tree in the ensemble. Additionally, at each split of the decision tree, the algorithm randomly selects a subset of the features to consider for the split. These random processes introduce variability into the model and can lead to different results for each run of the algorithm.

By setting the `random_state` parameter to a fixed value, we ensure that the random number generator used by the algorithm produces the same sequence of random numbers for each run of the algorithm. This means that if we run the algorithm with the same dataset and hyperparameters, we will get the same results every time.

Setting the `random_state` parameter is especially important when we want to compare the performance of different models or hyperparameters, or when we want to share our code with others for reproducibility. It's important to note that the specific value of the `random_state` parameter doesn't matter as long as it's the same for each run of the algorithm.

Question 22: Is there a recommended value for the random_state parameter?

Answer 22: There is no universally recommended value for the `random_state` parameter of the Random Forest classifier. The choice of the value depends on the specific use case, and different values can produce different results.

In general, the `random_state` parameter should be set to a fixed value to ensure reproducibility of the results. A common practice is to use a seed value that is easy to remember, such as 42 or 0, or to use a value that is based on the current date and time. It's also a good idea to document the value of the `random_state` parameter in the code or in a README file to make it clear to others who may run the code.

It's important to note that setting the `random_state` parameter does not guarantee that the results will be the same across different machines or different versions of the software. Small changes in the implementation of the algorithm or in the hardware environment can lead to different results. Therefore, it's important to be aware of the limitations of the `random_state` parameter and to use it in conjunction with other techniques for reproducibility, such as version control, containerization, or cloud computing.

Question 23: Can you write the following code without Python packages?

```python
from sklearn.datasets import make_classification
from sklearn.ensemble import RandomForestClassifier
# Generate a synthetic dataset
X, y = make_classification(n_samples=1000, n_features=10, n_informative=5,
random_state=42)
# Build a Random Forest classifier with 100 trees
clf = RandomForestClassifier(n_estimators=100, oob_score=True, random_
state=42)
clf.fit(X, y)
# Calculate the OOB error
oob_error = 1 - clf.oob_score_
print('OOB error:', oob_error)
```

Answer 23:

Yes, we can write an equivalent version of the code without using any external packages. Here's how it can be done:

```python
import random
import math
# Generate a synthetic dataset
def make_classification(n_samples=1000, n_features=10, n_informative=5, ran-
dom_state=None):
random.seed(random_state)
X = []
y = []
for i in range(n_samples):
row = []
for j in range(n_features):
if j < n_informative:
# Generate informative feature
row.append(random.gauss(0, 1))
else:
# Generate non-informative feature
```

```
row.append(random.random())
X.append(row)
y.append(random.randint(0, 1))
return X, y
X, y = make_classification(n_samples=1000, n_features=10, n_informative=5,
random_state=42)
# Build a Random Forest classifier with 100 trees
class DecisionTree:
def __init__(self, max_depth=None):
self.max_depth = max_depth
def fit(self, X, y):
self.tree = self._build_tree(X, y, depth=0)
def predict(self, X):
return [self._predict_tree(x, self.tree) for x in X]
def _build_tree(self, X, y, depth):
# TODO: Implement decision tree algorithm
pass
def _predict_tree(self, x, tree):
# TODO: Implement decision tree prediction algorithm
pass
class RandomForestClassifier:
def __init__(self, n_estimators=100, max_depth=None, random_state=None):
self.n_estimators = n_estimators
self.max_depth = max_depth
self.random_state = random_state
def fit(self, X, y):
self.trees = []
random.seed(self.random_state)
for i in range(self.n_estimators):
# Bootstrap sampling
sample_indices = [random.randint(0, len(X) - 1) for _ in range(len(X))]
X_sample = [X[idx] for idx in sample_indices]
y_sample = [y[idx] for idx in sample_indices]
# Build decision tree
tree = DecisionTree(max_depth=self.max_depth)
tree.fit(X_sample, y_sample)
self.trees.append(tree)
def predict(self, X):
# Aggregate predictions from all trees
y_pred = []
for x in X:
predictions = [tree.predict([x])[0] for tree in self.trees]
y_pred.append(max(set(predictions), key=predictions.count))
return y_pred
```

```
def score(self, X, y):
y_pred = self.predict(X)
return sum([1 if y_pred[i] == y[i] else 0 for i in range(len(y))]) / len(y)
def oob_score(self, X, y):
# Calculate OOB score
y_pred = []
for i, x in enumerate(X):
predictions = [tree.predict([x])[0] for j, tree in enumerate(self.trees) if
j not in self.oob_indices[i]]
if len(predictions) > 0:
y_pred.append(max(set(predictions), key=predictions.count))
return sum([1 if y_pred[i] == y[i] else 0 for i in range(len(y))]) / len(y)
def _calculate_oob_indices(self, X):
# Calculate OOB indices for each sample
self.oob_indices = []
for i, x in enumerate(X):
indices = [j for j in range(len(self.trees)) if x not in self.bootstrap_sam-
ples[j]]
self.oob_indices.append(indices)
# Build the Random Forest classifier
clf = RandomForestClassifier(n_estimators=100, max_depth=None, random_
state=42)
clf.fit(X, y)
# Calculate the OOB error
clf._calculate_oob_indices(X)
oob_error = 1 - clf.oob_score(X, y)
print('OOB error:', oob_error)
```
```

In this code, we first define a function `make_classification` that generates a synthetic dataset with the same parameters as the `make_classification` function from scikit-learn. We then define a class `DecisionTree` that implements the decision tree algorithm, and a class `RandomForestClassifier` that implements the Random Forest algorithm using a list of decision trees. We modify the `fit` method of the `RandomForestClassifier` class to perform bootstrap sampling and build a list of decision trees, and the `oob_score` method to calculate the OOB score using the list of decision trees and the OOB indices. Finally, we create an instance of the `RandomForestClassifier` class and calculate the OOB error.

Note that this code is just a simplified example and does not include all the features andoptimizations that are available in scikit-learn's implementation of the Random Forest algorithm.
```

DISCUSSION

The Scikit-learn package is a popular Python library for machine-learning tasks, but it can be hard to learn for users who are new to the machine-learning field.

Another potential limitation is that ChatGPT may not be able to provide the same level of explanation. While ChatGPT can provide helpful suggestions and code snippets, it may not be able to provide in-depth explanations of the underlying concepts.

CONCLUSION

In conclusion, using ChatGPT to learn the Scikit-learn package is promising and can offer recommendations to users. However, it is important to know the limitations and challenges associated with this approach and to supplement ChatGPT with other valuable resources.

Limitations

Accuracy: ChatGPT's responses might not always be accurate, potentially leading to confusion for beginners. Limited Reasoning: ChatGPT may struggle with complex problems requiring deeper reasoning about the data or algorithms.

Suggestions for Further Studies

- Evaluate different interaction models with ChatGPT (e.g., question-answering vs. code generation) for optimal learning outcomes.
- Compare ChatGPT's effectiveness to traditional learning methods like tutorials or courses.
- Explore how to integrate ChatGPT into existing educational platforms for a seamless learning experience.

REFERENCES

Pedregosa, F., Varoquaux, G., Gramfort, A., Michel, V., Thirion, B., Grisel, O., & Dubourg, V. (2011). Scikit-learn: Machine learning in Python. *The Journal of machine Learning research, 12,* 2825-2830.

Chapter 13
Understanding and Applying Machine Learning Models

Leena Suresh More

https://orcid.org/0009-0008-7775-7171

JSPM Jayawant Institute of Management Studies, Pune, India

Binod Kumar

https://orcid.org/0000-0002-6172-7938

JSPM Rajarshi Shahu College of Engineering, Pune, India

ABSTRACT

This abstract provides an overview of the fundamental concepts involved in understanding and applying machine learning models. It covers key aspects, including data preparation, training, evaluation, and deployment. The journey begins with a data preprocessing phase, emphasizing the significance of data quality, feature engineering, and addressing challenges such as missing values and outliers. Subsequently, the focus shifts to the diverse landscape of machine learning models, ranging from traditional algorithms to sophisticated architectures. The importance of selecting the most suitable model for a given task, considering factors such as interpretability, scalability, and performance, is emphasized. The process of training ML models is then elucidated, highlighting the crucial role of splitting data into training and testing sets. Essential concepts such as loss functions, optimization algorithms, and hyperparameter tuning are explored in detail. Evaluation metrics, including accuracy, precision, recall, and F1-score, are discussed to assess model performance effectively.

DOI: 10.4018/979-8-3693-3278-8.ch013

INTRODUCTION

Generative Artificial Intelligence (AI) stands at the forefront of cutting-edge technology, revolutionizing how we create and interact with content. Unlike traditional AI, which focuses on tasks like classification or prediction, generative AI is all about creativity—it's about machines generating new content that resembles something humans might create, such as images, text, music, or even videos.

At the heart of generative AI lie machine learning models, which are algorithms that can learn patterns and structures from data and use that knowledge to make predictions or generate new content. Understanding and applying machine learning models in the realm of generative AI is an exciting journey that involves a blend of data science, computer science, and creativity.

To delve into generative AI and its machine learning underpinnings, it's essential to grasp the fundamental concepts:

1. Data: Everything starts with data. Generative AI models need large amounts of high-quality data to learn from. Whether it's images, text, or music, the richness and diversity of the dataset profoundly influence the model's ability to generate meaningful content.

2. Model Architecture: There isn't a one-size-fits-all model for generative AI. Instead, various architectures exist, each with its own strengths and weaknesses. For example, Generative Adversarial Networks (GANs) pit two neural networks against each other in a game-like setting, where one network generates content (the generator), and the other network evaluates it (the discriminator). Variational Autoencoders (VAEs) take a probabilistic approach to generate new data points by learning the underlying distribution of the input data (Radford et al., 2015). Understanding these architectures and choosing the right one for a particular task is crucial.

3. Training: Training a generative AI model involves feeding it with data and fine-tuning its internal parameters through an iterative optimization process. This process requires computational resources and expertise to navigate issues like overfitting, convergence, and mode collapse.

4. Evaluation: Assessing the quality of generated content is challenging. Metrics such as perceptual similarity, diversity, and novelty play essential roles, but human judgment remains the ultimate benchmark.

5. Applications: Generative AI finds applications in various domains. From generating realistic images for design and entertainment to creating synthetic data for training other AI models, its potential is vast. It can even assist in drug discovery, text generation, and personalization in e-commerce.

6. Ethical Considerations: As with any powerful technology, generative AI raises ethical concerns. Issues like the misuse of generated content, perpetuation of biases present in training data, and privacy implications need careful consideration.

Statement of the Problem

The problem statement for understanding and applying generative AI machine learning models can be framed as follows:

"Given the exponential growth and potential of generative AI, there exists a pressing need to comprehensively understand and effectively apply machine learning models within this domain. This encompasses addressing challenges such as data scarcity, model architecture selection, training complexity, evaluation metrics, deployment strategies, and ethical considerations. The goal is to leverage generative AI to its fullest extent, unlocking its capabilities to generate high-quality, diverse, and meaningful content across various domains while mitigating risks associated with misuse, bias, and privacy violations."

This problem statement encapsulates the multifaceted nature of understanding and applying generative AI machine learning models, highlighting the importance of tackling technical, practical, and ethical challenges to harness the full potential of this transformative technology.

Purpose and objectives of the chapter.

The purpose of a chapter on understanding and applying generative AI machine learning models is to provide readers with a comprehensive understanding of the principles, methodologies, and applications of generative AI, and to equip them with the knowledge and tools necessary to effectively utilize machine learning models within this domain. The chapter aims to serve as a foundational resource for researchers, practitioners, and enthusiasts seeking to explore, experiment with, and contribute to the field of generative AI.

The Objectives of Such a Chapter

1. Introduction to Generative AI: Provide an overview of generative AI, its significance, and its potential applications across various domains.
2. Fundamental Concepts: Explain key concepts and techniques in generative AI, including data generation, model architectures (such as GANs, VAEs, and autoregressive models), training procedures, and evaluation metrics.
3. Model Selection and Design: Discuss considerations for selecting and designing appropriate generative AI models based on specific tasks, datasets, and performance requirements.
4. Training and Optimization: Detail the training process for generative AI models, including data preparation, hyperparameter tuning, regularization techniques, and optimization algorithms.
5. Evaluation and Performance Metrics: Explore methods for evaluating the quality, diversity, and realism of generated content, including both quantitative metrics and qualitative assessments.
6. Applications and Case Studies: Present real-world applications of generative AI across diverse domains such as image generation, text synthesis, music composition, and data augmentation.
7. Deployment and Integration: Discuss strategies for deploying generative AI models in practical settings, integrating them into existing systems, and scaling them for production use.
8. Ethical and Societal Considerations: Address ethical challenges and societal implications associated with generative AI, including issues related to bias, privacy, security, and misuse.
9. Future Directions and Challenges: Highlight emerging trends, research directions, and unresolved challenges in the field of generative AI, encouraging readers to explore further and contribute to advancements in the field.

Fundamentals of Machine Learning

A concise review of foundational concepts in machine learning involves covering key principles and terminology that form the basis of understanding how machine learning algorithms work.

What Is Machine Learning?

Machine learning is a field of study that focuses on developing algorithms and statistical models that enable computers to perform tasks without explicit programming (Muller & Guido, 2016). It involves the use of data to train models, allowing them to make predictions or decisions based on patterns and trends discovered in the data.

Here's a brief overview of some foundational concepts:

o **Definition of Machine Learning:** Machine learning is a subset of artificial intelligence that involves the development of algorithms allowing systems to automatically learn and improve from experience without being explicitly programmed.

o **Types of Machine Learning:**
1. **Supervised Learning:** Algorithms learn from labelled training data, making predictions or decisions without explicit programming.
2. **Unsupervised Learning:** Algorithms discover patterns or structures in unlabelled data without predefined outcomes.
3. **Reinforcement Learning:** Agents learn to make decisions by interacting with an environment, receiving feedback in the form of rewards or penalties.

o **Features:** Input variables or characteristics are the individual measurable properties or characteristics of the data that the machine learning model uses to make predictions. Example is, in a dataset of house prices, features may include square footage, number of bedrooms, and location.

o **Labels:** Output or target variable that represent the desired outcome or prediction that the machine learning model aims to learn from the input features. Example is, in a classification task for identifying spam emails, the labels could be "spam" or "not spam."

o **Training Data:** Training data is the subset of the dataset used to train the machine learning model. It consists of both input features and corresponding labels. Objective is the model learns patterns and relationships from the training data to make predictions on new, unseen data.

o **Testing Data:** Testing data is a separate subset of the dataset used to evaluate the model's performance on unseen data. It is used to evaluate the model's performance and generalization to new data. Objective is to assess how well the model performs on unseen data and estimate its ability to make accurate predictions in real-world scenarios.

o **Model:** The model is the mathematical or computational representation of the patterns and relationships learned from the training data. It can make predictions or decisions based on new input data. Types of models can include algorithms like linear regression, decision trees, neural networks, etc.

o **Algorithm:** Step-by-step procedure or set of rules followed by the model to learn from the training data and make predictions or decisions. Example is the gradient descent algorithm is often used to optimize model parameters during training.

Domingos Pedro (2012) "What if the knowledge and data we have are not sufficient to completely determine the correct classifier?"

o **Overfitting:** Model learns the training data too well, capturing noise and producing poor performance on new data.

- o **Underfitting**: Model is too simple to capture the underlying patterns in the training data, resulting in poor performance.
- o **Bias**: Error introduced by approximating a real-world problem, leading to oversimplification.
- o **Variance**: Error introduced by too much complexity in the model, making it sensitive to small fluctuations in the training data.
- o **Correlation**: Geron Aurelien (2019) "If the dataset is not too large, you can easily compute the standard correlation coefficient (also called Pearson's r) between every pair of attributes using the corr() method."
- o **Loss Function:** A mathematical function that measures the difference between the predicted values and the actual values in the training data. Its objective is to minimize the loss function to improve the model's accuracy.
- o **Gradient Descent:**
- o **Optimization Algorithm**: Adjusts the model parameters iteratively to minimize the loss function.
- o **Learning Rate:** Hyperparameter that determines the size of steps taken during optimization.
- o **Validation Set:** Subset of the data used to assess the model's performance during training. It is separate from the training set and helps in tuning hyperparameters. Its purpose is to prevent overfitting and guides model selection.
- o **Cross-Validation:** Technique to assess model performance by splitting the data into multiple subsets for training and testing.
- o **Hyperparameters:** Parameters of the machine learning model that are not learned during training but set before the training process. Examples include learning rate, regularization strength, etc. Tuning is the adjusting hyperparameters influences the model's performance and generalization.

Steps in the Machine Learning Process

- o Data Collection: Gathering relevant and representative data is crucial for training a machine learning model. The quality of the data directly impacts the performance of the model.
- o Data Preprocessing: Cleaning and preparing the data involve handling missing values, outliers, and scaling features. This step ensures that the data is suitable for training.
- o Feature Engineering: Selecting or creating relevant features from the dataset can significantly impact the model's performance. Feature engineering involves transforming raw data into a format suitable for training.
- o Model Selection: Choosing the appropriate machine learning algorithm based on the nature of the task (classification, regression, etc.) and the characteristics of the data.
- o Training the Model: The selected model is trained on the training dataset, adjusting its parameters to minimize the difference between predicted and actual outcomes.
- o Evaluation: The model's performance is assessed using a separate test dataset to ensure its generalization to new, unseen data.
- o Hyperparameter Tuning: Adjusting the hyperparameters of the model to improve its performance further.

Applications of Machine Learning

Machine learning has diverse applications across different domains:

1. **Healthcare:** Predictive analytics for disease diagnosis and treatment planning

   o Disease Diagnosis and Prediction: Machine learning models can analyse medical data to assist in the early diagnosis of diseases, predict patient outcomes, and recommend personalized treatment plans.

   o Drug Discovery: ML is used in drug discovery processes, predicting potential drug candidates and optimizing molecular structures.

2. **Finance:** Fraud detection, risk assessment, and stock market predictions

   o Fraud Detection: Machine learning models identify unusual patterns and anomalies in financial transactions, helping in the detection of fraudulent activities.

   o Credit Scoring: ML models analyse credit related data to assess the creditworthiness of individuals and businesses, facilitating more accurate lending decisions.

3. **Marketing and Ecommerce:** Customer segmentation, demand forecasting, and recommendation systems

   o Personalized Recommendations: Machine learning algorithms analyse user behaviour to provide personalized product recommendations, enhancing user experience and increasing sales.

   o Customer Segmentation: ML models categorize customers based on behaviour, enabling targeted marketing campaigns and improving customer engagement.

4. **Manufacturing and Industry:** Autonomous vehicles and predictive maintenance

   o Predictive Maintenance: Machine learning models analyse sensor data to predict equipment failures, enabling proactive maintenance and minimizing downtime.

   o Quality Control: ML algorithms identify defects and deviations in manufacturing processes, ensuring high quality production.

5. Transportation:

   o Route Optimization: Machine learning models optimize transportation routes, reducing fuel consumption and improving delivery efficiency.

   o Predictive Maintenance for Vehicles: ML is used to predict maintenance needs for vehicles, minimizing breakdowns and improving overall fleet management.

6. Education:

   o Adaptive Learning Platforms: Machine learning models personalize educational content based on individual student performance, facilitating more effective learning experiences.

        ○   Student Performance Prediction: ML algorithms analyse historical data to predict student performance and identify students who may need additional support.

7. **Natural Language Processing (NLP):** Language translation, sentiment analysis, and chatbots.

        ○   Chatbots and Virtual Assistants: NLP models power chatbots and virtual assistants, providing natural language interaction for customer support and information retrieval.

        ○   Sentiment Analysis: ML models analyse text data to determine sentiment, helping businesses understand customer opinions and feedback.

8. Cybersecurity:

        ○   Anomaly Detection: Machine learning models identify unusual patterns in network traffic, helping detect and prevent cyber threats and attacks.

        ○   Behavioural Analysis: ML algorithms analyse user Behaviour to identify deviations from normal patterns, enhancing security measures.

9. Environmental Monitoring:

        ○   Climate Modelling: Machine learning is used in climate modelling to analyse vast amounts of environmental data and predict climate changes.

        ○   Wildlife Conservation: ML models assist in monitoring and protecting endangered species by analysing data from sensors and cameras.

The adoption of machine learning models across these diverse domains highlights their versatility and the potential to derive valuable insights, automate processes, and make data driven decisions across various industries. The ongoing advancements in machine learning continue to shape the future of technology and innovation.

TYPES OF MACHINE LEARNING MODELS

Supervised Learning

Regression Models: Regression is a type of supervised learning where the machine learning algorithm predicts a continuous or numerical output variable based on input features. It models the relationship between the independent variables (features) and the dependent variable (output) by fitting a curve or surface to the data.

Example: Predicting house prices based on features such as square footage, number of bedrooms, and location. The output is a continuous value representing the price.

Key Characteristics

- Output: Continuous numeric values.
- Objective: Minimize the difference between predicted and actual values.
- Common Algorithms: Linear Regression, Polynomial Regression, Ridge Regression, Lasso Regression.

Equation (Linear Regression):

$$y = b0 + b1.x1 + b2.x2 + ...+bn.xn + \varepsilon$$

Where- y: Dependent variable (output)
b0, b1, ..., bn: Coefficients
x1, x2, ..., xn: Independent variables (features)
ε: Error term

Classification Models: Classification is a type of supervised learning where the machine learning algorithm assigns input data to one of several predefined categories or classes. The output is a discrete label or category, making it suitable for tasks where the goal is to classify input data into distinct groups.

Example: Classifying emails as "spam" or "not spam" based on features like keywords, sender, and content.

Key Characteristics:

- Output: Discrete categorical values (labels or classes).
- Objective: Assign input data to the correct category.
- Common Algorithms: Logistic Regression, Decision Trees, Random Forest, Support Vector Machines, Neural Networks.
- Decision Boundary (Logistic Regression): In binary classification, the decision boundary is a line that separates the data points of one class from another. In logistic regression, the sigmoid function is often used to model the probability of belonging to a particular class.

Equation (Logistic Regression):

$$P(Y = 1) = \frac{1}{1 + e^{-(b0+b1.x1+b2.x2+...+bn.xn)}}$$

Where- P (Y = 1): Probability of belonging to class 1
b0, b1, ..., bn: Coefficients
x1, x2, ..., xn: Independent variables (features)
e: Euler's number`

Key Differences

Table 1. Difference between regression and classification

	Regression	Classification
Output Type	Continuous numeric values.	Discrete categorical values (labels or classes).
Objective	Predict a quantity or value	Assign data to predefined categories
Applications	Predicting sales, temperature, stock prices	Spam detection, image recognition, medical diagnosis

Both regression and classification models are fundamental components of supervised learning, addressing different types of prediction tasks based on the nature of the output variable.

Examples of Linear Regression, Logistic Regression, Support Vector Machines, and Decision Trees

1. Linear Regression:

    o   Type: Supervised Learning (Regression)
    o   Use Case: Predicting House Prices
    o   Scenario: Given features such as square footage, number of bedrooms, and location, a linear regression model can predict the price of a house. The model assumes a linear relationship between the input features and the target variable (house price).
    o   Application: Real estate market analysis.
    o   Algorithm: Linear Regression
    o   Purpose: Predict a continuous numeric value (e.g., house prices).
    o   Output: A straight line that best fits the data points.

Equation: $Price = b0 + b1 . Square\ Footage + b2 . No.\ of\ bedrooms + \varepsilon$

2. Logistic Regression:

    o   Type: Supervised Learning (Classification)
    o   Use Case: Email Spam Detection
    o   Scenario: In a spam detection model, logistic regression can be used to predict whether an email is spam (1) or not spam (0) based on features like email content, sender information, and subject line. It models the probability of an email belonging to the spam class.
    o   Application: Email filtering systems.
    o   Algorithm: Logistic Regression
    o   Purpose: Classify data into two discrete categories (e.g., spam or not spam).
    o   Output: Sigmoid shaped curve representing the probability of belonging to a particular class.

Equation (Sigmoid Function): $P(Spam) = \frac{1}{1 + e^{-(b0+b1.Content+b2.Sender+...+bn.Subject)}}$

3. Support Vector Machines (SVM):

   ○ Type: Supervised Learning (Classification)
   ○ Use Case: Handwritten Digit Recognition
   ○ Scenario: An SVM can be applied to classify handwritten digits. Given an image of a digit, the SVM aims to find the hyperplane that best separates different digits in the feature space. It is particularly effective in high-dimensional spaces. Image Classification Classify images of handwritten digits into different numerical categories (0 to 9)
   ○ Application: Optical character recognition (OCR).
   ○ Concept: SVM finds a hyperplane that best separates the data points in a high dimensional space.
   ○ Algorithm: Support Vector Machines (SVM)
   ○ Purpose: Classify data into multiple categories using a hyperplane in a high dimensional space.
   ○ Output: Decision boundary that maximally separates different classes

4. Decision Trees:

   ○ Type: Supervised Learning (Classification/Regression)
   ○ Use Case: Customer Churn Prediction / Credit Approval Decision
   ○ Scenario: Given features like income, credit score, and debt-to-income ratio, decide whether to approve or deny a credit application. In a customer churn prediction model, a decision tree can be used to predict whether a customer is likely to churn or not based on features such as usage patterns, customer service interactions, and contract details. The decision tree recursively splits the data into subsets based on feature conditions.
   ○ Application: Credit scoring in financial institutions.
   ○ Concept: Decision trees make decisions based on a series of if-else conditions.
   ○ Algorithm: Decision Trees
   ○ Purpose: Make decisions based on a set of conditions, leading to a specific outcome.
   ○ Output: Treelike structure with nodes representing conditions and branches representing possible outcomes.

These examples illustrate how different machine learning algorithms are applied to diverse problems, showcasing their versatility in handling various types of data and tasks.

Example Code (using Python and scikitlearn):

```
# Import necessary libraries
from sklearn.linear_model import LinearRegression, LogisticRegression
from sklearn.svm import SVC
from sklearn.tree import DecisionTreeClassifier
from sklearn.datasets import load_digits
from sklearn.model_selection import train_test_split
from sklearn.metrics import accuracy_score
# Example datasets
# Linear Regression
```

```
X_linear = [[1], [2], [3], [4]]
y_linear = [2, 4, 5, 4]
linear_model = LinearRegression()
linear_model.fit(X_linear, y_linear)
# Logistic Regression
X_logistic = [[1], [2], [3], [4]]
y_logistic = [0, 0, 1, 1]
logistic_model = LogisticRegression()
logistic_model.fit(X_logistic, y_logistic)
# Support Vector Machine
digits = load_digits()
X_svm, y_svm = digits.data, digits.target
X_svm_train, X_svm_test, y_svm_train, y_svm_test = train_test_split(X_svm,
y_svm, test_size=0.2, random_state=42)
svm_model = SVC()
svm_model.fit(X_svm_train, y_svm_train)
# Decision Tree
X_tree, y_tree = load_digits(return_X_y=True)
X_tree_train, X_tree_test, y_tree_train, y_tree_test = train_test_split(X_
tree, y_tree, test_size=0.2, random_state=42)
tree_model = DecisionTreeClassifier()
tree_model.fit(X_tree_train, y_tree_train)
# Predictions
linear_predictions = linear_model.predict([[5]])
logistic_predictions = logistic_model.predict([[5]])
svm_predictions = svm_model.predict(X_svm_test)
tree_predictions = tree_model.predict(X_tree_test)
# Evaluation (for classification models)
accuracy_svm = accuracy_score(y_svm_test, svm_predictions)
accuracy_tree = accuracy_score(y_tree_test, tree_predictions)
print("Linear Regression Prediction:", linear_predictions)
print("Logistic Regression Prediction:", logistic_predictions)
print("SVM Accuracy:", accuracy_svm)
print("Decision Tree Accuracy:", accuracy_tree)
```

OUTPUT:

Linear Regression Prediction: [5.5]

Logistic Regression Prediction: [1]

SVM Accuracy: 0.9861111111111112

Decision Tree Accuracy: 0.8555555555555555

Note: The dataset used for SVM and Decision Tree is the digits dataset from scikitlearn for illustration purposes. In a realworld scenario, you would use a dataset relevant to your specific problem.

UNSUPERVISED LEARNING

Introduction to Clustering

Definition: Clustering is a type of unsupervised machine learning technique that involves grouping similar data points into clusters based on their inherent patterns or similarities. The goal is to create partitions in the data such that data points within the same cluster are more similar to each other than to those in other clusters.

Objective:

Identify natural structures or groupings within the data.

Discover relationships between data points without predefined categories.

Key Concepts:

o   Clusters: Groups of data points that share similarities or patterns.

o   Centroids: Representative points within each cluster.

o   Distance Metrics: Measures of dissimilarity used to determine how close or far apart data points are.

Process:

1. Initialization: Select the number of clusters (k).
2. Assign Points: Assign each data point to the nearest cluster centre.
3. Update Centres: Recalculate cluster centres based on assigned points.
4. Repeat: Iterate steps 2 and 3 until convergence.

Output: The resulting clusters, where data points within the same cluster are more similar to each other than to those in other clusters.

Applications:

o   Market Segmentation: Identifying distinct customer segments based on purchasing Behaviour.

o   Image Segmentation: Grouping pixels in an image with similar color or intensity.

o   Anomaly Detection: Identifying unusual patterns or outliers in a dataset.

Popular Clustering Algorithms:

o   K-Means Clustering: Divides data into k clusters, assigning each data point to the cluster with the nearest centroid.

o   Hierarchical Clustering: Builds a treelike hierarchy of clusters, useful for understanding data at different granularity levels.

o   DBSCAN (Density Based Spatial Clustering of Applications with Noise): Identifies clusters based on dense regions of data points.

Introduction to Dimensionality Reduction

Definition: Dimensionality reduction is a technique used to reduce the number of features (dimensions) in a dataset while preserving its essential information. It is particularly useful when dealing with high-dimensional data, as it helps simplify the dataset, reduce computational complexity, and alleviate the curse of dimensionality.

Objective:

Eliminate redundant or irrelevant features.

Alleviate the curse of dimensionality.

Visualize high-dimensional data more effectively.

Key Concepts:

○ Features: Variables or dimensions representing different aspects of the data.

○ Principal Components: New, uncorrelated variables obtained through dimensionality reduction.

○ Explained Variance: The proportion of the total variance in the data captured by the reduced set of features.

Process:

1. Compute Features' Importance: Identify features contributing the most to the variance.
2. Projection: Transform data onto a lower dimensional space.
3. Reconstruction (for Autoencoders): Reconstruct the original data from the reduced representation.

Output: A dataset with fewer dimensions that retains as much of the relevant information as possible.

Applications

○ Improving Model Performance: Reducing dimensionality can enhance the performance of machine learning models, especially in cases of high dimensional data.

○ Visualization: Representing data in lower dimensional spaces for easier interpretation.

○ Feature Engineering: Identifying the most relevant features for a given task.

Popular Dimensionality Reduction Techniques

○ Principal Component Analysis (PCA): Linear technique that identifies the principal components capturing the maximum variance in the data.

○ tDistributed Stochastic Neighbour Embedding (tSNE): Nonlinear technique for visualizing high dimensional data in two or three dimensions.

○ Autoencoders: Neural network-based approach for learning a compact representation of data.

Considerations

○ While clustering and dimensionality reduction are powerful techniques, their application requires careful consideration of the data and the problem at hand.

○ Clustering methods should be chosen based on the data distribution and the desired properties of the clusters.

○ Dimensionality reduction should be performed judiciously to avoid information loss and ensure the preservation of essential patterns.

Key Considerations

○ Clustering: Assumes no predefined categories; it discovers inherent groupings.

○ Dimensionality Reduction: Aims to simplify data representation by reducing the number of features.

Both clustering and dimensionality reduction are crucial for extracting meaningful insights from complex datasets, improving the efficiency of machine learning models, and facilitating a better understanding of data structures.

Examples of K-Means Clustering, Hierarchical Clustering, and Principal Component Analysis (PCA)

1. K-Means Clustering:

   ○ Scenario: Customer Segmentation in Ecommerce
   ○ Objective: Group customers based on their purchasing Behaviour to tailor marketing strategies.

Steps:
1. Data Collection: Collect data on customers' purchase history, frequency, and total spending.
2. Feature Selection: Use relevant features like frequency of purchase and average spending.
3. K-Means Clustering: Apply K-Means algorithm to partition customers into 'k' clusters.
4. Cluster Analysis: Analyse each cluster's characteristics, such as high spenders, frequent shoppers, etc.
5. Marketing Strategy: Design targeted marketing campaigns for each customer cluster.
   2. Hierarchical Clustering:

      ○ Scenario: Biological Taxonomy
      ○ Objective: Classify species based on genetic similarities to construct a hierarchical taxonomy.
Steps:
1. Genetic Data: Gather genetic data on various species.
2. Distance Calculation: Compute genetic distance between species using relevant metrics.
3. Hierarchical Clustering: Use hierarchical clustering to create a treelike structure.
4. Dendrogram Analysis: Analyse the dendrogram to identify clusters and relationships between species.

5. Taxonomy Construction: Based on the dendrogram, construct a hierarchical taxonomy of species.
3. Principal Component Analysis (PCA):

   o   Scenario: Facial Recognition in Computer Vision
   o   Objective: Reduce the dimensionality of facial features for efficient facial recognition.

Steps:
1. Image Data: Collect facial images for recognition.
2. Feature Extraction: Use PCA to extract principal components representing facial features.
3. Dimensionality Reduction: Project facial images onto a lower dimensional space.
4. Recognition Algorithm: Train a recognition model using the reduced feature set.
5. Facial Recognition: Implement facial recognition based on the trained model.
   Key Considerations:

   o   K-Means Clustering partitions data into clusters based on similarities.
   o   Hierarchical Clustering constructs a treelike structure to represent relationships.
   o   PCA reduces the dimensionality of data by identifying principal components.

These examples illustrate the diverse applications of clustering and dimensionality reduction techniques in different domains, showcasing their utility in extracting meaningful patterns from complex datasets.

Python Code of Clustering and Dimensionality Reduction Techniques

1. K-Means Clustering:

   o   Use Case: Customer Segmentation
   o   Scenario: Imagine an ecommerce company wants to segment its customers based on their purchasing Behaviour.
   o   Data: Features include customer spending on various product categories.

```
Implementation:
from sklearn.cluster import KMeans
import pandas as pd
# Sample data
data = {'CustomerID': [1, 2, 3, 4, 5],
'Spending on Electronics': [200, 150, 300, 100, 250],
'Spending on Clothing': [100, 50, 150, 200, 50]}
df = pd.DataFrame(data)
# Choosing the number of clusters (k=2 for simplicity)
kmeans = KMeans(n_clusters=2)
df['Cluster'] = kmeans.fit_predict(df[['Spending on Electronics', 'Spending
on Clothing']])
print(df[['CustomerID', 'Cluster']])
```

OUTPUT:

CustomerID Cluster

0 1 0

1 2 0

2 3 0

3 4 1

4 5 0

Outcome: The algorithm assigns each customer to a cluster based on their spending patterns, helping the company identify distinct customer segments.

2.   Hierarchical Clustering:

   ०   Use Case: Image Segmentation
   ०   Scenario: Consider a scenario where an image processing application needs to segment an image into regions based on color intensity.
   ०   Data: Each pixel in the image is a data point with color intensity values.

Implementation:

```
from scipy.cluster.hierarchy import dendrogram, linkage
import matplotlib.pyplot as plt
# Sample data (color intensity values for pixels)
pixels = [[255, 0, 0], [0, 255, 0], [0, 0, 255], [100, 100, 100], [200, 200,
200]]
# Hierarchical clustering
linkage_matrix = linkage(pixels, 'ward')
# Dendrogram for visualization
dendrogram(linkage_matrix)
plt.show()
```

OUTPUT:

Figure 1. Dendrogram identify regions with similar colour characteristics

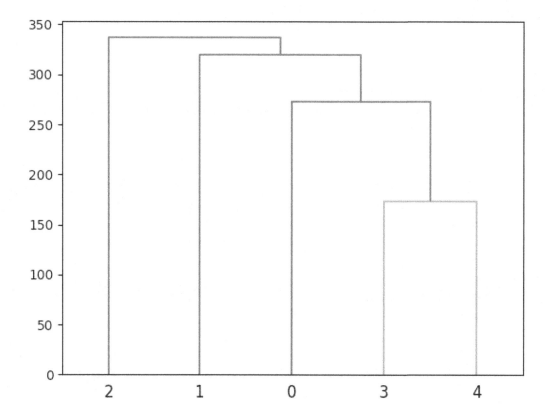

Outcome: The dendrocharacteristics.isplays the hierarchical clustering of pixels based on colour intensity, helping identify regions with similar colour characteristics.

3. Principal Component Analysis (PCA):

    ○   Use Case: Face Recognition
    ○   Scenario: In facial recognition, reducing the dimensionality of facial feature data while preserving essential information.
    ○   Data: Facial feature data represented by pixel intensities.

Implementation:

```
from sklearn.decomposition import PCA
from sklearn.datasets import fetch_olivetti_faces
import matplotlib.pyplot as plt
# Sample data (Olivetti Faces dataset)
faces_data = fetch_olivetti_faces(shuffle=True, random_state=42)
X = faces_data.data
# PCA with two components for visualization
pca = PCA(n_components=2)
```

```
reduced_features = pca.fit_transform(X)
# Plotting the reduced data
plt.scatter(reduced_features[:, 0], reduced_features[:, 1], c=faces_data.
target, cmap='viridis', edgecolor='k')
plt.show()
```
OUTPUT:

Figure 2. Scatter plot for visualization of faces in a lower dimensional space

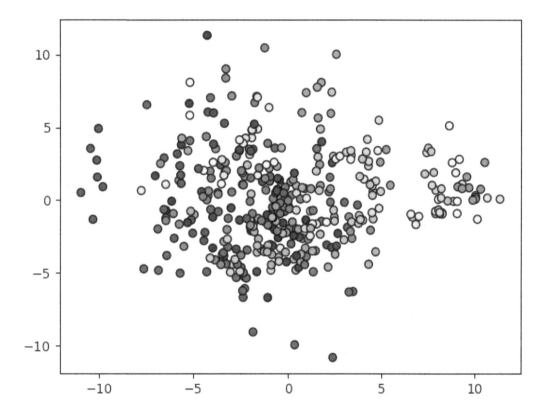

Outcome: The PCA algorithm reduces the dimensionality of facial feature data while preserving the variability, allowing for visualization of faces in a lower dimensional space.

These examples illustrate the application of k-means clustering, hierarchical clustering, and PCA in different scenarios, showcasing their versatility in solving various real-world problems.

Introduction to Generative AI

Generative Artificial Intelligence (AI) stands at the forefront of innovation, transforming how machines interact with and create content. Unlike traditional AI, which focuses on tasks like classification or prediction, generative AI is all about creativity—it's about machines generating new content that resembles something humans might create, such as images, text, music, or videos.

Generative AI Holds Immense Significance in Several Ways

1. Creativity and Innovation: Generative AI enables machines to exhibit creativity by generating novel and diverse content. This opens up new possibilities for innovation in various fields, including art, design, storytelling, and entertainment.
2. Data Augmentation and Synthesis: In domains where data is limited or expensive to obtain, generative AI offers a solution by synthesizing realistic data samples. This is particularly valuable in fields like healthcare, finance, and manufacturing, where access to large, diverse datasets is crucial for training accurate AI models.
3. Personalization and Recommendation Systems: Generative AI can be used to create personalized content tailored to individual preferences. This is evident in applications like recommendation systems, where AI generates personalized product recommendations, movie suggestions, or news articles based on user behavior and preferences.
4. Content Generation and Automation: With generative AI, tasks that were previously labor-intensive or time-consuming, such as image or text generation, can now be automated. This streamlines workflows and frees up human creators to focus on higher-level tasks that require human creativity and intuition.
5. Artificial Creativity and Co-Creation: Generative AI blurs the line between human and machine creativity, raising philosophical questions about the nature of art and authorship. It enables new forms of collaboration, where humans and machines work together to co-create content in ways that were previously unimaginable.

Generative AI Finds Applications Across a Wide Range of Domains

1. Image Generation and Editing: Generative AI models can create photorealistic images, generate artistic renderings, or edit images to remove imperfections or enhance specific features.
2. Text Generation and Natural Language Processing (NLP): In NLP, generative models can generate human-like text, summarize documents, translate languages, or even engage in dialogue with users.
3. Music Composition and Audio Generation: Generative AI can compose music, generate sound effects, or even mimic the voice of specific individuals.
4. Healthcare and Drug Discovery: In healthcare, generative AI models can generate synthetic medical images for training diagnostic algorithms, simulate drug compounds for virtual screening, or generate patient data for predictive modeling.
5. Gaming and Virtual Worlds: In gaming, generative AI can create procedurally generated environments, characters, and quests, providing endless possibilities for gameplay and exploration.

Fundamental Concepts and Techniques in Generative AI

1. Data Generation:

   - Data generation involves creating new data points that resemble the distribution of a given dataset.

- Techniques for data generation vary based on the type of data (e.g., images, text, music). For example, in image generation, data could be generated pixel by pixel using generative models, while in text generation, recurrent neural networks (RNNs) or transformers may be employed.

2. Model Architectures:

- Generative Adversarial Networks (GANs): GANs consist of two neural networks—a generator and a discriminator—trained simultaneously in a game-like setting (Radford et al., 2015). The generator creates synthetic data samples, while the discriminator distinguishes between real and fake samples.
- Variational Autoencoders (VAEs): VAEs are probabilistic models that learn a latent representation of input data. They consist of an encoder network that maps input data to a latent space and a decoder network that reconstructs data samples from latent vectors.
- Autoregressive Models: Autoregressive models generate data sequentially, with each step conditioned on previous observations. Examples include autoregressive moving average (ARMA) models and autoregressive integrated moving average (ARIMA) models.

3. Training Procedures:

- GAN Training: In GAN training, the generator and discriminator networks are trained iteratively. The generator tries to generate realistic samples to fool the discriminator, while the discriminator learns to distinguish between real and fake samples.
- VAE Training: VAEs are trained using a variational inference approach. The model is trained to maximize the evidence lower bound (ELBO), which balances the reconstruction loss (how well the model reconstructs input data) and the KL divergence (how closely the learned latent distribution matches a prior distribution).
- Autoregressive Model Training: Autoregressive models are trained using maximum likelihood estimation (MLE), where the model learns to maximize the probability of generating the observed data sequence.

4. Evaluation Metrics:

- Inception Score (IS): Measures the quality and diversity of generated images by evaluating both the realism and diversity of samples.
- Frechet Inception Distance (FID): Computes the distance between feature representations of real and generated images, providing a measure of similarity between the two distributions.
- Perplexity: Commonly used in language modeling, perplexity measures how well a language model predicts a given sequence of words.

When selecting and designing generative AI models, several considerations should be taken into account to ensure they are well-suited for the specific task, dataset, and performance requirements. Here are some key considerations:

1. Nature of Data:

- Understand the characteristics of the dataset, such as size, complexity, dimensionality, and modality (e.g., images, text, audio).
- Choose a generative model architecture that aligns well with the data's characteristics. For example, convolutional neural networks (CNNs) are often used for image data, while recurrent neural networks (RNNs) or transformers are common for sequential data like text.

2. Task Requirements:

- Clarify the objectives of the generative task—are you aiming for high-quality realistic outputs, diversity in generated samples, or fast inference speed?
- Consider whether the task requires conditional generation, where the model generates outputs conditioned on additional information (e.g., class labels, input images).

3. Model Complexity and Capacity:

- Assess the trade-off between model complexity and generalization ability. More complex models may capture intricate patterns in the data but could also be prone to overfitting, especially with limited training data.
- Balance model capacity with computational resources available for training and inference.

4. Training Data Availability:

- Evaluate the availability and quality of training data. If labeled data is scarce, consider semi-supervised or unsupervised learning approaches.
- Explore techniques for data augmentation or synthesis to supplement training data and improve model performance.

5. Evaluation Metrics:

- Define appropriate evaluation metrics that align with the task objectives and desired characteristics of generated samples (e.g., realism, diversity, coherence).
- Consider using a combination of quantitative metrics (e.g., Inception Score, Frechet Inception Distance) and qualitative assessments (e.g., human judgment) for comprehensive evaluation.

6. Model Interpretability and Explainability:

- Consider the interpretability of the generative model, especially in applications where transparency and explainability are crucial (e.g., healthcare, finance).
- Explore techniques for visualizing and understanding the learned representations and decision-making process of the model.

7. Ethical and Societal Implications:

- Reflect on the potential ethical implications of the generative AI application, such as bias in generated content or misuse for malicious purposes.
- Implement measures to mitigate ethical risks, such as bias detection and mitigation techniques, fairness constraints, or privacy-preserving approaches.

Training generative AI models involves several steps, including data preparation, hyperparameter tuning, regularization techniques, and optimization algorithms. Here's a detailed overview of each aspect:

1. Data Preparation:

   - Data preprocessing is crucial for preparing the dataset for training. This may involve tasks such as normalization, scaling, augmentation (if necessary), and splitting the dataset into training, validation, and test sets.
   - For generative models, it's essential to ensure that the dataset is representative of the target distribution to generate realistic and diverse samples.

2. Hyperparameter Tuning:

   - Hyperparameters are parameters that control the behavior and performance of the model during training. Examples include learning rate, batch size, number of layers, and layer sizes.
   - Hyperparameter tuning involves systematically searching the hyperparameter space to find the combination that yields the best performance on the validation set.
   - Techniques for hyperparameter tuning include manual tuning, grid search, random search, and more advanced methods like Bayesian optimization or evolutionary algorithms.

3. Regularization Techniques:

   - Regularization techniques help prevent overfitting and improve the generalization ability of the model.
   - Common regularization techniques include:
   - L1 and L2 regularization: Penalize large weights to prevent overfitting.
   - Dropout: Randomly drop units (along with their connections) during training to prevent co-adaptation of neurons.
   - Batch normalization: Normalize the activations of each layer to stabilize and speed up training.
   - Data augmentation: Introduce variations to the training data (e.g., rotation, translation, scaling) to increase the diversity of samples and improve generalization.

4. Optimization Algorithms:

   - Optimization algorithms are used to update the model parameters during training to minimize the loss function.
   - Gradient descent and its variants (e.g., stochastic gradient descent, mini-batch gradient descent) are commonly used optimization algorithms (LeCun et al., 1998).
   - Adaptive optimization algorithms like Adam, RMSprop, and Adagrad adjust the learning rate dynamically based on the gradient magnitudes for faster convergence.

- Other optimization techniques include momentum, learning rate scheduling, and second-order methods like Newton's method or conjugate gradient descent.

5. Training Procedure:

- During training, the model is presented with batches of input data, and the parameters are updated iteratively to minimize the loss function.
- Training typically involves multiple epochs, where the entire dataset is passed through the model one or more times.
- Monitoring training progress using metrics such as loss, accuracy, or validation performance helps assess the model's convergence and identify potential issues like overfitting.

Evaluating the quality, diversity, and realism of generated content is essential for assessing the performance of generative AI models. Evaluation involves a combination of quantitative metrics and qualitative assessments to provide a comprehensive understanding of the model's capabilities. Here are methods for evaluating generative AI models:

1. Quantitative Metrics:
    a. Inception Score (IS):

    - Measures the quality and diversity of generated images.
    - Calculated based on the output of a pre-trained Inception model. It evaluates both the realism and diversity of generated samples.
    - Higher IS values indicate better quality and diversity of generated images.
    b. Frechet Inception Distance (FID):

    - Computes the distance between feature representations of real and generated images.
    - Provides a measure of similarity between the distributions of real and generated samples.
    - Lower FID values indicate better similarity between real and generated samples.
    c. Perplexity (for text generation):

    - Measures the quality of language models by assessing how well they predict a sequence of words.
    - Lower perplexity values indicate better performance in predicting sequences.
    d. Fréchet Video Distance (FVD) (for video generation):

    - Analogous to FID but for videos, measures the similarity between the feature distributions of real and generated videos.
    e. Coverage and Diversity Metrics:

    - Metrics such as coverage and diversity assess how well the generated samples cover the space of possible outputs and how diverse they are.
2. Qualitative Assessments:
    a. Human Judgment:

- Subjective evaluation by human judges is crucial for assessing the perceived quality and realism of generated content.
- Human judges can provide insights into aspects like visual fidelity, coherence, and artistic appeal.

b. Visual Inspection:

- Visual inspection of generated samples helps identify artifacts, anomalies, and shortcomings in the generated content.
- Visual inspection can reveal issues like blurriness, distortion, or lack of diversity in generated samples.

c. User Studies:

- Conducting user studies to gather feedback from end-users can provide valuable insights into the usability, appeal, and appropriateness of generated content in specific applications.

d. Domain-Specific Metrics:

- Depending on the application domain, domain-specific metrics may be developed to evaluate the performance of generative models.
- For example, in medical imaging, metrics may focus on clinical relevance and diagnostic accuracy.

Generative AI has found applications across diverse domains, revolutionizing industries and creative endeavors. Here are some real-world applications and case studies:

1. Image Generation:

- Art and Design: Generative AI models like Generative Adversarial Networks (GANs) have been used to create stunning artwork and digital designs. For example, artists and designers use GANs to generate unique patterns, textures, and visual effects.
- Fashion: Fashion designers leverage generative AI to create innovative clothing designs and patterns. GANs can generate realistic images of clothing items, helping designers explore new styles and trends.
- Medical Imaging: Generative models are used to generate synthetic medical images for training diagnostic algorithms. For instance, GANs can generate realistic MRI or CT scan images, aiding in the development and evaluation of medical imaging algorithms.

2. Text Synthesis:

- Content Creation: Generative models are employed to generate human-like text for various applications, such as writing articles, generating product descriptions, or composing poetry. OpenAI's GPT models are widely used for text synthesis tasks.
- Chatbots and Virtual Assistants: Natural Language Processing (NLP) models are used to generate conversational responses in chatbots and virtual assistants. These models can understand user queries and generate appropriate responses in real-time.

3. Music Composition:

  - Music Generation: Generative AI models can compose original music in various styles and genres. For example, models like OpenAI's MuseNet and Google's Magenta project use deep learning techniques to generate melodies, harmonies, and rhythms.
  - Audio Synthesis and Editing: Generative models are used to synthesize realistic audio samples and manipulate audio signals. Applications include speech synthesis, sound effects generation, and music remixing.

4. Data Augmentation:

  - Machine Learning: Generative models are employed to augment training data for machine learning tasks. For instance, GANs can generate synthetic images or text samples to supplement the training dataset, improving the robustness and generalization of machine learning models.
  - Anomaly Detection: Generative models can be used to generate normal data samples for anomaly detection tasks. By learning the underlying distribution of normal data, these models can identify deviations or anomalies in new data samples.

5. Video Generation:

  - Animation and Visual Effects: Generative models are used to create animations and visual effects in movies, video games, and virtual reality experiences. GANs can generate realistic images and sequences, enhancing the visual quality of digital content.
  - Surveillance and Security: Generative models can generate synthetic video footage for training surveillance systems and security algorithms. By simulating various scenarios, these models help improve the accuracy and reliability of surveillance systems.

Deploying and integrating generative AI models into practical settings requires careful consideration of various factors, including infrastructure, scalability, performance, and compatibility with existing systems. Here are some strategies for deploying and integrating generative AI models effectively:

1. Infrastructure and Environment:

  - Set up a suitable infrastructure for deploying generative AI models, considering factors like computational resources, storage, and network bandwidth.
  - Choose an appropriate deployment environment, such as cloud-based platforms (e.g., AWS, Google Cloud Platform, Microsoft Azure) or on-premises servers, based on requirements like scalability, security, and cost.

2. Model Serving and Inference:

  - Implement a robust model serving architecture for handling inference requests efficiently. This may involve containerization using technologies like Docker or Kubernetes to encapsulate the model and its dependencies.

- Use frameworks like TensorFlow Serving, TensorFlow.js, or PyTorch Serve for serving and running inference on generative AI models.

3. Integration with Existing Systems:

   - Integrate generative AI models seamlessly into existing systems and workflows. This may involve developing APIs or SDKs for easy integration with other applications or services.
   - Ensure compatibility with existing data pipelines, databases, and software frameworks to facilitate data exchange and communication between different components.

4. Scalability and Performance:

   - Design generative AI models with scalability in mind to handle varying workloads and demand spikes. Consider distributed training techniques and model parallelism for training large-scale models efficiently.
   - Use optimization techniques like quantization, pruning, and model compression to reduce model size and inference latency without compromising performance.

5. Monitoring and Maintenance:

   - Implement robust monitoring and logging mechanisms to track model performance, resource utilization, and system health in real-time.
   - Set up alerting systems to detect anomalies, errors, or performance degradation and take timely actions to address them.
   - Establish a maintenance schedule for regularly updating models, addressing security vulnerabilities, and incorporating improvements based on feedback and new data.

6. Security and Privacy:

   - Implement security measures to protect sensitive data and prevent unauthorized access to generative AI models and their outputs.
   - Use encryption, access controls, and authentication mechanisms to secure communication channels and data storage.
   - Ensure compliance with privacy regulations (e.g., GDPR, HIPAA) and ethical guidelines when handling user data and generating content.

7. Versioning and Experimentation:

   - Implement version control and tracking for generative AI models to manage different model versions and experiments effectively.
   - Use techniques like A/B testing or multi-armed bandit algorithms to evaluate and compare the performance of different model variants in production.

Addressing ethical challenges and societal implications associated with generative AI is crucial to ensure responsible development and deployment of these technologies. Here are some key considerations:

1. Bias and Fairness:

    - Generative AI models can inherit biases present in the training data, leading to unfair or discriminatory outcomes.
    - Mitigate bias by carefully curating and diversifying training datasets, conducting bias audits, and using fairness-aware training techniques.
    - Implement fairness constraints and evaluation metrics to monitor and mitigate bias in generated content.

2. Privacy:

    - Generative AI models may inadvertently reveal sensitive information about individuals, especially when trained on personal data.
    - Protect privacy by anonymizing or de-identifying training data, implementing differential privacy techniques, and limiting access to sensitive model outputs.
    - Comply with privacy regulations (e.g., GDPR, CCPA) and obtain informed consent when collecting or using personal data for training generative models.

3. Security:

    - Generative AI models can be vulnerable to adversarial attacks, where malicious actors manipulate inputs to produce undesirable outputs.
    - Enhance security by robustly validating and sanitizing inputs, implementing model robustness techniques (e.g., adversarial training, input perturbation), and monitoring for suspicious activities.
    - Secure model deployment and communication channels to prevent unauthorized access, tampering, or data breaches.

4. Misuse and Malicious Applications:

    - Generative AI models can be misused for malicious purposes, such as creating deepfakes, spreading disinformation, or generating offensive content.
    - Implement safeguards and detection mechanisms to identify and mitigate misuse, including content moderation, authenticity verification, and traceability of generated content.
    - Foster awareness and education about the potential risks and ethical implications of generative AI among developers, users, and policymakers.

5. Transparency and Accountability:

    - Ensure transparency in the development and deployment of generative AI models, including documenting model architectures, training data, and decision-making processes.

- Establish mechanisms for accountability and responsible AI governance, including ethical guidelines, auditing processes, and mechanisms for redress in case of harm.

6. Social Impact and Human Well-being:

- Consider the broader societal impact of generative AI on jobs, economy, culture, and human well-being.
- Foster interdisciplinary collaboration and engage with diverse stakeholders to address societal concerns, promote inclusivity, and ensure that generative AI benefits society as a whole.

7. Continual Evaluation and Iteration:

- Regularly assess and evaluate the ethical implications of generative AI systems throughout their lifecycle.
- Iterate and adapt strategies based on evolving ethical norms, technological advancements, and feedback from stakeholders.

The field of generative AI is continuously evolving, presenting exciting opportunities and challenges. Here are some emerging trends, research directions, and unresolved challenges that shape the future of generative AI:

1. Continual Advancements in Model Architectures:

- Explore novel architectures and techniques for generative models, such as hierarchical models, attention mechanisms, and transformer-based architectures.
- Investigate ways to improve model efficiency, scalability, and interpretability while maintaining high-quality outputs.

2. Cross-Modal Generation:

- Research on generating content across multiple modalities, such as images, text, and audio, to enable richer and more immersive experiences.
- Explore techniques for cross-modal translation, style transfer, and multimodal fusion.

3. Unsupervised and Self-Supervised Learning:

- Advance unsupervised and self-supervised learning techniques for generative models to reduce reliance on labeled data and improve generalization.
- Investigate approaches for unsupervised domain adaptation, domain generalization, and zero-shot learning.

4. Ethical AI and Responsible Innovation:

- Address ethical challenges and societal implications of generative AI, including bias, privacy, security, and misuse.

- Foster interdisciplinary collaboration and develop frameworks for responsible AI governance, transparency, and accountability.

5. Interactive and Adaptive Generative Models:

   - Develop interactive generative models that can adapt to user preferences, feedback, and context in real-time.
   - Explore techniques for user-guided generation, co-creation with humans, and personalized content generation.

6. Robustness and Adversarial Defense:

   - Enhance the robustness of generative AI models against adversarial attacks and distributional shifts.
   - Investigate techniques for adversarial training, robust optimization, and model verification to improve resilience to attacks.

7. Generative AI for Scientific Discovery and Innovation:

   - Apply generative AI techniques to accelerate scientific discovery, drug design, material discovery, and other domains with complex data.
   - Collaborate with domain experts to develop domain-specific generative models and leverage AI for solving real-world challenges.

8. Interdisciplinary Collaboration and Diversity:

   - Foster interdisciplinary collaboration between researchers, practitioners, and stakeholders from diverse backgrounds to address complex challenges and unlock new opportunities.
   - Promote diversity and inclusivity in the development and deployment of generative AI technologies to ensure equitable access and representation.

Types of Generative AI Machine Learning Models

Generative AI encompasses a variety of machine learning models designed to generate new data samples that resemble the training data distribution (Goodfellow et al., 2014). Here are some types of generative AI machine learning models:

1. Generative Adversarial Networks (GANs):

   - GANs consist of two neural networks—the generator and the discriminator—trained simultaneously in a competitive setting.
   - The generator learns to produce realistic data samples (e.g., images, text) from random noise, while the discriminator learns to distinguish between real and fake samples.

       o   GANs have been widely used for image generation, video synthesis, style transfer, and data augmentation.

       o   The standard recurrent neural network language model (RNNLM) generates sentences one word at a time and does not work from an explicit global sentence representation (Bowman et al., 2016).

To implement Generative Adversarial Networks (GANs) using Python, you'll need to utilize deep learning frameworks such as TensorFlow or PyTorch (Aurelien, 2019). Here's a simple implementation using TensorFlow:

```python
import tensorflow as tf
from tensorflow.keras import layers, models, optimizers
import numpy as np
# Define the generator network
def build_generator(latent_dim):
model = models.Sequential([
layers.Dense(128, input_dim=latent_dim, activation='relu'),
layers.Dense(784, activation='sigmoid'), # Output layer for MNIST images
(28x28 = 784)
layers.Reshape((28, 28)) # Reshape to image dimensions
])
return model
# Define the discriminator network
def build_discriminator(input_shape):
model = models.Sequential([
layers.Flatten(input_shape=input_shape),
layers.Dense(128, activation='relu'),
layers.Dense(1, activation='sigmoid') # Output a single probability value
(real or fake)
])
return model
# Define the GAN model
def build_gan(generator, discriminator):
discriminator.trainable = False # Freeze discriminator weights during gener-
ator training
model = models.Sequential([
generator,
discriminator
])
return model
# Generate random noise samples for the generator
def generate_noise(batch_size, latent_dim):
return np.random.uniform(-1, 1, size=(batch_size, latent_dim))
# Load and preprocess the MNIST dataset
(x_train, _), (_, _) = tf.keras.datasets.mnist.load_data()
```

```python
x_train = x_train.astype('float32') / 255.0
x_train = np.expand_dims(x_train, axis=-1)
# Define model parameters
latent_dim = 100
input_shape = (28, 28, 1)
batch_size = 128
epochs = 10000
# Build and compile the generator and discriminator networks
generator = build_generator(latent_dim)
discriminator = build_discriminator(input_shape)
discriminator.compile(loss='binary_crossentropy', optimizer=optimizers.
Adam(), metrics=['accuracy'])
# Build and compile the GAN model
gan = build_gan(generator, discriminator)
gan.compile(loss='binary_crossentropy', optimizer=optimizers.Adam())
# Training loop
for epoch in range(epochs):
# Train discriminator
real_images = x_train[np.random.randint(0, x_train.shape[0], batch_size)]
fake_images = generator.predict(generate_noise(batch_size, latent_dim))
x = np.concatenate([real_images, fake_images])
y = np.concatenate([np.ones((batch_size, 1)), np.zeros((batch_size, 1))])
d_loss = discriminator.train_on_batch(x, y)
# Train generator
noise = generate_noise(batch_size, latent_dim)
y = np.ones((batch_size, 1))
g_loss = gan.train_on_batch(noise, y)
# Print training progress
if epoch % 100 == 0:
print(f"Epoch {epoch}, Discriminator Loss: {d_loss[0]}, Generator Loss: {g_
loss}")
# Generate and visualize synthetic images
import matplotlib.pyplot as plt
num_samples = 10
noise = generate_noise(num_samples, latent_dim)
generated_images = generator.predict(noise)
plt.figure(figsize=(num_samples, 1))
for i in range(num_samples):
plt.subplot(1, num_samples, i+1)
plt.imshow(generated_images[i], cmap='gray')
plt.axis('off')
plt.show()
```

This code sets up a simple GAN architecture using TensorFlow and trains it on the MNIST dataset for generating handwritten digit images. The generator and discriminator networks are defined, and the GAN model is compiled for training. The training loop alternates between training the discriminator and the generator. Finally, synthetic images are generated using the trained generator for visualization.

2. Variational Autoencoders (VAEs):

   o   VAEs are probabilistic generative models consisting of an encoder network and a decoder network.
   o   The encoder maps input data to a latent space, where the decoder reconstructs the input data from latent vectors sampled from a learned distribution.
   o   VAEs are used for tasks like image generation, anomaly detection, and unsupervised learning.

Implementing Variational Autoencoders (VAEs) using Python involves building and training a neural network architecture that consists of an encoder and a decoder. Here's a basic implementation using TensorFlow:

```python
import tensorflow as tf
from tensorflow.keras import layers, models, losses, optimizers
import numpy as np
# Define the VAE architecture
class VAE(models.Model):
def __init__(self, latent_dim):
super(VAE, self).__init__()
self.latent_dim = latent_dim
self.encoder = self.build_encoder()
self.decoder = self.build_decoder()
def build_encoder(self):
inputs = layers.Input(shape=(28, 28, 1))
x = layers.Flatten()(inputs)
x = layers.Dense(256, activation='relu')(x)
z_mean = layers.Dense(self.latent_dim)(x)
z_log_var = layers.Dense(self.latent_dim)(x)
return models.Model(inputs, [z_mean, z_log_var])
def build_decoder(self):
latent_inputs = layers.Input(shape=(self.latent_dim,))
x = layers.Dense(256, activation='relu')(latent_inputs)
x = layers.Dense(28 28, activation='sigmoid')(x)
outputs = layers.Reshape((28, 28, 1))(x)
return models.Model(latent_inputs, outputs)
def sample(self, z_mean, z_log_var):
batch = tf.shape(z_mean)[0]
dim = tf.shape(z_mean)[1]
epsilon = tf.keras.backend.random_normal(shape=(batch, dim))
return z_mean + tf.exp(0.5 z_log_var) epsilon
def call(self, inputs):
```

```
z_mean, z_log_var = self.encoder(inputs)
z = self.sample(z_mean, z_log_var)
reconstructed = self.decoder(z)
return reconstructed
# Define the VAE loss function
def vae_loss(inputs, reconstructed, z_mean, z_log_var):
reconstruction_loss = losses.binary_crossentropy(inputs, reconstructed)
reconstruction_loss = 28 28
kl_loss = 0.5 tf.reduce_sum(tf.exp(z_log_var) + tf.square(z_mean) - 1 - z_
log_var, axis=1)
  return tf.reduce_mean(reconstruction_loss + kl_loss)
  # Load and preprocess the MNIST dataset
  (x_train, _), (_, _) = tf.keras.datasets.mnist.load_data()
x_train = x_train.astype('float32') / 255.0
x_train = np.expand_dims(x_train, axis=-1)
  # Define model parameters
latent_dim = 10
batch_size = 128
epochs = 30
  # Instantiate the VAE model
vae = VAE(latent_dim)
  # Compile the VAE model
vae.compile(optimizer=optimizers.Adam(), loss=vae_loss)
  # Train the VAE model
vae.fit(x_train, x_train, batch_size=batch_size, epochs=epochs)
  # Generate and visualize reconstructed images
num_samples = 10
indices = np.random.randint(0, len(x_train), num_samples)
sample_images = x_train[indices]
reconstructed_images = vae.predict(sample_images)
import matplotlib.pyplot as plt
plt.figure(figsize=(num_samples, 2))
for i in range(num_samples):
plt.subplot(2, num_samples, i + 1)
plt.imshow(sample_images[i].squeeze(), cmap='gray')
plt.axis('off')
plt.subplot(2, num_samples, num_samples + i + 1)
plt.imshow(reconstructed_images[i].squeeze(), cmap='gray')
plt.axis('off')
plt.show()
```

In this implementation:

1. The `VAE` class defines the encoder and decoder networks as separate models. The encoder takes input images and outputs the mean and log variance of the latent space distribution. The decoder takes latent space samples as input and reconstructs the input images.

2. The `sample` method generates latent space samples using the reparameterization trick.
3. The VAE loss function consists of two components: the reconstruction loss and the KL divergence loss.
4. The VAE model is compiled with the custom VAE loss function and trained on the MNIST dataset.
5. Reconstructed images are generated using the trained VAE model and visualized alongside the original images for comparison.

This implementation demonstrates how to build and train a Variational Autoencoder using TensorFlow for reconstructing MNIST images.

3. Autoregressive Models:

- Autoregressive models generate data sequentially, with each step conditioned on previous observations.
- Examples include autoregressive neural networks, autoregressive moving average (ARMA) models, and autoregressive integrated moving average (ARIMA) models.
- Autoregressive models are commonly used for time series prediction, language modeling, and text generation.

4. Flow-Based Models:

- Flow-based models learn a invertible mapping between input data and latent space.
- They are trained to transform a simple distribution (e.g., Gaussian) into the data distribution, allowing for efficient sampling and density estimation.
- Flow-based models are used for tasks like image generation, density estimation, and data compression.

5. PixelCNN:

- PixelCNN is a type of autoregressive model specifically designed for generating images pixel by pixel.
- It predicts the conditional distribution of each pixel given the previous pixels in the image.
- PixelCNN is commonly used for image generation tasks where spatial coherence is important, such as generating high-resolution images.

6. Normalizing Flows:

- Normalizing flow models learn invertible transformations between data distributions.
- They are trained to transform a simple distribution (e.g., Gaussian) into the target data distribution using a sequence of invertible transformations.
- Normalizing flows are used for tasks like density estimation, variational inference, and image generation.

These are just a few examples of generative AI machine learning models, each with its own strengths, weaknesses, and applications. Depending on the specific task and data characteristics, different models may be more suitable for generating high-quality, diverse, and realistic content.

CONCLUSION

In conclusion, understanding and applying machine learning models involve a combination of theoretical knowledge, practical skills, and a thorough understanding of the specific problem domain. As technology continues to advance, machine learning will play an increasingly integral role in solving complex problems and driving innovation across various industries.

Machine learning models are not only shaping current research landscapes but are expected to be transformative in the future. Their ability to extract meaningful patterns from data, automate complex tasks, and contribute to a wide array of domains positions them as indispensable tools for advancing knowledge and driving innovation. Researchers across disciplines will increasingly leverage machine learning to unlock new insights, address complex challenges, and push the boundaries of what is possible in the realms of science, technology, and societal progress.

REFERENCES

Aurélien, G. (2019). *Hands-On Machine Learning with Scikit-Learn*. Keras, and TensorFlow.

Bowman, S. R., Vilnis, L., Vinyals, O., Dai, A. M., Jozefowicz, R., & Bengio, S. (2016). *Generating Sentences from a Continuous Space*. arXiv preprint arXiv:1511.06349. 10.18653/v1/K16-1002

Foster, D. (2019). *Generative Deep Learning: Teaching Machines to Paint, Write, Compose, and Play*. O'Reilly Media.

Goodfellow, I., Bengio, Y., & Courville, A. (2016). *Deep Learning*. MIT Press.

Goodfellow, I. J., Pouget-Abadie, J., Mirza, M., Xu, B., Warde-Farley, D., Ozair, S., & Bengio, Y. (2014). Generative adversarial nets. *Advances in Neural Information Processing Systems*, 27, 2672–2680.

Kingma, D. P., & Welling, M. (2013). *Auto-Encoding Variational Bayes*. arXiv preprint arXiv:1312.6114.

LeCun, Y., Léon, B., Yoshua, B., & Patrick, H. (1998). Gradient-Based Learning Applied to Document Recognition. *Proceedings of the IEEE*, 86(11), 2278–2324. 10.1109/5.726791

Müller Andreas, C. (2016). *Introduction to Machine Learning with Python: A Guide for Data Scientists*. Research Gate.

Pedro, D. (2012). A Few Useful Things to Know About Machine Learning. *Communications of the ACM*, 55(10), 78–87. 10.1145/2347736.2347755

Radford, A., Metz, L., & Chintala, S. (2015). *Unsupervised representation learning with deep convolutional generative adversarial networks*. arXiv preprint arXiv:1511.06434

Compilation of References

Abiodun, O., Jantan, A., Omolara, A., Dada, K., Mohamed, N., & Arshad, H. (2018). State-of-the-art in artificial neural network applications: A survey. *Heliyon*, 4(11), e00938. 10.1016/j.heliyon.2018.e0093830519653

Adams, R. (2019). Python and AI: A match made in heaven. *Journal of Computer Science and Technology*, 34(2), 215–230.

Aggarwal, C. C. (2018). *Neural Networks and Deep Learning: A Textbook*. Springer. 10.1007/978-3-319-94463-0

Aggarwal, D., Mittal, S., & Bali, V. (2021). Significance of non-academic parameters for predicting student performance using ensemble learning techniques. [IJSDA]. *International Journal of System Dynamics Applications*, 10(3), 38–49. 10.4018/IJSDA.2021070103

Aguinis, H., Beltran, J. R., & Cope, A. (2024). How to use generative AI as a human resource management assistant. *Organizational Dynamics*, 53(1), 101029. 10.1016/j.orgdyn.2024.101029

Ahmad, N., Hassan, N., Jaafar, H., & Enzai, N. I. M. (2021). Students' Performance Prediction using Artificial Neural Network. *IOP Conference Series. Materials Science and Engineering*, 1176(1), 12020. 10.1088/1757-899X/1176/1/012020

Ahmad, S., El-Affendi, M. A., Anwar, M. S., & Iqbal, R. (2022). Potential future directions in optimization of students' performance prediction system. *Computational Intelligence and Neuroscience*, 2022, 2022. 10.1155/2022/686495535619762

Ahmad, T., Zhang, D., Huang, C., Zhang, H., Dai, N., Song, Y., & Chen, H. (2021). Artificial intelligence in sustainable energy industry: Status Quo, challenges and opportunities. *Journal of Cleaner Production*, 289, 125834. 10.1016/j.jclepro.2021.125834

Ahn, J., Shin, H., & Guo, M. (2021). *Building a Deep Learning Model to Predict Academic Achievement*.

Ai, W. (2016, July 26). *Circle of animals / zodiac heads*. Carnegie Museum of Art. https://carnegieart.org/exhibition/ai-weiwei-circle-of-animals-zodiac/

AiArt. (2020). *Towards artificial intelligence art*. Research Gate. https://www.researchgate.net/publication/342642793_AiArt_Towards_Artificial_Intelligence_Art

Akhtar, Z. (2023). *Unsupervised learning: Types, applications & advantages*. Database Town. https://databasetown.com/unsupervised-learning-types-applications/ [Accessed: 26-03-2024].

Al Shuaeb, S. M. A., Alam, S., Rahman, M. M., & Matin, M. A. (n.d.). *Polytechnic Students' Academic Performance Prediction Based on Deep Neural Network*.

Albaghajati, Z. M., Bettaieb, D. M., & Malek, R. B. (2023). Exploring text-to-image application in architectural design: Insights and implications. Architecture. *Structures and Construction*, 3(4), 475–497. 10.1007/s44150-023-00103-x

Ali, H., & Aysan, A. F. (2023). What will ChatGPT revolutionize in financial industry? *Available atSSRN* 4403372.

Alpaydin, E. (2016). *Machine Learning: The New AI (The MIT Press Essential Knowledge series)*. The MIT Press.

Alqahtani, H., Kavakli-Thorne, M., & Kumar, G. (2021). Applications of generative adversarial networks (gans): An updated review. *Archives of Computational Methods in Engineering*, 28(2), 525–552. 10.1007/s11831-019-09388-y

Alzubi, J., Nayyar, A., & Kumar, A. (2018). Machine learning from theory to algorithms: An overview. *Journal of Physics: Conference Series*, 1142(1), 012012. 10.1088/1742-6596/1142/1/012012

Amrieh, E. A., Hamtini, T., & Aljarah, I. (2016). Mining educational data to predict student's academic performance using ensemble methods. *International Journal of Database Theory and Application*, 9(8), 119–136. 10.14257/ijdta.2016.9.8.13

Anantrasirichai, N., & Bull, D. (2022). Artificial intelligence in the creative industries: A review. *Artificial Intelligence Review*, 55(1), 589–656. 10.1007/s10462-021-10039-7

Arashpour, M., Golafshani, E. M., Parthiban, R., Lamborn, J., Kashani, A., Li, H., & Farzanehfar, P. (2023). Predicting individual learning performance using machine-learning hybridized with the teaching-learning-based optimization. *Computer Applications in Engineering Education*, 31(1), 83–99. 10.1002/cae.22572

Armstrong, E. G. (2013). A hybrid model of problem-based learning. In *The challenge of problem-based learning* (pp. 145–158). Routledge.

Arora, R., & Suman, S. (2012). Comparative analysis of classification algorithms on different datasets using WEKA. *International Journal of Computer Applications*, 54(13), 21–25. 10.5120/8626-2492

Arslan, Y., Allix, K., Veiber, L., Lothritz, C., Bissyandé, T. F., Klein, J., & Goujon, A. (2021, April). A comparison of pre-trained language models for multi-class text classification in the financial domain. In *Companion Proceedings of the Web Conference 2021* (pp. 260-268). ACM. 10.1145/3442442.3451375

Art's next medium. (2020). Christie's. https://www.christies.com/en/stories/a-collaboration-between-two-artists-one-human-one-a-machine-0cd01f4e232f4279a525a446d60d4cd1

Artrendex. (2021). Artrendex. https://www.artrendex.com/

Augenstein, I., Baldwin, T., Cha, M., Chakraborty, T., Ciampaglia, G. L., Corney, D., DiResta, R., Ferrara, E., Hale, S., Halevy, A., & Hovy, E. (2023). Factuality challenges in the era of large language models. arXiv:2310.05189.

Aurélien, G. (2019). *Hands-On Machine Learning with Scikit-Learn*. Keras, and TensorFlow.

Ayoola, O. O., Alenoghena, R., & Adeniji, S. (2023). ChatGPT impacts on access-efficiency, employment, education and ethics: The socio-economics of an AI language model. *BizEcons Quarterly*, 16, 1–17.

Azamfirei, R., Kudchadkar, S. R., & Fackler, J. (2023). Large language models and the perils of their hallucinations. *Critical Care (London, England)*, 27(1), 120. 10.1186/s13054-023-04393-x36945051

Azimi, S., Popa, C.-G., & Cucić, T. (2020). Improving Students Performance in Small-Scale Online Courses—A Machine Learning-Based Intervention. *ArXiv Preprint ArXiv:2012.01187*.

Babu, T., Gupta, D., Singh, T., Hameed, S., Zakariah, M., & Alotaibi, Y. A. (2021a). Robust magnification independent colon biopsy grading system over multiple data sources. *Computers, Materials & Continua*, 69(1), 99–128. 10.32604/cmc.2021.016341

Babu, T., & Nair, R. R. (2023). Colon cancer prediction with transfer learning and k-means clustering. In Frontiers of ICT in Healthcare [Springer.]. *Proceedings of EAIT*, 2022, 191–200.

Babu, T., Singh, T., & Gupta, D. (2020). Colon cancer prediction using 2dreca segmentation and hybrid features on histopathology images. *IET Image Processing*, 14(16), 4144–4157. 10.1049/iet-ipr.2019.1717

Babu, T., Singh, T., Gupta, D., & Hameed, S. (2021b). Colon cancer prediction on histological images using deep learning features and bayesian optimized svm. *Journal of Intelligent & Fuzzy Systems*, 41(5), 5275–5286. 10.3233/JIFS-189850

Badal, Y. T., & Sungkur, R. K. (2023). Predictive modelling and analytics of students' grades using machine learning algorithms. *Education and Information Technologies*, 28(3), 3027–3057. 10.1007/s10639-022-11299-836097545

Bahroun, Z., Anane, C., Ahmed, V., & Zacca, A. (2023). Transforming education: A comprehensive review of generative artificial intelligence in educational settings through bibliometric and content analysis. *Sustainability (Basel)*, 15(17), 12983. 10.3390/su151712983

Baidoo-Anu, D., & Ansah, L. O. (2023). Education in the era of generative artificial intelligence (AI): Understanding the potential benefits of ChatGPT in promoting teaching and learning. *Journal of AI*, 7(1), 52–62. 10.61969/jai.1337500

Bandi, A., Adapa, P. V. S. R., & Kuchi, Y. E. V. P. K. (2023). The Power of Generative AI: A Review of Requirements, Models, Input–Output Formats, Evaluation Metrics, and Challenges. *Future Internet*, 15(8), 260. 10.3390/fi15080260

Banh, L., & Strobel, G. (2023). Generative artificial intelligence. *Electronic Markets*, 33(1), 63. 10.1007/s12525-023-00680-1

Bannet Tumuhimbise, D. A. P., & Chidananda, K. (2021). Advanced Prediction of a student in a university using Machine Learning techniques. [TURCOMAT]. *Turkish Journal of Computer and Mathematics Education*, 12(14), 5913–5919.

Barletta, V. S., Caivano, D., Gigante, D., & Ragone, A. (2023). *A rapid review of responsible AI frameworks: How to guide the development of Ethical AI.* arXiv:2306.05003. 10.1145/3593434.3593478

Batool, S., Rashid, J., Nisar, M. W., Kim, J., Kwon, H.-Y., & Hussain, A. (2023). Educational data mining to predict students' academic performance: A survey study. *Education and Information Technologies*, 28(1), 905–971. 10.1007/s10639-022-11152-y

Bauer, A., Trapp, S., Stenger, M., Leppich, R., Kounev, S., Leznik, M., Chard, K., & Foster, I. (2024). Comprehensive exploration of synthetic data generation: A survey. arXiv preprint arXiv:2401.02524.

Bavaresco, R., Silveira, D., Reis, E., Barbosa, J., Righi, R., Costa, C., Antunes, R., Gomes, M., Gatti, C., Vanzin, M., Junior, S. C., Silva, E., & Moreira, C. (2020). Conversational agents in business: A systematic literature review and future research directions. *Computer Science Review*, 36, 100239. 10.1016/j.cosrev.2020.100239

Bendel, O. (2023). Image synthesis from an ethical perspective. *AI & Society*, 1–10.

Berabi, B., He, J., Raychev, V., & Vechev, M. (2021, July). Tfix: Learning to fix coding errors with a text-to-text transformer. In *International Conference on Machine Learning* (pp. 780-791). PMLR.

Bewersdorff, A., Hartmann, C., Hornberger, M., Seßler, K., Bannert, M., Kasneci, E., Kasneci, G., Zhai, X., & Nerdel, C. (2024). Taking the Next Step with Generative Artificial Intelligence: The Transformative Role of Multimodal Large Language Models in Science Education. arXiv:2401.00832.

Bhatt, U., Antorán, J., Zhang, Y., Liao, Q. V., Sattigeri, P., Fogliato, R., Melançon, G. G., Krishnan, R., Stanley, J., Tickoo, O., Nachman, L., Chunara, R., Srikumar, M., Weller, A., & Xiang, A. (2020). Uncertainty as a form of transparency: Measuring, communicating, and using uncertainty. In *arXiv[cs.CY]*. http://arxiv.org/abs/2011.07586

Bhutto, E. S., Siddiqui, I. F., Arain, Q. A., & Anwar, M. (2020). Predicting students' academic performance through supervised machine learning. *2020 International Conference on Information Science and Communication Technology (ICISCT)*, (pp. 1–6). IEEE. 10.1109/ICISCT49550.2020.9080033

Biswas, S. S. (2023). Role of chat gpt in public health. *Annals of Biomedical Engineering*, 51(5), 868–869. 10.1007/s10439-023-03172-736920578

Bloomberg. (n.d.). 50 billion parameter. *Bloomberg*. https://www.bloomberg.com/company/press/bloomberggpt-50-billion-parameter-llm-tuned-finance/

Bohr, A., & Memarzadeh, K. (2020). The rise of artificial intelligence in healthcare applications. In *Artificial Intelligence in Healthcare* (pp. 25–60). Elsevier. 10.1016/B978-0-12-818438-7.00002-2

Bommasani, R. (2021). On the Opportunities and Risks of Foundation Models (Report). arXiv:2108.07258.

Borden, B. (2023, May 4). *Driving transformation in banking with generative AI*. Microsoft Industry Blogs. https://www.microsoft.com/en-us/industry/blog/financial-services/2023/05/04/the-era-of-generative-ai-driving-transformation-in-banking/

Borji, A. (2019). Pros and cons of gan evaluation measures. *Computer Vision and Image Understanding*, 179, 41–65. 10.1016/j.cviu.2018.10.009

Boussioux, L. N., Lane, J., Zhang, M., Jacimovic, V., & Lakhani, K. R. (2023). *The Crowdless Future?* How Generative AI Is Shaping the Future of Human Crowdsourcing. The Crowdless Future.

Bowman, S. R., Vilnis, L., Vinyals, O., Dai, A. M., Jozefowicz, R., & Bengio, S. (2016). *Generating Sentences from a Continuous Space*. arXiv preprint arXiv:1511.06349. 10.18653/v1/K16-1002

Bozkurt, A., & Sharma, R. C. (2023). Challenging the status quo and exploring the new boundaries in the age of algorithms: Reimagining the role of generative AI in distance education and online learning. *Asian Journal of Distance Education*, 18(1).

Bozkurt, A., & Sharma, R. C. (2023). *Challenging the status quo and exploring the new boundaries in the age of algorithms: Reimagining the role of generative AI in distance education and online learning. Zenodo.* 10.5281/ZENODO.7755273

Brings together new 2024 papers. (2020). Ebin.Pub. http://ebin.pub

Brock, A., Donahue, J., & Simonyan, K. (2018). Large scale GAN training for high fidelity natural image synthesis. arXiv preprint arXiv:1809.11096.

Brown, A., & Green, T. (2021). Ethical considerations in AI-generated content: Navigating the new media landscape. *Ethics and Information Technology*, 23(4), 567–576.

Brown, T., Mann, B., Ryder, N., Subbiah, M., Kaplan, J. D., Dhariwal, P., & Amodei, D. (2020). Language models are few-shot learners. *Advances in Neural Information Processing Systems*, 33, 1877–1901.

Brundage, M., Avin, S., Wang, J., Belfield, H., Krueger, G., Hadfield, G., & Anderljung, M. (2020). Toward trustworthy AI development: mechanisms for supporting verifiable claims. *arXiv preprint arXiv:2004.07213*.

Bryan-Kinns, N., Zhang, B., Zhao, S., & Banar, B. (2024). Exploring variational auto-encoder architectures, configurations, and datasets for generative music explainable ai. *Machine Intelligence Research*, 21(1), 29–45. 10.1007/s11633-023-1457-1

Budhwar, P., Chowdhury, S., Wood, G., Aguinis, H., Bamber, G. J., Beltran, J. R., Boselie, P., Lee Cooke, F., Decker, S., DeNisi, A., Dey, P. K., Guest, D., Knoblich, A. J., Malik, A., Paauwe, J., Papagiannidis, S., Patel, C., Pereira, V., Ren, S., & Varma, A. (2023). Human resource management in the age of generative artificial intelligence: Perspectives and research directions on chatgpt. *Human Resource Management Journal*, 33(3), 606–659. 10.1111/1748-8583.12524

Bussell, C., Ehab, A., Hartle-Ryan, D., & Kapsalis, T. (2023). Generative ai for immersive experiences: Integrating text-to-image models in vr-mediated co-design workflows. In *International Conference on Human-Computer Interaction*, (pp. 380–388). Springer. 10.1007/978-3-031-36004-6_52

Bütüner, R., & Calp, M. H.BÜTÜNER. (2022). Estimation of the Academic Performance of Students in Distance Education Using Data Mining Methods. *International Journal of Assessment Tools in Education*, 9(2), 410–429. 10.21449/ijate.904456

Campus, W. (n.d.). *A Random Forest Students' Performance Prediction (RFSPP) Model Based on Students' Demographic.*

Cao, H., Tan, C., Gao, Z., Xu, Y., Chen, G., Heng, P. A., & Li, S. Z. (2024). A survey on generative diffusion models. *IEEE Transactions on Knowledge and Data Engineering*, 1–20. 10.1109/TKDE.2024.3361474

Caroline Clabaugh, D. M., & Pang, J. (2022). *Neural networks – architecture - feed-forward networks.* Stanford. https://cs.stanford.edu/people/eroberts/courses/soco/projects/neural-networks/Architecture/feedforward. html

Celard, P., Iglesias, E. L., Sorribes-Fdez, J. M., Romero, R., Vieira, A. S., & Borrajo, L. (2023). A survey on deep learning applied to medical images: From simple artificial neural networks to generative models. *Neural Computing & Applications*, 35(3), 2291–2323. 10.1007/s00521-022-07953-436373133

Chahal, A., & Gulia, P. (2019). Machine Learning and Deep Learning. *International Journal of Innovative Technology and Exploring Engineering*, 8(12), 4910–4914. 10.35940/ijitee.L3550.1081219

Chan, E. R., Lin, C. Z., Chan, M. A., Nagano, K., Pan, B., De Mello, S., & Wetzstein, G. (2022). Efficient geometry-aware 3d generative adversarial networks. In *Proceedings of the IEEE/CVF conference on computer vision and pattern recognition* (pp. 16123-16133). IEEE.

Chandra, V., & Hareendran, A. (2014). *Artificial Intelligence and Machine Learning.* PHI Learning.

Chang, C.-H., & Kidman, G. (2023). The rise of generative artificial intelligence (ai) language models-challenges and opportunities for geographical and environmental education. *International Research in Geographical and Environmental Education*, 32(2), 85–89. 10.1080/10382046.2023.2194036

Chawla, Y., Shimpo, F., & Sokołowski, M. M. (2022). Artificial intelligence and information management in the energy transition of India: Lessons from the global IT heart. *Digital Policy Regulation and Governance*, 24(1), 17–29. 10.1108/DPRG-05-2021-0062

Chen, W. (2020). *AiArt: Towards artificial intelligence art.* Research Gate. https://www.researchgate.net/publication/342642793_AiArt_Towards_Artificial_Intelligence_Art

Cheng, L., & Liu, X. (2023). From principles to practices: The intertextual interaction between AI ethical and legal discourses. *International Journal of Legal Discourse*, 8(1), 31–52. 10.1515/ijld-2023-2001

Cheng, Y., & Duan, M. (2020, December). Chinese grammatical error detection based on BERT model. In *Proceedings of the 6th Workshop on Natural Language Processing Techniques for Educational Applications* (pp. 108-113). ACM.

Chen, X., Ding, M., Wang, X., Xin, Y., Mo, S., Wang, Y., Han, S., Luo, P., Zeng, G., & Wang, J. (2024). Context autoencoder for self-supervised representation learning. *International Journal of Computer Vision*, 132(1), 208–223. 10.1007/s11263-023-01852-4

Chen, X., Xie, H., Zou, D., & Hwang, G.-J. (2020). Application and theory gaps during the rise of artificial intelligence in education. *Computers and Education: Artificial Intelligence*, 1, 100002. 10.1016/j.caeai.2020.100002

Chen, Y., Koch, T., Lim, K. G., Xu, X., & Zakiyeva, N. (2021). A review study of functional autoregressive models with application to energy forecasting. *Wiley Interdisciplinary Reviews: Computational Statistics*, 13(3), e1525. 10.1002/wics.1525

Chiu, T. K. (2023). The impact of Generative AI (GenAI) on practices, policies and research direction in education: A case of ChatGPT and Midjourney. *Interactive Learning Environments*, 1–17. 10.1080/10494820.2023.2253861

Chowdhery, A., Narang, S., Devlin, J., Bosma, M., Mishra, G., Roberts, A., & Fiedel, N. (2023). Palm: Scaling language modeling with pathways. *Journal of Machine Learning Research*, 24(240), 1–113.

Chui, M., Roberts, R., & Yee, L. (n.d.). *Generative AI is here: How tools like ChatGPT could change your business*. Mckinsey.com. https://www.mckinsey.com/capabilities/quantumblack/our-insights/generative-ai-is-here-how-tools-like-chatgpt-could-change-your-business

Condon, D. M. and M ottus, R. (2021). A role for information theory in personality modeling, assessment, and judgment. In *Measuring and modeling persons and situations*. Elsevier.

Cook, J., & Sasse, G. (2020). The challenge of deepfakes and the threat to democracy. *Media Culture & Society*, 42(7-8), 1152–1171.

Correlation Coefficient Formula. (n.d.). GeeksforGeeks. https://www.geeksforgeeks.org/correlation-coefficient-formula/

Creating the impossible statue. (2023, April). Sandvik. https://www.home.sandvik/en/stories/articles/2023/04/creating-the-impossible-statue/

Creswell, A., White, T., Dumoulin, V., Arulkumaran, K., Sengupta, B., & Bharath, A. A. (2018). Generative adversarial networks: An overview. *IEEE Signal Processing Magazine*, 35(1), 53–65. 10.1109/MSP.2017.2765202

Creswell, J. W., & Creswell, J. D. (2018). *Research design: Qualitative, quantitative, and mixed methods approaches* (5th ed.). Sage Publications.

Croitoru, F. A., Hondru, V., Ionescu, R. T., & Shah, M. (2023). Diffusion models in vision: A survey. *IEEE Transactions on Pattern Analysis and Machine Intelligence*, 45(9), 10850–10869. 10.1109/TPAMI.2023.326198837030794

Dasborough, M. T. (2023). Awe-inspiring advancements in AI: The impact of ChatGPT on the field of Organizational Behavior. *Journal of Organizational Behavior*, 44(2), 177–179. 10.1002/job.2695

De Angelis, L., Baglivo, F., Arzilli, G., Privitera, G. P., Ferragina, P., Tozzi, A. E., & Rizzo, C. (2023). ChatGPT and the rise of large language models: The new AI-driven infodemic threat in public health. *Frontiers in Public Health*, 11, 1166120. 10.3389/fpubh.2023.116612037181697

Decelle, A., & Furtlehner, C. (2021). Restricted boltzmann machine: Recent advances and mean-field theory. *Chinese Physics B*, 30(4), 040202. 10.1088/1674-1056/abd160

Deepart Io. (n.d.). (2023). *Creativity with AI*. https://creativitywith.ai/deepartio/

DeepDream. (2015, July). *A code example for visualizing neural networks*. Google AI Blog. https://ai.googleblog.com/2015/07/deepdream-code-example-for-visualizing.html

Deiana, G., Dettori, M., Arghittu, A., Azara, A., Gabutti, G., & Castiglia, P. (2023). Artificial intelligence and public health: Evaluating ChatGPT responses to vaccination myths and misconceptions. *Vaccines*, 11(7), 1217. 10.3390/vaccines1107121737515033

Deisenroth, M. P., Faisal, A. A., & Ong, C. S. (2024). *Mathematics for Machine Learning*. Cambridge University Press.

Della Sciucca, L., Balloni, E., Mameli, M., Frontoni, E., Zingaretti, P., & Paolanti, M. (2022, May). StyleTrendGAN: A Deep Learning Generative Framework for Fashion Bag Generation. In *International Conference on Image Analysis and Processing* (pp. 191-202). Cham: Springer International Publishing. 10.1007/978-3-031-13324-4_17

Dengov, V. V., Zvarikova, K., & Balica, R. S. (2023). Generative Artificial Intelligence and Movement and Behavior Tracking Tools, Remote Sensing and Cognitive Computing Systems, and Immersive Audiovisual Content in Virtually Simulated Workspace Environments. *Analysis and Metaphysics*, 22(0), 274–293. 10.22381/am22202315/

Deng, Z., Zhang, H., Liang, X., Yang, L., Xu, S., Zhu, J., & Xing, E. P. (2017). Structured generative adversarial networks. *Advances in Neural Information Processing Systems*, 30.

Dessalgn, A. W., Sharma, R., Chung, Y. K., & Sungheetha, A. (2022). Generative Adversarial Network-Based Visual-Aware Interactive Fashion Design Framework. *Implementing and Leveraging Blockchain Programming*, 63-78.

Devlin, J., Chang, M. W., Lee, K., & Toutanova, K. (2018). Bert: Pre-training of deep bidirectional transformers for language understanding. arXiv preprint arXiv:1810.04805.

DeYoung, J., Jain, S., Rajani, N. F., Lehman, E., Xiong, C., Socher, R., & Wallace, B. C. (2019). ERASER: A benchmark to evaluate rationalized NLP models. arXiv preprint arXiv:1911.03429.

Dhariwal, P., & Nichol, A. (2021). Diffusion models beat gans on image synthesis. *Advances in Neural Information Processing Systems*, 34, 8780–8794.

Di Chio, C. (Ed.). (2011). *Generative art is the ceding of control by the artist to an autonomous system.*

DigitalCommons@UNO. (2021). *The institutional repository of the University of Nebraska Omaha.* Unomaha.edu. http://digitalcommons.unomaha.edu

Ding, Z. (2024, March). Advancing GUI for Generative AI: Charting the Design Space of Human-AI Interactions through Task Creativity and Complexity. In *Companion Proceedings of the 29th International Conference on Intelligent User Interfaces* (pp. 140-143).

Ding, M., Yang, Z., Hong, W., Zheng, W., Zhou, C., Yin, D., & Tang, J. (2021). Cogview: Mastering text-to-image generation via transformers. *Advances in Neural Information Processing Systems*, 34, 19822–19835.

DIO - Artist. Ben Snell. (2018). This AI-generated sculpture is made from the shredded remains of the computer that designed it. The Verge. https://www.theverge.com/tldr/2019/4/12/18306090/ai-generated-sculpture-shredded-remains-ben-snell-dio

Doe, J. (2020). Generative AI in media production: Opportunities and challenges. *Media Innovations Journal*, 17(3), 89–104.

Doersch, C. (2016). Tutorial on variational autoencoders. arXiv preprint arXiv:1606.05908.

Duan, Y., Zhou, J., Wang, Z., Chang, Y. C., Wang, Y. K., & Lin, C. T. (2023). *Domain-specific denoising diffusion probabilistic models for brain dynamics.* arXiv preprint arXiv:2305.04200.

Dubey, A., Bhardwaj, N., Abhinav, K., Kuriakose, S. M., Jain, S., & Arora, V. (2020). *AI Assisted Apparel Design.* arXiv preprint arXiv:2007.04950.

Du, N., Huang, Y., Dai, A. M., Tong, S., Lepikhin, D., Xu, Y., & Cui, C. (2022, June). Glam: Efficient scaling of language models with mixture-of-experts. In *International Conference on Machine Learning* (pp. 5547-5569). PMLR.

Dwivedi, Y. K., Kshetri, N., Hughes, L., Slade, E. L., Jeyaraj, A., Kar, A. K., Baabdullah, A. M., Koohang, A., Raghavan, V., Ahuja, M., Albanna, H., Albashrawi, M. A., Al-Busaidi, A. S., Balakrishnan, J., Barlette, Y., Basu, S., Bose, I., Brooks, L., Buhalis, D., & Wright, R. (2023). Opinion Paper: "So what if ChatGPT wrote it?" Multidisciplinary perspectives on opportunities, challenges and implications of generative conversational AI for research, practice and policy. *International Journal of Information Management*, 71(102642), 102642. 10.1016/j.ijinfomgt.2023.102642

Edwards, C., Zhai, C., & Ji, H. (2021, November). Text2mol: Cross-modal molecule retrieval with natural language queries. In *Proceedings of the 2021 Conference on Empirical Methods in Natural Language Processing* (pp. 595-607). ACL. 10.18653/v1/2021.emnlp-main.47

Elarabawy, A., Kamath, H., & Denton, S. (2022). *Direct inversion: Optimization-free text-driven real image editing with diffusion models.* arXiv preprint arXiv:2211.07825.

Eloundou, T., Manning, S., Mishkin, P., & Rock, D. (2023). Gpts are gpts: An early look at the labor market impact potential of large language models. *arXiv preprint arXiv:2303.10130.*

Ernst, D., & Louette, A. (2024). Introduction to reinforcement learning. Feuerriegel, S., Hartmann, J., Janiesch, C., and Zschech, P. (2024). Generative ai. *Business & Information Systems Engineering*, 66(1), 111–126.

Esser, P., Rombach, R., & Ommer, B. (2021). Taming transformers for high-resolution image synthesis. In *Proceedings of the IEEE/CVF conference on computer vision and pattern recognition* (pp. 12873-12883). IEEE.

Evtikhiev, M., Bogomolov, E., Sokolov, Y., & Bryksin, T. (2023). Out of the bleu: How should we assess quality of the code generation models? *Journal of Systems and Software*, 203, 111741. 10.1016/j.jss.2023.111741

Fang, J., Gu, X., & Tan, M. (2020). Fashion-sketcher: A model for producing fashion sketches of multiple categories. In *Pattern Recognition and Computer Vision: Third Chinese Conference*. Springer International Publishing.

Fang, W., Ding, Y., Zhang, F., & Sheng, J. (2019). Gesture recognition based on CNN and DCGAN for calculation and text output. *IEEE Access : Practical Innovations, Open Solutions*, 7, 28230–28237. 10.1109/ACCESS.2019.2901930

Fang, W., Wen, X. Z., Zheng, Y., & Zhou, M. (2017). A survey of big data security and privacy preserving. *IETE Technical Review*, 34(5), 544–560. 10.1080/02564602.2016.1215269

Farrokhnia, M., Banihashem, S. K., Noroozi, O., & Wals, A. (2023). A SWOT analysis of ChatGPT: Implications for educational practice and research. *Innovations in Education and Teaching International*, 1–15. 10.1080/14703297.2023.2195846

Fast, E., & Horvitz, E. (2017). Long-term trends in the public perception of artificial intelligence. *Proceedings of the ... AAAI Conference on Artificial Intelligence.AAAI Conference on Artificial Intelligence, 31*(1). 10.1609/aaai.v31i1.10635

Fei, Z., Fan, M., Zhu, L., & Huang, J. (2022). *Progressive Text-to-Image Generation.* arXiv preprint arXiv:2210.02291.

Ferrara, E. (2023). *GenAI Against Humanity: Nefarious Applications of Generative Artificial Intelligence and Large Language Models.* arXiv:2310.00737.

Floridi, L., & Chiriatti, M. (2020). GPT-3: Its nature, scope, limits, and consequences. *Minds and Machines*, 30(4), 681–694. 10.1007/s11023-020-09548-1

Foster, D. (2019). *Generative Deep Learning: Teaching Machines to Paint, Write, Compose, and Play.* O'Reilly Media.

Fox, A. (2020, May 5). Bronze Age chieftain's remains found beneath U.K. skate park. *Smithsonian Magazine.* https://www.smithsonianmag.com/arts-culture/daniel-rozin-interactive-art-180974810/

Framework, C. S. I. (2019). Ganpaint.Io. https://ganpaint.io/

Frederico, G. F. (2023). ChatGPT in supply chains: Initial evidence of applications and potential research agenda. *Logistics*, 7(2), 26. 10.3390/logistics7020026

Frey, C. B., & Osborne, M. (2023). Generative AI and the future of work: A reappraisal. *The Brown Journal of World Affairs*, 1–12.

Frolov, S., Hinz, T., Raue, F., Hees, J., & Dengel, A. (2021). Adversarial text-to-image synthesis: A review. *Neural Networks*, 144, 187–209. 10.1016/j.neunet.2021.07.01934500257

Fuhr, A. S., & Sumpter, B. G. (2022). Deep generative models for materials discovery and machine learning-accelerated innovation. *Frontiers in Materials*, 9, 865270. 10.3389/fmats.2022.865270

Fui-Hoon Nah, F., Zheng, R., Cai, J., Siau, K., & Chen, L. (2023). *Generative ai and chatgpt: Applications, challenges, and ai-human collaboration*. geeksforgeeks. https://www.geeksforgeeks. org/variational-autoencoders/

Fui-Hoon Nah, F., Zheng, R., Cai, J., Siau, K., & Chen, L. (2023). Generative AI and ChatGPT: Applications, challenges, and AI-human collaboration. *Journal of Information Technology Case and Application Research*, 25(3), 277–304. 10.1080/15228053.2023.2233814

Gallego, V. (2022). *Personalizing text-to-image generation via aesthetic gradients*. arXiv preprint arXiv:2209.12330.

Gal, R., Patashnik, O., Maron, H., Bermano, A. H., Chechik, G., & Cohen-Or, D. (2022). Stylegan-nada: Clip-guided domain adaptation of image generators. *ACM Transactions on Graphics*, 41(4), 1–13. 10.1145/3528223.3530164

Ganesh, P., Chen, Y., Lou, X., Khan, M. A., Yang, Y., Sajjad, H., Nakov, P., Chen, D., & Winslett, M. (2021). Compressing large-scale transformer-based models: A case study on bert. *Transactions of the Association for Computational Linguistics*, 9, 1061–1080. 10.1162/tacl_a_00413

García-Peñalvo, F., & Vázquez-Ingelmo, A. (2023). *What do we mean by GenAI? A systematic mapping of the evolution, trends, and techniques involved in Generative AI*.

Garg, S., Sinha, S., Kar, A. K., & Mani, M. (2022). A review of machine learning applications in human resource management. *International Journal of Productivity and Performance Management*, 71(5), 1590–1610. 10.1108/IJPPM-08-2020-0427

Geetha, R., Padmavathy, T., & Anitha, R. (2021). Prediction of the academic performance of slow learners using efficient machine learning algorithm. *Advances in Computational Intelligence*, 1(4), 1–12. 10.1007/s43674-021-00005-9

Gefen, D., & Arinze, O. (2023). ChatGPT and usurping academic authority. *Journal of Information Technology Case and Application Research*, 25(1), 3–9. 10.1080/15228053.2023.2186629

GenAI. (n.d.). *Gen A. I. Forum*. https://genaiforum.org

Gill, J. K. (2023, December 15). Generative AI in telecom industry. *Xenonstack.com*. https://www.xenonstack.com/blog/generative-ai-telecom-industry

Gillioz, A., Casas, J., Mugellini, E., & Abou Khaled, O. (2020, September). Overview of the Transformer-based Models for NLP Tasks. In *2020 15th Conference on Computer Science and Information Systems (FedCSIS)* (pp. 179-183). IEEE. 10.15439/2020F20

Goodfellow, I. (2016). *Nips 2016 tutorial: Generative adversarial networks*. arXiv preprint arXiv:1701.00160.

Goodfellow, I., Bengio, Y., & Courville, A. (2016). *Deep Learning*. MIT Press.

Goodfellow, I., Pouget-Abadie, J., Mirza, M., Xu, B., Warde-Farley, D., Ozair, S., & Bengio, Y. (2014). Generative adversarial nets. *Advances in Neural Information Processing Systems*, 27.

Goodfellow, I., Pouget-Abadie, J., Mirza, M., Xu, B., Warde-Farley, D., Ozair, S., Courville, A., & Bengio, Y. (2020). Generative adversarial networks. *Communications of the ACM*, 63(11), 139–144. 10.1145/3422622

Gragnaniello, D., Marra, F., & Verdoliva, L. (2022). Detection of AI-generated synthetic faces. In *Handbook of Digital Face Manipulation and Detection* (pp. 191–212). Springer International Publishing. 10.1007/978-3-030-87664-7_9

Guo, Z., Zhu, Z., Li, Y., Cao, S., Chen, H., & Wang, G. (2023). Ai assisted fashion design: A review. *IEEE Access : Practical Innovations, Open Solutions.*

Guo, Z., Zhu, Z., Li, Y., Cao, S., Chen, H., & Wang, G. (2023). AI Assisted Fashion Design: A Review. *IEEE Access : Practical Innovations, Open Solutions.*

Gupta, P., Ding, B., Guan, C., & Ding, D. (2024). Generative ai: A systematic review using topic modelling techniques. *Data and Information Management*, 8(2), 100066. 10.1016/j.dim.2024.100066

Gu, S., Chen, D., Bao, J., Wen, F., Zhang, B., Chen, D., & Guo, B. (2022). Vector quantized diffusion model for text-to-image synthesis. In *Proceedings of the IEEE/CVF Conference on Computer Vision and Pattern Recognition* (pp. 10696-10706). IEEE. 10.1109/CVPR52688.2022.01043

Gutiérrez, L., Flores, V., Keith, B., & Quelopana, A. (2019). Using the Belbin method and models for predicting the academic performance of engineering students. *Computer Applications in Engineering Education*, 27(2), 500–509. 10.1002/cae.22092

Haarika, R., Babu, T., & Nair, R. R. (2023). Insect classification framework based on a novel fusion of high-level and shallow features. *Procedia Computer Science*, 218, 338–347. 10.1016/j.procs.2023.01.016

Haase, J., & Hanel, P. H. (2023). Artificial muses: Generative artificial intelligence chatbots have risen to human-level creativity. *Journal of Creativity*, 33(3), 100066. 10.1016/j.yjoc.2023.100066

Hacker, P., Engel, A., & Mauer, M. (2023). Regulating ChatGPT and other Large Generative AI Models. In *Proceedings of the 2023 ACM Conference on Fairness, Accountability, and Transparency (FAccT '23).* Association for Computing Machinery. 10.1145/3593013.3594067

Haenlein, M., & Kaplan, A. (2019). A Brief History of Artificial Intelligence: On the Past, Present, and Future of Artificial Intelligence. *California Management Review*, 61(4), 5–14. 10.1177/0008125619864925

Hallgren, M., Olhager, J., & Schroeder, R. G. (2011). A hybrid model of competitive capabilities. *International Journal of Operations & Production Management*, 31(5), 511–526. 10.1108/01443571111126300

Haluza, D., & Jungwirth, D. (2023). Artificial intelligence and ten societal megatrends: An exploratory study using GPT-3. *Systems*, 11(3), 120. 10.3390/systems11030120

Harbinja, E., Edwards, L., & McVey, M. (2023). Governing ghostbots. *Computer Law & Security Report*, 48, 105791. 10.1016/j.clsr.2023.105791

Harshvardhan, G. M., Gourisaria, M. K., Pandey, M., & Rautaray, S. S. (2020). A comprehensive survey and analysis of generative models in machine learning. *Computer Science Review*, 38, 100285. 10.1016/j.cosrev.2020.100285

Hartwig, S., Engel, D., Sick, L., Kniesel, H., Payer, T., & Ropinski, T. (2024). *Evaluating text to image synthesis: Survey and taxonomy of image quality metrics.* arXiv preprint arXiv:2403.11821.

Hatzius, J. (n.d.). *The potentially large effects of artificial intelligence on economic growth (Briggs/kodnani).* Gspublishing. com. https://www.gspublishing.com/content/research/en/reports/2023/03/27/d64e052b-0f6e-45d7-967b-d7be35fabd16 .html

Hemeida, A., Hassan, S., Mohamed, A., Alkhalaf, S., Mahmoud, M., Senjyu, T., El-Din, A., & Alsayyari, A. (2020). Nature-inspired algorithms for feed-forward neural network classifiers: A survey of one decade of research. *Ain Shams Engineering Journal*, 11(3), 659–675. 10.1016/j.asej.2020.01.007

Hertz, A., Mokady, R., Tenenbaum, J., Aberman, K., Pritch, Y., & Cohen-Or, D. (2022). *Prompt-to-prompt image editing with cross attention control*. arXiv preprint arXiv:2208.01626.

Hess, P., Drüke, M., Petri, S., Strnad, F. M., & Boers, N. (2022). Physically constrained generative adversarial networks for improving precipitation fields from earth system models. *Nature Machine Intelligence*, 4(10), 828–839. 10.1038/s42256-022-00540-1

Heusel, M., Ramsauer, H., Unterthiner, T., Nessler, B., & Hochreiter, S. (2017). Gans trained by a two time-scale update rule converge to a local nash equilibrium. *Advances in Neural Information Processing Systems*, 30.

Hinton, G. E., & Salakhutdinov, R. R. (2006). Reducing the dimensionality of data with neural networks. *science, 313*(5786), 504-507.

Ho, J., & Salimans, T. (2022). Classifier-free diffusion guidance. arXiv preprint arXiv:2207.12598.

Ho, J., Chan, W., Saharia, C., Whang, J., Gao, R., Gritsenko, A., & Salimans, T. (2022). Imagen video: High definition video generation with diffusion models. arXiv preprint arXiv:2210.02303.

Ho, J., Jain, A., & Abbeel, P. (2020). Denoising diffusion probabilistic models. *Advances in Neural Information Processing Systems*, 33, 6840–6851.

Ho, J., Salimans, T., Gritsenko, A., Chan, W., Norouzi, M., & Fleet, D. J. (2022). Video diffusion models. *Advances in Neural Information Processing Systems*, 35, 8633–8646.

Hong, F., Zhang, M., Pan, L., Cai, Z., Yang, L., & Liu, Z. (2022). Avatarclip: Zero-shot text-driven generation and animation of 3d avatars. arXiv preprint arXiv:2205.08535.

Hou, X., Zhao, Y., Liu, Y., Yang, Z., Wang, K., Li, L., Luo, X., Lo, D., Grundy, J., & Wang, H. (2023). Large language models for software engineering: A systematic literature review. arXiv:2308.10620.

Huang, N., Tang, F., Dong, W., & Xu, C. (2022, October). Draw your art dream: Diverse digital art synthesis with multimodal guided diffusion. In *Proceedings of the 30th ACM International Conference on Multimedia* (pp. 1085-1094). ACM. 10.1145/3503161.3548282

Huang, N., Zhang, Y., Tang, F., Ma, C., Huang, H., Dong, W., & Xu, C. (2024). Diffstyler: Controllable dual diffusion for text-driven image stylization. *IEEE Transactions on Neural Networks and Learning Systems*, 1–14. 10.1109/TNNLS.2023.334264538198263

Hu, C., Ji, Y., & Ma, C. (2023). Joint two-stage multi-innovation recursive least squares parameter and fractional-order estimation algorithm for the fractional-order input nonlinear output-error autoregressive model. *International Journal of Adaptive Control and Signal Processing*, 37(7), 1650–1670. 10.1002/acs.3593

Hughes, R. T., Zhu, L., & Bednarz, T. (2021). Generative adversarial networks–enabled human–artificial intelligence collaborative applications for creative and design industries: A systematic review of current approaches and trends. *Frontiers in Artificial Intelligence*, 4, 604234. 10.3389/frai.2021.60423433997773

IBSE. (2019). Iitm.Ac.In. http://ibse.iitm.ac.in

Inceptionism: Going deeper into neural networks. (2015, June). Google AI Blog. https://ai.googleblog.com/2015/06/inceptionism-going-deeper-into-neural.html

Indrakumari, R., Poongodi, T., & Singh, K. (2021). *Introduction to deep learning. Advanced Deep Learning for Engineers and Scientists: A Practical Approach.*

Inyang, U. G., Eyoh, I. J., Robinson, S. A., & Udo, E. N. (2019). Visual association analytics approach to predictive modelling of students' academic performance. *International Journal of Modern Education \&. Computer Science*, 11(12), 1–13.

Is artificial intelligence set to become art's next medium? (n.d.). (2023). Christie's. https://www.christies.com/features/A-collaboration-between-two-artists-one-human-one-a-machine-9332-1.aspx

Iskender, A. (2023). Holy or unholy? Interview with open AI's ChatGPT. *European Journal of Tourism Research*, 34, 3414. 10.54055/ejtr.v34i.3169

Jabbar, A., Li, X., & Omar, B. (2021). A survey on generative adversarial networks: Variants, applications, and training. *ACM Computing Surveys*, 54(8), 1–49. 10.1145/3463475

Jain, R. (2021). Dreamscape: Using ai to create speculative vr environments. In *Proceedings of the Future Technologies Conference (FTC) 2020*. Springer.

Jain, A. K., & Mao, J. (1996). Artificial Neural Networks: A Tutorial. *Computer*, 29(3), 31–44. 10.1109/2.485891

Jain, A., Mildenhall, B., Barron, J. T., Abbeel, P., & Poole, B. (2022). Zero-shot text-guided object generation with dream fields. In *Proceedings of the IEEE/CVF conference on computer vision and pattern recognition* (pp. 867-876). IEEE. 10.1109/CVPR52688.2022.00094

Jain, A., Xie, A., & Abbeel, P. (2023). Vectorfusion: Text-to-svg by abstracting pixel-based diffusion models. In *Proceedings of the IEEE/CVF Conference on Computer Vision and Pattern Recognition* (pp. 1911-1920). IEEE. 10.1109/CVPR52729.2023.00190

Jain, D. K., Zareapoor, M., Jain, R., Kathuria, A., & Bachhety, S. (2020). GAN-Poser: An improvised bidirectional GAN model for human motion prediction. *Neural Computing & Applications*, 32(18), 14579–14591. 10.1007/s00521-020-04941-4

Jang, Y., Choi, S., Jung, H., & Kim, H. (2022). Practical early prediction of students' performance using machine learning and eXplainable AI. *Education and Information Technologies*, 27(9), 12855–12889. 10.1007/s10639-022-11120-6

Janiesch, C., Zschech, P., & Heinrich, K. (2021). Machine learning and deep learning. *Electronic Markets*, 31(3), 685–695. 10.1007/s12525-021-00475-2

Jarrahi, M. (2018). Artificial intelligence and the future of work: Human-AI symbiosis in organizational decision making. *Business Horizons*, 61(4), 577–586. 10.1016/j.bushor.2018.03.007

Jatana, N., Wadhwa, D., Singh, N. K., Hassen, O. A., Gupta, C., Darwish, S. M., Mohammed, S. M., Farhan, D. A., & Abdulhussein, A. A. (2024). Future frame prediction using generative adversarial networks. *Karbala International Journal of Modern Science*, 10(1), 2. 10.33640/2405-609X.3338

Javapoint (2022). *Supervised machine learning*. Javapoint. https://www.javatpoint.com/supervised-machine-learning

Jenitha, T., Santhi, S., & Jeba, J. M. P. (2021). Prediction of Students' Performance based on Academic, Behaviour, Extra and Co-Curricular Activities. *Webology*, 18(Special Issue 01, SI01), 262–279. 10.14704/WEB/V18SI01/WEB18058

Jesuthasan, R. (2023, April 14). *Here's how companies can navigate generative AI in their work*. World Economic Forum. https://www.weforum.org/agenda/2023/04/how-companies-should-navigate-generative-ai-in-future-of-work/

Jia, C., Yang, Y., Xia, Y., Chen, Y. T., Parekh, Z., Pham, H., & Duerig, T. (2021, July). Scaling up visual and vision-language representation learning with noisy text supervision. In *International conference on machine learning* (pp. 4904-4916). PMLR.

Johnson, M., & Li, S. (2022). Python's role in the next generation of AI development. *Advanced Computing Review*, 28(1), 47–65.

Johri, P., Khatri, S. K., Al-Taani, A. T., Sabharwal, M., Suvanov, S., & Kumar, A. (2021). Natural language processing: History, evolution, application, and future work. In *Proceedings of 3rd International Conference on Computing Informatics and Networks: ICCIN 2020*. Springer. 10.1007/978-981-15-9712-1_31

Jussupow, E., Spohrer, K., Heinzl, A., & Gawlitza, J. (2021). Augmenting medical diagnosis decisions? An investigation into physicians' decision-making process with artificial intelligence. *Information Systems Research*, 32(3), 713–735. 10.1287/isre.2020.0980

K'uppers, E. U. (2023). Cybernetic systems in practice. In *A Transdisciplinary Introduction to the World of Cybernetics: Basics, Models, Theories and Practical Examples*. Springer.

Kahambing, J. G. (2023). ChatGPT, public health communication and 'intelligent patient companionship'. *Journal of Public Health (Oxford, England)*, 45(3), e590–e590. 10.1093/pubmed/fdad02837036209

Kanbach, D. K., Heiduk, L., Blueher, G., Schreiter, M., & Lahmann, A. (2023). The genai is out of the bottle: Generative artificial intelligence from a business model innovation perspective. *Review of Managerial Science*, 1–32.

Kasneci, E., Sessler, K., Küchemann, S., Bannert, M., Dementieva, D., Fischer, F., Gasser, U., Groh, G., Günnemann, S., Hüllermeier, E., Krusche, S., Kutyniok, G., Michaeli, T., Nerdel, C., Pfeffer, J., Poquet, O., Sailer, M., Schmidt, A., Seidel, T., & Kasneci, G. (2023). ChatGPT for good? On opportunities and challenges of large language models for education. *Learning and Individual Differences*, 103(102274), 102274. 10.1016/j.lindif.2023.102274

Kato, N., Osone, H., Sato, D., Muramatsu, N., & Ochiai, Y. (2018, March). Deepwear: a case study of collaborative design between human and artificial intelligence. In *Proceedings of the Twelfth International Conference on Tangible, Embedded, and Embodied Interaction* (pp. 529-536). ACM. 10.1145/3173225.3173302

Kaviani, S., & Sohn, I. (2021). Application of complex systems topologies in artificial neural networks optimization: An overview. *Expert Systems with Applications*, 180, 115073. 10.1016/j.eswa.2021.115073

Kavitha, R. K., Jaisingh, W., & Devi, S. K. K. (2021). Applying Learning Analytics to Study the Influence of Fundamental Computer Courses on Project Work and Student Performance Prediction using Machine Learning Techniques. *2021 International Conference on Advancements in Electrical, Electronics, Communication, Computing and Automation (ICAECA)*, (pp. 1–5). IEEE. 10.1109/ICAECA52838.2021.9675517

Kenton, J. D. M. W. C., & Toutanova, L. K. (2019, June). Bert: Pre-training of deep bidirectional transformers for language understanding. In *Proceedings of naacL-HLT* (*Vol. 1*, p. 2).

Khan, M. I., Khan, Z. A., Imran, A., Khan, A. H., & Ahmed, S. (2022). Student Performance Prediction in Secondary School Education Using Machine Learning. *2022 8th International Conference on Information Technology Trends (ITT)*, (pp. 94–101). IEEE.

Kim, G., & Ye, J. C. (2021). *Diffusionclip: Text-guided image manipulation using diffusion models*. Academic Press.

Kim, C. D., Kim, B., Lee, H., & Kim, G. (2019, June). Audiocaps: Generating captions for audios in the wild. In *Proceedings of the 2019 Conference of the North American Chapter of the Association for Computational Linguistics: Human Language Technologies*, (pp. 119-132).

Kim, G., & Chun, S. Y. (2023). Datid-3d: Diversity-preserved domain adaptation using text-to-image diffusion for 3d generative model. In *Proceedings of the IEEE/CVF Conference on Computer Vision and Pattern Recognition* (pp. 14203-14213). IEEE. 10.1109/CVPR52729.2023.01365

Kim, T., Cha, M., Kim, H., Lee, J. K., & Kim, J. (2017, July). Learning to discover cross-domain relations with generative adversarial networks. In *International conference on machine learning* (pp. 1857-1865). PMLR.

Kingma, D. P., & Welling, M. (2013). *Auto-Encoding Variational Bayes*. arXiv preprint arXiv:1312.6114.

Kingma, D. P., & Welling, M. (2013). Auto-Encoding Variational Bayes. In *arXiv[stat.ML]*. http://arxiv.org/abs/1312.6114

Kishore, S., Nair, R. R., Mehra, V., & Babu, T. (2023). A generalized framework for brain tumor and pneumonia detection using streamlite application. In *2023 4th International Conference for Emerging Technology (INCET)*. IEEE.

Kobyzev, I., Prince, S., & Brubaker, M. A. (2019). Normalizing flows: Introduction and ideas. *Stat, 1050*, 25.

Kobyzev, I., Prince, S. J., & Brubaker, M. A. (2020). Normalizing flows: An introduction and review of current methods. *IEEE Transactions on Pattern Analysis and Machine Intelligence*, 43(11), 3964–3979. 10.1109/TPAMI.2020.299293432396070

Korinek, A. (2022). *How innovation affects labor markets: An impact assessment*. (Brookings Center on Regulation and Markets Working Paper).

Kumar, T. R., Vamsidhar, T., Harika, B., Kumar, T. M., & Nissy, R. (2019). Students performance prediction using data mining techniques. *2019 International Conference on Intelligent Sustainable Systems (ICISS)*, 407–411. kumar, Y., & Sahoo, G. (2012). Analysis of Parametric & Non Parametric Classifiers for Classification Technique using WEKA. *International Journal of Information Technology and Computer Science*, 4(7), 43–49. 10.5815/ijitcs.2012.07.06

Kumar, Y., Koul, A., Singla, R., & Ijaz, M. F. (2023). Artificial intelligence in disease diagnosis: A systematic literature review, synthesizing framework and future research agenda. *Journal of Ambient Intelligence and Humanized Computing*, 14(7), 8459–8486. 10.1007/s12652-021-03612-z35039756

Kwon, M., Jeong, J., & Uh, Y. (2022). *Diffusion models already have a semantic latent space*. arXiv preprint arXiv:2210.10960.

Lazaroiu, G., & Rogalska, E. (2023). How generative artificial intelligence technologies shape partial job displacement and labor productivity growth. *Oeconomia Copernicana*, 14(3), 703–706. 10.24136/oc.2023.020

LeCun, Y., Léon, B., Yoshua, B., & Patrick, H. (1998). Gradient-Based Learning Applied to Document Recognition. *Proceedings of the IEEE*, 86(11), 2278–2324. 10.1109/5.726791

Ledig, C., Theis, L., Huszár, F., Caballero, J., Cunningham, A., Acosta, A., & Shi, W. (2017). Photo-realistic single image super-resolution using a generative adversarial network. In *Proceedings of the IEEE conference on computer vision and pattern recognition* (pp. 4681-4690). IEEE. 10.1109/CVPR.2017.19

Lee, D., Kim, C., Kim, S., Cho, M., & Han, W. S. (2022). Autoregressive image generation using residual quantization. In *Proceedings of the IEEE/CVF Conference on Computer Vision and Pattern Recognition* (pp. 11523-11532). IEEE.

Lee, H. (2022). The impact of artificial intelligence on media and communication. *Future Media Research*, 5(2), 134–150.

Lee, M., & Seok, J. (2019). Controllable generative adversarial network. *IEEE Access : Practical Innovations, Open Solutions*, 7, 28158–28169. 10.1109/ACCESS.2019.2899108

Lee, Y. K. (2022). How complex systems get engaged in fashion design creation: Using artificial intelligence. *Thinking Skills and Creativity*, 46, 101137. 10.1016/j.tsc.2022.101137

Leippold, M. (2023). Thus spoke GPT-3: Interviewing a large-language model on climate finance. *Finance Research Letters*, 53, 103617. 10.1016/j.frl.2022.103617

Lester, J., Choudhury, T., Kern, N., Borriello, G., & Hannaford, B. (2005). *A hybrid discriminative/generative approach for modeling human activities*.

Levy, A. (2023, May 10). *2 companies are using generative AI to supercharge revenue.* The Motley Fool. https://www .fool.com/investing/2023/05/10/companies-using-generative-ai-supercharge-revenue/

Li, G., Zheng, H., Wang, C., Li, C., Zheng, C., & Tao, D. (2022). 3ddesigner: Towards photorealistic 3d object generation and editing with text-guided diffusion models. arXiv preprint arXiv:2211.14108.

Li, J., Cao, H., Lin, L., Hou, Y., Zhu, R., & Ali, A. E. (2023). *User experience design professionals' perceptions of generative artificial intelligence.* arXiv preprint arXiv:2309.15237.

Liam, M. O. (2020, October 6). *The next Rembrandt developed by AI.* Liam M OBrien. https://www.liammobrien.com/ rembranbt-ai/

Liang, D., Krishnan, R. G., Hoffman, M. D., & Jebara, T. (2018, April). Variational autoencoders for collaborative filtering. In *Proceedings of the 2018 world wide web conference* (pp. 689-698). 10.1145/3178876.3186150

Lin, J., Men, R., Yang, A., Zhou, C., Ding, M., Zhang, Y., & Yang, H. (2021). *M6: A chinese multimodal pretrainer.* arXiv preprint arXiv:2103.00823.

Lin, M., Chen, Q., & Yan, S. (2014). Network In Network. *arXiv preprint arXiv:1312.4400.* https://doi.org//arXiv.1312 .440010.48550

Lin, T., Pfister, H., & Wang, J. H. (2024). GenLens: A Systematic Evaluation of Visual GenAI Model Outputs. arXiv preprint arXiv:2402.03700. 10.1109/PacificVis60374.2024.00044

Lin, C. H., Gao, J., Tang, L., Takikawa, T., Zeng, X., Huang, X., & Lin, T. Y. (2023). Magic3d: High-resolution text-to-3d content creation. In *Proceedings of the IEEE/CVF Conference on Computer Vision and Pattern Recognition* (pp. 300-309). IEEE.

Lin, T. Y., Maire, M., Belongie, S., Hays, J., Perona, P., Ramanan, D., & Zitnick, C. L. (2014). Microsoft coco: Common objects in context. *Computer Vision–ECCV 2014: 13th European Conference, Zurich, Switzerland, September 6-12, 2014Proceedings*, 13(Part V), 740–755.

Li, S., Chen, J., Shen, Y., Chen, Z., Zhang, X., Li, Z., Wang, H., Qian, J., Peng, B., Mao, Y., & Chen, W. (2022). Explanations from large language models make small reasoners better. arXiv:2210.06726.

Liu, Y., Han, T., Ma, S., Zhang, J., Yang, Y., Tian, J., He, H., Li, A., He, M., Liu, Z., Wu, Z., Zhao, L., Zhu, D., Li, X., Qiang, N., Shen, D., Liu, T., & Ge, B. (2023). Summary of ChatGPT-Related research and perspective towards the future of large language models. *Meta-Radiology, 1*(2). 10.1016/j.metrad.2023.100017

Liu, Z., Huang, Y., Yu, X., Zhang, L., Wu, Z., Cao, C., & Li, X. (2023). Deid-gpt: Zero-shot medical text de-identification by gpt-4. *arXiv preprint arXiv:2303.11032.*

Liu, B., Bubeck, S., Eldan, R., Kulkarni, J., Li, Y., Nguyen, A., Ward, R., & Zhang, Y. (2023). TinyGSM: achieving> 80% on GSM8k with small language models. arXiv:2312.09241.

Liu, L., Wang, Y., & Xu, Y. (2024). A practical guide to counterfactual estimators for causal inference with time-series cross-sectional data. *American Journal of Political Science*, 68(1), 160–176. 10.1111/ajps.12723

Liu, Q., Allamanis, M., Brockschmidt, M., & Gaunt, A. (2018). Constrained graph variational autoencoders for molecule design. *Advances in Neural Information Processing Systems*, 31.

Liu, T., Fan, J., Li, G., Tang, N., & Du, X. (2024). Tabular data synthesis with generative adversarial networks: Design space and optimizations. *The VLDB Journal*, 33(2), 255–280. 10.1007/s00778-023-00807-y

Liu, T., Wang, K., Sha, L., Chang, B., & Sui, Z. (2018, April). Table-to-text generation by structure-aware seq2seq learning. *Proceedings of the AAAI Conference on Artificial Intelligence*, 32(1). 10.1609/aaai.v32i1.11925

Liu, V., & Chilton, L. B. (2021). Design guidelines for prompt engineering text-to-image generative models. In *arXiv[cs. HC]*. http://arxiv.org/abs/2109.06977

Long, D., & Magerko, B. (2020). What is AI Literacy? Competencies and Design Considerations. *Proceedings of the 2020 CHI Conference on Human Factors in Computing Systems*. 10.1145/3313831.3376727

Long, X. (2023). *Common features of Henri Matisse's painting concept and ancient Chinese pictorial thought.* Человек и Культура.

López Zambrano, J., Lara Torralbo, J. A., & Romero Morales, C. (2021). Early prediction of student learning performance through data mining: A systematic review. *Psicothema.*34297676

Lucas, A., Lopez-Tapia, S., Molina, R., & Katsaggelos, A. K. (2019). Generative adversarial networks and perceptual losses for video super-resolution. *IEEE Transactions on Image Processing*, 28(7), 3312–3327. 10.1109/TIP.2019.289576830714918

Luo, J. (2024). A critical review of GenAI policies in higher education assessment: A call to reconsider the "originality" of students' work. *Assessment & Evaluation in Higher Education*, 1–14.

Lv, Z. (2023). Generative artificial intelligence in the metaverse era. Cognitive Robotics. Gupta, P., Ding, B., Guan, C., & Ding, D. (2024). Generative AI: A systematic review using topic modelling techniques. *Data and Information Management*, ●●●, 100066.

Lyu, H., Sha, N., Qin, S., Yan, M., Xie, Y., & Wang, R. (2019). Advances in neural information processing systems. *Advances in Neural Information Processing Systems*, 32.

Mʻuggenburg, J. (2021). From learning machines to learning humans: how cybernetic machine models inspired experimental pedagogies. *History of Education, 50*(1), 112–133.

Machado, P., Romero, J., & Greenfield, G. (2021). *Artificial intelligence for designing games. Artificial Intelligence and the Arts: Computational Creativity.* Artistic Behavior, and Tools for Creatives.

Magazine, S. (2023). Arts & culture. *Smithsonian Magazine.* https://www.smithsonianmag.com/category/arts-culture/

Mamaghani, M. (2021, March 26). *Detecting financial fraud using GANs at swedbank with hopsworks and NVIDIA GPUs.* NVIDIA Technical Blog. https://developer.nvidia.com/blog/detecting-financial-fraud-using-gans-at-swedbank -with-hopsworks-and-gpus/

Manco, I., Benetos, E., Quinton, E., & Fazekas, G. (2021, July). Muscaps: Generating captions for music audio. In *2021 International Joint Conference on Neural Networks (IJCNN)* (pp. 1-8). IEEE.

Mandal, M. (2022). *Introduction to convolutional neural networks.* Analytics Vidhya. https://www.analyticsvidhya.com/blog/2021/05/convolutional-neural-networks-cnn/

Mandapuram, M., Gutlapalli, S. S., Bodepudi, A., & Reddy, M. (2018). Investigating the Prospects of Generative Artificial Intelligence. *Asian Journal of Humanity. Art and Literature*, 5(2), 167–174.

Mansimov, E., Parisotto, E., Ba, J. L., & Salakhutdinov, R. (2015). *Generating images from captions with attention.* arXiv preprint arXiv:1511.02793.

Manufacturing skills gap study. (2018, November 13). Deloitte United States. https://www2.deloitte.com/us/en/pages/manufacturing/articles/future-of-manufacturing-skills-gap-study.html

Marchandot, B., Matsushita, K., Carmona, A., Trimaille, A., & Morel, O. (2023). ChatGPT: The next frontier in academic writing for cardiologists or a pandora's box of ethical dilemmas. *European Heart Journal Open*, 3(2), oead007. 10.1093/ehjopen/oead00736915398

MathWorks. (2022). *What is a convolutional neural network?* Mathworks. https://www.mathworks.com/discovery/convolutional-neural-network.html#:~ text=A%20convolutional%20neural%20network%20(CNN,%2Dseries%2C%20and%20signal%20data [Accessed: 26-03-2024].

Matisse, H. (2023, November 15). Creativity takes courage. *The Socratic Method*. https://www.socratic-method.com/quote-meanings-french/henri-matisse-creativity-takes-courage

Matzavela, V., & Alepis, E. (2021). Decision tree learning through a predictive model for student academic performance in intelligent m-learning environments. *Computers and Education: Artificial Intelligence*, 2, 100035. 10.1016/j.caeai.2021.100035

McCormack, J., Gifford, T., & Hutchings, P. (2019). Autonomy, authenticity, authorship and intention in computer generated art. In *Computational Intelligence in Music, Sound, Art and Design* (pp. 35–50). Springer International Publishing. 10.1007/978-3-030-16667-0_3

Meghji, A. F., Mahoto, N. A., Unar, M. A., & Shaikh, M. A. (2019). Predicting student academic performance using data generated in higher educational institutes. *3c Tecnolog{\'\i}a. Glosas de Innovación Aplicadas a La Pyme*, 8(1), 366–383.

Meher, S. K., & Panda, G. (2021). Deep learning in astronomy: A tutorial perspective. *The European Physical Journal. Special Topics*, 230(10), 2285–2317. 10.1140/epjs/s11734-021-00207-9

Meitz, M., Preve, D., & Saikkonen, P. (2023). A mixture autoregressive model based on student'st–distribution. *Communications in Statistics. Theory and Methods*, 52(2), 499–515. 10.1080/03610926.2021.1916531

Meng, C., Trinh, L., Xu, N., Enouen, J., & Liu, Y. (2022). Interpretability and fairness evaluation of deep learning models on MIMIC-IV dataset. *Scientific Reports*, 12(1), 7166. 10.1038/s41598-022-11012-235504931

Merchant, A., Shenoy, N., Bharali, A., & Kumar, M. A. (2022). Predicting Students' Academic Performance in Virtual Learning Environment Using Machine Learning. *2022 Second International Conference on Power, Control and Computing Technologies (ICPC2T)*, (pp. 1–6). IEEE. 10.1109/ICPC2T53885.2022.9777008

Meyers, J., Fabian, B., & Brown, N. (2021). De novo molecular design and generative models. *Drug Discovery Today*, 26(11), 2707–2715. 10.1016/j.drudis.2021.05.01934082136

Mildenhall, B., Srinivasan, P. P., Tancik, M., Barron, J. T., Ramamoorthi, R., & Ng, R. (2021). Nerf: Representing scenes as neural radiance fields for view synthesis. *Communications of the ACM*, 65(1), 99–106. 10.1145/3503250

Mirza, M., & Osindero, S. (2014). Conditional generative adversarial nets. arXiv preprint arXiv:1411.1784.

Mishra, P., Warr, M., & Islam, R. (2023). Tpack in the age of chatgpt and generative ai. *Journal of Digital Learning in Teacher Education*, 39(4), 235–251. 10.1080/21532974.2023.2247480

Mitchell, T. M. (1997). Does Machine Learning Really Work? *AI Magazine*, 18(3), 11–20. 10.1609/aimag.v18i3.1303

Mohamad Razi, N. F., Baharun, N., & Omar, N. (2022). Machine learning predictive model of academic achievement efficiency based on data envelopment analysis. [MIJ]. *Mathematical Sciences and Informatics Journal*, 3(1), 86–99. 10.24191/mij.v3i1.18284

Mokady, R., Hertz, A., Aberman, K., Pritch, Y., & Cohen-Or, D. (2023). Null-text inversion for editing real images using guided diffusion models. In *Proceedings of the IEEE/CVF Conference on Computer Vision and Pattern Recognition* (pp. 6038-6047). IEEE. 10.1109/CVPR52729.2023.00585

Monarch, R. (munro). (2021). *Human-in-the-Loop Machine Learning: Active learning and annotation for human-centered AI*. Simon and Schuster.

Moraffah, R., Sheth, P., Karami, M., Bhattacharya, A., Wang, Q., Tahir, A., Raglin, A., & Liu, H. (2021). Causal inference for time series analysis: Problems, methods and evaluation. *Knowledge and Information Systems*, 63(12), 3041–3085. 10.1007/s10115-021-01621-0

Morra, J. (2023, April 10). *System-level PCB design tool embraces "generative" AI*. Electronic Design. https://www.electronicdesign.com/technologies/eda/article/21263574/electronic-design-system-level-pcb-design-tool-embraces-generative-ai

Mourtzis, D. (2023). The Metaverse in Industry 5.0: A Human-Centric Approach towards Personalized Value Creation. *Encyclopedia*, 3(3), 1105–1120. 10.3390/encyclopedia3030080

Mueller, J. P., & Massaron, L. (2016). *Machine Learning for Dummies*. John Wiley & Sons.

Müller Andreas, C. (2016). *Introduction to Machine Learning with Python: A Guide for Data Scientists*. Research Gate.

Muruganandam, S., Joshi, R., Suresh, P., Balakrishna, N., Kishore, K. H., & Manikanthan, S. (2023). A deep learning based feed forward artificial neural network to predict the k-barriers for intrusion detection using a wireless sensor network. *Measurement. Sensors*, 25, 100613. 10.1016/j.measen.2022.100613

Muthukumar, P., & Zhong, J. (2021). *A stochastic time series model for predicting financial trends using nlp*. arXiv preprint arXiv:2102.01290.

Nair, R. R., Babu, T., Singh, T., Duraisamy, P., & Mehra, V. (2023). Class room student attentiveness model based on yolo. In *2023 14th International Conference on Computing Communication and Networking Technologies (ICCCNT)*. IEEE. 10.1109/ICCCNT56998.2023.10306686

Nair, R. R., Singh, T., Basavapattana, A., & Pawar, M. M. (2022). Multi-layer, multi-modal medical image intelligent fusion. *Multimedia Tools and Applications*, 81(29), 42821–42847. 10.1007/s11042-022-13482-y

Nair, R. R., Singh, T., Sankar, R., & Gunndu, K. (2021). Multi-modal medical image fusion using lmf-gan-a maximum parameter infusion technique. *Journal of Intelligent & Fuzzy Systems*, 41(5), 5375–5386. 10.3233/JIFS-189860

Nam, S., Jeon, S., Kim, H., & Moon, J. (2020). Recurrent gans password cracker for iot password security enhancement. *Sensors (Basel)*, 20(11), 3106. 10.3390/s2011310632486361

Narasimhan, A., & Rao, K. P. A. V. (2021). *Cgems: A metric model for automatic code generation using gpt-3*. arXiv preprint arXiv:2108.10168.

Nichol, A., Dhariwal, P., Ramesh, A., Shyam, P., Mishkin, P., McGrew, B., & Chen, M. (2021). *Glide: Towards photorealistic image generation and editing with text-guided diffusion models*. arXiv preprint arXiv:2112.10741.

Nichol, A. Q., & Dhariwal, P. (2021, July). Improved denoising diffusion probabilistic models. In *International conference on machine learning* (pp. 8162-8171). PMLR.

Nicholls, J., Kuppa, A., & Le-Khac, N.-A. (2021). Financial cybercrime: A comprehensive survey of deep learning approaches to tackle the evolving financial crime landscape. *IEEE Access : Practical Innovations, Open Solutions*, 9, 163965–163986. 10.1109/ACCESS.2021.3134076

Nielsen, M. (1994). Neural networks and deep learning. In Clark, A., & Millican, P. (Eds.), *Neural networks and deep learning: Contemplating minds: A forum for artificial intelligence* (pp. 11–25). MIT Press.

Niet, I., van Est, R., & Veraart, F. (2021). Governing AI in electricity systems: Reflections on the EU artificial intelligence bill. *Frontiers in Artificial Intelligence*, 4, 690237. 10.3389/frai.2021.69023734396090

Nishant, R., Kennedy, M., & Corbett, J. (2020). Artificial intelligence for sustainability: Challenges, opportunities, and a research agenda. *International Journal of Information Management*, 53(102104), 102104. 10.1016/j.ijinfomgt.2020.102104

Niu, K., Lu, Y., Peng, X., & Zeng, J. (2022). Fusion of sequential visits and medical ontology for mortality prediction. *Journal of Biomedical Informatics*, 127, 104012. 10.1016/j.jbi.2022.10401235144001

NSynth. (2017, April 6). *Neural audio synthesis.* Magenta. https://magenta.tensorflow.org/nsynth

Ntoutsi, E., Fafalios, P., Gadiraju, U., Iosifidis, V., Nejdl, W., Vidal, M. E., Ruggieri, S., Turini, F., Papadopoulos, S., Krasanakis, E., Kompatsiaris, I., Kinder-Kurlanda, K., Wagner, C., Karimi, F., Fernandez, M., Alani, H., Berendt, B., Kruegel, T., Heinze, C., & Staab, S. (2020). Bias in data-driven artificial intelligence systems—An introductory survey. *Wiley Interdisciplinary Reviews. Data Mining and Knowledge Discovery*, 10(3), e1356. 10.1002/widm.1356

NVivo. (2020). *NVivo qualitative data analysis software.* QSR International.

O'Connor, J. (2023). Undercover algorithm: A secret chapter in the early history of artificial intelligence and satellite imagery. *International Journal of Intelligence and CounterIntelligence*, 36(4), 1337–1351.

Oguine, O. C., Oguine, K. J., & Bisallah, H. I. (2022). Big Data and Analytics Implementation in Tertiary Institutions to Predict Students Performance in Nigeria. *ArXiv Preprint ArXiv:2207.14677.*

Okaiyeto, S. A., Bai, J., & Xiao, H. (2023). Generative AI in education: To embrace it or not? *International Journal of Agricultural and Biological Engineering*, 16(3), 285–286. 10.25165/j.ijabe.20231603.8486

Ooi, K.-B., Tan, G. W.-H., Al-Emran, M., Al-Sharafi, M. A., Capatina, A., Chakraborty, A., Dwivedi, Y. K., Huang, T.-L., Kar, A. K., Lee, V.-H., Loh, X.-M., Micu, A., Mikalef, P., Mogaji, E., Pandey, N., Raman, R., Rana, N. P., Sarker, P., Sharma, A., & Wong, L.-W. (2023). The potential of generative artificial intelligence across disciplines: Perspectives and future directions. *Journal of Computer Information Systems*, 1–32. 10.1080/08874417.2023.2261010

Open, A. I., Achiam, J., Adler, S., Agarwal, S., Ahmad, L., Akkaya, I., Aleman, F. L., Almeida, D., Altenschmidt, J., Altman, S., Anadkat, S., Avila, R., Babuschkin, I., Balaji, S., Balcom, V., Baltescu, P., Bao, H., Bavarian, M., Belgum, J., & Zoph, B. (2023). GPT-4 Technical Report. In *arXiv[cs.CL].* http://arxiv.org/abs/2303.08774

Oreski, G. (2023). Synthesizing credit data using autoencoders and generative adversarial networks. *Knowledge-Based Systems*, 274, 110646. 10.1016/j.knosys.2023.110646

Pan, Z., Yu, W., Yi, X., Khan, A., Yuan, F., & Zheng, Y. (2019). Recent progress on generative adversarial networks (GANs): A survey. *IEEE Access: Practical Innovations, Open Solutions*, 7, 36322–36333. 10.1109/ACCESS.2019.2905015

Pan, Z., Zhou, X., & Tian, H. (2023). Arbitrary style guidance for enhanced diffusion-based text-to-image generation. In *Proceedings of the IEEE/CVF Winter Conference on Applications of Computer Vision* (pp. 4461-4471). IEEE. 10.1109/WACV56688.2023.00444

Pavan Kumar, M., & Jayagopal, P. (2021). Generative adversarial networks: A survey on applications and challenges. *International Journal of Multimedia Information Retrieval*, 10(1), 1–24. 10.1007/s13735-020-00196-w

Pavez, V., Hermosilla, G., Silva, M., & Farias, G. (2023). Advanced Deep Learning Techniques for High-Quality Synthetic Thermal Image Generation. *Mathematics*, 11(21), 4446. 10.3390/math11214446

Pavlik, J. V. (2023). Collaborating with ChatGPT: Considering the implications of generative artificial intelligence for journalism and media education. *Journalism & Mass Communication Educator*, 78(1), 84–93. 10.1177/10776958221149577

Pawar, S. (2024, January 25). Unveiling the future: Exploring the wonders of generative AI and its applications. *Medium*. https://medium.com/@sureshkumar.pawar/unveiling-the-future-exploring-the-wonders-of-generative-ai-and-its-applications-c0fb0cae09c6

Pearson, K. (1901). LIII. On lines and planes of closest fit to systems of points in space. *The London, Edinburgh and Dublin Philosophical Magazine and Journal of Science*, 2(11), 559–572. 10.1080/14786440109462720

Pedregosa, F., Varoquaux, G., Gramfort, A., Michel, V., Thirion, B., Grisel, O., & Dubourg, V. (2011). Scikit-learn: Machine learning in Python. *The Journal of machine Learning research, 12,* 2825-2830.

Pedro, D. (2012). A Few Useful Things to Know About Machine Learning. *Communications of the ACM*, 55(10), 78–87. 10.1145/2347736.2347755

Pont-Tuset, J., Uijlings, J., Changpinyo, S., Soricut, R., & Ferrari, V. (2020). Connecting vision and language with localized narratives. *Computer Vision–ECCV 2020: 16th European Conference, Glasgow, UK, August 23–28, 2020Proceedings*, 16(Part V), 647–664.

Poole, B., Jain, A., Barron, J. T., & Mildenhall, B. (2022). Dreamfusion: Text-to-3d using 2d diffusion. arXiv preprint arXiv:2209.14988.

Qadir, J., Islam, M. Q., & Al-Fuqaha, A. (2022). Toward accountable human-centered AI: Rationale and promising directions. *Journal of Information Communication and Ethics in Society*, 20(2), 329–342. 10.1108/JICES-06-2021-0059

Qiao, T., Zhang, J., Xu, D., & Tao, D. (2019). Mirrorgan: Learning text-to-image generation by redescription. In *Proceedings of the IEEE/CVF conference on computer vision and pattern recognition* (pp. 1505-1514). IEEE.

Quintans-Júnior, L. J., Gurgel, R. Q., Araújo, A. A. D. S., Correia, D., & Martins-Filho, P. R. (2023). ChatGPT: The new panacea of the academic world. *Revista da Sociedade Brasileira de Medicina Tropical*, 56, e0060–e2023. 10.1590/0037-8682-0060-202336888781

R, G., Pati, P. B., Singh, T., & Nair, R. R. (2022). A framework for the prediction of diabtetes mellitus using hyper-parameter tuned xgboost classifier. In *2022 13th International Conference on Computing Communication and Networking Technologies (ICCCNT)*. Research Gate.

Rader, E., Cotter, K., & Cho, J. (2018). Explanations as mechanisms for supporting algorithmic transparency. *Proceedings of the 2018 CHI Conference on Human Factors in Computing Systems*. 10.1145/3173574.3173677

Radford, A., Metz, L., & Chintala, S. (2015). *Unsupervised representation learning with deep convolutional generative adversarial networks*. arXiv preprint arXiv:1511.06434

Radford, A., Metz, L., & Chintala, S. (2015). *Unsupervised representation learning with deep convolutional generative adversarial networks*. arXiv preprint arXiv:1511.06434.

Radford, A., Wu, J., Child, R., Luan, D., Amodei, D., & Sutskever, I. (2019). Language models are unsupervised multitask learners. *OpenAI blog, 1*(8), 9.

Radford, A., Kim, J. W., Hallacy, C., Ramesh, A., Goh, G., Agarwal, S., & Sutskever, I. (2021, July). Learning transferable visual models from natural language supervision. In *International conference on machine learning* (pp. 8748-8763). PMLR.

Raffel, C., Luong, M. T., Liu, P. J., Weiss, R. J., & Eck, D. (2017, July). Online and linear-time attention by enforcing monotonic alignments. In *International conference on machine learning* (pp. 2837-2846). PMLR.

Raffel, C., Shazeer, N., Roberts, A., Lee, K., Narang, S., Matena, M., & Liu, P. J. (2020). Exploring the limits of transfer learning with a unified text-to-text transformer. *Journal of Machine Learning Research*, 21(140), 1–67.

Raisch, S., & Krakowski, S. (2021). Artificial intelligence and management: The automation–augmentation paradox. *Academy of Management Review*, 46(1), 192–210. 10.5465/amr.2018.0072

Rajendran, S. (2021). Predicting Factors Impacting Student Academic Performance using Machine Learning Algorithms. *Available at SSRN* 3898302. 10.2139/ssrn.3898302

Ramdas, B. R., Machhindra, M. B., Kailas, W. P., & Raut, M. V. (2019). *Tracking and Predicting Student Performance Using Machine Learning.*

Ramdurai, B., & Adhithya, P. (2023). The impact, advancements and applications of generative AI. *International Journal on Computer Science and Engineering*, 10(6), 1–8. 10.14445/23488387/IJCSE-V10I6P101

Ramdurai, B., & Adhithya, P. (n.d.). The impact, advancements and applications of generative. *AI*. 10.14445/23488387/IJCSEV10IP10

Ramesh, A., Dhariwal, P., Nichol, A., Chu, C., & Chen, M. (2022). Hierarchical text-conditional image generation with clip latents. arXiv preprint arXiv:2204.06125.

Ramesh, A., Pavlov, M., Goh, G., Gray, S., Voss, C., Radford, A., & Sutskever, I. (2021, July). Zero-shot text-to-image generation. In *International conference on machine learning* (pp. 8821-8831). PMLR.

Ramezanian-Panahi, M., Abrevaya, G., Gagnon-Audet, J.-C., Voleti, V., Rish, I., & Dumas, G. (2022). Generative models of brain dynamics. *Frontiers in Artificial Intelligence*, 5, 807406. 10.3389/frai.2022.80740635910192

Ramzan, S., Iqbal, M. M., & Kalsum, T. (2022). Text-to-Image Generation Using Deep Learning. *Engineering Proceedings*, 20(1), 16.

Rane, N. (2023). ChatGPT and Similar Generative Artificial Intelligence (AI) for Smart Industry: role, challenges and opportunities for industry 4.0, industry 5.0 and society 5.0. *Challenges and Opportunities for Industry, 4.*

Rane, N. L., Anand, A., & Deepak, K. (2023). Evaluating the Selection Criteria of Formwork System (FS) for RCC Building Construction. *International Journal of Engineering Trends and Technology*, 71(3), 197–205. 10.14445/22315381/IJETT-V71I3P220

Rane, N. L., & Attarde, P. M. (2016). Application of value engineering in commercial building projects. *International Journal of Latest Trends in Engineering & Technology : IJLTET*, 6(3), 286–291.

Rashid, T. (2016). *Make Your Own Neural Network*. CreateSpace Independent Publishing Platform.

Rathore, B. (2023). Future of textile: Sustainable manufacturing & prediction via chatgpt. *Eduzone: International Peer Reviewed/Refereed Multidisciplinary Journal, 12*(1), 52-62.

Ray, P. P. (2023). ChatGPT: A comprehensive review on background, applications, key challenges, bias, ethics, limitations and future scope. *Internet of Things and Cyber-Physical Systems*, 3, 121–154. 10.1016/j.iotcps.2023.04.003

Razavi, A., Van den Oord, A., & Vinyals, O. (2019). Generating diverse high-fidelity images with vq-vae-2. *Advances in Neural Information Processing Systems*, 32.

Reed, S., Akata, Z., Lee, H., & Schiele, B. (2016). Learning deep representations of fine-grained visual descriptions. In *Proceedings of the IEEE conference on computer vision and pattern recognition* (pp. 49-58). IEEE. 10.1109/CVPR.2016.13

Reed, S., Akata, Z., Yan, X., Logeswaran, L., Schiele, B., & Lee, H. (2016, June). Generative adversarial text to image synthesis. In *International conference on machine learning* (pp. 1060-1069). PMLR.

Regis, M., Serra, P., & van den Heuvel, E. R. (2022). Random autoregressive models: A structured overview. *Econometric Reviews*, 41(2), 207–230. 10.1080/07474938.2021.1899504

Reinke, A., Tizabi, M. D., Sudre, C. H., Eisenmann, M., Rädsch, T., Baumgartner, M., & Maier-Hein, L. (2021). Common limitations of image processing metrics: A picture story. arXiv preprint arXiv:2104.05642.

Ren, Y., Ruan, Y., Tan, X., Qin, T., Zhao, S., Zhao, Z., & Liu, T. Y. (2019). Fastspeech: Fast, robust and controllable text to speech. *Advances in Neural Information Processing Systems*, 32.

Riedl, M. O. (2019). Human-centered artificial intelligence and machine learning. *Human Behavior and Emerging Technologies*, 1(1), 33–36. 10.1002/hbe2.117

Rivas, P., & Zhao, L. (2023). Marketing with chatgpt: Navigating the ethical terrain of gpt-based chatbot technology. *AI*, 4(2), 375–384. 10.3390/ai4020019

Rombach, R., Blattmann, A., & Ommer, B. (2022). *Text-guided synthesis of artistic images with retrieval-augmented diffusion models.* arXiv preprint arXiv:2207.13038.

Rombach, R., Blattmann, A., Lorenz, D., Esser, P., & Ommer, B. (2022). High-resolution image synthesis with latent diffusion models. In *Proceedings of the IEEE/CVF conference on computer vision and pattern recognition* (pp. 10684-10695). IEEE. 10.1109/CVPR52688.2022.01042

Ronneberger, O., Fischer, P., & Brox, T. (2015). U-net: Convolutional networks for biomedical image segmentation. In *Medical image computing and computer-assisted intervention–MICCAI 2015: 18th international conference, Munich, Germany, October 5-9, 2015, proceedings, part III 18* (pp. 234-241). Springer International Publishing.

Roy, D., Mahmood, M. A., & Roy, T. J. (2021). *An Analytical Model for Prediction of Heart Disease using Machine Learning Classifiers.* TechrXiv. 10.36227/techrxiv.14867175

Russell, S. J., & Norvig, P. (2010). *Artificial Intelligence: A Modern Approach.* Prentice Hall.

Sætra, H. S. (2023). Generative AI: Here to stay, but for good? *Technology in Society*, 75, 102372. 10.1016/j.techsoc.2023.102372

Saharia, C., Chan, W., Saxena, S., Li, L., Whang, J., Denton, E. L., & Norouzi, M. (2022). Photorealistic text-to-image diffusion models with deep language understanding. *Advances in Neural Information Processing Systems*, 35, 36479–36494.

Saharia, C., Ho, J., Chan, W., Salimans, T., Fleet, D. J., & Norouzi, M. (2022). Image super-resolution via iterative refinement. *IEEE Transactions on Pattern Analysis and Machine Intelligence*, 45(4), 4713–4726.36094974

Sai, S., Gaur, A., Sai, R., Chamola, V., Guizani, M., & Rodrigues, J. J. (2024). Generative ai for transformative healthcare: A comprehensive study of emerging models, applications, case studies and limitations. *IEEE Access : Practical Innovations, Open Solutions*, 12, 31078–31106. 10.1109/ACCESS.2024.3367715

Saleem, F., Ullah, Z., Fakieh, B., & Kateb, F. (2021). Intelligent decision support system for predicting student's e-learning performance using ensemble machine learning. *Mathematics*, 9(17), 2078. 10.3390/math9172078

Salehi, P., Chalechale, A., & Taghizadeh, M. (2020). *Generative adversarial networks (GANs): An overview of theoretical model, evaluation metrics, and recent developments.* arXiv preprint arXiv:2005.13178.

Sánchez-Pozo, N. N. Mej\'\ia-Ordóñez, J. S., Chamorro, D. C., Mayorca-Torres, D., & Peluffo-Ordóñez, D. H. (2021). Predicting High School Students' Academic Performance: A Comparative Study of Supervised Machine Learning Techniques. *2021 Machine Learning-Driven Digital Technologies for Educational Innovation Workshop*, (pp. 1–6). IEEE.

Sandamini, A., Jayathilaka, C., Pannala, T., Karunanayaka, K., Kumarasinghe, P., & Perera, D. (2022, November). An Augmented Reality-based Fashion Design Interface with Artistic Contents Generated Using Deep Generative Models. In *2022 22nd International Conference on Advances in ICT for Emerging Regions (ICTer)* (pp. 104-109). IEEE. 10.1109/ICTer58063.2022.10024084

Särmäkari, N., & Vänskä, A. (2022). 'Just hit a button!'–fashion 4.0 designers as cyborgs, experimenting and designing with generative algorithms. *International Journal of Fashion Design, Technology and Education*, 15(2), 211–220. 10.1080/17543266.2021.1991005

Sarwat, S., Ullah, N., Sadiq, S., Saleem, R., Umer, M., Eshmawi, A., Mohamed, A., & Ashraf, I. (2022). Predicting students' academic performance with conditional generative adversarial network and deep SVM. *Sensors (Basel)*, 22(13), 4834. 10.3390/s2213483435808330

Savitha, R., Ambikapathi, A., & Rajaraman, K. (2020). Online rbm: Growing restricted boltzmann machine on the fly for unsupervised representation. *Applied Soft Computing*, 92, 106278. 10.1016/j.asoc.2020.106278

Sbai, O., Elhoseiny, M., Bordes, A., LeCun, Y., & Couprie, C. (2018). Design: Design inspiration from generative networks. In *Proceedings of the European Conference on Computer Vision (ECCV) Workshops* (pp. 0-0). EC.

Scheerder, A., Van Deursen, A., & Van Dijk, J. (2017). Determinants of Internet skills, uses and outcomes. A systematic review of the second-and third-level digital divide. *Telematics and Informatics*, 34(8), 1607–1624. 10.1016/j.tele.2017.07.007

Schick, T., Dwivedi-Yu, J., Jiang, Z., Petroni, F., Lewis, P., Izacard, G., & Riedel, S. (2022). Peer: A collaborative language model. arXiv preprint arXiv:2208.11663.

Schuhmann, C., Vencu, R., Beaumont, R., Kaczmarczyk, R., Mullis, C., Katta, A., & Komatsuzaki, A. (2021). Laion-400m: Open dataset of clip-filtered 400 million image-text pairs. arXiv preprint arXiv:2111.02114.

Sharma, N., Sharma, R., & Jindal, N. (2021). Machine learning and deep learning applications: A vision. *Global Transitions Proceedings*, 2(1), 24–28. 10.1016/j.gltp.2021.01.004

Shen, Y., Borowski, J. E., Hardy, M. A., Sarpong, R., Doyle, A. G., & Cernak, T. (2021). Automation and computer-assisted planning for chemical synthesis. *Nature Reviews. Methods Primers*, 1(1), 1–23. 10.1038/s43586-021-00022-5

Siau, K. (2018). *Education in the Age of Artificial Intelligence How Will Technology Shape Learning. The global analyst, 7, 22-24. - references - scientific research publishing*. Scirp.org. https://www.scirp.org/reference/referencespapers?referenceid=2988977

Siau, K., & Wang, W. (2020). Artificial intelligence (AI) ethics: Ethics of AI and ethical AI. *Journal of Database Management*, 31(2), 74–87. 10.4018/JDM.2020040105

Simian, D., & Husac, F. (2022, October). Challenges and Opportunities in Deep Learning Driven Fashion Design and Textiles Patterns Development. In *International Conference on Modelling and Development of Intelligent Systems* (pp. 173-187). Cham: Springer Nature Switzerland.

Singer, U., Polyak, A., Hayes, T., Yin, X., An, J., Zhang, S., & Taigman, Y. (2022). Make-a-video: Text-to-video generation without text-video data. arXiv preprint arXiv:2209.14792.

Singh, M., Bajpai, U., v, V., & Prasath, S. (2019). Generation of fashionable clothes using generative adversarial networks: A preliminary feasibility study. *International Journal of Clothing Science and Technology*, 32(2), 177–187. 10.1108/IJCST-12-2018-0148

Sinha, P., Shastri, A., & Lorimer, S. E. (2023, March 31). How generative AI will change sales. *Harvard Business Review*. https://hbr.org/2023/03/how-generative-ai-will-change-sales

Smith, J. (2021). Transforming creativity: The revolutionary potential of AI in content creation. *Creative Technologies Journal*, 12(1), 22–35.

Smola, A., & Vishwanathan (2008). *Introduction to Machine Learning*. Cambridge University Press.

Sohl-Dickstein, J., Weiss, E., Maheswaranathan, N., & Ganguli, S. (2015, June). Deep unsupervised learning using nonequilibrium thermodynamics. In *International conference on machine learning* (pp. 2256-2265). PMLR.

Sohn, I. (2021). Deep belief network based intrusion detection techniques: A survey. *Expert Systems with Applications*, 167, 114170. 10.1016/j.eswa.2020.114170

Sohn, K., Sung, C. E., Koo, G., & Kwon, O. (2020). Artificial intelligence in the fashion industry: Consumer responses to generative adversarial network (GAN) technology. *International Journal of Retail & Distribution Management*, 49(1), 61–80. 10.1108/IJRDM-03-2020-0091

Song, J., Meng, C., & Ermon, S. (2020). *Denoising diffusion implicit models*. arXiv preprint arXiv:2010.02502.

Song, Y., & Ermon, S. (2019). Generative modeling by estimating gradients of the data distribution. *Advances in Neural Information Processing Systems*, 32.

Song, Y., & Ermon, S. (2020). Improved techniques for training score-based generative models. *Advances in Neural Information Processing Systems*, 33, 12438–12448.

Sood, A., Forster, R. A., Archer, B. J., and Little, R. C. (2021). Neutronics calculation advances at los alamos: Manhattan project to monte carlo. *Nuclear Technology, 207*(sup1), S100–S133.

StatusNeo. (2022, September 18). *Accelerated time to value*. StatusNeo - Cloud Native Technology Services & Consulting. http://statusneo.com

Su, J., & Yang, W. (2023). Unlocking the power of ChatGPT: A framework for applying generative AI in education. *ECNU Review of Education*, 6(3), 355–366. 10.1177/20965311231168423

Suleiman, R., & Anane, R. (2022). Institutional data analysis and machine learning prediction of student performance. *2022 IEEE 25th International Conference on Computer Supported Cooperative Work in Design (CSCWD)*. IEEE.

Sun, W., Bappy, J. H., Yang, S., Xu, Y., Wu, T., & Zhou, H. (2019). *Pose guided fashion image synthesis using deep generative model*. arXiv preprint arXiv:1906.07251.

Sun, J., Liao, Q. V., Muller, M., Agarwal, M., Houde, S., Talamadupula, K., & Weisz, J. D. (2022). Investigating explainability of generative AI for code through scenario-based design. In *arXiv[cs.HC]*. http://arxiv.org/abs/2202.04903

Susarla, A., Gopal, R., Thatcher, J. B., & Sarker, S. (2023). The Janus effect of generative AI: Charting the path for responsible conduct of scholarly activities in information systems. *Information Systems Research*, 34(2), 399–408. 10.1287/isre.2023.ed.v34.n2

Susnjak, T. (2022). ChatGPT: The end of online exam integrity? *arXiv preprint arXiv:2212.09292*.

Susnjak, T. (2022). ChatGPT: The end of online exam integrity? 10.48550/ARXIV.2212.09292

Taeihagh, A. (2021). Governance of artificial intelligence. *Policy and Society*, 40(2), 137–157. 10.1080/14494035.2021.1928377

Taeihagh, A., Ramesh, M., & Howlett, M. (2021). Assessing the regulatory challenges of emerging disruptive technologies. *Regulation & Governance*, 15(4), 1009–1019. 10.1111/rego.12392

Taigman, Y., Polyak, A., & Wolf, L. (2016). Unsupervised cross-domain image generation. arXiv preprint arXiv:1611.02200.

Tambe, P., Cappelli, P., & Yakubovich, V. (2019). Artificial intelligence in human resources management: Challenges and a path forward. *California Management Review*, 61(4), 15–42. 10.1177/0008125619867910

The Global Partnership on Artificial Intelligence (GAPI). (n.d.). *Home*. GPAI. https://gpai.ai

Thibault, M., Kivikangas, T., Roihankorpi, R., Pohjola, P., & Aho, M. (2023, October). Who am AI?: Mapping Generative AI Impact and Transformative Potential in Creative Ecosystem. In *Proceedings of the 26th International Academic Mindtrek Conference* (pp. 344-349). ACM. 10.1145/3616961.3617804

Thoppilan, R., De Freitas, D., Hall, J., Shazeer, N., Kulshreshtha, A., Cheng, H. T., & Le, Q. (2022). *Lamda: Language models for dialog applications*. arXiv preprint arXiv:2201.08239.

Thorp, H. H. (2023). ChatGPT is fun, but not an author. *Science*, 379(6630), 313–313. 10.1126/science.adg787936701446

Tlili, A., Shehata, B., Adarkwah, M. A., Bozkurt, A., Hickey, D. T., Huang, R., & Agyemang, B. (2023). What if the devil is my guardian angel: ChatGPT as a case study of using chatbots in education. *Smart Learning Environments*, 10(1), 15. 10.1186/s40561-023-00237-x

Trajtenberg, M. (2018). *AI as the next GPT: a Political-Economy Perspective* (No. w24245). National Bureau of Economic Research.

Tripathi, A., Singh, T., & Nair, R. R. (2021). Optimal pneumonia detection using convolutional neural networks from x-ray images. In *2021 12th International Conference on Computing Communication and Networking Technologies (ICCCNT)*. IEEE. 10.1109/ICCCNT51525.2021.9580140

Tumanyan, N., Geyer, M., Bagon, S., & Dekel, T. (2023). Plug-and-play diffusion features for text-driven image-to-image translation. In *Proceedings of the IEEE/CVF Conference on Computer Vision and Pattern Recognition* (pp. 1921-1930). IEEE. 10.1109/CVPR52729.2023.00191

Ullah, U., Lee, J. S., An, C. H., Lee, H., Park, S. Y., Baek, R. H., & Choi, H. C. (2022). A review of multi-modal learning from the text-guided visual processing viewpoint. *Sensors (Basel)*, 22(18), 6816. 10.3390/s2218681636146161

Van Den Oord, A., Kalchbrenner, N., & Kavukcuoglu, K. (2016, June). Pixel recurrent neural networks. In *International conference on machine learning* (pp. 1747-1756). PMLR.

Van Den Oord, A., & Vinyals, O. (2017). Neural discrete representation learning. *Advances in Neural Information Processing Systems*, 30.

Van Dijk, J. A. (2006). Digital divide research, achievements and shortcomings. *Poetics*, 34(4-5), 221–235. 10.1016/j.poetic.2006.05.004

van Dis, E. A. M., Bollen, J., Zuidema, W., van Rooij, R., & Bockting, C. L. (2023). ChatGPT: Five priorities for research. *Nature*, 614(7947), 224–226. 10.1038/d41586-023-00288-736737653

Van Rossum, G. (2020). *The Python Language Reference, version 3.8*. Python Software Foundation.

Vaswani, A., Shazeer, N., Parmar, N., Uszkoreit, J., Jones, L., Gomez, A. N., Kaiser, L., & Polosukhin, I. (2017). Attention is all you need. In *arXiv[cs.CL]*. http://arxiv.org/abs/1706.03762

Vaswani, A., Shazeer, N., Parmar, N., Uszkoreit, J., Jones, L., Gomez, A. N., & Polosukhin, I. (2017). Attention is all you need. *Advances in Neural Information Processing Systems*, 30.

Vignac, C., Krawczuk, I., Siraudin, A., Wang, B., Cevher, V., & Frossard, P. (2022). *Digress: Discrete denoising diffusion for graph generation.* arXiv preprint arXiv:2209.14734.

Villavicencio, C. N., Macrohon, J. J. E., Inbaraj, X. A., Jeng, J. H., & Hsieh, J. G. (2021). Covid-19 prediction applying supervised machine learning algorithms with comparative analysis using weka. *Algorithms*, 14(7), 201. 10.3390/a14070201

Vincent, J. (2019, April 12). This AI-generated sculpture is made from the shredded remains of the computer that designed it. *The Verge*. https://www.theverge.com/tldr/2019/4/12/18306090/ai-generated-sculpture-shredded-remains-ben-snell-dio

Votto, A. M., Valecha, R., Najafirad, P., & Rao, H. R. (2021). Artificial intelligence in tactical human resource management: A systematic literature review. *International Journal of Information Management Data Insights*, 1(2), 100047. 10.1016/j.jjimei.2021.100047

Wallace, B., Gokul, A., & Naik, N. (2023). Edict: Exact diffusion inversion via coupled transformations. In *Proceedings of the IEEE/CVF Conference on Computer Vision and Pattern Recognition* (pp. 22532-22541). IEEE. 10.1109/CVPR52729.2023.02158

Wan, W. Y., Tsimplis, M., Siau, K. L., Yue, W. T., Nah, F. F.-H., & Yu, G. M. (2022). Legal and regulatory issues on artificial intelligence, machine learning, data science, and big data. In *Lecture Notes in Computer Science* (pp. 558–567). Springer Nature Switzerland. 10.1007/978-3-031-21707-4_40

Wang, W., & Siau, K. (2019). Artificial intelligence, machine learning, automation, robotics, future of work and future of humanity: A review and research agenda. *Journal of Database Management*, 30(1), 61–79. 10.4018/JDM.2019010104

Waqas, A., Bui, M. M., Glassy, E. F., El Naqa, I., Borkowski, P., Borkowski, A. A., & Rasool, G. (2023). Revolutionizing digital pathology with the power of generative artificial intelligence and foundation models. *Laboratory Investigation*, 103(11), 100255. 10.1016/j.labinv.2023.10025537757969

Watkins, J., Fabielli, M., & Mahmud, M. (2020). SENSE: A Student Performance Quantifier using Sentiment Analysis. *Proceedings of the International Joint Conference on Neural Networks*. IEEE. 10.1109/IJCNN48605.2020.9207721

We like to build AI things. (2024, February 24). Growthsetting. http://growthsetting.com

Weidinger, L., Mellor, J., Rauh, M., Griffin, C., Uesato, J., Huang, P. S., & Gabriel, I. (2021). Ethical and social risks of harm from language models. *arXiv preprint arXiv:2112.04359.*

Wei, J., Tay, Y., Bommasani, R., Raffel, C., Zoph, B., Borgeaud, S., Yogatama, D., Bosma, M., Zhou, D., Metzler, D., & Chi, E. H. (2022). Emergent abilities of large language models. arXiv:2206.07682.

Weng, L. (2022). *What are diffusion models?* GitHub. https://lilianweng.github.io/posts/2021-07-11-diffusion-models/f

Wessel, M., Adam, M., Benlian, A., & Thies, F. (2023). Generative AI and its transformative value for digital platforms. *Journal of Management Information Systems.*

What's the next word in large language models? (2023). *Nature Machine Intelligence*, 5(4), 331–332. 10.1038/s42256-023-00655-z

Wijmans, J. G., & Baker, R. W. (1995). The solution-diffusion model: A review. *Journal of Membrane Science*, 107(1-2), 1–21. 10.1016/0376-7388(95)00102-I

Wikipedia contributors. (2024, February 4). *A picture is worth a thousand words.* Wikipedia, The Free Encyclopedia. https://en.wikipedia.org/w/index.php?title=A_picture_is_worth_a_thousand_words&oldid=1203266294

Wong, L.-W., Tan, G. W.-H., Lee, V.-H., Ooi, K.-B., & Sohal, A. (2023). Psychological and system-related barriers to adopting blockchain for operations management: An artificial neural network approach. *IEEE Transactions on Engineering Management*, 70(1), 67–81. 10.1109/TEM.2021.3053359

Wong, Y., Fan, S., Guo, Y., Xu, Z., Stephen, K., Sheoran, R., Bhamidipati, A., Barsopia, V., Liu, J., & Kankanhalli, M. (2022). Compute to tell the tale: Goal-driven narrative generation. *Proceedings of the 30th ACM International Conference on Multimedia*. ACM. 10.1145/3503161.3549202

Wu, C. H., & De la Torre, F. (2022). *Unifying Diffusion Models' Latent Space, with Applications to CycleDiffusion and Guidance*. arXiv preprint arXiv:2210.05559.

Wu, X. (2022, October). Creative painting with latent diffusion models. In *Proceedings of the Second Workshop on When Creative AI Meets Conversational AI* (pp. 59-80). Academic Press.

Wu, J., & Wu, L. (2023). Bayesian local likelihood estimation of time-varying dsge models: Allowing for indeterminacy. *Computational Economics*, 1–40. 10.1007/s10614-023-10478-0

Wu, Q., Zhu, B., Yong, B., Wei, Y., Jiang, X., Zhou, R., & Zhou, Q. (2021). ClothGAN: Generation of fashionable Dunhuang clothes using generative adversarial networks. *Connection Science*, 33(2), 341–358. 10.1080/09540091.2020.1822780

Wu, W., Huang, F., Kao, Y., Chen, Z., & Wu, Q. (2021). Prediction Method of Multiple Related Time Series Based on Generative Adversarial Networks. *Information (Basel)*, 2021(12), 55. 10.3390/info12020055

Xarhoulacos, C.-G., Anagnostopoulou, A., Stergiopoulos, G., & Gritzalis, D. (2021). Misinformation vs. situational awareness: The art of deception and the need for cross-domain detection. *Sensors (Basel)*, 21(16), 5496. 10.3390/s2116549634450937

Xiao, Z., Kreis, K., & Vahdat, A. (2021). Tackling the generative learning trilemma with denoising diffusion gans. arXiv preprint arXiv:2112.07804.

Xiaotong, D., & Peng, Z. (2024). Exploring the intersection of data and ethics: Seeking a societal role for artificial general intelligence. *Journal of the Humanities and Social Sciences*, 7(3), 1–11.

Xie, T., Fu, X., Ganea, O. E., Barzilay, R., & Jaakkola, T. (2021). Crystal diffusion variational autoencoder for periodic material generation. arXiv preprint arXiv:2110.06197.

Xu, L., & Liu, Y. (2022, December). Application of Generative Adversarial Network Tabular Data Synthesis for Federal Learning-based Thermal Process Performance Prediction. In *2022 IEEE 8th International Conference on Computer and Communications (ICCC)* (pp. 430-434). IEEE. 10.1109/ICCC56324.2022.10065986

Xu, T., Zhang, P., Huang, Q., Zhang, H., Gan, Z., Huang, X., & He, X. (2018). Attngan: Fine-grained text to image generation with attentional generative adversarial networks. In *Proceedings of the IEEE conference on computer vision and pattern recognition* (pp. 1316-1324). IEEE. 10.1109/CVPR.2018.00143

Xu, Y., Liu, X., Cao, X., Huang, C., Liu, E., Qian, S., Liu, X., Wu, Y., Dong, F., Qiu, C.-W., Qiu, J., Hua, K., Su, W., Wu, J., Xu, H., Han, Y., Fu, C., Yin, M., Liu, M., & Zhang, J. (2021). Artificial intelligence: A Powerful paradigm for Scientific Research. *Innovation (Cambridge (Mass.))*, 2(4), 100179. 10.1016/j.xinn.2021.10017934877560

Y\ild\iz, M., & Börekci, C. (2020). Predicting academic achievement with machine learning algorithms. *Journal of Educational Technology and Online Learning*, 3(3), 372–392.

Yang, K., & Liu, J. (2024). *If LLM Is the Wizard, Then Code Is the Wand: A Survey on How Code Empowers Large Language Models to Serve as Intelligent Agents*. arXiv:2401.00812.

Yang, L., Zhang, Z., Song, Y., Hong, S., Xu, R., Zhao, Y., Zhang, W., Cui, B., & Yang, M. H. (2023). Diffusion models: A comprehensive survey of methods and applications. *ACM Computing Surveys*, 56(4), 1–39. 10.1145/3626235

Yan, H., Zhang, H., Liu, L., Zhou, D., Xu, X., Zhang, Z., & Yan, S. (2022). Toward intelligent design: An ai-based fashion designer using generative adversarial networks aided by sketch and rendering generators. *IEEE Transactions on Multimedia*.

Young, P., Lai, A., Hodosh, M., & Hockenmaier, J. (2014). From image descriptions to visual denotations: New similarity metrics for semantic inference over event descriptions. *Transactions of the Association for Computational Linguistics*, 2, 67–78. 10.1162/tacl_a_00166

Younis, E. M., Mohsen, S., Hussein, E. H., & Ibrahim, O. A. S. (2024). Machine learning for human emotion recognition: A comprehensive review. *Neural Computing & Applications*, 36(16), 1–47. 10.1007/s00521-024-09426-2

Your all-in-one collaborative workspace. (2024). Coda. http://coda.io

Yousafzai, B. K., Khan, S. A., Rahman, T., Khan, I., Ullah, I., Ur Rehman, A., Baz, M., Hamam, H., & Cheikhrouhou, O. (2021). Student-performulator: Student academic performance using hybrid deep neural network. *Sustainability (Basel)*, 13(17), 9775. 10.3390/su13179775

Yu, J., Li, X., Koh, J. Y., Zhang, H., Pang, R., Qin, J., & Wu, Y. (2021). Vector-quantized image modeling with improved vqgan. arXiv preprint arXiv:2110.04627.

Yu, J., Xu, Y., Koh, J. Y., Luong, T., Baid, G., Wang, Z., & Wu, Y. (2022). Scaling autoregressive models for content-rich text-to-image generation. arXiv preprint arXiv:2206.10789, 2(3), 5.

Yuan, C., & Moghaddam, M. (2020). *Garment design with generative adversarial networks.* arXiv preprint arXiv:2007.10

Yuan, L., Chen, D., Chen, Y. L., Codella, N., Dai, X., Gao, J., & Zhang, P. (2021). Florence: A new foundation model for computer vision. arXiv preprint arXiv:2111.11432.

Zarifhonarvar, A. (2023). Economics of ChatGPT: A labor market view on the occupational impact of artificial intelligence. SSRN *Electronic Journal*. https://doi.org/10.2139/ssrn.4350925

Zhang, B., & Dafoe, A. (2019). Artificial intelligence: American attitudes and trends. SSRN *Electronic Journal*.

Zhang, C., Zhang, C., Zhang, M., & Kweon, I. S. (2023). Text-to-image Diffusion Models in Generative AI: A Survey. arXiv 2023. arXiv preprint arXiv:2303.07909.

Zhang, C., Zhang, C., Zhang, M., & Kweon, I. S. (2023a). *Text-to-image diffusion model in generative ai: A survey.* arXiv preprint arXiv:2303.07909.

Zhang, T., Wang, Z., Huang, J., Tasnim, M. M., & Shi, W. (2023). *A Survey of Diffusion Based Image Generation Models: Issues and Their Solutions.* arXiv preprint arXiv:2308.13142.

Zhang, H., Goodfellow, I., Metaxas, D., & Odena, A. (2019, May). Self-attention generative adversarial networks. In *International conference on machine learning* (pp. 7354-7363). PMLR.

Zhang, H., Xu, T., Li, H., Zhang, S., Wang, X., Huang, X., & Metaxas, D. N. (2017). Stackgan: Text to photo-realistic image synthesis with stacked generative adversarial networks. In *Proceedings of the IEEE international conference on computer vision* (pp. 5907-5915). IEEE. 10.1109/ICCV.2017.629

Zhang, R., Isola, P., Efros, A. A., Shechtman, E., & Wang, O. (2018). The unreasonable effectiveness of deep features as a perceptual metric. In *Proceedings of the IEEE conference on computer vision and pattern recognition* (pp. 586-595). IEEE. 10.1109/CVPR.2018.00068

Zhang, Y., Zhang, Y., Yan, D., Deng, S., & Yang, Y. (2023b). Revisiting graph based recommender systems from the perspective of variational auto-encoder. *ACM Transactions on Information Systems*, 41(3), 1–28. 10.1145/3573385

Zhang, Z., & Schomaker, L. (2024). Optimizing and interpreting the latent space of the conditional text-to-image gans. *Neural Computing & Applications*, 36(5), 2549–2572. 10.1007/s00521-023-09185-6

Zhang, Z., Zhu, J., Zhang, S., & Gao, F. (2023c). Process monitoring using recurrent kalman variational auto-encoder for general complex dynamic processes. *Engineering Applications of Artificial Intelligence*, 123, 106424. 10.1016/j.engappai.2023.106424

Zhao, R., & Shi, Z. (2021). Text-to-remote-sensing-image generation with structured generative adversarial networks. *IEEE Geoscience and Remote Sensing Letters*, 19, 1–5.

Zhou, L. (2021). Intelligence augmentation: Towards building human- machine symbiotic relationship. *AIS Transactions on Human-Computer Interaction, 13*(2), 243–264. 10.17705/1thci.00149

Zhou, R., Jiang, C., & Xu, Q. (2021). A survey on generative adversarial network-based text-to-image synthesis. *Neurocomputing*, 451, 316–336. 10.1016/j.neucom.2021.04.069

Zhu, M., Pan, P., Chen, W., & Yang, Y. (2019). Dm-gan: Dynamic memory generative adversarial networks for text-to-image synthesis. In *Proceedings of the IEEE/CVF conference on computer vision and pattern recognition* (pp. 5802-5810). IEEE.

Zhuo, T. Y., Huang, Y., Chen, C., & Xing, Z. (2023). Red teaming chatgpt via jailbreaking: Bias, robustness, reliability and toxicity. *arXiv preprint arXiv:2301.12867.*

Zhuo, T. Y., Huang, Y., Chen, C., & Xing, Z. (2023). *Red teaming ChatGPT via jailbreaking: Bias, Robustness, Reliability and toxicity.* 10.48550/ARXIV.2301.12867

Zhu, X., Ye, Y., Zhao, L., & Shen, C. (2021). MOOC Behavior Analysis and Academic Performance Prediction Based on Entropy. *Sensors (Basel)*, 21(19), 6629. 10.3390/s2119662934640949

Zodiac: A graphic memoir. (2023). Ai Weiwei Films. https://www.aiweiwei.com/zodiac

About the Contributors

Susanta Das is a seasoned educator with a proven record of teaching and mentoring diverse students, working at multiple institutions, and providing service to the various initiatives of organizations. He received his Ph.D. and M.A. degrees from Western Michigan University (WMU), USA, and M.Sc. degree from Banaras Hindu University (BHU), India all in Physics. He continued his research as a Marie-Curie post-doctoral fellow at Stockholm University, Stockholm, Sweden on beam diagnostics for the DESIREE (Double ElectroStatic Ion Ring ExpEriment) in the project DITANET (Diagnostic Techniques for particle Accelerators – a Marie-Curie initial training NETwork), at the Indian Institute of Science Education and Research-Kolkata, India on high-pressure physics as a Project Scientist-B, and at the University of Electro-Communications, Tokyo, Japan on ion-surface interactions as a Post-doctoral fellow. Throughout his career, Dr. Das worked and collaborated with many researchers, Ph.D., master, and visiting students from different countries. He further visited many countries to discuss research and an international conference participant (UK, Italy, Germany, Greece, Belgium, Bulgaria, Romania, Brazil etc.). He co-authored several research articles in WoS/Scopus indexed international journals, conference proceedings, and scholarly book chapters published by renowned international publishing houses. Beyond his research endeavors, Dr. Das has a storied history of service to academic and administrative committees, exhibiting his commitment to the growth and development of educational institutions. His experience includes tenure at Central University South Bihar, Sri Sri University, and P.K. University before assuming his current role at Ajeenkya DY Patil University. He received the Marie-Curie post-doctoral fellowship in Sweden, Science Academies' Summer Research Fellowship in India, Gwen Frostic Doctoral Fellowship, Department Graduate Research and Creative Scholar Award by WMU, and Leo R. Parpart Doctoral Fellowship by Dept. of Physics, WMU, among many others, throughout his academic journey. At present, Dr. Das continues to delve into cutting-edge fields, with a keen interest in nanotechnology, quantum computing, and data science. His multifaceted contributions, spanning teaching, research, and administrative leadership, showcase a dedicated professional who is instrumental in advancing the vision and mission of the institutions he serves.

Pooja Dehankar is working as Assistant Professor in School of Engineering, Ajeenkya DY Patil University, Pune. She has completed BE in Computer Engineering from Priyadarshini College of Engineering, Nagpur and ME in Information Technology from Sinhgad College of Engineering, Pune. She has done Post Graduate Diploma in Advance Computing from Pune. She has 15 years of experience in academics. Her area of interest are Artificial Intelligence, Cyber Security and Data Mining. She has published papers in Scopus indexed Journals. Furthermore,she has published several book chapters. She actively participates in workshops, faculty development programs, short term training programs, conferences and webinars. She is committed to continuous learning by expanding her knowledge, and skills. She has completed NPTEL online course on Internet of Things, Cloud Computing, Demystifying Networking and Enhancing soft skill and personality. She had organized many Guest Lectures and workshops. Her hobbies are Playing Harmonium, Gardening and Photography. Her goal is to make a positive difference in the world through her work.

Vishal Jain is presently working as an Associate Professor at Department of Computer Science and Engineering, Sharda School of Engineering and Technology, Sharda University, Greater Noida, U. P., India. Before that, he has worked for several years as an Associate Professor at Bharati Vidyapeeth's Institute of Computer Applications and Management (BVICAM), New Delhi. He has more than 16 years of experience in the academics. He obtained Ph.D (CSE), M.Tech (CSE), MBA (HR), MCA, MCP and CCNA. He has more than 1350 research citation indices with Google Scholar (h-index score 18 and i-10 index 34). He has authored more than 100 research papers in reputed conferences and journals, including Web of Science and Scopus. He has authored and edited more than 45 books with various reputed publishers, including Elsevier, Springer, DeGruyter, IET, River Publishers, Apple Academic Press, CRC, Taylor and Francis Group, Scrivener, Wiley, Emerald, NOVA Science, Bentham Books and IGI-Global. He is life member of CSI, ISTE and senior member of IEEE. His research areas include information retrieval, semantic web, ontology engineering, data mining, ad hoc networks, and sensor networks. He received a Young Active Member Award for the year 2012–13 from the Computer Society of India, Best Faculty Award for the year 2017 and Best Researcher Award for the year 2019 from BVICAM, New Delhi.

Umesh Chandra Jaiswal was born in 1967, India. He received the B. E. degree in Computer Science and Engineering from Madan Mohan Malaviya Engineering College, Gorakhpur, in 1988 and M. Tech. degree in Computer Science and Engineering from the Indian Institute of Technology, Delhi, in 1994. He has completed Ph.D. degree in Computer Science and Engineering, from Madan Mohan Malaviya engineering collage, Gorakhpur, in 2011. His research interests include natural language processing, design and analysis of algorithms, parallel Algorithms, machine learning.

Seema Khanum is a distinguished scientist renowned for her exemplary contributions to the field of cybersecurity. With a career spanning over five years, she has solidified her reputation as a visionary leader and expert in her domain. Born with an innate curiosity for technology, Seema embarked on her academic journey with a firm resolve to explore the depths of computer science. She pursued her undergraduate studies in Computer Science and Engineering, laying a robust foundation for her future endeavors. Her passion for cybersecurity ignited during this period, propelling her towards a career dedicated to safeguarding digital landscapes. After completing her undergraduate degree with distinction, Seema ventured into the dynamic realm of cybersecurity, joining the esteemed Indian Computer Emergency Response Team (CERT-In). From the onset, she exhibited exceptional prowess in identifying vulnerabilities and devising effective strategies to mitigate cyber threats. Her astute analytical skills and meticulous approach earned her recognition as a promising talent within the organization.

Binod Kumar is Professor and Dean(International Relations) at JSPM's Rajarshi Shahu College of Engineering (MCA Dept.), Pune, affiliated with Savitribai Phule Pune University, India. He received the IEEE Pune Section Senior Member of the Year 2023 Award. He received Dignitary Fellow of International Organization for Academic and Scientific Development (IOASD) in year 2023. He received the National Level Award GURU SHAKTI SAMMAN For EXCELLENCE IN ACADEMICS 2023 by Research Education Solution on 5th September 2023. He received Excellence Award 2020" by Institute of Scholars and "Best Researcher Award" under International Scientist Award 2021 on Engineering, Science and Medicine by VDGOOD Technology Factory. He received an amount of Rs 93000 Under AICTE Quality Improvement Scheme for FDP titled AI-Diving in IOT & Computer Vision (Jan 17-22, 2022) . He worked as an associate professor at the School of Engineering and Computer Technology, Quest International University, MALAYSIA .He published 12 patents .He has conducted PhD viva-voice as External Expert of 12 students at different universities. Under his supervision 07 students have completed PhD and 06 students are pursuing PhD at SPPU, Pune, India. .He is reviewer of Journals like Elsevier, Springer and TPC of various IEEE sponsored conferences. He is an editorial board member of 45 International Journals. He is senior member of IEEE and ACM.I have published four books, two book chapters in IGI Global, USA and one book chapter in Wiley Publications, and nearly 45 papers in International & National Journals (25 Scopus)/Conferences.

Sweety Kumari is a driven student pursuing her undergraduate studies in Computer Science and Engineering, specializing in Internet of Things and Cybersecurity at C. V. Raman Global University. While her academic pursuits primarily focus on IoT and cybersecurity, Sweety harbors a deep interest in the transformative potential of artificial intelligence. Motivated by a curiosity to explore emerging technologies, Sweety actively engages in research and projects that bridge the gap between IoT, cybersecurity, and AI. She is passionate about leveraging innovative technologies to address pressing societal challenges and is dedicated to honing her skills to become a proficient AI practitioner. With a strong foundation in computer science and a thirst for knowledge, Sweety is poised to make significant contributions to the field of artificial intelligence.

Smruti Pratisruti Maharana is an ambitious student enrolled in the Department of Computer Science and Engineering, specializing in Internet of Things and Cybersecurity at C. V. Raman Global University. While her academic focus lies in IoT and cybersecurity, Smruti possesses a keen interest in the broader landscape of technology and innovation. Eager to explore the realms of artificial intelligence, Smruti actively seeks opportunities to expand her knowledge and skills in AI-related disciplines. She believes in the power of interdisciplinary collaboration and aims to leverage her expertise in IoT and cybersecurity to contribute meaningfully to the advancement of AI-driven solutions.

Anjana Mishra is an Assistant Professor in the Department of Computer Science and Information Technology at C.V. Raman Global University. With a focus on machine learning, data mining, and sentiment analysis, she brings over seven years of teaching experience to her role. Anjana is committed to leveraging technology to address real-world challenges and is dedicated to nurturing the next generation of AI and machine learning professionals. Her research contributions include over 30 publications in prestigious journals, conference papers, book chapters, and patents, highlighting her expertise and commitment to advancing the field.

Archan Mitra is an Assistant Professor at School of Media Studies (SOMS) at Presidency University, Bangalore. He is the author of two book "Cases for Classroom Media and Entertainment Business" and "Multiverse and Media", he also has other several edited books to his credit. He has done his doctorate from Visva-Bharati Santiniketan, West Bengal in the field of "environmental informatics and communication for sustainability". In addition to that he is a certified Science Communicator and Journalism from Indian Science Communication Society (ISCOS), certified Corporate Trainer with Amity Institute of Training and Development, Certified Social Media Network Analyst. He has a strong interest in environmental communication. He was awarded certificate of merit by PRSI, Kolkata Chapter and Medal of Honor by Journalistic Club of Kolkata. He was working as a research assistant with the World Bank's "Environmental Capacity Building in Southeast Asia" project at IIM Kashipur. He was instrumental in launching the World Bank's Green MBA MOOC, he has also assisted in the research project on Uttarakhand disaster mitigation by ICSSR, the leading research on Uttarakhand disaster.

Leena Rahul Deshmukh (Leena Suresh More) is an Asst Professor at JSPM's Jayawant Institute of Management Studies, Pune affiliated with Savitribai Phule Pune University, India. She has more than 25 years of experience in the field of academics (PG Courses-MCA) and industrial. She has presented more than 12 papers in various national and international conferences also published papers in various journals. She has developed ERP software for JSPM institutes. She has delivered expert sessions in various colleges on AI, ML, Python Programming, Mobile Computing and many more. She has guided more than 100 projects at PG Level. She has attended and participated in more than 50 national and international seminars, workshops. Her research interest includes AI, ML, DL.

Rabi Shankar is currently pursuing B. Tech in Computer Science & Engineering with a specialization in Artificial Intelligence & Machine Learning at C. V. Raman Global University, Bhubaneswar. Rabi has cultivated a deep curiosity and strong interest in Machine Learning, Deep Learning, Generative AI, and Natural Language Processing (NLP), Rabi is eager to dive into the emerging field of Quantum AI. Committed to leveraging advanced AI techniques to develop innovative solutions, Rabi aims to address and solve pressing real-world issues, demonstrating a profound dedication to both academic excellence and practical application.

Rajneesh Ranjan is an enthusiastic student pursuing a Bachelor's degree in Computer Science and Engineering, specializing in Artificial Intelligence and Machine Learning (CSE-AIML) at C. V. Raman Global University. With a keen interest in the transformative potential of AI, Rajneesh is dedicated to expanding his knowledge and expertise in cutting-edge technologies. Alongside his academic pursuits, he actively engages in research and projects related to AI and machine learning, aiming to contribute to the development of innovative solutions for real-world challenges.

Atharva Saraf is pursuing his B.Tech. in Computer Science and Engineering in the School of Engineering of Ajeenkya DY Patil University, Pune, Maharashtra, India. His research interests are cybersecurity, deep learning, machine learning, neural network, and artificial intelligence.

Richard Shan is a consultant and a thought leader in the field of emerging technologies, with extensive experience in enabling organizations to adopt and leverage cutting-edge solutions such as GenAI, LLMOps, Edge Computing, MLOps, and more. His hands-on expertise and forward-thinking vision help drive and empower businesses to incubate and harness the power of disruptive technologies for growth and acceleration. He is a regular speaker at international conferences and events, where he shares his insights and best practices on digital transformation and innovation. He is also a startup founder and author of books, along with regularly publishing articles in trade journals.

Neha Singh was born in Gorakhpur, India, in 1995. She received the B. Tech. degree in Computer Science Engineering from Institute of Technology and Management Gida, Gorakhpur, in 2018 and M. Tech. degree in Information Technology from the Madan Mohan Malaviya University of Technology, Gorakhpur, in 2020. She is currently pursuing Ph.D. degree in Information Technology from Madan Mohan Malaviya University of Technology, Gorakhpur. Her research interests include natural language processing and machine learning.

Ritu Singh was born in Gorakhpur India in 1995.She received the B. Tech. degree in Computer Science Engineering from Institute of Technology and Management Gida, Gorakhpur, in 2018 and M. Tech. degree in Information Technology from the Madan Mohan Malaviya University of Technology, Gorakhpur, isn 2020. Her research interests include computer network.

Index

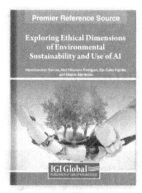

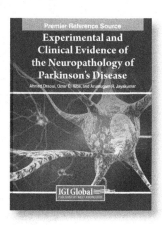
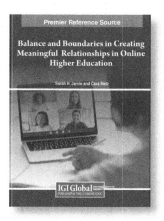

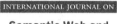
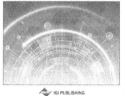

Individual Article & Chapter Downloads
US$ 37.50/each

Easily Identify, Acquire, and Utilize Published Peer-Reviewed Findings in Support of Your Current Research

- Browse Over *170,000+ Articles & Chapters*

- *Accurate & Advanced* Search

- Affordably Acquire *International Research*

- *Instantly Access* Your Content

- Benefit from the *InfoSci® Platform Features*

THE UNIVERSITY
of NORTH CAROLINA
at CHAPEL HILL

Printed in the United States
by Baker & Taylor Publisher Services